D1523074

Asian Contagion

Asian Contagion

The Causes and Consequences of a Financial Crisis

EDITED BY

Karl D. Jackson

Westview Press
A Member of the Perseus Books Group

Copyright © 1999 by Westview Press, A Member of the Perseus Books Group

Published in 1999 in the United States of America by Westview Press, 5500 Central Avenue, Boulder, Colorado 80301-2877, and in the United Kingdom by Westview Press, 12 Hid's Copse Road, Cumnor Hill, Oxford OX2 9JJ

A CIP catalog record for this book is available from the Library of Congress.
ISBN 0-8133-9033-8 (hc) — ISBN 0-8133-90354 (pb)

The paper used in this publication meets the requirements of the American National Standard for Permanence of Paper for Printed Library Materials Z39.48-1984.

10   9   8   7   6   5   4   3   2

This book is dedicated to

P. C. F. Hu
Lifelong Friend

Contents

Tables and Figures

Preface

For me, this book is the tale of two rivers: New River in Fort Lauderdale, Florida, in the 1950s and the Chao Phraya in Bangkok in the mid-1990s. On January 8, 1994, I had spent the day exploring the ruins of Ayuthaya, the former capital city of Thailand fifty miles north of modern Bangkok. I was returning to bustling Bangkok by air conditioned boat along the Chao Phraya on that sunny Saturday, when I first sensed the advent of what would become known as the Asian financial collapse of 1997–1998.

I had grown up in Fort Lauderdale in the mid-1950s. At that time, white stone bridges were still connected to vacant residential plots that had become mangrove swamps again after the collapse of the real estate boom of the 1920s. The white bridges along the canals of "the Venice of America" were monuments to the real estate developers who had gone bust because they had planned luxurious residential developments for a marketplace that would not catch up with their dreams for another thirty years.

Two things impressed me during that afternoon boat trip between Ayuthaya and Bangkok in 1994. The first was the degree to which the urban sprawl of Bangkok had expanded far beyond the city I had known when I lived in Thailand during the late 1970s. In "the Venice of the Orient," canals had been paved over to accommodate ever-expanding vehicular traffic in the capital city of the world's most rapidly growing economy. Bangkok was growing rapidly upward, as well as outward, in an exploding urban sprawl. Second, during the leisurely trip down the river, I spied several new, luxurious—and thoroughly empty—thirty-story apartment buildings that had been built on the assumption that large numbers of wealthy buyers would rapidly be produced by the ever-increasing Thai prosperity. Thus, my first inkling of the coming collapse of Asian assets came from mingling the images of empty Bangkok buildings in the 1990s with memories of equally bold real estate developers of South Florida who had so woefully misjudged the marketplace of the 1920s.

On a subsequent trip to Bangkok, inkling became hypothesis. In the company of business colleague Rod Porter, I returned to Bangkok in September 1994. Representing a New York foreign exchange firm, we were attempting to interest Thai institutional investors and wealthy individuals in the firm's foreign exchange risk management services. The businessmen with whom we spoke were polite but non-committal. After all, the value of the baht would "never" change; hence, there was little risk to be reduced. My colleague's morning jog that Sunday morning passed numerous construction sites. Later, he hypothesized with me that there was no way the Bangkok market could absorb all of the modern offices and luxury condominiums being opened or under construction. To test our hypothesis, after returning to the United States we obtained basic data on current office space, the amount of new space coming on-line, and the vacancy and absorption rates. From these data we concluded that even at 8.5% per annum growth rates, Bangkok was on the verge of a real estate crisis that would have a substantial negative impact on the banking system. In a January 1995 letter, conveyed indirectly and informally to the highest levels of the Bank of Thailand, we predicted a crisis similar to the American Savings & Loan debacle of the late 1980s. We warned of a negative impact on the banks similar to the aftermath of the collapse of the bubble economy in Tokyo.

During 1995–1996, an informal collaborative group formed to devise plans for achieving a "soft landing" for Thailand. Pornpimol Kanchanalak, Tom Kendall, Tadashi Maeda, John Merante, Rod Porter, John R. Taylor, and a number of exceptionally astute Thai friends contributed their time, pro bono, to this effort. With each plan (dutifully passed along to Thai authorities), we learned more about the depth and breadth of the crisis. It became clear that the glutted real estate market accounted for only a third of the non-performing loans threatening the banking system. Non-performing loans also had appeared throughout the modern manufacturing sector.

A further trip led me into a series of interviews with bankers and several Thai financial analysts. Most of the individuals admitted there was a non-performing loan problem, but they claimed it was not serious and that only one bank, the Bangkok Bank of Commerce, was in deep trouble. Only one person suggested the problem was large, involving the property companies, the finance companies, and ultimately the banks. The officials with whom I shared my findings did not take offense but gently indicated the problems would be handled "the Thai way," behind the scenes, through compromises among builders, bankers, and regulators, thereby precluding both slow growth and financial panic.

Repeated trips to Bangkok clarified the political fact of life that for each proposal there was always another special interest group standing in the way of rational policy choices. Sophisticated technocrats, with advanced degrees from the most prestigious universities in the United States and Western Europe, remained solidly embedded in their own business culture. They proved unable to begin unraveling "the Thai way," by which personal relationships supplied the only real collateral for business loans. Long before the baht crashed, business began to sour. Poor business decisions became non-performing loans and, in the absence of a binding foreclosure law, the financial sector could not clear its books.

Thailand had also become a democracy, and the political will required for tough decisions could only be assembled, it seemed, once the failure of the entire system had become evident to the whole world. Action could not be taken until the threat was obvious to all, and by that point a "soft landing" was no longer a real option. Particularly in 1995 and 1996, the interests of property owners did not coincide with the interests of the finance companies, which in turn differed in important ways from those of the banks. Rather than reigning in a runaway boom, those responsible for regulating the system instead sought to be responsive by keeping the boom going.

Like the Florida developers of the 1920s and the Tokyo speculators of the late 1980s, Bangkok's developers, financiers, bankers, and government leaders had all adopted a linear view of history. They assumed that the economy would expand indefinitely and that the baht would remain permanently pegged at the current rate. Therefore, they reasoned, the prosperity of the last twenty years could safely be projected far into the future, without fear of a possible cyclical downturn that would be financially lethal to those who had borrowed too extensively abroad. Thai and other Asian entrepreneurs had no lack of skill, daring, and sophistication; but they did not understand the boom could not last forever.

Regardless of location—in time or cultural space—the booms that precede financial panics are always characterized by beliefs about the uniqueness of a particular time or place and the incomparable skills of the business elite. This was equally true of Tokyo, Shanghai, Bangkok, and Kuala Lumpur, where foreigners were continually assured that special qualities precluded the application of standard business practices. Likewise, in the spectacular 1998 failure of Long Term Capital Management of Greenwich, Connecticut, neither sophisticated derivatives nor Nobel prize winners in economics were sufficiently unique substitutes for sound business judgement about the real value of underlying assets. Judgement, rather than intellect, is the rarest of commodities when markets begin to unwind in unprecedented ways. In business, as in other fields of endeavor, hubris comes before a fall.

Books always involve a group effort. Michael Carns, Executive Director of the Center for International Political Economy, encouraged this project throughout and supplied funding for the on-going policy seminar at the Paul H. Nitze School of Advanced International Studies (SAIS) where most of the chapters were originally presented. Yasusuke Tsukagoshi, of the Japan Center for International Finance, supported the research for the chapters on China, Indonesia, India, and Thailand. My colleague, Fred Brown, was involved from start to finish, and the volume would not have been possible without his good judgement and unstinting support. Lois Weiss, Program Office Coordinator for SAIS Southeast Asia studies, oversaw the entire enterprise with competence and good humor. David Timberman arranged the contract with the publisher. Martin Lasater labored long and hard as the copy editor; without his skill and efficiency the production schedule would have been lengthened considerably. Diligent and skillful research assistance was supplied by Sampriti Ganguli, Tracy Henry, Suzanne Jessop, and Jae Ku. I owe a special intellectual debt to my business colleagues, Thomas Kendall, John Merante, Rod Porter, and John R. Taylor, who taught me just enough to comprehend what was going on, but mercifully not enough to allow me to meddle too extensively in the practical affairs of finance that will determine the future of Asia. Finally, none of this would have been possible without the insights of friends and associates in

Tokyo and especially in Bangkok. They offered their time and their wisdom, and I hope the product is in some ways worthy of their effort.

Karl D. Jackson
Washington, D.C.
September 1998

About the Contributors

David L. Asher has been involved in Japan affairs for over a decade, spending his first extended period there in 1988 as a researcher inside the Japanese Diet. During 1990–1993 he worked as a staff specialist on Asian affairs and international trade in the U.S. House of Representatives. From 1994 to 1995 he was a staff researcher at the Institute for Defense Analyses and was later assigned to the Japan Desk in the Office of the Secretary of Defense in support of policy planning and analysis. Since 1996 he has been a doctoral candidate in international relations at the University of Oxford, writing a thesis on the failure of economic liberalization and financial crisis management in Japan during the 1920s. He works as a consultant on Japan market strategy and economic analysis for securities companies, investment banks, and research organizations. He is the author of numerous reports, chapters, and articles on Japanese economic policy and on U.S.-Japan relations.

Surjit S. Bhalla is President of O[x]US Research and Investments in India. He has more than twenty-years experience working on economics, especially developing economics, at the following institutions: World Bank (fourteen years), Brookings Institution, Rand Corporation, Delhi School of Economics, and as Executive Director of The Policy Group in New Delhi, India.

Eugene R. Dattel has been directly involved with Japanese financial institutions for over a decade as an investment banker and financial consultant. He is author of *The Sun That Never Rose: The Inside Story of Japan's Failed Attempt at Global Financial Dominance.*

Richard F. Doner is Associate Professor of Political Science at Emory University and a specialist on the political economy of Southeast Asia. He is author of *Driving a Bargain: Automotive Jndustrialization and Japanese Firms in Southeast Asia,* as well as several articles and chapters on Thai economic development.

Karl D. Jackson is Director of the Southeast Asia Program of the School of Advanced International Studies of Johns Hopkins University. He has served as Assistant to the Vice President for National Security Affairs, Special Assistant to the President for National Security Affairs at the National Security Council, and Deputy Assistant Secretary of Defense for East Asia. He is author of *Traditional Authority, Islam and Rebellion: A Study of Indonesian Political Behavior* and is the editor or co-editor of several studies on Indonesia, Cambodia, ASEAN, and U.S.-Thailand relations.

Nicholas R. Lardy is a Senior Fellow in the Foreign Policy Studies program at the Brookings Institution where he is studying the Chinese banking system and the economic consequences of deferring reform in the state-owned sector. He has written and edited numerous books and articles on the Chinese economy. Prior to joining Brookings, he was director of the Henry M. Jackson School of International Studies at the University of Washington.

Ross H. McLeod is a Research Fellow in the Indonesia Project at Australian National University and a Director of Ricardo, Smith Pty. Ltd, a financial consulting firm. He is author of numerous articles and book chapters on the Indonesian economy. Currently, he is writing a book on the evolution of economic policy making in Indonesia.

Manual F. Montes is a Senior Fellow at the Institute of Southeast Asian Studies in Singapore and Co-Director of a UN University project on short-term capital movements and balance of payments crises. He is the author of numerous articles and book chapters on the Philippine economy, capital flows, and economic policy making.

Hak K. Pyo is a Visiting Professor in Asian Studies at the Paul H. Nitze School Advanced of International Studies. He is the author of numerous articles and research papers on the political economy of Korea, trade effects and the effects of capital market liberalization, economic forecasts for Asian industrializing regions, and many other subjects relating to economic factors in Korea and East Asia. Dr. Pyo has been a Professor of International Economics at Seoul National University since 1981.

Ansil Ramsay is a Professor of Government at St. Lawrence University. He has authored numerous journal articles on Thai politics and economic policy making and is co-editor of *Thailand-US Relations: Changing Political, Strategic and Economic Factors*.

Andrew Smithers is Chairman of Smithers & Co., Ltd., an economic consultancy based in London, providing advice to some seventy fund management companies in Japan, the United States, and the United Kingdom. His research reports are frequently cited in such leading business publications as the *Financial Times* and *Wall Street Journal*. He also writes a weekly economics column for the *Evening Standard* newspaper. He has held several other top management positions and lived and worked in Japan from 1986 to 1989.

William Turley is a Professor of Political Science at Southern Illinois University at Carbondale, where he teaches international relations, international political economy, and comparative politics. His publications include *The Second Indochina War 1954–1975*, the edited volumes *Reinventing Vietnamese Socialism: Doi Moi in Comparative Perspective and Vietnamese Communism in Comparative Perspective*, plus dozens of articles and book chapters on Vietnamese politics, foreign affairs, and political economy. He is currently collaborating on a study of the political economy of reform in Vietnam and a comparison of the political implications of economic opening in Ho Chi Minh City and Guangzhou.

1

Introduction:
The Roots of the Crisis

Karl D. Jackson

From 1945 to 1997 the Asian economic miracle fueled the greatest expansion of wealth, for the largest number of persons, in the history of mankind. Prognosticators spoke confidently of the advent of "an Asian century." By 2020 Asians were expected to produce 40 percent of the world's GDP while the U.S. and European shares would recede to 18 percent and 14 percent, respectively. Some market researchers predicted that Asia's middle and lower middle classes would grow to more than a billion people by the turn of the century, powering the greatest explosion of consumption the world had ever seen (see Rohwer 1995).

Regional Impact of Crisis

In mid-summer 1997, a half-century of economic progress came to a crashing halt. In direct contradiction to conventional wisdom, several Asian economies previously praised for balanced budgets, high savings and investment rates, low inflation and openness to the world marketplace, went into free fall. What became a region-wide panic struck first in Thailand before spreading to Malaysia, the Philippines, Indonesia, and eventually to Korea. Stock markets and currencies plummeted, prompting central banks to mount expensive currency defenses through buying forwards, raising interest rates to unprecedented levels, or both. The magnitude and volatility of the crisis dealt a sharp blow to fragile and over-extended banking systems, while devastating those manufacturing establishments dependent on cheap capital and foreign inputs for their production. During the first year of the crisis, the currencies of the five affected countries depreciated by 35-80 percent, diminishing substantially the wealth of the five miracle economies (Table 1.1).

TABLE 1.1   Impact of the Crisis: Exchange Rates and GNP

Country	Exchange Rates to U.S. Dollars		GNP in U.S. Billion Dollars	
	June 1997	July 1998	June 1997	July 1998
Thailand	24.5 baht	41	170	102
Indonesia	2,380 rupiah	14,150	205	34
Philippines	26.3 peso	42	75	47
Malaysia	2.5 ringgit	4.1	90	55
Korea	850 won	1,290	430	283

Source: Updated version from a table in R. J. Cheetham, "Asia Crisis," June 1, 1998.

On a human scale, the Crash of 1997 shook the confidence of foreign investors and domestic entrepreneurs, while decreasing the wealth of the newly emergent middle classes and impoverishing the non-agricultural labor force. The number of people living on less than one U.S. dollar per day in the five affected countries was approximately 40 million prior to the crisis, and they were concentrated in Indonesia and the Philippines (Cheetham 1998). During the first year of the crisis the number of Asians living in absolute poverty more than doubled in countries without elaborate social safety nets, and pockets of absolute poverty reappeared in Korea and Thailand. In Indonesia, the "good news" was that the government and the international agencies were actively moving to acquire the millions of tons of rice needed to prevent starvation.

The affected middle classes had formerly been known for their automobiles, cell phones, and a materialistic lifestyle that had never been available before in South-east Asia outside of the narrowest upper reaches of the elite. The middle classes of the affected countries worked hard, and their upwardly mobile children were acquiring educational tools in universities at home and abroad. Educational statistics are not yet available on the impact of the crisis, but the number of families incapable of paying school fees has escalated rapidly, thereby diminishing the prospect for white collar jobs for a whole generation of citizens who realistically expected them. If economic nationalism results from the Crash of 1997, it will be generated by formerly upwardly mobile people who have suddenly been denied access to the status, power, and wealth they had come to expect.

As a result of the crisis, governments throughout the area now find their political legitimacy challenged by groups and individuals who, until recently, had been willing to tolerate cronyism and familism so long as governments delivered the economic goods.[1] With remarkable speed, democratic and non-democratic governments were overturned during the first twelve months of the crisis. In Korea, former political prisoner Kim Dae Jung ousted the ruling political party, even though he had long been considered too extreme to be acceptable to important factions of the Korean elite. In Thailand, the dominance of up-country rural politicians was at least temporarily eclipsed with the promulgation of a new constitution and the installation of the government of Chuan Leekpai in November 1997. In Indonesia, a thirty-two-year regime ended abruptly when the military asked for President Suharto's resignation in the wake of student protests and urban looting directed against the Indonesian Chinese community. In the Philippines, the electorate rejected the chosen successor of President Fidel Ramos and chose the most anti-establishment candidate, Joseph Estrada, over the objections of the Catholic Church and the traditional elite power holders. As a result of the LDP's poor showing in Japan's Upper House elections on July 12, 1998, Prime Minister Ryutaro Hashimoto was forced to resign from office. Depending on the duration and severity of the crisis across Asia, other formerly secure governments may be toppled at the ballot boxes or in the streets in the political aftermath of the severe economic downturn.

Roots of the Crisis

Initially, the financial crisis was perceived almost exclusively as an exchange rate problem, being blamed alternatively on governments (for maintaining fixed exchange rates and allowing currencies to become overvalued) or on greedy foreign speculators who, in a matter of days, supposedly had undone the hard work of generations of Asians. In the early months of the crisis, commentators clung to the language of the Asian miracle by depicting the crisis as temporary, chanting the mantra of the "strong fundamentals of the Asian Tigers." At the same time, some Asian nationalists voiced conspiracy theories suggesting Asia was being put in its place by wily global capitalists using sophisticated speculative tools to deflate the value of all Asian assets in a plot to buy everything Asians had built but at fire sale prices. The frustration and resentment of Asian nationalism is captured in Mahathir's August 23, 1997, statement, "All these countries have spent forty years to build up their economies and a moron like Soros comes along" (Loh 1997).

In reality, the simultaneous crises affecting much of Asia are as multifaceted as they are tied to fundamental problems within the economic structure of each country. Excessive borrowing abroad (primarily by the private sector) is the hallmark of this crisis. In the five years prior to the crisis, the borrowings of banks and non-banks in the affected countries grew very rapidly. In particular, banks in each country rapidly increased their net foreign liabilities by large percentages during the four years prior to the crisis. By the time the crisis broke in mid-July 1997, total external indebtedness had reached large proportions, exceeding 50 percent of GDP in Thailand, Indonesia, and the Philippines (Figure 1.1).

FIGURE 1.1   External Debt as a Percent of 1996 GDP

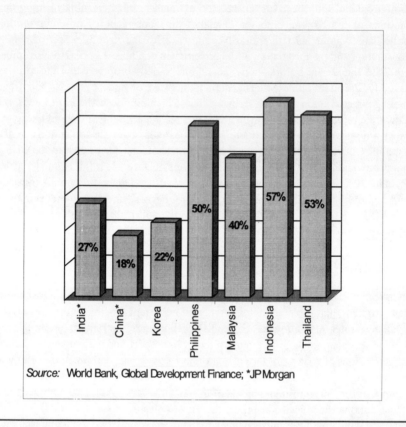

Source: World Bank, Global Development Finance; *JP Morgan

Particularly in Thailand, Malaysia, and the Philippines it was the private sector, rather than the governments, who were responsible for incurring these large overseas obligations.

As reflected in Figure 1.2, not only was the amount of foreign indebtedness large as a proportion of GDP, but in several instances there were large amounts of short-term borrowings. As Korea, Indonesia, and Thailand approached the year of crisis, they were burdened by short-term loans equal to 13, 14, and 22 percent of their respective GDPs. In the ensuing period of plummeting currency values, these short-term loans, with principal and interest due in less than one year, became a crushing burden for all three countries.

FIGURE 1.2 Total External Debt in US$ Billions in 1996

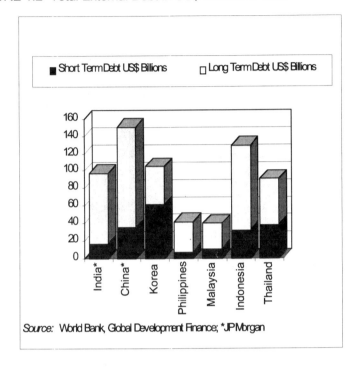

Source: World Bank, Global Development Finance; *JP Morgan

Although external aspects (fixed exchange rates, high interest rates, and excessive borrowing from abroad) are among the important causal factors in this crisis, the crisis would not have occurred without internal weaknesses as well: inadequate supervisory institutions, traditional banking practices, and, most of all, poor investment decisions made by the private sector of each country. Foreign borrowing led to a domestic lending boom across all of Asia, which generated multiple asset bubbles, especially in stock markets and real estate.[2] If it had not been for pre-existing internal weakness throughout the private sector, the Asian contagion would never have spread so far or had such a lasting impact in individual countries. The variants of corporate familism found in Asian businesses, pre-existing forms of business-government relations, and a tendency to follow investment fads rather than market demand created over-capacity in production in similar sectors across Asia. There was simply too much foreign money chasing too few sound investments that were capable of earning foreign exchange sufficient to service the principal and interest on the debt. Instead of exercising restraint, local banks re-lent monies borrowed abroad to speculative investments in real estate (which earned no foreign exchange) or to protected and noncompetitive enterprises such as steel and petrochemicals. The speed of the investment buildup can be seen in Figure 1.3, which shows domestic credit expansion as a percentage of GDP for several Asian countries.

The failure of entire business sectors to meet global standards regarding financial regulation, auditing, and corporate governance became critical in undermining foreign confidence once earnings began to fall rapidly as a result of glutted markets in real estate, steel, automobiles, petrochemicals, and semiconductors. Domestic investors were first to react to the downturn. As they became unable to meet payments to domestic bank creditors on stalled or unprofitable projects, they also began pulling capital out of local stock markets. These factors became exacerbated by capital flight in Indonesia, Thailand, Malaysia, Korea, and the Philippines once foreign and domestic investors sensed the deep-seated weakness of the financial sector in each country. Sharply falling stock and property markets reinforced one another in a downward spiral that devastated local financial systems.

Asia had profited greatly during the late 1980s and early 1990s from massive amounts of domestic and foreign investment. Across the region governments maintained fixed exchange rates minimizing the foreign exchange risk for domestic borrowers and foreign investors.[3] Local banks borrowed offshore at low, short-term rates and lent the money for long terms at a substantial premium to manufacturers and real estate developers. Unfortunately, the abundance of inexpensive capital, in combination with local bank loans based on personal relationships rather than real business plans, resulted in the widespread misallocation of capital into speculative and noncompetitive sectors and enterprises. Returns on investments fell steadily during the 1990s in Korea, Indonesia, and Thailand until large numbers of projects no longer generated income sufficient to meet both principal and interest payments.

Asian firms often perceived market share to be the most important indicator of success. In their search for increased market share, firms borrowed heavily to fund plant expansion and acquired unsustainable debt/equity ratios. Heavy debts meant that a slight downturn in national or regional economic growth (not to mention the possibility of currency devaluation) would mean insolvency. The worst examples of excessive borrowing prior to the crisis are found in Korea, when in 1996 the five largest chaebols (producing 30 percent of the GDP) had debt/equity ratios averaging 3.9. As a group, the top thirty chaebols had even higher debt/equity ratios along with barely positive returns on capital. High debt/equity ratios, when combined with wafer thin profits, were simply unsustainable. Seven of the chaebols folded during the first year of the crisis (Pyo 1999).

Before the currency crisis struck the region, poorly conceived investments turned into non-performing loans, effectively curtailing the ability of banking systems to maintain the economic expansion through continued lending. In Thailand, Indonesia, and Korea the proportion of bank loans that became nonperforming skyrocketed, probably reaching more than 20 percent of the total loan

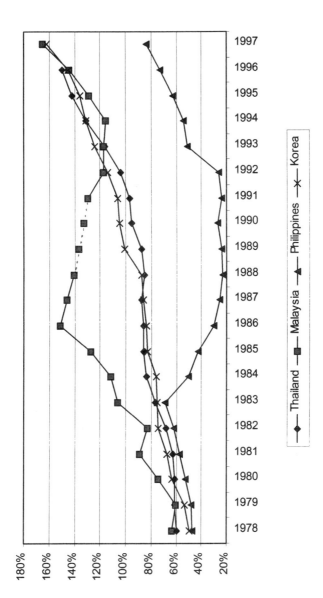

FIGURE 1.3 Domestic Credit, 1978–1997 in Percent of GDP. *Source:* IMF International Financial Statistics. Data for Malaysia between 1989–1991 is incomplete and has been estimated using trend.

portfolio of many banks and finance companies, rendering them technically insolvent prior to the advent of the currency crisis.[4] The combination of unhedged foreign liabilities, non-performing domestic assets, and the absence of institutions capable of supervising the banks and protecting small depositors created near perfect conditions for a classic banking panic. In essence, most of the banks in Asia were technically insolvent before the run on the baht in mid-1997.[5]

The oversupply of Asia's export markets in the late-1990s also contributed to the Crisis of 1997. Three factors account for this oversupply:

1. capital from Western Europe, North America, and especially Japan, flowing into Asia as foreign direct investments designed to produce exports;[6]
2. the assumption of foreign and domestic investors that expansion of inter-Asian trade would continue to boost exports at double digit figures for the foreseeable future; and
3. a belief that the marketplace could absorb an almost infinite supply of shoes, textiles, semiconductors, petrochemicals, steel, automobiles, and automobile parts.

The seemingly endless export boom began having problems in the mid-1990s.[7] Thailand was the first country in Southeast Asia to experience virtually zero growth in its export markets, signaling to speculators the vulnerability of Thai foreign exchange reserves that had become dependent on foreign borrowings rather than on foreign trade earnings.

In Thailand, only one-third of the non-performing loans that crushed the financial sector came from investments in property. An additional one-third originated from manufacturing. Although not directly related to export industries, estimated levels of industrial oversupply for Thailand in early 1997 indicate a manufacturing establishment poised on the brink of collapse. According to Saicheua (1997), Thailand's automotive industry had an oversupply level of 192 percent; modern housing in Bangkok had an oversupply of 200 percent; petrochemicals an oversupply of 195 percent; steel bar production an oversupply of 150 percent; and private hospital beds had an oversupply of 300 percent.

If misjudging the markets had been characteristic of only Thai entrepreneurs and their bankers, the financial crisis would not have become a region-wide event featuring an eventual collapse of inter-Asian trade. Rapid expansion of domestic lending in similar industries also led to excess capacity in China, where a 1995 survey of capacity utilization showed 60 percent utilization rates for 900 major industrial products (see Lardy 1999). Part of this stemmed from the chronic inefficiency of the older, state-owned enterprises (SOEs). Serious oversupply conditions also were apparent in more recent investments such as automobile production and the varied products of the township and village enterprises (TVEs) that had been responsible for most new employment opportunities in China during the late 1980s and 1990s. One seasoned observer estimated production levels in the TVEs had fallen approximately 50 percent by the end of 1997. The construction boom, especially in Shanghai and Beijing, had far exceeded market demand by late 1996. By 1999, Shanghai will have as many upscale office spaces as Hong Kong, with most financed by domestic lending. The conclusion of the construction boom caused an immediate contraction in employment, while sharply elevating non-performing loans of the major Chinese banks.

Chinese auto production slowed prior to the advent of the Asian crisis, working at only half capacity in late 1996 (Wards Auto World December 1996). Likewise in Thailand, car buying dropped off at the beginning of the year before the outside world sensed any serious economic downturn. In Korea, domestic sales of automobiles and commercial vehicles had fallen by 13 percent in the first five months of 1997, well before the crisis. After the crash these markets became chronically saturated with automobiles. In Japan, by the first half of 1998 domestic automobile production on a monthly basis had declined by 25 percent in comparison to the year before. Toyota's exports to ASEAN in January 1998 fell by 42 percent from the same period in 1997, while Nissan's sales to ASEAN shrank by 40 percent and Mazda's by 52 percent (Indonesian Commercial Newsletter, March 16, 1998). Likewise, Japanese machine tool domestic sales were down by more than 15 percent in the first half of 1998 compared to a year earlier.

Neither Asian entrepreneurs nor major Western investors should have been caught unaware by the events of 1997. By the early 1990s the misallocation of investments that would bring the great Asian boom to a halt was visible to the naked eye in cities such as Bangkok and Shanghai (see Ramo 1998).[8] In early 1995, Bangkok was becoming a city of dark towers, where completed buildings stood empty against the night sky while finance companies and real estate developers continued to borrow and build (Figure 1.4). Everyone assumed the expansion would never stop, and many assumed that an 8.5 percent annual expansion of the GDP had become a permanent parameter of the business environment. Such a high rate of expansion could absorb any number of office spaces and condominiums, petrochemical complexes, steel plants, and semiconductor factories. Practically down to the month the balloon burst in Bangkok, macroeconomic statistics (with the exception of the current account deficit) continued to mislead observers because glutted real estate and manufacturing markets were masked by balanced budgets, low inflation, and high rates of savings and investment.

Theories of Causality

The Asian financial crisis illustrates the absence of unified theory among social scientists. Each discipline remains tied to its own partial explanations, rejecting the

FIGURE 1.4 Asia Pacific Office Vacancy Rates, 1996–1998

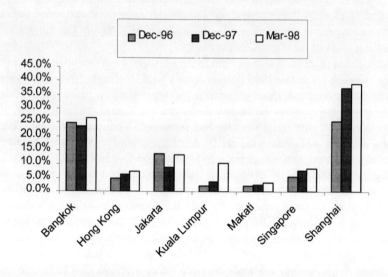

Source: Jones, Lang, Wooten

explanations drawn from other disciplines. In reality, there are three complementary streams of causality rising from political science, economics, and investment banking.

For example, political scientists and journalists tend to depict the crisis in Jakarta as being almost solely the product of familism and cronyism. According to this logic, if only the Suharto family had not taken so much, for so long, from so many, and had not concentrated such a large portion of the national wealth in its own hands, then the Indonesian economy might not have collapsed. This represents, at best, only part of the story. Primitive business practices (e.g., absence of accounting standards, overestimation of asset values, and disguised liabilities) are found throughout the Indonesian business and banking systems; they are not limited to institutions controlled by the Suharto family and its cronies.

On the other hand, economists saw the plummeting rupiah as the product of a regional panic and an overvalued currency. Relatively scant consideration was given to either the internal economic weaknesses flowing from gross misallocation of investments or the political interests which both facilitated the misallocation and precluded unwinding them prior to a political transition. Especially during the initial stages of the crisis, economists portrayed the crisis as a panic and assumed things would calm down quickly once the market realized the underlying macro-economic strengths of the economy and recognized that the market had overshot in devaluing the rupiah. Concentration on macroeconomic models tended to blind economists to the microeconomic mess which, on a firm-by-firm basis, had under-mined the foundations of the Asian economic miracle.[9]

Finally, market analysts perceived the crisis as involving weak banks and real estate speculation, in addition to fixed exchange rates, partially overvalued currencies, and political uncertainty. More than others, market analysts sensed the degree to which the Asian miracle was, in fact, a house of cards. By virtue of being directly involved in commerce, financial analysts sensed glutted markets and vulnerable financial structures. Market analysts and foreign exchange traders have been special targets of economic nationalists like Prime Minister Mahathir, but it was the financial analysts who first predicted boom turning into gloom and rapidly moved their resources elsewhere. They did not cause the crash but simply identified it, and, through their reactions, further accelerated it.

Market analysts, however, were not without their own blinders. They were often the other half of loans that should not have been made, either because they believed biased information provided by corporations and governments or because they believed (quite amorally) that there was one last deal to be made before rushing for the market exit. Market analysts tended to neglect good governance issues ranging from the underdeveloped government regulatory and supervisory capacities, the absence of modern planning and control mechanisms at the corporate level (detailed business plans based on realistic projections, transparent auditing procedures, etc.), and the ways in which competition among interest groups can immobilize governments in the early stages of a financial crisis, thereby precluding a soft landing.

Both economists and market analysts tended to be relatively insensitive to the political dimensions that would exacerbate the crisis once it broke. In Thailand and Indonesia, for instance, the most acute aspects of the crisis might have been avoided if each country, in its own way, had not been politically immobilized. As the crisis broke, Thai democracy was controlled by a coalition of up-country politi-cians who had little interest in fixing Bangkok's financial institutions and pro-tecting the Bangkok middle class from economic ruin. Only after a new constitu-tion had been adopted and a new government had taken office in November 1997 did Thailand begin to put in place the painful reforms required to regain the confidence of the international marketplace. In Indonesia, no Suharto cabinet could unwind the special interests choking the marketplace, because the web of special interests constituted almost the entire base of the government's political support. Reforms could not be adopted because their content threatened the regime's very existence.

A Comprehensive Approach

Understanding and explaining what came to be known as the Asian contagion requires abandoning the certainties of disciplinary parochialism in favor of a more comprehensive approach to all facets of the Asian crisis. Since no single cause is both necessary and sufficient to explain the contagion's spread within or among countries, this volume contains several case studies. Included are the country where the first symptoms of the crisis appeared in the early 1990s (Japan); three of the most prominent victims of the Asian crisis (Thailand, Indonesia, and Korea); two of the most notable exceptions (China and India); the Philippines, where reforms instituted during previous crises partially precluded a disaster of the proportions experienced in Thailand and Indonesia; and an economy partly insulated from the Asian contagion by it own isolation and relatively low level of economic development (Vietnam).

Understanding why some countries became victims while others remained relatively healthy requires analyzing the political, economic, and financial aspects of each case. Thailand, Indonesia, and Korea fell victim because all five of the following factors were present simultaneously:

- Capital account convertibility
- Fixed exchange rates
- Excessive expansion of domestic lending accompanied by gross misallocation of investments by the private sector
- Absence of regulatory and supervisory capacities to control excesses in the financial sector
- Paralysis of political decision making at the onset of the crisis.

Thailand, Indonesia, and Korea manifested all five elements, whereas China and India shared several but not all of the same characteristics. For this reason, China and India have not fallen victim to the Asian financial crisis, but each remains susceptible because it possesses several of the main underlying weaknesses. The Chinese economy, for example, suffers from misallocation of investments and massive insolvency within its banking system; but it has remained economically stable during the first year of the crisis for several reasons. First, its currency is not freely convertible and therefore is not susceptible to attack by speculators (except by proxy via the Hong Kong dollar). Second, although China—like Thailand, Indonesia, and Korea—has expanded its domestic lending at a torrid pace, its banking system is saddled with relatively little short-term foreign debt. Third, China has emphasized foreign direct investment and accumulated record trade surpluses and foreign reserve holdings. Finally, China has benefited from relatively decisive political leadership, which has reacted to the Asian crisis by undertaking financial reforms designed to preempt any onset of the crisis inside China itself.

China has not yet fallen victim to the Asian financial flu, but it might do so in the future because of misallocation of investment, overproduction, insolvent banks, and declining rates of internal economic growth.

Likewise, the Indian economy hosts a fragile banking system and the inefficient post-infant industries that are the products of forty years of centralized planning in combination with isolation from the global economy. Only in the 1990s, under the reforms initiated by the Rao government, have large amounts of foreign direct investment begun to flow into India. The speculative boom characterizing much of Asia simply did not have sufficient time to develop the excesses necessary to bring down the entire economic system. Also, the group of technocrats guiding the Indian economy have been particularly adept during the 1990s, creating high levels of growth which have legitimized the whole process of internal economic reform. Further, India (like China) has the stability conferred by the size of its internal market as well as the relative isolation of its economy. India and China (like Vietnam) had no capital account convertibility. The economic isolation of India may have constrained the upside of economic expansion but it also limited the downside of potential economic catastrophe.

Lessons from the Afflicted Asian Tigers

Thailand, Indonesia, and Korea illustrate the combination of external and internal factors that have created Asia's worst economic decline in three decades. First, all three countries had overextended banks, which were caught in a vice between domestic borrowers who could not pay, and foreign lenders who became increasingly reluctant to lend. Second, all three countries experienced massive capital flight as soon as the crisis began. Credit lines dried up and foreign banks became increasingly reluctant to roll over previously extended short-term loans. Third, all three countries had relatively immobilized political systems at the time the crisis struck. The constellation of vested interests in these counries precluded bold policy responses which might have mitigated the sharp decline in domestic and international confidence.

In Thailand, Korea, Malaysia, and the Philippines (although not in Indonesia), the fall in the stock market was one telltale sign of the coming of the overall crisis (Figure 1.5). By January 1997, well before the baht came under pressure, the Stock Exchange of Thailand (SET) had already fallen 51 percent from its 1993 high. Likewise, the Korean stock market fell 36 percent between 1994 and 1996. Although the stock market of Malaysia had fallen by 24 percent in 1994 and remained down in 1995, it had almost recovered in 1996 before falling again at the beginning of 1997—months prior to the crisis.[10]

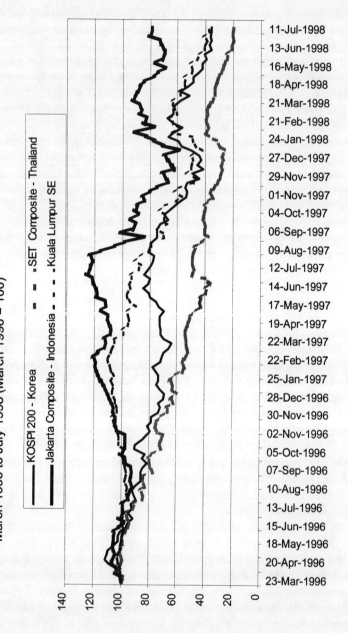

FIGURE 1.5   Stock Market Indices for Korea, Thailand, Indonesia, and Malaysia
March 1996 to July 1998 (March 1996 = 100)

The fate of property market indices, rather than indices for whole markets, proved an even more reliable predictor of the oncoming crash. Between 1993 and 1996, property stocks in Indonesia, Malaysia, and Thailand had fallen 33 percent, 20 percent, and 73 percent, respectively, before plunging into oblivion in 1997.[11] The rapid decline of property stocks was a harbinger of doom for finance companies and those banks which had lent heavily to property companies during the late 1980s and early 1990s. The fact that property stock fell earlier and more steeply than stock markets in general probably means that domestic capital began to exit the stock markets first. In more general studies, declining equity prices have also been shown to correlate with the breakdown of fixed exchange rate systems (Kaminsky, Lizondo, and Reinhart 1997; Taylor 1998).

The movements of international capital, in turn, multiplied the impact of the crisis once it had begun. There was a contagious loss of confidence by domestic elites across Asia, leading them to move liquid assets to more secure havens in North America and Western Europe. Within the first year of the Asian crisis, over $200 billion had fled from the five affected Asian markets, amounting to roughly 18 percent of the combined GDPs of the five countries (Severino 1998). Markets can punish and they can forgive; restoration of foreign confidence had been partially achieved by Thailand and Korea in early 1998 before local equity markets returned to record lows in early summer.

Thailand, Indonesia, and Korea were all required by the IMF to adopt policies that were more appropriate to Latin America in the 1980s than to Southeast Asia in the 1990s. In spite of the fact that before the crisis the Asian Tigers had balanced budgets, the IMF required belt-tightening monetary and fiscal policies, including budget surpluses. This requirement crushed consumer demand and brought the current account rapidly into surplus—but at the expense of kindling a deep recession and a substantial decline in inter-Asian trade. Subsequent discussions led the IMF to relax the budget surplus requirements, but not before unemployment in the major cities had spiked to record levels.

Both Thailand and Indonesia were at the end of a building boom when the crisis struck. Poorly financed property companies had built too many upscale offices and high-priced condominiums on the assumption that rapid economic expansion was a continuing certainty. When growth collapsed, even existing office space began to empty with the result being that central business area office vacancy rates in Jakarta and Bangkok will be approximately 20 percent in 1998–1999. Once the pain of the property companies was transferred to the banking system, non-performing loan balances resulted which precluded further loans to virtually any business by any bank. Non-performing loan balances were already critically high prior to the onset of the crisis; and when foreign credit lines and domestic deposits both dried up, the banking systems melted down. Loans for normal business activity became almost impossible. Banks, with inadequate capital reserves, simply could not lend and normal commerce stopped. Even export financing for businesses with signed contracts could not be obtained from the banks, thereby limiting the ability of each country to export its way out of the crisis.

Thailand and Indonesia both suffer from a legacy of political clientelism. Until 1973, when the students first brought down the military, Thailand was a bureaucratic polity, that is, a state ruled by and for the benefit of a narrow circle of officials, both uniformed and civilian, who comprised the upper levels of the civil and military bureaucracies. Neither political parties nor voluntary organizations existed which were capable of disciplining or sharing power with the civil and military bureaucrats. In the 1940s and 1950s, the entire Sino-Thai business community was exploited as a source of rent by the ruling bureaucratic elite. The expansion of the Thai economy was brought about in an atmosphere of "competitive clientelism" in which different portions of the business elite competed for the patronage from different parts of the bureaucratic elite (see Doner and Ramsay 1999).

During the 1950s and 1960s, the wealth of the Bangkok business elite grew substantially. Prestige eventually flowed toward money, even while the essence of political power remained in the Thai bureaucratic community. The expansion of university education, the growth of the Thai middle class, and the extension of economic and communication networks into the hinterland, all further populated the Thai political stage with new actors. In a gradual process, extending from the student uprising of 1973 through the democracy movement of 1992, these new forces seized control of the Thai political system. In doing so they transformed it from a bureaucratic polity into a democracy. The basis of modern Thai democracy remains clientelist, however. Politics is based on neither ideology nor permanent organizational membership, but on constantly changing cliques of patrons and shifting groups of clients. Politics in present-day Thailand remains democratic and particularistic, a search for benefits for one's own patron-client grouping, rather than the pursuit of generalized legal change designed to benefit all members of a wider social grouping.

The expansion of participation beyond the confines of narrow elite politics has had two important effects on Thailand. First, military rule has ceased being a long-term option. Although military rule might not be out of the question if Thailand descended into chaos, it is no longer the normal form of government that it was from 1932 to 1973. Second, democracy has meant one-man, one-vote and this has shifted power away from the civilian side of the Bangkok bureaucracy to political party leaders drawn largely from the provinces (Robertson 1995). Technocrats can now wield real power only if they are also political leaders with genuine, grassroots constituencies. Three-quarters of the wealth of Thailand is located in the cities (primarily Bangkok), while three-quarters of the votes remain in the countryside (Laothamatas 1996). Under democracy, Bangkok has lost its automatic preeminence, and unsophisticated rural politicians have dominated three out of the five democratic governments. The Bangkok elite, as reflected by the Bangkok mass media, refused to accept the leadership or legitimacy of the Chatchai, Banharn, or Chavalit governments. The very acceptability to Bangkok of the first and second Chuan governments provides one important root of ongoing political instability. Paradoxically, in the past it is His Royal Majesty, King Bhumiphol, who has been absolutely critical to insuring the survival of clean governments that were backed by Bangkok, and thus far he seems to be quietly using his immense authority to support the second Chuan government.

Suharto's Indonesia was a presidential variant of bureaucratic polity in which power to influence the most important decisions of the state was concentrated almost exclusively in the ruling circle of officers and bureaucrats in nearest proximity to the President (Jackson 1978). Patron-client relationships were the most important form of political glue tying Suharto's Indonesia together. State enterprises and the state budget were dispensed as the personal largesse of the President. While clientelism in Thailand featured competitive bureaucratic and business cliques, clientelism in Indonesia became monopolistic. In the end, this is what dramatically weakened President Suharto along with the economic modern-ization which had bred the beginnings of a middle class. At the end of the day, President Suharto had very few clients who were actually willing to fight to maintain his power. The problem was that corruption had ceased being sufficiently widespread. When it became limited to cronies and family members only, the power base of the regime shrank dramatically. After thirty-two years in power, Suharto had become so weak that not even a significant armed confrontation proved necessary to bring down the regime. President Suharto in the aftermath of the Crash of 1997, like Ferdinand Marcos in the Philippines in the wake of the commodities recession of the early 1980s, fell rather quickly: performance regimes that lack other (noneconomic) sources of legitimacy tend to collapse during sharp economic downturns.

The Future

The relative emphasis here on domestic factors is not meant to deny the rele-vance of international sources of the contagion. Bhalla (1999) has written exten-sively concerning the degree to which China's exports undercut Southeast Asia's after China's devaluation in 1994. According to his theory, the financial crisis in Southeast Asia was set in motion when Southeast Asian export markets were undercut by China's 7 percent devaluation on January 1, 1994. By contrast, Ferald, Edison, and Loungani (1999) contend the sharp downturn in demand for ASEAN exports had relatively little to do with China's 1994 nominal devaluation, which was actually a minor downward adjustment in a 60 percent appreciation of the Chinese currency in real exchange rate terms during 1993–1996. They argue that slower economic growth rates in Japan and Western Europe, a downturn in worldwide demand for computer chips, and the depreciation of the yen were more directly related to the declining rate of ASEAN export growth. Furthermore, China's gains in the export markets have come at the expense of the newly industrialized economies (Korea, Singapore, and Taiwan) rather than at the expense of Thailand, Indonesia, Malaysia, and the Philippines.

Each of these theories may be partially true. China's 100 percent increase in exports from 1993 to 1996 may have caused significant problems for Southeast Asia, but mainly because of a general oversupply in Asia rather than as a result solely of falling exchange rates. Support for this compromise interpretation can be found in the list of industries where China accumulated excess capacity in the 1990s: office buildings, automobiles and auto parts, steel, petrochemicals, and so forth. These are precisely the areas into which Southeast Asian nations, like Thailand, were mistakenly pouring investments during the 1990s.

This is not to deny the destabilizing impact, especially in the short term, of competitive devaluation. During the first stage of the Asian crisis, Singapore and Taiwan both refused to protect the value of their currencies and allowed them instead to depreciate by approximately 20 percent. This preserved their international competitiveness but also created pressure on the Hong Kong dollar and the Korean won. A major destabilizing factor in 1998 will continue to be the weakening yen and the increasing pressure this is creating for a Chinese devaluation at the beginning of 1999 (Figure 1.6).

Although the conventional wisdom during the first half of 1998 assumed China would not devalue its currency, the continuing slowdown of the Chinese economy, sharply declining production in the employment-producing township and village enterprises, and the collapse of much of inter-Asian trade have forced analysts to reassess this line of thinking. Virtually all agree there are circumstances under which the yuan will be devalued. In what may have been a trial balloon to condition the international marketplace, a high-ranking official of the People's Bank of China wrote on May 6, 1998:

> There are difficulties associated with the strategy of maintaining the exchange rate and the consequences of slowing exports to the domestic economy could be far-reaching. First, falling export competitiveness may affect those foreign investors, particularly small and medium size firms, who use China mainly as an export production base. As a result, inflows of foreign investment may slow down. Second, with a drop in export revenue and a slowdown in capital inflows, supporting an overvalued exchange rate could be costly and result in a substantial reduction in official exchange reserves. Third, a setback to export growth is likely to cap economic growth in the next two years making the current structural adjustments even more difficult (Yi Gang 1998:5-6).

The most powerful arguments against further devaluation of the yuan are that many of China's exports are based on foreign inputs and that a Chinese devaluation

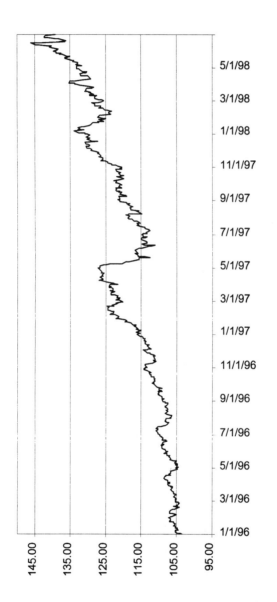

FIGURE 1.6 US Dollar / Japanese Yen Exchange Rate, January 1996–June 1998

also would imperil the prospects of Hong Kong. According to this argument, a Chinese devaluation would be followed by competitive devaluations throughout the rest of Asia, which would prevent China from gaining any real advantage from a devaluation. Unfortunately, these arguments are more frequently voiced in New York, London, and Washington than in Beijing. On the eve of President Clinton's July 1998 trip to China, the U.S. government initiated a large-scale intervention in the currency markets to prop up the value of the yen in order to stave off a devaluation of the yuan during the president's visit. The joint American and Japanese intervention was prompted by statements from Beijing indicating that China would not be able to maintain the yuan if the yen continued to depreciate against the dollar.

The near universal fear among policymakers and currency traders alike is that a Chinese devaluation, perhaps combined with an adjustment of the Hong Kong dollar peg, would lead to a further round of downwardly cascading exchange rates throughout Asia. A Chinese devaluation in late 1998 or early 1999 might set off another set of devaluations in Asia. This would continue until valuations were reached at which world markets would absorb a sufficient portion of the over-capacity produced throughout Asia by the heady investment boom of the 1990s. Such an event would probably mark the bottom of the Asian financial crisis from which the recovery of drastically devalued Asian assets would begin.[12]

In any case, the Asian crisis is now more than a year old and appears far from over. Fixed exchange rates have been replaced by floating ones, and current accounts have moved from deficit to surplus. The afflicted economies remain in deep recession, bordering on depression (see Severino 1998). The standard IMF medicine did not work well in Thailand, where it has been the most successful, or in Indonesia where the results, for both political and economic reasons, have been disastrous. The economies under the direct care of the IMF doctor currently remain in the economic equivalent of an intensive care ward.

Talk of the crisis being over in eighteen months now seems far-fetched. Asia, unlike Mexico, does not border on the most dynamic economy in the world, and Asia is not likely to be admitted to NAFTA any time soon. The logical engine for pulling Asia out of the crisis is Japan, but this would-be economic locomotive is itself stalled at the station. It suffers from the "Five-Ds": debt, deflation, default, demography, and the absence of deregulation (see Asher and Smithers 1999). Both government and corporate debt have reached levels that will be difficult to sustain in the long run. Average debt/equity ratios in corporate Japan at present are at least 4 to 1, resembling more closely Korean rather than U.S. corporations. In 1997 real public debt in Japan (from all sources) probably exceeded 150 percent of GDP, higher on a per capita basis than the public debt of Italy. The assets of Japan will continue to deflate, especially domestic real estate and the stock market, as will the holdings of corporate Japan in Southeast Asia and Hong Kong. At present the sum of bankruptcies, as a percentage of GDP, have reached a post-World War II high;

the current level exceeds that in the U.S. at the depth of the Great Depression. The banks are encumbered with $600 billion to $1 trillion in non-performing loans, and the government has yet to chart a clear course for auctioning non-performing loans to clear the markets to allow economic growth to begin again.

With Asia's fastest aging population, new entrants to the economy will not be a stimulus for a high rate of growth. Although Japanese manufacturing institutions are highly efficient, labor productivity elsewhere, particularly in services and in agriculture, remains low in comparison to the remainder of the industrial world. Nowhere is low efficiency more crippling than in the Japanese financial sector, which needs to be de-bureaucratized rather than just de-regulated (see Dattel 1999). Land, labor, and capital—as factors in production—must be deregulated, exposing them to levels of competition capable of creating world-class performance standards. In spite of having saved more than any economy in the world, Japan must either embark on fundamental economic reform or it will be condemned to a slow but inexorable decline (Asher and Smithers 1999).

Lurking behind the "Five D's" is a sixth D: indecisiveness. Since the end of the bubble economy, the Japanese political system has been incapable of extricating the system from crisis. This is partly because the vast majority of Japanese do not perceive the fundamental ills of the system and partly because "the 1955 system" (comprised of a dominant, multi-factional Liberal Democratic Party and an un-electable Socialist Party) has ended, but with no strong system of government to take its place. Japan remains basically a one-party system in search of a viable alternative governing party. Furthermore, the bureaucrats, who along with the major corporations ran Japan during the post-World War II era, have lost prestige and power because their leadership has been inadequate in coping with the demands of a highly competitive, globalized economy, especially in the field of finance (see Dattel 1999). In addition, scandals have destroyed the legitimacy of Tokyo bureaucrats as a group for honest public service. In sum, MOF no longer rules, but nobody else does either. The result is policy paralysis rather than the kind of decisiveness required to move the world's second largest economy back to the path of robust growth.

In Thailand, Indonesia, and Korea (and one suspects, Japan), macroeconomic policies alone have not brought and will not bring recovery rapidly enough to quell pressures for more radical change (economic nationalism of the left or right). The financial crisis was basically caused by a defective Asian banking system, which led to vast misallocation of investments by the private sector. As a result, the banking systems deserve a significant share of the blame, but their recovery requires public resources, and without state-induced recovery of the banking system general economic recovery will be impossible. Only when the banks are healthy and begin to lend again to private businesses can the economies return to growth and industrial workers to their jobs.

In Thailand, Indonesia, and Korea, the size of the hole in the financial system created by domestic and foreign debt remains enormous. Non-performing loans in Thailand equal approximately one-quarter of the GDP. In Korea, returning private firms to a 2:1 debt/equity ratio would require in excess of $400 billion in new equity. Japan has both the largest banking problem (measured in absolute size) and the largest savings resources with which to deal with it. China, on the other hand, carries a massive load of bad bank debt on the books but as yet has not faced a crisis of confidence internationally or among its depositors (see Lardy 1999).

One solution is nationalization of the banking systems. This is being done partially in Korea and Thailand. Moral hazard notwithstanding, the only workable alternative may be to nationalize some of the banks, while simultaneously guaranteeing the savings (at least of small depositors), stripping out the bad assets of the banks, and clearing the markets by selling these assets. In addition, the newly nationalized banks should themselves be privatized at the earliest possible moment. The budgetary resources of most nations will not be sufficient to accomplish these arduous tasks. Furthermore, in each of these newly democratic societies, there is substantial popular resistance to bailing out banking institutions widely perceived to have been both incompetent and corrupt.

Policy Implications

What is to be done? There are at least seven requirements. First, reality must be recognized. The Asian crisis is a threat to global economic well-being, and governments in Washington and Tokyo must move beyond denial. The problems described above are found in virtually every Asian financial system, with the partial exceptions of Hong Kong, Singapore, and Taiwan, and the impact will continue to spread unless a credible multinational effort is mounted by the capital rich countries.

Second, policymakers must squarely confront the primarily private sector nature of this crisis. Not only must the banks be fixed, but also the problems of the real sector must be dealt with through complex restructuring that only the private sector can adequately accomplish. Beyond the banking sector, only company-by-company restructuring, complete with management changes and loan write-downs, can return companies and employees to work. This requires a massive recapitalization effort, a partnership between the state (changing regulations and the economic parameters) and the private sector (both foreign and domestic). Recovery must primarily be a private sector solution. But resolution cannot come without a strong public policy component, because current owners will not sell out at rock bottom prices and need the state to shoulder, at least temporarily, part of the debt burden to facilitate fast, as well as fair, restructuring.

Third, the private sector *alone* cannot supply all of the answers, at least not in sufficient time to preclude a more generalized global slowdown and the possible political instabilities that would flow from it. Private capital from Europe and North America remains reluctant to reinvest the $200 billion withdrawn from the five affected Asian countries during the last year until it can see at least the beginning of the end of the crisis. An initial wave of recapitalization was undertaken during the first half of 1998. The losses (in share values) to the new investors of early 1998 in several instances exceed 50 percent after just three months. Major intermediaries, burned in early 1998, will be twice reluctant later in the year unless new international measures are adopted to reassure the market.

Fourth, Washington must recognize that not one of the economically afflicted systems—not Japan, not China, not Korea, not Indonesia, and not Thailand—has the political will, *on its own*, to make the necessary financial changes rapidly enough to preclude its own destruction at the polls. Good governments and bad tend to lose elections when economies collapse. Altering the national leadership may lead to an improved response to the financial crisis (as in Thailand and Korea) or to continued drift (as in Indonesia and Japan). An appropriately designed multilateral institution could bolster economic reform policies regardless of which political party or faction comes to power.

Fifth, Asian elites can only enforce the required sacrifices if a new international financial institution is created to support the tough decisions necessary to restructure broken banking systems.[13] The day-to-day workings of an international restructuring agency would alter the culture of Asian finance, requiring it to move away from the personalism/familism of relationship-based banking to credit-based decisions emphasizing independent audits and honest asset evaluation. The new international structure should be designed to transfer to Asia the financial technologies created by the private sector during the 1980s and 1990s. Bringing new financial vehicles to Asia (from venture capital funds to leveraged buy outs) is at least as important as transferring particular lessons learned from the Swedish banking crisis and the American S & L debacle of the 1980s.

Sixth, the United States should take the lead in organizing such a new financial institution by rallying the resources of the G-7 to supply the capital inputs necessary to prevent the Crash of 1997 from becoming an Asian depression.

Seventh, the alternative to bold action may be a depth of socioeconomic and political instability in Asia in the next twenty years that will be reminiscent of the period 1930–1960. Can anyone conceive of a decade long depression not creating an outburst of economic nationalism in Indonesia? Likewise, would it not be prudent to create an international institution capable of dealing with a massive banking crisis before, rather than during, the next banking crisis (perhaps in China in 2001)?

Even though at present public opinion throughout the G-7 countries remains riveted on the reality of its own prosperity, the long-term global political risks of the Crash of 1997 remain of historic proportions. Economic liberalization of the global marketplace is already threatened, and if only one of the major political systems (for instance, Indonesia or China) becomes radicalized as a result of an unchecked crisis, the levels of expenditure required to contain the political consequences will dwarf the scale of preventive measures that might now be taken.

The years 1997 and 1998 have witnessed a vast reversal of economic fortunes in Asia. The worst may be yet to come, depending on when, whether, and how the yuan is devalued. The political stability and long-term economic viability of Asia in the first quarter of the twenty-first century will depend on the quantity and quality of the international public and private response. At this point the stakes are very high, but policymakers, at least in Washington, remain remarkably uninvolved, believing the crisis will take care of itself or that acting incisively might involve them in "moral hazard," or that as leaders, they are simply powerless to act internationally in the post-Cold War world. Unfortunately, it may be too late politically in Asia before the West fully realizes that neglect is not benign at this historic juncture, and that an opportunity to establish itself as the model for politics and commerce for the next century may be lost for lack of insight and fortitude.

Notes

1. Familism is defined as a disproportionate attention to the interests of the nuclear, (and in Asia, the extended) family at the expense of considering the good of the community as a whole. The predatory behaviors of the Marcos and Suharto families remain difficult to comprehend without reference to amoral familism, the tendency to maximize only the wealth and well-being of one's family and to behave largely without scruples whenever something comes into conflict with the interests of the family. On the concept of amoral familism, see Banfield (1958).

2. The magnitude of the boom in the stock markets of Southeast Asia was obvious in the early 1990s. The indices of the stock exchanges of Indonesia, Malaysia, the Philippines, and Thailand for 1991–1993, increased by 37 percent, 50 percent, 58 percent, and 56 percent per annum for three consecutive years. In this casino-like atmosphere, all manner of phony valuations and chain listings of the same assets for multiple companies created massive equity bubbles based on unrealistic valuations. Of the five affected economies, only Korea showed moderate increases of 8 percent per annum for the period 1991–1994. Interestingly, the very markets that ascended so quickly leveled off and, with the exception of Indonesia, moved systematically downward. This indicated the boom had really begun to fade domestically in 1994, long before the collapse of the currencies in mid-1997. For a diametrically different view regarding asset bubbles and the import of private sector mismanagement, see Bhalla (1999).

3. The truly pernicious interaction between managed exchange rates and responsible fiscal polices is described in detail by Bhalla (1999).

4. Precise figures on the proportion of non-performing loans remain elusive because each banking system had its own criteria for defining them. The 20 percent figure seems

reasonable, however, if non-performance is defined as non-payment of principal and interest for ninety days and if finance companies are included in the calculation.

5. If 50 cents on the dollars can theoretically be recovered on the 20 percent of loans that are non-performing, this means a loss of 10 percent of total loan portfolio—which is probably more than the total equity of most banks at a given point in time.

6. Declining economic growth and low rates of return in both Europe and Japan in the early 1990s made Asia a particularly attractive alternative, and over time hundreds of billions of dollars in outside private capital became available to the emerging markets. Japanese government attempts to escape from slow growth included lowering interest raes to near zero. This meant that Japanese seeking returns needed to look abroad for higher returns on loans than could be obtained onshore in Japan.

7. Bhalla (1999) strongly believes that the Chinese devaluation of 1994 led directly to the collapse of Southeast Asian export growth and that this, in turn, set off the Crisis of 1997.

8. After a trip to Bangkok in December 1994 and as a result of analyzing the Jones, Lang, and Wooten data on the office real estate market, my colleague at FX Concepts, Inc., R. Roderick Porter, and I passed a letter indirectly to the Governor of the Bank of Thailand. It stated: "As of 9/30/94 the supply of office space in the Bangkok area was 4,054,582 square meters. Of that, 2,528,730 square meters (62%) was completed since the beginning of 1992. Even more extraordinarily, an additional 3,087,730 square meters is likely to enter the market before the end of 1997. That will bring the supply to 7,142,325 square meters of which 79% will have been completed since 1992."

"With Bangkok's current office vacancy running at around 20%, it is clear that it will be difficult to absorb the additional space no matter how fast Thailand's economic growth proves to be. These statistics indicate the Bangkok may be on the verge of a real estate crisis like the Savings and Loan crisis in the United States and the non-performing real estate loan problem currently crippling banks in Japan. We believe that devising a game plan early which utilizes the experience gained in the American real estate/banking crisis could minimize the damage to Thailand."

9. Eugene Dattel's work places emphasis on the importance of firm-by-firm analysis and the degree to which each country's business organizations and practices are an outgrowth of their own culture (see Dattel 1994 and 1999).

10. With floating exchange rates there is virtually no correlation on a day-to-day basis between the strength of a currency and the fluctuations of its stock market. As John R. Taylor (1998) has pointed out, in countries which are capital poor and which have fixed exchange rates, the local stock market serves as a proxy for the strength or weakness of the currency. Government operations to maintain the peg suppress any movement in the currency's value until it suddenly explodes out of the official band. Equity markets are not as controlled by the government, and the end of the game is nigh when the stock markets move precipitously downward, indicating that investors have withdrawn their vote of confidence from the business sector and that, if given the chance, they will move a substantial portion of their investments into liquid assets or actually move them out of country.

11. Interestingly, the Shanghai building frenzy also peaked in mid-1993 (see Ramo 1998:68).

12. This optimistic view rests on the assumption of continued robust economic growth in the United States. A sharp stock market correction or a recession in the United States would greatly complicate and delay the reemergence of Asian economic growth.

13. Although an independent agency might be ideal, the most important thing is to make restructuring the banks and closing those that are beyond help the number one priority of the international financial system. Neither the IMF (whose charter is to maintain currency stability) nor the World Bank (a development institution) was designed to act as an international equivalent of the Resolution Trust Corporation. Neither institution has the specialized experience or the skilled manpower required to produce the desired outcome.

References

Asher, D., and A. Smithers. 1999. Japan's Key Challenges for the 21st Century. In *The Asian Contagion*, ed. K. D. Jackson. Boulder, CO: Westview.

Banfield, E. 1958. *The Moral Basis of a Backward Society*. New York: Free Press.

Bhalla, S. S. 1999. Domestic Follies, Investment Crises: East Asian Lessons for India. In *The Asian Contagion*, ed. K. D. Jackson.

Cheetham, R. 1998. Asia Crisis. Paper presented at conference, U.S.-ASEAN-Japan Policy Dialogue. School of Advanced International Studies of Johns Hopkins University, June 7-9, in Washington, D.C.

Dattel, E. R. 1994. *The Sun That Never Rose: The Inside Story of Japan's Failed Attempt at Global Financial Domination*. Chicago: Probus.

——. 1999. Reflections of a Market Participant: Japanese and Asian Financial Institutions. In *The Asian Contagion*, ed. K. D. Jackson.

Doner, R., and A. Ramsay. 1999. Thailand: From Economic Miracle to Economic Crisis. In *The Asian Contagion*, ed. K. D. Jackson.

Ferald, J., H. Edison, and P. Loungani. 1999. Was China the First Domino? Assessing Links Between China and the Rest of Emerging Asia. Board of Governors of the Federal Reserve System, International Finance Discussion Paper No. 604.

Indonesian Commercial Newsletter. 1998. March 16.

Jackson, K. 1997. Thailand and the Crash of '97. Unpublished monograph. December.

——, ed. 1999. *The Asian Contagion: The Causes and Consequences of a Financial Crisis*. Boulder, CO: Westview.

Jackson, K., and L. Pye, eds. 1978. *Political Power and Communications in Indonesia*. Berkeley, CA.: University of California Press.

Kaminsky, G., S. Lizondo, and C. Reinhart. 1997. Leading Indicators of Currency Crises. Working Paper of the International Monetary Fund. July.

Kindleberger, C. 1996. *Manias, Panics, and Crashes: A History of Financial Crises*. New York: John Wiley.

Laothamatas, A. 1996. A Tale of Two Democracies: Conflicting Perceptions of Elections and Democracy in Thailand. In *The Politics of Elections in Southeast Asia*. ed. R. Taylor. New York: Cambridge University Press.

Lardy, N. R. 1999. China and the Asian Financial Contagion. In *The Asian Contagion*, ed. K. D. Jackson.

Loh, Hui Yin. 1997. "Mahathir Calls Soros 'Moron' in War of Words." *Business Times*. August 25.

Pyo, H. K. 1999. The Financial Crisis in South Korea: Anatomy and Policy Imperatives. In *The Asian Contagion*, ed. K. D. Jackson.

Ramo, J. 1998. The Shanghai Bubble. *Foreign Policy*. Summer.

Robertson, P. 1996. The Rise of the Rural Network Politician: Will Thailand's New Elite Endure? *Asian Survey* 36, no. 9.

Rohwer, J. 1995. *Asia Rising: Why America Will Prosper as Asia's Economies Boom*. New York: Simon and Schuster.

Severino, J. M. 1998. Speech at the International Herald Tribune Summit, June 16, in Melbourne, Australia.

Sicheua, S. 1997. The Way Out of the Economic Crisis. Unpublished paper. September 30.

Taylor, J. R. 1998. Paper presented at conference, The Dilemma of Emerging Markets Currency Risk Management. International Foreign Exchange Concepts Conference, June 22, in Auckland, New Zealand.

Wards Auto World. 1996. December.

Yi Gang and Song LiGang. 1998. East Asia in Crisis: From Being a Miracle to Needing One? Paper presented (The full text of a paper given by Yi Gang from the People's Bank of China and Song Ligang from Australia National University.) May 6.

2

Japan's Key Challenges for the 21st Century

David L. Asher and Andrew Smithers

Introduction

With the 21st century looming on the horizon, Japan's economy is in severe trouble. Despite recurrent waves of optimism that a sustainable recovery would be "just around the corner," Japanese economic performance in the 1990s has been a marked disappointment. Fifty years of prodigious growth have ended in a prolonged period of stagnation and asset market collapse. The government has expended tremendous fiscal energy since the beginning of the decade trying to extricate the economy from its immobile situation, only to find that the once mighty Japanese economy appears permanently mired in a bog.

The lead story on the cover of the *Nihon Keizai Shimbun* on New Year's Day 1997, traditionally a time of face-forward celebration in Japan as elsewhere, summed up the pressing situation: "Reform is going nowhere, while we're aging fast, becoming internationally isolated, and turning inward as a people." The article was the first in a twenty-part series on the nation's economic prospects looking toward 2020 subtitled disparagingly, "Japan is disappearing."[1]

By the beginning of 1998, Japan had slipped back into recession. The economy faced negative growth for the first time since 1974, three of its largest financial companies had gone under, and both consumer and producer confidence had sunk into record low territory. The world was left to wonder if Japan's once fabled economic might would disappear a lot sooner than by 2020.

The purpose of this chapter is to consider what the future may hold for the Japanese economy in the early part of the 21st century. Will Japan's economic power keep declining from here on? Or is the rising sun going to emerge from the darkness and blindside the other major world economies in the not-too-distant future with a mighty competitive resurgence as some pundits contend?[2] For those trying to sort out all the talk of doom and gloom from the chatter of comeback theorists, at root what factors are most likely to determine Japan's economic trajectory in the coming years? Furthermore, what are the key issues and hard choices facing policymakers and the Japanese people as they look ahead?

This analysis highlights five key challenges for Japan's economy looking toward the 21st century: (1) debt—very high levels of outstanding debt to GDP and debt to equity both in the private and public sectors; (2) deflation—distorted and deflating asset markets; (3) default—rising levels of business failures and unemployment; (4) demography—the growing financial burden of a rapidly aging population on society; and (5) deregulation—over-regulated and inefficient labor, land, and capital markets.

In order to achieve sustainable economic growth at a rate in excess of 1.5% per year these "five D's" will have to be systematically addressed in the near future. Unfortunately, we have only limited confidence in the ability and willingness of the Japanese government and business community to adjust to the nation's new economic realities and to take the necessary steps for restructuring and revitalization. Much hope is being placed on a "big bang" opening of Japan's financial markets. Insufficient attention is being paid, however, to the inevitable initial downside of financial deregulation in an economic environment plagued by chronic excess capacity, poor profitability, and unsustainably high degrees of leverage in industry. Although financial deregulation is critical to improving Japan's capital productivity and potential growth, unless it is accompanied by a restructuring of corporate balance sheets, the "big bang" is likely to turn out to be the "big bankruptcy" for a good many firms that have hitherto been thought too big to fail in a wide range of industries.

Our conclusion is that the policy failures of the post-bubble period indicate that a soft landing has become more or less impossible. Like a patient suffering from a slowly metastasizing cancer, Japan can opt for a very painful, though probably effective, course of treatment or accept gradual decline under the numbing influence of monetary and fiscal sedation. The longer Japan waits to decide what to do, however, the bleaker its chances are for a full recovery and the greater the damage to its economic health.

As things stand, the long-term prospects for growth are poor. Absent a radical reorientation of Japan's economic system away from debt toward equity, from producers toward consumers, and from excess state interference in markets toward freer competition, a large portion of Japan's considerable wealth and economic potential stands to be frittered away in the coming decades, just as they were in the 1990s.

Japan's Economy: Entering the 21st Century

Below we review in depth four key structural features of the contemporary Japanese economy that are likely to grow in prominence in the early part of the 21st

century: debt, deflation, default, and demography. Thereafter we consider Japan's long-range prospects for growth in light of a fifth "D," deregulation.

Japanese Debt: Even More than Meets the Eye

The long-term vitality of Japan's entire economic system is being sapped by a debt burden of truly gigantic proportions. Excessive debt is a problem that affects both the private sector and the public sector, threatening to sap rates of consumption, new investment, and capital accumulation for many years to come. Getting out of the debt trap is a prerequisite for a sustainable and balanced economic recovery.

The Private Sector: (1) Gross Leverage. By any comparative standard, Japanese corporations are highly leveraged. On a book value basis, Ministry of Finance data for companies with ¥10 million or more of capital indicates a debt/equity ratio of 4 to 1. In contrast, for U.S. companies the ratio is 1.5 to 1 on a book value basis and 1 to 1 in terms of replacement cost (an all-time high).[3]

Moreover, the situation of net indebtedness for Japanese companies may in fact be even worse than these figures suggest, due to the widespread use of equity cross-shareholdings as the cement for the well-known *keiretsu* system of intercorporate relations in Japan (well over 60% of the stock of companies listed on Japan's lead Nikkei 225 index is owned for "relationship reasons"). The existence of cross-shareholdings appears to increase the equity base of corporations without really doing so, as if it was all done with mirrors. This can be illustrated by assuming that two companies decide to create additional shares and proceed to swap them with one another. No new equity capital is raised by the corporate sector, but the data will give the appearance that gearing ratios have fallen.

(2) Grossly Underfunded Corporate Pensions. Underfunding of corporate pensions in Japan exacerbates the problem of excess leverage. The level of assets in Japan's private pension schemes is very low by the standards of the United States and United Kingdom. The proportion of private sector workers covered by corporate schemes appears to be similar in Japan to the situation in the United Kingdom and the United States, while the assets of the funds are only one seventh as large. Even allowing for their relative immaturity and other differences, this discrepancy suggests serious underfunding. The balance sheets of the twenty-four Japanese non-financial companies that file U.S. accounting statements confirm such a view. These companies have pension liabilities of ¥6.7 trillion but assets of only ¥4.0 trillion. They are 40% underfunded, a shortfall amounting to 17% of these corporations' net assets. Allowing for increased contributions to fund the gap over seven years, published profits overstated their true level by 34% in fiscal year 1995 (hereafter FY95).

However, the real situation is likely to be even worse than this data implies. The published shortfalls assume that future returns on pension investments will vary between 4 and 5.5%. From an actuarial viewpoint, it is unsatisfactory to assume, in advance, that different funds will achieve different returns; so it is desirable to use a standard rate for all. The rate of 5.5% has been the standard assumed in Japan in the past, but it has proved to be well beyond that actually achieved. It also is clearly too high in light of current long-term bond yields and the fact that one-third of corporate pension assets are invested through insurance companies, which currently offer an average return of only 2.5%. Even if a revised rate of 3.5% is accepted for all companies, the degree of overstatement of profits still rises to 43%. Thus, Japanese corporations not only will be under pressure from shareholders to reduce debt and increase returns on equity in the coming years, they also will be saddled with the task of paying a large percentage of their profits into their underfunded employee pensions.

The Government's "True" Level of Debt: (1) Grossly Unsettling Debt. A very high level of debt, of course, is not simply a problem for the private sector in Japan. It is a marked feature of the official Japanese government balance sheet, and it would stand out much more if Japanese government accounting practices were scrutinized to a greater degree.

Although all G5 countries have high gross debt/GDP ratios, Japan stands out as being 50% worse than the others, even when measured conventionally. Yet the nature of public finance in Japan is far from conventional. A great deal of the public sector investment in Japan is financed not by tax revenue and bond issuance but via government use of funds deposited in the nation's postal savings and life insurance schemes and in the state pension system. The vehicle for controlling these investments is the nearly ¥400 trillion Fiscal Investment and Loan Program (FILP). The FILP investment plan functions as Japan's "second budget." Each year the Ministry of Finance (MOF) prepares it alongside the general government budget. The FILP budget has come to be about two-thirds the size of the regular government budget (in FY96 the FILP's new investment authorization was over ¥40 trillion). Although the government manages FILP investments and the money is raised (essentially by *borrowing* from the people's savings accounts) with a state guarantee, the cost of this investment is not included in the figures for government borrowing. This a highly dubious and potentially deleterious practice.[4]

(2) The Scary Truth about the Japanese Government Debt. If FILP funds are treated as government borrowing rather than investment and the liabilities of the system are added to the national debt, Japan's public sector financial situation appears much worse than is commonly thought. For FY97 the OECD calculates that general government gross debt is nearly 90% of GDP. If one adds to this sum the liabilities of the Ministry of Finance's Trust Fund Bureau (the central funding conduit for the FILP)—after netting off the portion of the Bureau's assets which already are included in the figure for government debt—Japan's public sector level exceeds 150% of GDP. By this measure, Japan is the most indebted nation in the entire OECD.[5]

(3) The State's Combined Liabilities. Still, the big picture of government debt must include an estimate of the total liabilities it is obligated to repay—not just those it carries on (or off) its official books. Governments make, on behalf of taxpayers, two major promises with regard to future payments. The first is to pay the interest and principal on government debt, The second is to pay pensioners. The greater the combined liabilities, the more difficult it will be to meet both commitments.

Figure 2.1 estimates the total obligations of Japan's public sector towards both its debtors and its prospective pensioners in 1996.[6] In aggregate it is likely that they now exceed 250% of GDP. It is sometimes claimed that the size of Japan's debt/GDP ratio is overstated, because so much of the current debt is owned by the state pension scheme. It therefore should be emphasized that the above estimate of aggregate debt is net of these assets. It clearly will be difficult to meet such large obligations in full, and Japan's ability to do so will be largely dependent on the strength of its budgetary position.

(4) Budgetary Bobbling. Making matters worse, the enormity of dealing with the combined national debt and pension burden is compounded by the fact that Japan's budgetary position also is in peril. The central government's projected budget deficit for FY98 is around 7% of GDP. Although this level of budgetary shortfall seems bad, the number does not adequately convey the severity of Japan's budget crunch. Much more important is the fact that the cost of debt service (as of FY98) occupies 47% of retained central government tax revenue (i.e., after central government transfers to regional governments) while the ratio of outstanding long-term debt to retained tax revenues is worsening rapidly. For the central government, it is likely to exceed eleven times in FY98 (versus an average of five times from 1980–1992). These figures show that the dimensions of Japan's public debt problem are worse than those found in Italy (which under the pressure of the Mastricht criteria is pursuing fiscal reform), even before the off-balance FILP liabilities are accounted for. As we will explain later, to even begin to handle the government's acknowledged deficits (let alone address the problem of off-balance liabilities), either the ratio of tax to GDP will need to rise over the next few years by around 8% from 33% to 41%, or equivalent cuts will be needed in government expenditure.

Kunji Okue, an economist at Dresdner Kleinwort Benson Securities in Tokyo, points out the dire implications of this trend in the event of an economic recovery or a deterioration in the Japanese government bond market:

> Should interest rates rise going forward, debt service would balloon. If interest rates had remained at FY90 levels (average 10-year JGB yield 7.4%), the ratio of debt service to retained tax revenues in FY98 would likely have exceeded 60%. 60% of retained taxes dedicated to repaying debt means that spending would have to be covered with the remaining 40%. This would be impossible. In such a situation, the government would be unable to pay even half of the public servant payroll.[7]

FIGURE 2.1   Japan's Real Public Debt Burden (percent of GDP)

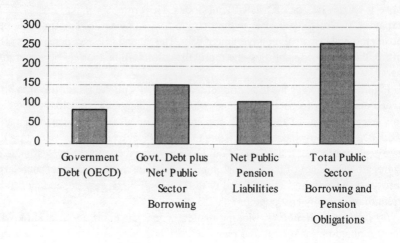

Source: Smithers & Co., London

Japan: A Nation in Deflation

The force of continued asset deflation magnifies Japan's debt problems. Since 1990 land and stock values have eroded precipitously, falling to levels last seen in the early 1980s. Moreover, there appears to be a long way to go before prices hit bottom.

The Land Market: Structurally Distorted and Still Falling

The irony of Japan's troubled real estate market is that land prices remain massively over-valued (see Figure 2.2). Since peaking in 1990, the official index of commercial land in six major cities has fallen by 73%. Yet, even after this dramatic fall, real estate prices in Japan are still very high by international standards. Office property prices in Tokyo, for example, are more than ten times higher than in New York in terms of available floor area.

Why, then, is Japanese real estate so expensive? Despite the commonly held view to the contrary, the very high price of land has never been "natural" in that it somehow reflected a lack of usable land in "resource-less Japan" (*mu-shigen koku Nippon*). In fact, despite its apparently limited land space and dense population, Tokyo is far from being as highly developed as Hong Kong, London, New York, or Seoul. According to the Ministry of Construction, the average building height in the Tokyo metropolitan area remains less than three stories. Many third world

FIGURE 2.2 Land Prices in Japan: Comparisons over Time and Space

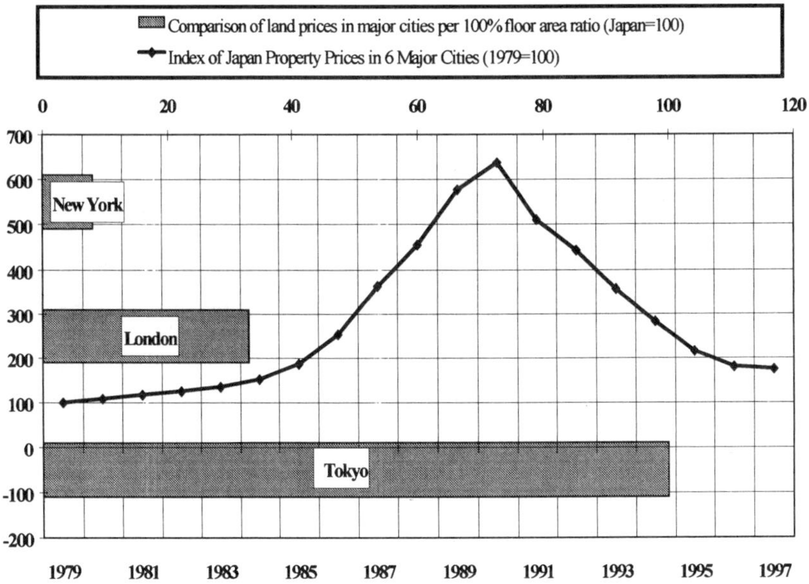

Note: Land prices have fallen 73% from their peak, but Tokyo prices are still three times more expensive than in London. *Source: Financial Times.*

cities are taller.[8] Moreover, land typically is not utilized to its full potential, even within the current, very restrictive zoning regulations. Overall, Tokyo is "underbuilt" by more than 50% compared to allotted floorspace ratios. Even central Tokyo office buildings utilize only around 85% of permitted floor area.[9]

Given such considerable inefficiency, the underlying reality is that the almost constantly inflating land market in pre-1990s Japan was always a house of cards destined eventually to collapse. The glue that held the cards together was easy money, while the foundation upon which the house sat was made up of stringent regulations on the use of land and near punitive tax disincentives against transactions.[10] When the Bank of Japan started raising interest rates in October 1989 to slow down asset inflation, the glue began melting away, triggering a collapse.

With the government committed to removing the myriad zoning limitations on building height, footprints, basement construction, etc., while also cutting the high capital gains tax on real estate transactions and improving the rights of landlords over tenants, the remaining foundations of the postwar property market pyramid are crumbling away. If reforms are fully implemented, no longer will myriad perverse disincentives keep property from changing hands in line with underlying supply and demand conditions and no more will the population be forced by policy to underutilize their supposedly scarce land resources. The implication is that, with the available supply of land increasing markedly at the same time it is more efficiently utilized, Japanese urban property prices are likely to continue falling in real terms well into the next century.

Stock Market Overvaluation

As with the price of land, Japan's beleaguered equity markets remain remarkably overvalued and liable to a further collapse. Many analysts seem infatuated with the view that, after so many bad years, Japanese stocks must somehow be a "buy." Nonetheless, by almost all conventional measures—e.g., price to earnings ratios (P/E) and return on equity (ROE)—Japanese stock prices remain tremendously inflated in comparative and historical perspective, even when excluding companies in the financial sector. Japan's lingering "valuation bubble" is shown clearly in Figure 2.3.

Direct pressure on equity prices is exerted not only by the insufficiency of underlying value, but also by the increased supply of shares on the market. For most of the post-Occupation era, the supply of "free floating" shares declined in Japan. From 1965 to 1990 there was a steady rise in the proportion of the stock market owned by corporate investors while the holdings of individuals, who were formerly the dominant group of shareholders, fell substantially. A prime factor behind this shifting makeup of ownership was the solidification of the so-called *keiretsu* system of equity cross-shareholding between companies. In a nutshell, as capital liberalization began to be implemented in the early 1970s and made the threat of foreign takeovers greater, companies possessing long-term business affiliations (usually related to their identity with one of the prewar *zaibatsu* business groups) aggressively began to acquire shares in each other as a form of "self-protection" (read by many foreign firms as simply a form of protectionism from unfriendly takeovers).[11]

Among other things, the buildup of cross-holdings had the effect of pushing up the stock market to a level well beyond that which could be justified by normal value criteria. It thus provided capital at an extremely low cost. Furthermore, cross-holdings also enabled linked companies to have extremely long-time horizons in doing business, allowing them to place the expansion of market share over that of profitability since their friendly shareholders did not have to be sensitive to prices-to-earnings ratios and the like.

However, such insider capitalist "logic," out of which so many myths of Japanese invincibility in the face of foreign competition were spun, applied only

FIGURE 2.3 Japanese Stocks: Still a Long Way to Fall

The Global Overvaluation Olympics: And the Winner Still Is . . .

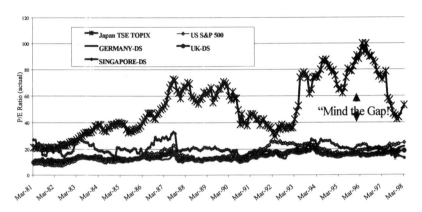

Still Governed by Historical Standards

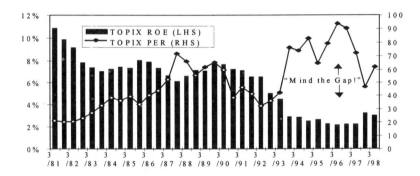

Source: Datastream.

as long as the equity market was rising. Once the bubble burst, the financial losses entailed by cross-shareholdings far exceeded any non-financial benefits. Since 1990 the percentage of stocks held for "relationship reasons" has been in decline and the rate of unwinding is accelerating. The percentage of stock *not* held for relationship reasons has increased from the 1987 low point of around 25% to nearly 37% by mid-1998.

We expect that bad-debt-laden, capital-deficient Japanese corporations, particularly in the two industries that dominate market holdings, banking and insurance, will be net sellers of accumulated equities well into the first decade of the coming century. Meanwhile, if the present situation persists, the only net buyers are likely to continue to be foreigners and Japanese institutional fund investors, and only when fundamentals present themselves in a more rational fashion. We thus predict the equity market in Japan will fall over time until share prices attain valuations that can be justified by prospective risk-adjusted returns, without any allowance for special corporate relationships. We estimate that this would mean the stock market selling around 10,000 on the leading Nikkei 225 index, but the reaction from the previous overvaluation could obviously entail the market falling well below this level as it adjusts.[12]

Default: Japan Heading Toward Depression?

The third, increasingly prominent, feature of the Japanese economy as it approaches the millennium is the rapidly rising levels of business bankruptcy and loan default. In calendar year 1997 corporate bankruptcy losses exceeded ¥14 trillion, up 75% from the previous year and reaching the largest amount in Japanese history. The net liabilities of bankrupt companies have come to occupy a much larger share of GDP in post-bubble Japan than they did in the United States at the height of the Great Depression in the early 1930s (see Figure 2.4). They also well exceed the very high levels reached when the U.S. government finally foreclosed on insolvent banks and thrifts in the early 1990s, temporarily sending corporate bankruptcy rates skyrocketing.[13]

Despite such a scary backdrop, the rate of bankruptcy and loan default is likely to rise further in the coming years as indebted companies and individuals struggle in the midst of slow economic growth, increased competition due to financial market deregulation, and continuing asset price declines. Of particular concern are companies within three of Japan's largest economic sectors: banking, insurance, and property.

Bad, Bad Banks

The loan problems that plague Japan's once considered mighty banks are well known. After years of denying massive worst-case estimates for problem loans emerging from foreign brokerage houses, Ministry of Finance officials unexpectedly announced at the end of 1997 that banks in Japan held a combined ¥76.70 trillion in loans for which "recovery may be difficult, or is deemed quite doubtful

FIGURE 2.4 Japan in the Great Recession vs. U.S. in the Great Depression (Corporate Bankruptcy Liabilities as a % of GDP)

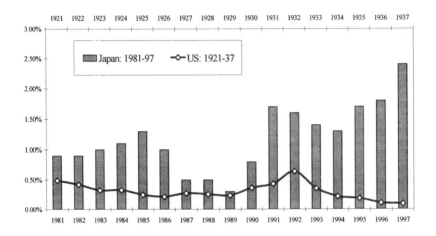

Notes: U.S. data through 1993 includes net liabilities of bankrupt financial and real estate instutitions as well as all other companies. Japanese data for FY97 is estimated based on annualizing the first half numbers. (The real figure is likely to be higher given the rash of bankruptcies in the second half.) *Sources:* Historical Statistics of the United States (1976); U.S. Statistical Abstract (1936); and Teikoku Databank.

or nearly impossible." The figure accounted for 12% of the banks' total loans and loan guarantees and was 3.5 times the value of total non-performing loans the MOF officially unveiled at the end of September 1996. The new total covered large city and trust banks as well as first- and second-tier lending institutions. For comparison, at the apex of the U.S. bank and savings and loan crisis in the late 1980s, the comparable figure was 5.6%.

Yet even the massive new official bad-loan numbers are likely to substantially underestimate the real situation. Japanese companies in the financial services world are legendary for their practices of hiding insolvent assets on the books of offshore subsidiaries and for misleading creditors and government credit investigators regarding their real state of operational health. For example, when Hyogo Bank went bankrupt in September 1995, it was found that its bad debts were more than double the "full figure" it had given government inspectors earlier in the year. Similarly, the revealed net liabilities on the books of Nissan Life Insurance increased by nearly six-fold following its closure.

Given the startling losses involved, much attention has been paid to the size of the loan crisis in Japan. Nonetheless, lurking in the background of the lending disaster is a more fundamental problem that is sure to become evident as the big bang proceeds: the poor operational performance of Japanese financial institutions.

As reflected in Figure 2.5, although massive in size, in terms of return on assets (ROA), returns on shareholders' equity (ROE), and margins on lending, even the top banks in Japan are in poor condition compared to their dominant western rivals.[14] Furthermore, they are exposed en masse to companies with high credit risks. As pointed out earlier, Japanese companies have even worse balance sheets than their American competitors, even though the latter show record leverage. Japanese banks must therefore expect higher levels of bankruptcy from their clients, now that they are no longer protected by rapid economic growth and ever rising land prices. To allow for this risk, Japanese banks require even higher margins on their lending than American lending institutions, not substantially lower ones.

Rather than having emerged as world-beaters (as widely predicted in the late 1980s), Japan's financial institutions (JFIs) have become worldwide losers. Eugene Dattel, a former senior American investment banker in Japan and author of a book highly critical of Japanese financial management, writes:

> Unlike many of Japan's manufacturers, JFIs are inept, unprofessional, and uncom-
> petitive. When [in the 1980s] the JFIs moved out of their protected, cozy domestic
> market where they had been granted regulated franchises, their weaknesses were
> exposed to the harsh realities of the deregulated open international markets. The JFIs
> resemble ossified government bureaucracies more than private sector industries.[15]

Even if the bad-loan burden is removed from the backs of these institutions as a result of loan securitization, yield-curve-induced operating profit gains, and a colossal government bail-out, Japanese banks will remain in danger. A further large wave of consolidation and failure in the face of heightened local and foreign competition seems inevitable.

Imperiled Life Insurers

Although Japan's banking problems are better known, the ills of Japan's giant life insurance industry—source of more than 40% of worldwide premium income—are equally significant. Wracked by investment and loan losses and poor capital management practices, the industry began contracting in FY96, as shown in Figure 2.6. Premium and investment incomes are falling, while payments on maturing policies are rising at 14% yearly. The cancellation of pension contracts is increasing rapidly.

The combination of losses and poor cash flow makes the weaker life insurers extremely vulnerable. One of them, Nissan Life Insurance, went bankrupt in 1997. An assessment of the valuation of Japanese life insurance assets and liabilities by

FIGURE 2.5 The Myth of Japanese Financial Competitiveness

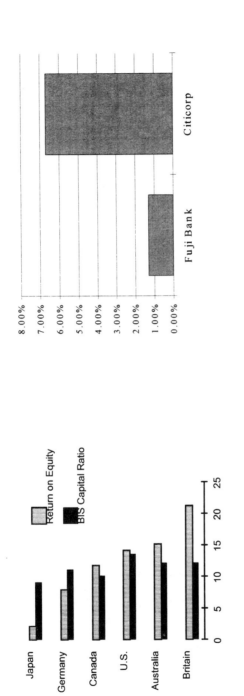

Major Banks BIS Ratios and ROE in International Perspective

Revenue Return on Assets: Japan vs. USA

Source: ING Barings

Source: Goldman Sachs

FIGURE 2.6 Running Out of Life? Life Insurance Companies' Cash Flow

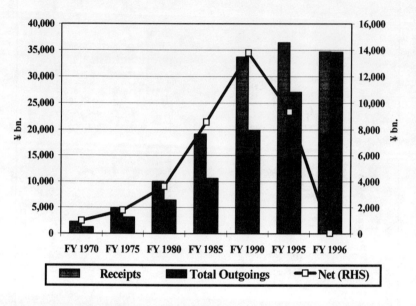

Source: Smithers & Co., London

Smithers & Co. with the assistance of Tillinghast consulting actuaries, suggests that the industry's liabilities probably exceed its capital.[16] The collateral damage of further bankruptcies could be very large indeed. Life insurers own nearly ¥45 trillion of listed Japanese equities, more than 11% of the total stock market, and have almost ¥10 trillion invested in property. Their perilous condition thus poses a very big threat to the Japanese share and property markets.

The Looming Destruction of the Construction and Real Estate Industries

During the bubble economy, construction and real estate spending skyrocketed on the back of the boom in property speculation. However, so did the liabilities of companies in the property sector. With the land market having collapsed and the number of new projects to bid on in decline, an increasing number of companies find themselves unable to service their debts. More than one-fourth of interest bearing liabilities in the non-financial part of the economy are in the construction and real estate industries (see Figure 2.7). Moreover, the cost of paying interest on outstanding loans for companies in these two industries is on the verge of exceeding net cash flow. Thus, it is no surprise that more than half of all bankrupt-

FIGURE 2.7 Ratio of Interest Bearing Liabilities to Cash Flow:
Construction and Real Estate versus the Rest

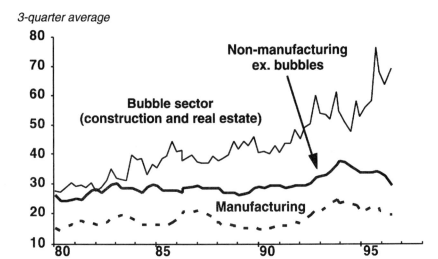

3-quarter average

Source: JP Morgan

cies filed since the beginning of the 1990s have been by contractors and real estate developers.

They face two big problems: (1) Japanese banks are under great pressure to cut their exposure to companies like contractors and developers with a high risk of default, and (2) the government, which accounts for more than 40% of construction contracts and serves as the sole net provider of real estate project loans, is determined to cut such spending back by 10% each year from 1998 to 2001. Thus,the potential looms for further swelling in the number and size of failures. Furthermore, given the generally low educational and technical skill levels of most of the over 6 million employees in the construction industry, the effect of such failures could push up Japan's unemployment rate much higher.

Demography: The Fourth "D"

As Japan moves into the 21st century, the problems of excess debt, deflating asset markets, and growing rates of default will be made all the more difficult to solve by a dramatic shift in its demographic structure. Examining changes in the ratio of those aged between 15 and 64 to those aged over 65, Figure 2.8 illustrates

FIGURE 2.8   Aging Population in G5 Countries (Population aged over 65 as
a percentage of those aged 15-64)

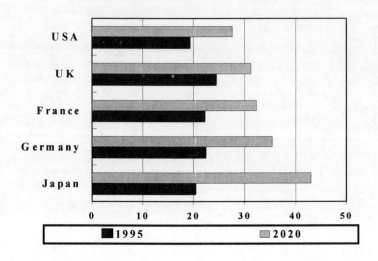

Source: IMF, Occasional Paper 147.

how rapidly the population of Japan will age. From 1995 to 2020 the change in the
ratio will be much more rapid for Japan than for any of the other major industrial
countries. Each person of working age will have to support more than twice as
many elderly people as they do today.

Demography, Labor Productivity, and Growth Potential

There are 126 million Japanese, of whom 64 million are available for work. This
is 77% of those aged between 15 to 64 and represents, together with the United
States, the highest labor participation rate among the G5 countries. Over the next
two decades, the total population will be stable while the working population will
be falling steadily. This will be a significant change from the past, as the labor
force has risen at 1.1% annually since 1980. From around the turn of the century,
the Japanese government projects that the labor force will begin to decline at
around 0.6% a year.

With the working population in decline, there is relatively little scope for
increasing the size of the labor force, without cutting back on the number of people
in full-time education, increasing the age of retirement, or allowing mass immigration. Immigration seems unlikely, as there is a widespread wish in Japan to
preserve the homogeneity of the population and the national culture. If the economy were to boom and labor shortages became a brake on growth, immigration

policy might change, but an unchanged policy and thus a steady fall in the working population is the most reasonable assumption to make.

It is impossible to predict the impact of the demographic shift on Japan's long-term economic growth rate with any degree of certainty. However, given that the supply of labor is falling, the relative increase or decrease in labor productivity will have a critical influence on whether growth can be revived and sustained at a relatively high level. As demonstrated in Figure 2.9, labor productivity has been decelerating for the last three decades. So has the rate of economic expansion. In the early 1970s output per worker grew yearly by over 2.5% on average, helping keep economic growth above 8%. Then between 1974 and 1992, labor productivity increases averaged 1.1% (while the economy grew at an average of slightly over 4%). Since 1992, the rate of increase in labor productivity has faltered. The implication of the past correlation between productivity improvement and GDP is that the underlying growth potential has fallen to between 1 and 1.5%.

The Impact of Aging on Savings, Investment, and Trade

There are no real precedents for the behavior of a modern industrial economy whose labor force is declining. The probable impact on savings, investment, and trade is thus unknown. Nonetheless, we can make some assumptions based upon the available data and draw some tentative conclusions.

An especially controversial issue is whether Japan eventually will turn from a nation of big savers to a nation of big spenders as the society demographically matures. Most analysts apparently support the view that Japan will spend down its surplus of savings in the 21st century. It is, however, far from clear that this will happen. First, such a prediction appears to be based on a confusion between the national and household savings rates. Second, the evidence, at least regarding Japan, that the latter necessarily slows with age is itself questionable.

The national savings rate is the sum of government saving, corporate saving, and household saving (with the last category usually divided into discretionary and non-discretionary saving). Currently, government saving in Japan is heavily negative because the budget deficit is so large. Boldly assuming a long-term improvement in the budget position (which the government says it is committed to obtaining at all costs), public sector saving should rise again in the future. As for corporate savings, it is generally believed that the low return on assets currently being achieved by corporations must be raised through higher profits to placate investors. This points to a rise in the corporate savings rate, unless there is a radical change in dividend payout ratios.

The response of the household sector to aging is disputed; differing approaches have led to widely divergent conclusions.[17] We believe that it is sensible to conclude from the evidence on savings in Japan so far assembled, that household discretionary saving is likely to decline somewhat as the population ages, especially

FIGURE 2.9 Japanese Labor Productivity, 1990–1996

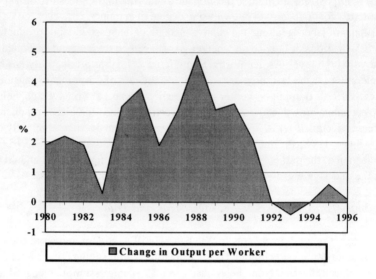

Source: Smithers & Co., London

from 2010 forward (when the first baby boomers will begin retiring). However, we forecast this decline will be less substantial than many analysts expect, especially given the need to make up for pension under funding.

One factor that could help absorb the high household savings rate would be a rise in housing related personal consumption. Given the poor state of Japan's housing stock, the potential relaxation of zoning and construction regulations (such as rules against building basements or inhibiting extensions) could help trigger a home improvement and land redevelopment boom someday. However, much depends on whether the cost of housing can be significantly lowered by a further large drop in land prices and the deregulation of the collusive construction industry. Furthermore, even if household savings do fall, any drop will be more than made up by the increased savings in the government and corporate sectors. Thus, overall, it appears likely that Japan will remain a nation of large-scale savers even as the demographic shift progresses (Figure 2.10).

Lastly, consider the outlook for the trade and current account surpluses. As the rate of savings is unlikely to decline substantially, Japan is likely to remain a major capital exporter for a long time to come. The decline in the working population implies that Japan will find it increasingly difficult to absorb a large amount of investment in the domestic economy. The only alternative to exporting its excess

FIGURE 2.10 Japanese Savings and Investment as Percent of GDP:
          Still Strong

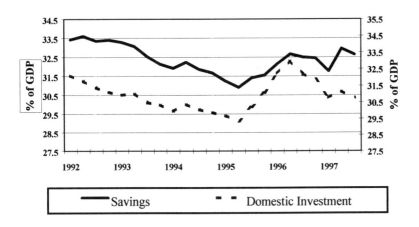

Source: Smithers & Co., London

savings is to run a huge budget deficit. However, this is not a feasible solution given the massive problem presented by the government's existing debts.

Equally, the yen is likely to weaken on the basis of enlarged capital outflow, thus retarding imports while improving export competitiveness. The return on capital in Japan is very low compared to the returns available in Europe and America and the last remaining regulatory restrictions on capital mobility are set to be removed in FY98. Thus, private capital can be expected to flow from Japan until the risk adjusted returns earned at home equalize with those obtainable abroad.

Left alone, the normal forces of economics will tend to push up the trade surplus unless and until the macroeconomic and structural situation changes. Japan's trade surplus for the fourth quarter of 1997 exceeded 3.7% of GDP (measured in seasonally adjusted 1990 prices), well above the 2.5% "threshold of tolerance" announced by the U.S. Treasury Department earlier in the year. However, Japan has little choice but to run a large surplus, given its economic structural problems and shifting demographic factors. Without a greater degree of acceptance of this fact by Japan's main trading partners, international trade relations threaten to be very stormy in the years ahead.

Deregulation: The Promise and the Pitfalls

What would it take for Japan to be able to find its way out of its financial problems, meet its demographic challenges, and rise again to be a growth leader in the early 21st century? Below we argue that increasing Japan's productivity, economic growth potential, and standard of living will depend greatly on the removal of structural impediments in Japan's labor, land, and capital markets and the deregulation of the service sector.

Increasing Labor, Land, and Capital Efficiency: Ways, Means, and Costs

Japanese Underproductivity: Labor, Capital, and Land. Why is it that since the beginning of the 1990s Japanese economic growth has stagnated while rates of savings and investment have remained above 30% of GDP? The irony of Japan's maturing growth rate is that, despite such high rates of investment, the economy overall no longer achieves high levels of productivity, in aggregate, compared to many of its leading competitors (Figure 2.11). This is even the case in terms of labor productivity, where Japan is conventionally seen to excel. True, Japanese manufacturers, by most measures and in most industries, still display relatively impressive levels of labor productivity (although when adjusted for sector specific purchasing power the numbers do not look quite as favorable). However, by all accounts, labor productivity in the Japanese service sector, which accounts for 60% of employment and GDP, remains remarkably low. This drags down aggregate labor productivity considerably.

Labor markets increasingly are warped by features formerly referred to as Japan's "three sacred jewels" (*sanshuu no jingi*): lifetime employment (*shushin koyou-sei*), the wage-seniority system (*nenko joretsu-sei*), and enterprise labor unions (*kigyou-betsu kumiai*). Lifetime employment, admittedly, applies to fewer and fewer workers and is only formally accepted by the largest companies. However, for the firms that adhere to it, in times when white-collar workforce reduction is needed, the only major options are halting new hires or granting costly early retirement to senior employees. Similarly, the wage-seniority system fails to provide incentives to productive, dynamic young workers to attempt to excel in their occupations while it protects the salaries of unproductive "window sitters" (*madogiwa zoku*) in upper-middle management. Last, although enterprise unions have served to reinforce the "company as family" image prevalent in Japan, they also have contributed to the immobility of labor. Very often industries in need of more labor cannot get it, while those facing labor surpluses cannot fire workers. Thus, many "sacred" labor relations practices that were once regarded as contributing to Japanese growth more and more seem to stand in its way.[18]

FIGURE 2.11 Japan's Labor Productivity Deficit: (Japan 1994 = 100)

Better<===>Worse

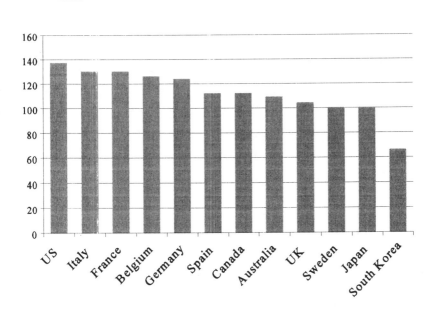

Source: Japan Productivity Center for Socio-Economic Development

Japanese capital productivity is even more problematic. Although Japan's rate of capital productivity growth was relatively strong compared to the U.S. and other leading economies of the miracle years of 1960s and early 1970s, returns on physical and financial capital have dwindled since then. This has had a direct effect on long-term growth prospects (since the rate of investment divided by the capital-to-output ratio over time correlates with GDP). Figure 2.12 shows that by the early mid-1990s Japanese capital productivity lagged behind the United States and Germany both on the aggregate level and in a multitude of important sectors. One result of capital inefficiency is that Japanese inventory levels are far in excess of U.S. levels—a radical turnabout from the 1980s, when Japanese industry was seen as "lean and mean" and U.S. companies were portrayed as "fat and slow."

Japan's financial market inefficiency and irregularity remain central barriers to productivity improvement and long-term growth. Overt government attempts at stock market "price-keeping" have led to immobilization of the market as a means of raising capital for all others. On top of this, Japan's Ministry of Finance still sets the standard for administrative irregularity, ambiguity, and irrationality in its management of capital markets.[19] Even on the eve of the big bang in January 1998,

FIGURE 2.12 Capital Productivity and Capital Inefficiency: An International Comparison

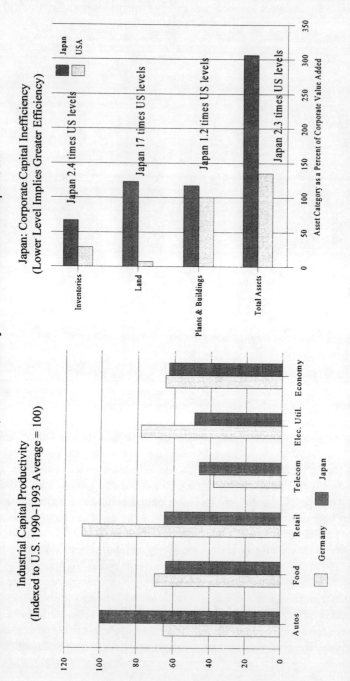

Note: The real internal rate of return on Japanese capital from 1988–1998 has been negative. *Source*: McKinsey Global Institute, 1996.

Note: Japan's bubble era capital investments appear to have been squandered on land speculation and capacity expansion in saturated market segments. *Source*: Smithers & Co., London.

as the MOF heralded the arrival of a market system that is "free, fair, and global," the weakness of its rhetorical commitments was plainly evident. It could be found threatening to ban short-selling, promising to punish those in the financial community who issue "unfounded research" that indicates that financial institutions "may be weak," and advocating the postponement of prompt corrective action measures that could lead to further bank failures (thus undermining their essential purpose).

Land remains an artificially illiquid and unexploitable resource whose lack of supply distorts productivity and pricing in the entire economy. Japan's land market is more constrained than probably any other in the OECD. The exorbitant cost of land stands in the way of new investment by raising start-up costs for outsiders and the cost of living for all in Japan. Furthermore, it lowers the capital costs of insiders who can borrow against land collateral. Property market distortions discourage entrepreneurship and risk-taking, necessitate an unusually high level of savings to offset the cost of being in Japan, and facilitate tendencies to speculate.

Purchasing Power Disparity. A relative lack of purchasing power convergence seems to mirror the lack of productivity convergence in Japan. Although it is frequently argued that high costs are a fact of life in Japan, somehow derived from Japanese consumer preference for quality, the absurdity of such a view is obvious. Aggregate purchasing power parity on average in 1997 was only around ¥165 to the dollar. Although this is an improvement over the past, a significant gap remains between the prices Japanese companies and consumers pay at home versus when abroad (Figure 2.13). Numerous studies have shown that this price gap is almost entirely due to the effect of over-regulation and high land prices.[20]

The Promise of Deregulation. Assuming that the debt problem was somehow solved, what would then happen if Japan were to truly free up the flow of assets and labor in its economy while also ridding itself of most sector-specific barriers? In June 1997 Japan's Ministry of International Trade and Industry published the findings of a major econometric study it did on the estimated impact of deregulation of sector-specific barriers in five industries: logistics, energy, information and telecommunications, finance, and distribution. The study's model used 1995 as a base year and assumed that all effects of deregulation will have emerged by 2001. It concluded that growth on average would by pushed up yearly by around 1.2% between the beginning of 1996 and 2001, if the sectors were opened as much as in the United States.[21] Other studies have abstracted even larger benefits from reform.[22] The MITI study results are summarized in Table 2.1.

Undoubtedly, much fat could profitably be trimmed away in Japan. The key is to find a means to do so without upsetting the body politic. Two final points can be said in this regard. First, without a systematic effort to encourage private sector debt reduction, the process of greater market opening could lead to extraordinarily high levels of business failure and unemployment. Second, unless the Japanese government gets its own finances in order, it eventually will be hard pressed to take the necessary fiscal measures to soften the impact of structural adjustment.

FIGURE 2.13   Purchasing Power Disparity: (Yen / Dollar)

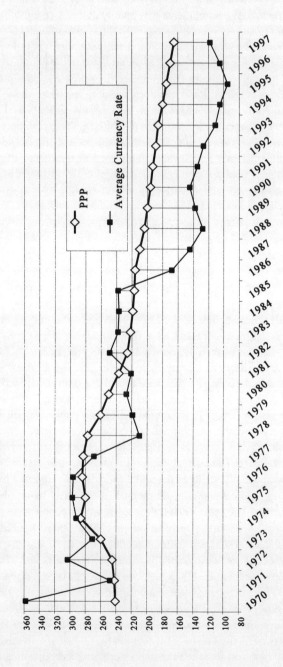

Source: JP Morgan

TABLE 2.1   MITI Deregulation Study Results

Assumptions	Cumulative Results 1996–2000
The following will be fulfilled by 2001: 1. Logistics: Controls on supply-demand adjustments will be abolished in areas of road cargo transport, rail, coastal shipping, and port transport. 2. Energy: Internationally comparable cost levels will be achieved. 3. Information/Telecommunications: Internationally competitive telecommunications services industry on par with the U.S. in terms of cost and productivity will be developed. 4. Finance: Japan's financial market will be as open and dynamic as those found in London. 5. Distribution (retail/wholesale): A trend toward deregulation and lifting restrictions on large-scale stores will be maintianed.	1. Real GDP pushed up by 6%. Deregulation encourages economic growth by increasing productivity, which lowers prices and creates new demand for good and services. 2. ¥39 trillion increase in plant and equipment investment. New investment in plant and equipment leads to a cumulative increase of 2.6% of GDP. 3. 3.4% drop in consumer prices leads to an income return effect of around ¥16.9 trillion (approximately ¥370,000 per household). Deregulation increases productivity, which in turn causes prices to fall, increasing consumers purchasing power. 4. Major fluctuation in number of employees by industry. While deregulation will create new employment, particularly in telecommunications (+170,000 jobs) and services (+70,000), employment will decrease in the wholesale (-220,000), financial (-80,000), and transport (-10,000) sectors.

Source: MITI, June 1997.

Conclusion

The bottom line for Japan looking toward the 21st century is that it must choose between the creative destruction of its current economic structure or simply accept the likelihood of continued stagnation. While accepting the former choice may be a quasi-revolutionary act with uncertain consequences for social and political stability, yielding to the latter could lead to an economic tragedy. This is Japan's core dilemma.

To ensure that it does not face a future where average economic growth remains trapped below 1.5%, Japan needs to adopt a comprehensive strategy designed to address the following five key problems we have detailed in this report:

1. Extremely high levels of outstanding debt to GDP and debt to equity both in the private and public sectors.
2. Distorted and deflating asset markets.
3. Rising levels of bankruptcy and the potential for a surge in unemployment.
4. The growing financial burden of a rapidly aging population on society.
5. Over-regulated and inefficient labor, land, and capital markets.

As the world's second largest economy, the ramifications of Japan's myriad problems are not merely domestic but also global. The world must realize the dimensions of the dilemma Japan faces. Japan's trading partners should stop urging it to irresponsibly stimulate its economy simply as a means of keeping the trade surplus down. Demographics alone points to a large surplus, and there is little Japan can do to avoid running one for a very long time to come. Nonetheless, the Japanese must push forward tough structural reforms as a quid pro quo for foreign tolerance. Unfortunately, we are not optimistic that either Japan or the world is ready for the challenges that lie ahead. A tragedy appears in the making.

Notes

1. "2020 no Keishou: Susmanu Kaikaku, Oi-hayaku: Sekai de koritsu, kojin wa kodoku" ("Warning bells from 2020: Reform is going no where, while we're aging fast, becoming internationally isolated, and turning inward as a people"), *Nihon Keizai Shimbun*, January 1, 1997, p.1.

2. See Eamonn Fingleton, *Blindside: Why Japan is Still on Track to Overtake the U.S. by the Year 2000* (New York: Simon and Schuster, 1995).

3. Japan has had no inflation with regard to productive assets since 1985 so the book value figures are similar to those at replacement cost and thus are best compared with the U.S. data on a replacement basis. Furthermore, the U.S. data covers all companies in the economy whereas the Japanese data excludes the numerous and collectively important limited liability companies (*yugengaisha*), whose inclusion would probably raise debt ratios further.

4. Making things all the more worrying is the fact that an increasingly large portion of the FILP investments are in danger of default. Details on the FILP and its fund management problems can be found in the report on which this chapter is based. See David Asher and Andrew Smithers, "Japan's Key Challenges for the 21st Century: Debt, Deflation, Default, Demography, and Deregulation," SAIS Policy Forum Series (Washington, DC: The John Hopkins University, Paul H. Nitze School of Advanced International Studies, March 1998).

5. We derive that the real public sector gross debt level for Japan exceeds 150% of GDP by combining the gross liabilities of the general government (local plus central), which according to the OECD for FY97 are 87% (based on over-optimistic growth and government revenue projections), with the 63% of GDP in estimated FY96 liabilities in the MOF Trust Fund Bureau (TFB). (We use the previous year's data since the undoubtedly larger FY97 number is not yet available.) In the more conservative methodology used in the appendix to our earlier SAIS study (see note 4), we only used the debts of the central government and did not include the debts of the various prefectures. Here we do so, recognizing that the Japanese central government is legally responsible for the viability of regional government finances.

To the 150% in gross public sector debt we can add the over 8% projected flow of funds in the public sector borrowing requirement for FY97 (which is not included in the 86.7%). However, if we move into FY98 we can include as well an estimated additional 10% of GDP in "hidden debt" (that has already been taken out of the TFB so we are not double counting). Although only about half of this will be assumed on the books in FY98, the full sum is officially acknowledged and thus should be accounted for in total. (We do not support more financial smoke and mirrors in Japan.) When the projected deficits produced by the 1998 regular budget, the large supplemental budget, tax cuts, and the bank bail-out are included, it seems likely that by this methodology Japan's gross public sector deficit will exceed 170% in FY98.

It is important to remember that our approach in calculating Japan's public sector gross debt is to treat the Trust Fund Bureau as *borrowing* money from the public pension, postal savings, and postal life insurance systems and then *investing* these funds in government projects. The government raises funds from these captive sources that otherwise would have to be raised via government bond issues or additional revenue. The responsibility for full repayment and fund management falls in the lap of the government. Thus, this obligation should be accounted for on its books even if only a portion of the FILP investments can be identified as bad.

6. The figure for net pension obligations is taken from the *IMF Occasional Paper 147*, published in December 1996.

7. See Kunji Okue, "Japan's Rating in the Balance, " *Japan Policy Monitor* (Tokyo: Dresdner Kleinwort Benson Securities, April 27, 1998), p. 2.

8. For comparative data see Yukio Noguchi and James M. Poterba, eds., *Housing in the United States and Japan* (Chicago: University of Chicago Press, 1994).

9. For a chart illuminating this point, see John Haley and Kozo Yamamura, eds., *Land Issues in Japan: A Policy Failure* (Seattle, WA: Society for Japanese Studies, 1992), p.17.

10. On the details of the postwar property tax and land use regime, see Kazuo Sato, "Economic Laws and the Household Economy in Japan: Lags in Policy Response to Economic Changes," in Gary Saxonhouse and Kozo Yamamura, eds., *Law and Trade Issues of the Japanese Economy* (Tokyo: Tokyo University Press, 1986), pp. 3-55. For discussion of how the tax system inhibits supply, see Noguchi Yukio, *Tochi no Keizaigaku* (*The Economics of Land*) (Tokyo: Tokyo University Press, 1989), pp.130-53. An excellent number of papers reviewing the whole land problem (*tochi mondai*) can be found in Haley and Yamamura, eds., *Land Issues in Japan: A Policy Failure*.

11. Shares were acquired by the *keiretsu* companies through a combination of rights issues and buy-backs, while the MOF imposed large minimum-block share purchase requirements that made it all but impossible for most individuals to afford buying equities as stock prices rose. Also, among other discriminatory practices, new listings typically were allocated to insiders *before* being made available to individuals or foreigners. For more detail on how the stock market became, in effect, re-regulated against foreigners and individuals and in favor of large Japanese *keiretsu*-affiliated companies, see Robert Zielinsky and Nigel Holloway, *Unequal Equities: Power and Risk in Japan's Stock Market* (Tokyo, 1991), pp. 21-40; Robert J. Ballon and Iwao Tomita, *The Financial Behavior of Japanese Companies* (Tokyo: Kodansha, 1988), especially pp. 50-53); and T. F. M. Adams and Iwao Hoshii, *A Financial History of the New Japan* (Tokyo: Kodansha, 1972), pp. 190-94.

12. One factor that could get in the way of such a rational downward price adjustment is increased Japanese government interference in the stock market in the form of so-called price keeping operations (PKOs). Typically, PKOs are carried out by the MOF ordering that funds in publicly-controlled accounts (such as public pension or postal life insurance) be used to make share purchases, indiscriminate of underlying value, while also directly or indirectly restricting the flow of new issues into the market. Frequent PKOs have had the

effect of holding the stock market above its natural clearing level, and this has had the unfortunate consequence of inhibiting the issue of new equity. Thus, the government has choked off one of the least painful ways available to reduce Japan's excess debt problems. The Ministry of Finance has seen PKOs as a solution to Japan's financial difficulties, while in practice it has added greatly to them. The PKOs have been one of the worst of the many policy errors of the 1990s. However, with the MOF under growing scrutiny for its manipulative practices and with deregulation making it harder for it to dictate how public (and private) pension funds are specifically invested, it may be much harder to control the equity prices in the future.

13. For reference, at their peak in 1991 U.S. net bankruptcy liabilities hit 1.65% of GDP thereafter to fall back into the fifteen-year trend rate of between 0.4% -.5% of GDP, where levels stood as of 1997.

14. David Atkinson of Goldman-Sachs in Tokyo has done an extensive comparison of the balance sheet of Fuji Bank versus that of Citicorp (parent of Citibank). Among other things, he found that Fuji Bank uses 619.8% of Citicorp 's capital per employee to generate a return of only 197.9% of a Citicorp employee. In absolute terms Fuji Bank uses 137.2% of Citicorp's capital to generate only 43.8% of the return. Citicorp's operating profit return to assets is 2.6% versus Fuji Bank's minuscule 0.6%, while its ROA is 6.7% in contrast with only 1.3% yielded by its Japanese competitor. No wonder that foreign bankers "smell blood" in Japan. See David Atkinson, David Richards, and Robert Albertson, "Fuji Bank versus Citicorp" (Tokyo: Goldman-Sachs Global Research, January 17, 1996.)

15. Quoted in Chalmers Johnson, Eugene Dattel, Henny Sender, and David Asher, "A Debate on the Japanese 'Miracle'," *Orbis*, Summer 1996, p. 436. Dattel's book is *The Sun That Never Rose: The Inside Story of Japan's Failed Attempt at Global Financial Dominance* (Chicago: Probus, 1994).

16. See Smithers & Co. Ltd. Report No. 112, "Japanese Life Insurance Industry: More Bankruptcies Likely," November 1997.

17. For an exceptionally well-grounded study criticizing the so-called life cycle approach to saving (i.e., that people dis-save in their retirement years) as applied to Japan, see Kurt W. Tong, "Applied Research on Japan's Household Savings Rate Using Prefectural Panel Data," *Nihon Keizai Kenkyuu*, no.34 (April 1997) (in Japanese). For a defense of the aging/dis-saving hypothesis, see, Naohiro Yashiro, Takashi Oshio, and Mantaro Matsuya, "Macroeconomic and Fiscal Impacts of Japan's Aging Population with a Specific Reference to Pension Reforms" (Tokyo: Japanese Economic Planning Agency Research Institute, September, 1997).

18. Prominent Japanese labor economist, Shimada Haruo, has written in detail about all of these points. See, for example, his *Nihon Keizai Mujun to Saisei* (Japan's Economic Contradictions and Rebirth) (Tokyo: Chikuma Shobo, 1991), pp. 49-117.

19. See Benn Steil, *Illusions of Liberalization: Securities Regulation in Japan and the EC* (London: Royal Institute of International Affairs, March 1995).

20. See, for example, *Second Annual Report of the US-Japan Working Group on the Structural Impediments Initiative* (Washington, DC: Department of State, July 30, 1992); and the Economic Planning Agency, *White Paper on the Japanese Economy* (Tokyo: Ministry of Finance Printing Bureau, 1993).

21. "Summary Report of the Study Group on the Economic Effects of Deregulation" (Tokyo: Ministry of International Trade and Industry, June 15, 1997).

22. For example, a widely cited Keidanren (Japan Federation of Economic Organizations) study from late 1994 predicted that an aggressive deregulation policy would lower Japanese prices to world levels (i.e., dollar PPP) and would push up economic growth by 1.7% a year, adding ¥177 trillion to GDP over a six-year period and bringing a net increase of 740,000 jobs. See "Keidanren Deregulation Forecast" (Tokyo: Keidanren, November 1994).

3

Reflections of a Market Participant: Japanese and Asian Financial Institutions

Eugene R. Dattel

In the past, (Japanese financial) markets were manipulated, prices rigged, and fictitious transactions were common . . . (the Japanese) in general are not informed and have only a rudimentary idea of the mechanics of markets.

—T.C.F. Adams 1953

(The Japanese financial bureaucracy has) . . . an already nocuous administrative arbitrariness without improving actual conditions.

—T.C.F. Adams 1964

History matters. It matters not just because we can learn from the past, but because the present and future are connected to the past by the continuity of a society's institutions.

—Douglas North 1990[1]

Japan's financial turmoil has finally focused the world's attention on the severe short-comings of Japanese financial institutions (JFIs). The financial debacle created by the JFIs is one of the major business and government failures of the twentieth century. The sheer scale of this financial tragedy and the incompetence which permeated this saga have few precedents in financial history. Although the Asian economic crisis has exposed flaws in many financial systems in the region, the primary concern of this chapter is Japan.

Americans were conditioned to fear the power and size of the JFIs in the 1980s. Now, the JFIs are viewed as dysfunctional and as having a negative impact on the world economy. Since 1990, the seemingly endless flow of problems—the stock market debacle, the $600 billion equivalent of non-performing loans held by Japanese banks, the loss compensation scandals endemic to Japanese securities firms, the Daiwa Bank trading fiasco, bribes at the Ministry of Finance and the Bank of Japan, the collapse of Yamaichi Securities, the failure of Hokkaido

Takushoku Bank, several conspicuous suicides within the Japanese government, and a host of other travails—have conditioned the American public, and even the Japanese public, to the existing quagmire. Japan's stagnant growth record during this period is now causally associated with the chronic weaknesses of its financial sector. But for years this stream of events was viewed benignly as a series of isolated, and not terribly important, phenomena.

Less obvious because of the lack of drama, though extremely damaging, were JFI-induced market distortions. Both domestically and overseas, the JFI's—the world's largest financial institutions—caused various markets to rise temporarily to ridiculously expensive levels. When the JFIs ceased purchasing various assets, reality asserted itself with a vengeance and asset values plummeted. The JFIs' under performance thus resulted in the subsequent loss of billions of dollars.

In 1994 one of Japan's foremost financial mandarins, Yasushi Mieno, a former Governor of the Bank of Japan, issued a stinging indictment of Japan's commercial banks. He berated the banks for their "pack mentality, their inability to evaluate financial risks, and their unwillingness to innovate." Clearly, Mr. Mieno was part of the group of financial mandarins who were considered to be "the best and the brightest," especially by foreigners. What had this elite actually created?

Public Perceptions of Japan's Financial Problem

Current Views

The much discussed Japanese financial crisis has been reduced to simple terms by the numerous commentators, analysts, economists, and politicians who regularly offer so-called expert opinion. Commentary on Japan rarely focuses on previous opinions held by the same experts. In many cases, these self-styled experts have merely ignored their prior mistakes, rationalized their blunders, or indulged in intellectual dishonesty. Few want to explore the past, which is rough country for many commentators. So discussion of Japan usually starts from today with little concern for the legacies that were created over prior decades. Avoiding the development and context of JFIs and the interpretation of that past, economists and policy officials just want to "fix Japan."[2]

The problems, we are told, are an over regulated financial sector, the lack of adequate financial supervision, the absence of accountability, an incestuous relationship between financial regulators and their constituency (the banks, insurance companies, and the securities firms), the failure to confront the bad loan situation, and the lack of transparency within the financial system. This list has been repeated so often that the contents have become clichés, preempting a substantive discussion.

In general, we are told, Japan and Asia should concentrate on developing a rule of law, emphasizing democracy, jettisoning crony capitalism, and becoming open societies. Political reformation is viewed as the cure for the various ailments which seem to afflict Japan and Asia. Courageous political leaders are needed to implement these reforms.

Japan's economic foibles have united American government officials, public policy analysts, the media, economists, and throngs of commentators who all cajol Japan to reform. President Clinton has pressed Japan to stimulate and reform its economy. Treasury Secretary Robert Rubin has demanded that Japan stimulate its economy and deregulate promptly. Interestingly, President Clinton is particularly fond of quoting Lester Thurow's book, *Head to Head: The Coming Economic Battle Among Japan, Europe, and America*. Mr. Thurow's book was a misguided, sensationalist account of Japan's economic threat to America. *The New York Times* and *Business Week*, after worshipping the coming triumph of the Japanese economic model in the 1980s, have become vocal critics of Japan. *The Wall Street Journal* urges Japan to cut taxes and deregulate, as if some elementary mechanistic approach will coax Japan to the promised land of the free market.

Past Perceptions

Many of the traits condemned today were viewed as Japanese strengths within the past decade. We were told that Japan was a model for the United States; Japan had developed a "public private partnership" which should be emulated; Japan had created a government planning apparatus that avoided America's adversarial, confrontational, and often messy private sector process; and that Japan had developed a benign paternalistic system, a model of harmony. It was noted that Japan's financial institutions were big; thus they must be efficient, powerful, fearsome, and threatening. Japan had proved that massive government intervention in the economy and society in general was indeed positive. Japan had shown the world the proper way for a society to adjust. In short, Japan had built institutions in the private and public sector which were the envy of the world. Other Asian countries used Japan as the model and were likewise prospering.

Dial 1-800-Fix-Japan/Asia (Now!)

Proposed quick solutions to Japan's current economic problems abound. Japan, after all, is the second largest economy in the world. Many other countries within the Asian region have experienced enormously high growth rates and made substantial economic progress. Japan and her neighbors could not have attained their current positions without skill, intelligence, and hard work. So why did Japan and other Asian countries not anticipate their current problems? When the problems surfaced, why were they not dealt with expeditiously? There is even a facile operative analogy with the United States, with Japan's banking crisis likened to the U.S. Savings and Loan debacle. America was forced to bailout its financial institutions, so Japan has a near perfect model for solving its non-performing loan dilemma. If the solution is so simple, why has Japan not followed the American example?

There is no shortage of advice for Japan:

- Reorganize the Ministry of Finance (MoF) along the lines of the U.S. Securities and Exchange Commission.
- Promote transparency by increasing the amount of financial information available.
- Allow foreign investment banks and foreign investment advisors full access to Japanese investors.
- Dismantle the regulatory framework stifling the JFIs.
- Increase JFI accountability.

The list is formidable. The U.S. government even sponsored a lecture series in several Japanese cities in March 1998 to promote financial reform. Financial reform is indeed a popular topic in Japan. The Japanese currently have seized upon America's Citicorp as their role model. Previous American role models have included J. P. Morgan, Merrill Lynch, and Salomon Brothers. In the late 1960s, teams of Nomura personnel visited the New York headquarters of Salomon to unlock the mysteries of financial research. Armed with cameras, the Nomura men practiced a form of economic espionage—but with no consequence.

All of these reforms are an attempt to move Japan towards the American system. Several critical issues remain, however: (1) Is it appropriate for Japan to adopt the American system or parts of the American system? (2) Can Japan adopt the American system or parts of the system? (3) If Japan can adopt only parts of the American system, will the result be effective?

Clearly, Japan has been able to graft parts of the American industrial economy onto an indigenous system, and the results, in many cases, have been staggeringly successful. The Japanese financial system, however, has, thus far, not been able to adapt the strategies and practices of American financial institutions. Two factors have been powerful forces in preventing this adaptation: (1) the difference in cultural environments between Japan and the United States, and (2) the particular dynamics of financial institutions as opposed to manufacturing entities.

The Japanese Reformation:
Manufacturers vs. Financial Institutions

As the second largest economy in the world, Japan has undeniable strengths. Many Japanese manufacturers are world class and, in many cases, the envy of the world. To date, many of these manufacturers and distribution companies are adjusting effectively to a competitive environment, while the country's rigid financial system has been impervious to change. *The Sun That Never Rose* (Dattel

1994) makes a clear distinction between the dynamics of Japan's world of manufacturing and the world of finance. Why are the financial institutions failing to adjust properly? After all, they are part of the same system that produced Toyota, Sony, and Matsushita—companies that are revered for their excellence and their adaptability.

The outside world tends to perceive Japanese manufacturing and financial institutions as a monolith. In fact, these institutions remain systematically different. Manufacturers make physical products; financial institutions deal in abstractions. It is difficult to hide a defect in a physical product. If Toyota built a flawed car, no one would purchase it. But the JFIs regularly conspired with the MoF to hide mistakes through secrecy and misinformation. A forty-five-year bull market in equities and real estate masked the decaying structure of Japan's financial institutions.

The distinction between manufacturers and financial institutions should be emphasized, not ignored. Any visitor who tours a Toyota or General Motors factory will instantly understand the activity being performed. A door fitted to a frame or a paint job are immediately recognizable. By contrast, a visitor who gazes at a vast investment banking trading room would have difficulty describing the activity being conducted by the hordes of young people with headsets seemingly glued to their ears.

Regrettably, the vocabulary of manufacturing is often superimposed on the activities of financial institutions. The standard manufacturing lexicon—efficiency, market share, productivity, economies of scale, performance, production, relationships, and time horizons—cannot be applied to financial institutions without qualification.

The extent of the confusion is revealed in an example from journalist Eamonn Fingleton. In an article written for the *New York Times* on April 9, 1994, Mr. Fingleton claimed that the (then) largest Japanese commercial bank, Dai-Ichi Kangyo (DKB) was "more productive than Citibank because DKB (needs) only 19,000 employees to manage $503 billion assets; whereas, Citicorp employs 81,000 to handle $217 billion." He confused manufacturing output and financial output. Bank performance and efficiency can be measured to a great extent by return ratios, which were shockingly low for DKB. At the time, DKB had a 0.16 percent return on total assets, whereas the Citibank figure was 1.3 percent, roughly eight times as high. Nor was it surprising that Citibank should be labor intensive, since it, unlike DKB, was a retail bank.

Financial Institutions: The Legacy

In general, analyses of Japan's financial crisis have erred by focusing mainly on macro rather than micro events. Commentators with an eye on Japanese real estate and stock and currency prices tend to dwell on money supply, trade policy, fiscal stimulus, and government bailouts. Although such topics are significant, they mask the real problems embedded in Japan's dysfunctional financial institutions. The internal workings, performance, and capability of each firm is important, not just its macro economic statistics. In Japan, as well as in other Asian countries, the financial crisis will require a firm-by-firm workout in the context of each country. In addition, each country should look carefully at the lack of diversity of financial institutions—a common, but little understood, feature in Asian countries.

Therefore, the critical questions should be: "What should Nippon Life do? What should Mitsubishi Trust do?" *The Sun That Never Rose*, based on both experience and practice, outlined a framework for examining the JFIs. Unfortunately, its harsh critique remains valid today.[3] Its warning that "one can safely say that the structural issues which have been outlined are not understood by the Japanese political and financial establishment" went unheeded in Japan. With regard to Japanese financial involvement in other Asian countries:

> (The JFIs were looking) to increase their presence in Asia, where they think they understand "the Oriental mind" better than they comprehend "Western ways." In some ways, Asia will actually be more difficult than the U.S. because of the lack of publicly available information, obstacles in developing a reliable network of business contacts and controls and legal structure.

Both cultural and regulatory factors contribute to Japan's malfunctioning financial system. Although commentators allude to the dark side of Japan's culture, they do not recognize the dark side of JFIs. Peer pressure, rigid hierarchy, suppression of individual recognition, inability to assimilate, an emphasis on rote memory in school, avoidance of confrontation, and an obsession with ritual and control are all inhibiting features. Cultural limitations, socioeconomic factors, and isolation from market forces have produced homogeneous organizations with distinct patterns of behavior. Connecting the dots between socioeconomic factors and the management of JFIs is a prerequisite to understanding the systemic nature of Japan's financial crisis.

An experienced observer has no difficulty identifying the JFIs' structural weaknesses. There are four mutually reinforcing, culturally derived problems. In order to explore these structural flaws, it is necessary to go inside the JFIs. The complimentary and reinforcing practices must be understood if we are to understand why the JFIs have remained so primitive and why they have not adjusted. The organizational structure of the JFIs should be seen from several different angles.

The Formal Personnel Rotation System

Specialization is anathema in the JFIs because formal Japanese organizational behavior emphasizes subordination of individual identity.[4] Employees of financial institutions rotate jobs in a formal, ritualistic manner approximately every three years. Even though some JFIs are tinkering with this practice, it remains a core institutional norm. Although usually unremarked upon, this practice has led to an extremely short-term approach to business. The generalist manager is idealized and the specialist is condemned for his Western individualism so loathed by group-oriented Japanese. In financial institutions, this generalist mentality has precluded the development of technological, analytical, and managerial skills.

This negative attitude towards the technology departments in most Japanese financial institutions in the 1980s is instructive. Although the integration of advanced technology is critical to trading, data processing, information retrieval, securities clearance, and risk control, the JFIs emphasis on the rotation system denigrated the role of technical specialists. During the 1980s, technology departments were insignificant appendages whose frustrated staffs were not taken seriously. Instead, the financial institutions were always looking for a formula for investment purposes that could be memorized or copied.

Perhaps this approach was a by-product of the Japanese educational system. JFIs have not learned that technology, while supporting the decision making process, is not the process itself. The purpose of technology was replication of entire classes of transactions rather than analysis of particular business opportunities. It is ironic that Japan, probably the most mathematically literate nation in the world, has not integrated technology into its financial system.

The three-year rotation practice also means that an employee's horizon does not extend past his rotation schedule. His goal is the avoidance of political mistakes, since economic failures can be tolerated. He does not need to achieve, but he must avoid interfering with other departments. As a result, duplication, waste, and inefficiency are rampant. Once an employee is transferred to another department, he is not responsible for previous errors. His promotions are purely routine. He resembles a bureaucrat more than a businessman. The personnel rotation system is a bonanza for consultants. Each JFI rotation presents an entirely new client list within the same organization.

JFIs, unlike Japan's manufacturers, have no institutional memory because the rotation system undermines the transfer of knowledge and skills. The Japanese manufacturing sector was able to co-opt ideas and technology, but no such process took place in the abstract and rapidly evolving financial services area.

Extreme Provincialism

In the 1980s, both Japan's critics and even some apologists agreed that the employees of JFIs lacked skill and knowledge, especially in managing assets.[5] It was widely assumed that the JFIs could easily rectify their deficiencies by acquiring needed expertise from foreigners who could be bought. Implicit in such thinking was a belief in Japan's legendary adaptability. Also, there was an assumption that Japan, and indeed Asia, were always moving forward in a linear fashion.

The JFIs' overseas operations were to play a critical role in technology transfer: they employed Americans and formed joint ventures with Americans. The JFIs would absorb foreign technology and foreign knowledge, and then the foreigners would become expendable. The closed nature of Japanese society prevented the full assimilation of foreigners and their ideas. In this way, the Japanese cultural concern for uniqueness and self-sufficiency presented barriers in finance.

As a variation of this theme, the recent joint ventures and associations between Bankers Trust and Nippon Credit Bank, Union Bank of Switzerland and the Long Term Credit Bank, and the Industrial Bank of Japan and Nomura have been greeted as harbingers of substantial change. Still, a certain amount of caution should be used when describing financial joint ventures, as financial history is littered with the bodies of dead joint ventures.

Excessive Centralization

In a society that considers decentralization anathema, the ill effects of over centralization tend to go unnoticed.[6] JFIs are highly centralized organizations. Because centralization implies central planning, it would be natural to assume that this control would result in coordinated organizations. Quite the contrary occurred. Department-by-department centralization produced a fragmented vertical system that fosters duplication of effort, wasteful political struggles, and defective risk monitoring systems.

Free from having to meet performance criteria, the centralized and hierarchical JFIs focused on fashionable trends. Joint ventures, investments, and acquisitions were undertaken to gain publicity, without a specific strategy for gaining genuine business advantage. American financial institutions are not immune to this type of behavior, but the systemic and embedded nature of the Japanese problem is qualitatively distinct.

As is now obvious, the JFIs justified their behavior by pointing to increased market share. The pursuit of market share in the financial services area can be meaningless and dangerous, even within the context of a proper strategy. Remarkably, the JFIs did not even have a strategy.

Bureaucratic Rot

All organizations are to some extent bureaucratic, but the JFIs represent bureaucracy in its purest and most unadulterated form.[7] Bureaucratic tendencies seen as indefensible elsewhere were applauded in Japan. The deliberate approach of the JFIs was deemed to promote consensus, but this too was a flaw. Their slow reaction time was rationalized as necessary attention to detail and as essential to long-term planning. The reality, however, was quite different. JFIs were subject to bureaucratic rot with consequences even more damaging than at Western firms because of the total absence of individual, departmental, or firm accountability.

The absence of protection for investors, the rotation system, the lack of competition, the lack of diversity among financial institutions, the protection offered by the MoF, and the absence of performance standards removed any checks from the system. No entrepreneurial firms or people existed to challenge the slothful establishment. As a result, JFIs were unable to properly evaluate transactions. The consensus-building process avoided both individual and departmental accountability.

The physical nature of a Japanese manufacturing product meant that a defect would be exposed; no feedback existed in the financial arena. If enough people left their footprints on a transaction, everyone was safe—no one would risk alienating fellow employees for the sake of performance. Transactions were subject to approval, not a decision making process. Seen in this light, the much-admired Japanese consensus-building technique, *nemawashi*, appears less than admirable.

The JFIs' involvement with their related companies was marred by incestuous non-economic behavior, which led to disastrous consequences. Westerners had applauded the cooperation between related companies as an advantage, often contrasting the harsher arms length approach of American companies. Rather than a positive feature of Japanese organizational structure, however, the cooperation should be viewed as a non-economic incentive for wasteful behavior.

Bureaucratic tendencies were further encouraged by a lack of objective analysis. Here, socioeconomic and cultural influences were at work, for the Japanese educational system discouraged confrontation, critical thinking, and the open flow of information that would threat the control jealously guarded by Japanese authorities. Experimentation, innovation, entrepreneurship, and critical awareness were smothered by business reduced to ritual ceremony.

The Ministry of Finance

In large measure, the Ministry of Finance (MoF) created the artificial and protected world of the JFIs. The omnipotent MoF regulated every aspect of a JFIs' existence, controlling the flow of financial information and answering to no one. MoF personnel were obsessed with their major goal—control—and their tenacity was directed through intimidation unchecked by performance criteria, accountability, public information, or a legal system. The method was quite simple. The MoF granted franchises to the JFIs who, in return for protection, were obedient and loyal. The JFIs developed a mind-set of chronic dependence on the MoF. Professionalism was not required in the artificial world administered by the MoF. JFIs lived in a time warp in which they remained dormant since World War II. The legacy of the Faustian bargain between MoF and the JFIs are the structurally flawed JFIs of today.

Foreigners revered the MoF, and the myth of the infallible Japanese government bureaucrat was alive and well until recently. In a 1995 article in *Foreign Affairs*, Eammon Fingleton described MoF employees as being of "noble-caliber, brilliant, creative, tenacious, public spirited." Jeffery Garten, a former Undersecretary of Commerce and currently the dean of the Yale School of Management, gave in 1992 an unqualified endorsement of Japan's bureaucrats as "skillful" and "highly professional."

In reality, however, MoF officials bear little resemblance to the caricatures invented by admiring Westerners. They are basically polemicists whose competence and professionalism have been vastly overrated. MoF personnel are often rotating amateurs who have little understanding of financial markets, financial institutions, or financial asset allocation. Power and prestige have produced an almost universal arrogance among MoF employees. After a few years, even the most well meaning young MoF man succumbs.

Again, it is assumed that MoF personnel are Japan's "best and brightest." This characterization is misleading and simplistic. What special kind of skill, intelligence, and personality do MoF personnel have? What development occurs within the confines of a Japanese financial or governmental organization?[8] Attendance at a prestigious university is clearly no substitute for hands-on knowledge of the marketplace.[9] The MoF's acquiescence in fraudulent practices, market manipulation, market distortions, and "loss compensation payments" reveal its true character to be that of a government agency concerned with vested interests and control.

Every participant in the Japanese financial system, both foreign and domestic, has encountered the vagueness and inconsistency of "administrative guidance," a procedure which gives MoF officials discretion to rule arbitrarily on matters. In essence, a bureaucrat has the discretion to approve or disapprove a particular practice or transaction. In reality, since there is an absence of specific guidelines and no recourse to legal apparatus, the process of administrative guidance is arbitrary. A market participant generally is forced to contact the MoF for approval of a particular practice. This habit of visiting MoF inhibits experimentation and creates uncertainty, reinforcing MoF's power. Admiring Westerners such as Jeffrey Garten have viewed Japan's "informal understandings" as a positive alternative to the confrontational American legal approach. The American system is far from perfect, but Japan's informal system of administrative guidance has resulted in a system of mutual obligations without a foundation of business competence. This process produces unchecked control and an environment of circumvention, obfuscation, and secrecy.

There is a virtual absence of legal recourse. Market participants were forced to go to the MoF for administrative guidance on all matters. As a foreign participant, I often consulted lawyers about a particular practice or possible transaction. In each case, the advice always contained a directive to "go to the MoF." In other words, MoF was the only source of approval. Legal precedent was absent. Legal recourse was absent. A judicial apparatus was absent. Legal rights were absent.

The result was a highly artificial system that nullified experimentation, entrepreneurship, innovation, and performance. Predictability and fairness were not priorities. The system was rigid in terms of administrative procedure but inconsistent in terms of content. Form clearly triumphed over substance in the MoF.

The Japanese Success Story: A Linear View

A mountain of reform literature has been generated since 1990 for transforming the JFIs. Each government reform proposal or package has been greeted with massive media coverage, market moves, and extensive commentary. Yet, relatively little has happened to change the system. There have been bank consolidations; Yamaichi Securities and Hokkaido Takushoku have failed; and the Long Term Credit Bank was forced, by its own insolvency, to consider merging with Sumitomo Trust. But the institutional structure of the JFIs has undergone no systemic change. Each package is followed by Westerners' conjecture that the Japanese are "serious this time."

As the financial condition of individual JFIs has deteriorated, foreign firms have purchased assets. Merrill Lynch purchased Yamaichi Securities branches. Travelers purchased a stake in Nikko Securities. American securities firms have been interested because Japanese investors purchase American assets, especially U.S. bonds. In a sense, the Japanese institutional and individual investors, who are faced with 1 percent yields in the domestic Japanese bond market, are forced to go overseas in search of higher yields.

Why has there been no resolve to deal with the financial problems? Conventional wisdom holds that the JFIs were part of the system which built the Japanese postwar miracle and therefore they played a positive role. It is assumed that changing conditions will force the JFIs to adjust in a manner befitting Japan's legendary ability to adapt. The Meiji Restoration, the postwar economic boom, and the oil shock adjustment of the 1970s are invariably offered as examples. In contrast, Japan's inability to find an appropriate means of adjusting to the 1930s is generally overlooked in such analyses.

This linear view implies that there is no cause for concern; Japan will gradually solve the present difficulties. Comparisons between Japan's financial institutions and those of the United States retrogressed. Japan's banks a few years ago were compared to U.S. banks in the 1970s, then the 1950s. Now the comparison is with the 1930s. No matter how distant the comparisons in time, the linear view presumes Japan eventually will move successfully along a U.S. trajectory.

Even journalists like Bill Emmott, the current editor of *The Economist,* who called attention to Japan's overvalued equity and real estate markets in his 1989 book, *The Sun Also Sets*, fell into the optimistic linear trap. "What (Japanese) fund managers had in common when the surplus (capital in the 1980s) flooded them was ignorance." Emmott correctly portrayed Japan as "a nation of speculators," but he also implied that once the problem had been identified a solution would readily be implemented:

> (Japanese) fund managers have learned fast because they had to. . . . The Japanese government hopes that domestic firms will learn from foreign firms, either through competition or tie-ups. More apparent than that have been investments in fund managers and investment banks overseas in order to gain training and experience for Japanese fund managers. . . . All are buying brain power, not control.

What is missing here is a full appreciation of the degree to which the JFIs resist structural change, especially within the protected environment created by the MoF. There is similarity between JFI problems today and descriptions forty years ago. Adams in 1953 described the Japanese security market as "rigged" and later spoke of the "administrative arbitrariness" of the Japanese financial bureaucracy (Adams 1964). In reality, the JFIs seem not to have changed much since these earlier analyses. In the financial arena, Japan's economic progress has not been linear. Some economists have been forced into the seemingly mushy cultural arena to explain Japan's financial system. Economists in general are not particularly comfortable discussing culture.

David S. Landes, the economic historian, in *The Wealth and Poverty of Nations* remarked: "Such terms as 'values' and 'culture' are not popular with economists, who prefer to deal with quantifiable (more definable) factors. Still, life being what it is, onemust talk about these things" (Landes 1998: 215). Such was the problem for Robert Feldman, the Japan economist for Morgan Stanley. In 1986 Mr. Feldman wrote a typical quantitative macro-text, *Japanese Financial Markets*, which was directed towards highly specialized economists. By 1996, however, Mr. Feldman was forced to confront Japan's cultural obstacles in a report about the Japanese economy. After describing Japan's financial industry, Feldman opines: "It is surprising, in fact, that the Japanese economy has done as well as it has in the post-war period."

Japan's economy did do very well in the postwar period, but financial institutions were only part of the economy. Those who think that the JFIs were a positive influence take comfort in the fact that this opinion can neither be proved nor refuted. But the assumption that JFIs served their purpose for fifty years means there will be little fundamental change without a crisis or intense competition. The current JFIs are the institutional legacy of Japan's culture and public policy. The question remains, "What should be done?"

The Asian Success Story: A Linear View

A similar problem of viewing financial institutions in a linear fashion can be found in analyses of the Asian crisis in general. Many of the nations in Asia experiencing financial turmoil were until last year regarded as economic success stories. Indeed, the Asian economic model had entered the lexicon of world business. Thailand, Korea, Malaysia, and Indonesia were part of a group of emerging market countries targeted by institutional investors and investment bankers around the world for their investment potential.

To some extent, Asian countries are confronting similar problems in the current financial turmoil. Asian financial institutions, both public and private, have proven themselves incapable of allocating financial resources without suffering massive losses. Furthermore, the range of their financial institutions is not nearly as diverse as in Europe and North America. The clichés—lack of transparency, accountability, a proper legal apparatus, and a proper regulatory apparatus; improper business motives; incestuous relationships between government and business; institutional ossification; and unprofessional conduct—are all part of the Asian landscape. In that general sense, Asian financial institutions throughout the region resemble the financial institutions of Japan.

Beyond that, each country, each financial system, and each government should be analyzed separately for their individual characteristics. It would be quite convenient if there were a standard financial blueprint to be applied to each of the Asian countries affected by the financial crisis. But in truth, there is no macroeconomic handbook or panacea applicable to all affected countries.

Nonetheless, the optimistic linear view of the inevitable evolution of Japan's financial institutions toward a more European or North American model has recently been attached to the other rapidly developing economies of Asia. Western commentators actually plot Asian countries on a Western, especially American, trajectory. Episodes in European or American history have become reference points for Asia countries. For example, the *New York Times* reported on May 20, 1998, that the Asian financial crisis signified a historic "landmark" in Asian society, in the same way that the popular uprisings of 1848 marked the eclipse of the old social and political order in Europe. Similarly, Paul Krugman in the May-June 1998 issue of *Foreign Affairs* compared the Asia financial crisis to the "crisis-prone" American economy between the Civil War and World War I.

Likewise, Fareed Zakaria in *Foreign Affairs* in November-December 1997 superimposed the Western historical trajectory on East Asia, noting that the "mix of democracy, liberalism, capitalism, oligarchy, and corruption" in East Asia today was analogous to the West "circa 1900." A *Forbes* article about India written in March 1998 suggested that doing business in India at this time must be like "business must have been . . . in the U.S." at the end of the nineteenth century. An American money manager in *Barron's* on May 25, 1998, emphatically asserted, "Japan today is where the United States was during the Great Depression." As previously mentioned, JFIs have been compared to American financial institutions from the 1930s to the 1970s, and similar historical templates are now being applied to much of the remainder of Asia.

But should Europe or America be the benchmark for Asia? Are these analogies really appropriate given the wide divergence in cultures and organizational modes, not only between Japan and the West, but among Asian nations themselves? It is as if young American economists and financial analysts were bent upon creating a new index whereby all countries would be quantitatively compared on an "Approaching America Market Index" (AAMI).

Practical Men Offer Practical Solutions

There are two distinct issues confronting Japan and the troubled Asian economies: (1) concrete immediate issues including short-term liquidity problems, bad loan dilemmas, or a combination of both; and (2) long-term development of effective public and private financial institutions.

The structural issues, which underlie the development of an effective financial system, are of primary concern in this essay. There have been attempts to isolate root causes of the Asian financial systems and there have been attempts to look at these financial systems comprehensively. In general, solutions and suggestions relate to political structures and government regulation. Very little attention is paid to the organizational structure of financial institutions. Financial institutions in Asia are rightly perceived to be governmental, quasi-governmental, or heavily dependent on the government. At some point, financial institutions should be allowed to function independent of inappropriate government oversight so that they can make market judgments rather than quasi-governmental judgments which lead them to investments that do not perform financially.

The Macro Solution

In the *Wall Street Journal* of December 17, 1997, Milton Friedman recently pointed an accusing finger at Japan's monetary policy, which he views as the root cause of Japan's financial woes: "Seemingly small numerical differences are enough to convert a healthy economy into a sick one. The surest road to a healthy economic recovery (for Japan) is to increase the rate of monetary growth."

Financial institutions, ossified government bureaucracies, culture, and a variety of factors—in addition to money supply—profoundly effect the economy. Precious little attention is paid to the roles and types of financial institutions and the way they evolve. Financial institutions play the critical role in allocating capital within an economy, both as disciplinarian and as sponsor. They are a vital adjustment mechanism. Dysfunctional financial institutions and a lack of diversity will most assuredly have a negative impact on an economy.

Lax Oversight vs. Overregulation

Clever Japanese bureaucrats now assert that there are too few regulators and bureaucrats. This, it should be noted, is asserted in the midst of Japan's rhetoric about loosening the reigns of government. The MoF complains that Japan has several hundred people, whereas U.S. financial regulators number in the thousands. For those following the machinations of MoF for years, these claims hold a certain irony. We had been told that the all-powerful MoF had total control of the JFIs. Now, we are told that lax oversight is the problem. One such spokesman, Joseph Stiglitz, the chief economist for the World Bank, stated, "inadequate oversight, not overregulation, caused these (Asia's financial) problems."[10] While Dr. Stiglitz was speaking about Asia, the same observation has been made about Japan.

The problem is not the lack of oversight but the wrong kind of oversight. MOF oversight is far too extensive and not sufficiently rooted in specialized knowledge of the marketplace to make it relevant and useful. The very MOF bureaucrats expecting to reform the old system and oversee the new are wedded, in fact, to the system of bureaucratized financial institutions that caused the financial crisis in the first place. Eisuke Sakakibara, currently the MoF's most visible figure, is the author of the 1993 book, *Beyond Capitalism*, a paean to Japan's uniqueness and the superiority of the Japanese system. The document is hardly a manifesto for change.

The Asian Debt Market Requirement

Davies Simon in the *Financial Times* of December 3, 1997, lectured Asian countries about "the region's most urgent task," a need to develop a bond market capable of correcting the unchecked power of local banks. The article said, "most of the requirements for a regional market are already in place." Yet, a half-year later, another journalist at the *Financial Times* was forced to admit, "Asia's bid to develop a regional bond market has been thwarted by many issues."[11] The financial secretary of Hong Kong, Donald Tsang, is yet another Asian bond market advocate. In July 1998 Mr. Tsang issued his call by stating, "now is the time to create a real Asian bond market."[12] Japan actually tried to construct a foreign currency bond market in the 1980s. The result—an artificial, highly stylized market called the "Shogun market"—parodied a real market, and after the usual opening fanfare, was doomed to failure and historical obscurity. The creation of an effective capital market cannot be mandated by government officials. The proposed capital market solution will be difficult to implement. Notions of gradual evolutionary development are naive.

The American Model

The Japanese and other Asian countries are in effect being told to adopt the American (or Anglo-American) financial system. American commentators and government officials are eager to superimpose American vocabulary on the existing Japanese system. The Japanese, accustomed to revering stability, are asked to emulate the messy and confrontational world of American finance.

Americans are forever preaching the gospel of deregulation to the Japanese. American free market purists view deregulation as a panacea. In response, Japan's bureaucrats adopted the phrase, "Big Bang," to indicate the dismantling of some of the rules which have controlled the JFIs and rendered them dependent on MoF. "Big Bang" was a term laden with baggage, exempting the user from the requirement to identify specifics and analyze the actual terms and the impact of the proposed deregulation.

The issues are, in fact, much more complex than the hordes of both experienced and newly minted Asian commentators might suspect. Extensive deregulation ultimately requires creating full disclosure, free flows of information, and an effective legal system. The JFIs and the MoF's ability to use information effectively is highly suspect, because Japan's private financial institutions resemble government bureaucracies more than private corporations.

To date, deregulation and market forces have brought some consolidation with the banking system. The trend has been hailed as positive—a portent of the arrival of a leaner and meaner Japanese financial system. The resulting JFIs are larger than ever; whether they are better than before is still doubtful. They are a powerful force, however. The JFIs retain a valuable franchise in the second largest economy in the world, and parts of the Japanese economy remain extremely formidable.

Can the American system or parts of the American system be transported to Japan or the rest of Asia? American traits—openness, accountability, confrontation, individualism, assimilation, decentralization, objective analysis, legal recourse, and checks and balances—are integral to the U.S. financial system. To a varying extent, these norms and organizational mechanisms are absent from the financial institutions of Japan and much of the rest of Asia. Cultural factors will make the wholesale adoption of American practices very difficult without a significant shock. Market forces, a crisis, or severe economic dislocation will be necessary to create an environment for substantial change in financial institutions.

American Financial Institutions

When America's financial institutions are compared to the JFIs, commentators generally take bits and pieces of the American system. For example, it is often said that Japan needs an independent regulatory body like the rather effective American Securities and Exchange Commission (SEC). It is asserted that Japan could allocate capital more effectively if American investment bankers such as Merrill Lynch or Morgan Stanley Dean Witter were allowed to roam more freely in the financial markets. According to this logic, the investment process will benefit dramatically from the advent of American fund managers, such as Fidelity.

In reality, straightforward comparisons between Japan or Asia and the United States are treacherous. The ubiquitous analogy between the Japanese banking crisis and the American S&L debacle is oversimplified and misleading. At the same time, truly useful comparisons between Japanese, Asian, and American financial firms are usually ignored.

If the American system is accepted as a model, the Japanese and other Asians should understand that the United States has a diverse group of financial institutions. For example, JFIs consist of banks, insurance companies, securities firms, and non-bank banks. The United States, on the other hand, has developed a fragmented, deregulated, and democratized financial system. Traditional banks, insurance companies, and securities firms are only part of the story. There are a myriad of American specialized investment firms, venture capital firms, leveraged buyout firms (LBOs), hedge funds, vulture funds, and real estate investment firms. Even large firms like Citicorp and Prudential Insurance can have separate or semi-autonomous departments, which operate with a great deal of independence. At times, these firms compete with each other; at other times, they complement one another in a complex and often messy interaction. These institutions operate on both a national and regional basis. It is difficult to explain this diversity to the Japanese.

In addition, there is an enormous separate supporting industry in the United States, including law firms, accounting firms, and multiple evaluation firms. Of course, the media, especially in the midst of America's ebullient markets, has a large involvement in the financial arena. The media's presence ranges from sophistication to ignorance, from integrity to manipulation, from objective coverage to sensationalist distortion. The role of the LBO movement is a case in point. Much of the publicity surrounding the restructuring of American industry focused on egregious examples like the RJR Nabisco transaction, which spawned books and movies. We became well acquainted with the antiheroes of American business like Michael Milken. Nevertheless, the LBO movement was an integral part of the process, forcing adjustments in the economy which Asia has found so difficult.

American financial institutions, unlike the JFIs, have spawned entrepreneurs like Henry Kravis of KKR, Fred Smith of FedEx, and Michael Bloomberg, who had tremendous impact on their respective organizations. In most cases, American entrepreneurs must challenge the establishment, an act of defiance found difficult by the Japanese.

The American financial services industry is constantly evolving, and the dynamics of the financial world can generate excesses very quickly. American financial history is filled with serious panics and crises. Charles Kindleberger's well-known book, *Manias, Panics and Crashes* reveals the frequency of American financial crises, which occurred in 1818, 1837, 1857, 1873, 1893, 1907, and 1929. A legal and regulatory apparatus evolved (and is still evolving) to deal with the issues which gave rise to abuses. In periods where there are sustained strong markets—whether in Japan, the United States, or elsewhere—patterns of behavior reflect the assumption that positive markets will continue indefinitely. This ingrained optimism, as we know, leads to mistakes.

Emerging market debt provides a useful example, as in the case of Russian bonds, where the attraction of extra yield induces investors to speculate in high country risk. The need for extra yield often causes fund managers to "rationalize" yield. In this process, the fund manager finds a way to justify purchases of bonds without fully accounting for risk. It is psychologically easier to rationalize the purchase of emerging market fixed income securities, as opposed to equities. The institutional investor—perhaps an insurance company—may yearn to buy an emerging market bond when there is little justification, and investment bankers are only too willing to aid and abet.

As we know, American fund managers are not immune to blunders based on greed, lax management, misjudgments of risk, or violations of laws. Investment bankers, as intermediaries and as principals have encouraged or even been responsible for financial blunders. The very success of an investment, market sector, or institution can produce devastating excesses as individuals and institutions irrationally commit funds, thus driving prices to unsustainable levels. Inevitably, there are failures and accidents. The S&L crisis, the Orange County insolvency, and the Long Term Capital Management debacle are unfortunate examples. Unlike Japan's financial miscues, however, public information in the United States reveals the extent of the damage and what happened. Participants will be held at least somewhat accountable. The problems are not structural; institutions will adjust. A satisfactory exploration of the strengths and weaknesses of American financial institutions would require a separate chapter.

Joseph de la Vega in his 1688 treatise, *Confusion de Confusiones*, described the speculation and trading in the seventeenth century Amsterdam stock and options market. His observations are still relevant: "(Finance is) the fairest and most deceitful (business) . . . the famous and most infamous . . . the finest and the most vulgar . . . the quintessence of academic learning and a paragon of fraudulence."

American investment banks function effectively within the American system, where there are numerous checks and balances in addition to a proper legal apparatus. Investment banks, in their intermediary (broker or conduit), corporate finance, and trading roles need to be monitored and viewed with a healthy skepticism. Profit incentives and gamesmanship can produce an amoral environment in which individuals rather than institutions should be trusted. Often, investment banker conduct reflects the sophistication or lack of sophistication of the client. Examples abound. Transcripts of the lawsuit brought by the state of West Virginia against Morgan Stanley reveal the unsavory side of Wall Street. The Normandy America deal in 1995 illustrates Salomon Brothers' appalling lack of diligence. After trading for one day, this ludicrous deal was canceled and the money refunded to investors. In June 1998, Merrill Lynch reimbursed Orange County for losses which were incurred because of Merrill's involvement. These

American investment banks are the same firms which the American government has been attempting to foist upon the Japanese as their financial saviors.

American investment banking firms spew forth reams of information, some of which is driven by self-serving marketing considerations. In their enthusiasm for generating income, investment banks have created a research apparatus for the emerging market bond market. Emerging market bond research, at times, consists of flights of fancy in superimposing the language applicable to the American bond market to the bonds of emerging countries. How do you evaluate credits—both sovereign and private—in markets with different accounting practices, disclosure procedure, legal systems, and business customs? Why do investment banking firms compare yields on particular bond markets such as Russia or Korea to the yield of U.S. treasury bonds? The folly of the American credit rating agencies foray into these markets is well documented. Standards established for the domestic U.S. market have had no predictive value in the recent Asian turmoil. Common sense would be an excellent antidote to the abuses of emerging market bond research.

American money managers should also be viewed with skepticism. To some extent their recent success is a function of ebullient U.S. markets. They will be tested by a number of conditions—difficult markets, size, performance, overseas activity, infrastructure costs, competition, pressure on fees, and a host of unforeseen events. In short, American firms should not be viewed as nor play the role of financial missionaries. Their strengths and weaknesses must be understood. Any comparison between the U.S. and the Japanese or Asian financial systems must include the goals, standards, and society in which each operates. Each country must decide for itself whether the American system can or should be adopted.

Long-term solutions for the actual structural problems which plague Asian finance require an analysis of private financial institutions, in addition to the current emphasis on the role of government. American financial institutions and regulatory bodies will provide useful examples, both positive and negative. There are many questions which need to be asked: What should Nippon Life do? What should Mitsubishi Trust do? What kinds of financial institutions are needed? How do financial institutions promote growth? How do financial institutions discipline companies? How do various financial institutions evaluate risk versus reward? To what extent can technology be used? What are the economies and diseconomies of scale within the financial services industry? How does the experimentation process work? The restructuring of Asia's financial institutions will be extremely complex. In part, the process will reflect a cultural conflict between the more closed and indirect Asian societies and the more open and confrontational American society.

Information Processing

The Japanese and Asian financial saga vividly illustrate the flaws in the processing of information about financial institutions. It is extremely important to understand why foreigners had such erroneous views about JFIs. We need to look no further than their sources of information—the books and articles written about Japan in the 1980s and 1990s. Visible foreigners—such as Paul Kennedy, the Yale historian, Jeffrey Garten, former Undersecretary of Commerce and currently dean of the Yale School of Management, and Clyde Prestowitz, a Washington commentator on foreign trade—wrote books with grossly misleading descriptions of JFIs.[13]

Concluding Thoughts

Events in the current Asian financial turmoil should force, or at least strongly encourage, structural change in the region's financial institutions, both private and public. Discussion and analysis should proceed on a case-by-case basis as each country presents a separate economic, political, legal, educational, and cultural challenge. The strengths and weaknesses of these countries should be dissected on an industry by industry basis.

In Japan there have been several consequences for JFIs. First, several such as Yamaichi Securities and Hokkaido Takushoku have been eliminated through insolvency. Second, financially troubled entities such as the Long Term Credit Bank (LTCB) have been forced to seek merger partners. In addition, there have been consolidations within the Japanese banking system, and joint ventures also have resulted. The long-term success of these endeavors will depend on many factors. Foreign entities have been active as well. Merrill Lynch acquired the branches of the defunct Yamaichi Securities. Travelers through its securities arm Salomon Smith Barney purchased a stake in Nikko Securities. General Electric Capital purchased an equity position in Toho Life Insurance. Each of these transactions represents to some extent a "distressed" sale by a JFI. The most compelling logic for the foreign purchaser has been added distribution capability in Japan. Currently, they are at the experimentation stage.

It will be difficult for the JFIs to reform themselves. An external shock such as a crisis would certainly provoke change. The advent of foreigners will alter the financial landscape, but the consequences of increased foreign influence in the Japanese market has yet to be seen. In general, the financial services industry is highly opportunistic; products, market discrepancies, and market strategies are constantly being altered because of economic or market conditions. Risk and reward criteria from an investment or trading position always contain an important subjective component.

The Japanese government has been unwilling and unable to deal with the short-term and long-term problems confronting the Japanese financial system. The institutional inertia, cultural limitations, and regulatory incompetence have retarded developmental change of the JFIs to cope with a rapidly evolving world financial arena. If financial deregulation is the obvious solution to the JFI dilemma, why have Japanese politicians and the MoF not enacted a broad range of proposals that would reform the financial institutions? As noted in this chapter, the issues are much more complex than most commentators suspect.

The U.S. government is attempting to play a greater role in the Japanese and Asian financial quagmire, but it is unclear how extensively or effectively the United States could be involved in the domestic affairs of Japan and other countries in the region. It also is unclear how much intervention the host countries will tolerate. In the past, the U.S. government misjudged the nature of the Japanese and Asian economic and financial environments. The U.S. government has switched from aggressive trade intervention rhetoric to aggressive rhetoric about domestic financial reform in Asia. Debates are heard over financial bailouts for Japan and Asia rather than over economic threats from the region.

Analysts should avoid the pitfalls of isolating a single cause of the Asian financial crisis. There are a variety of factors that contributed to the present drama. It should also be remembered that a society's culture has a profound impact on its economy. Culture can evolve or change, but caution is advisable when reflecting upon a nation's structures and institutions. America provides useful examples —positive and negative—to be studied in a dynamic environment, but certainly it is no role model to be blindly copied. Although it is tempting to search for an economic blueprint of quantitative or political simplicity, the long-term structural flaws within Asia's financial institutions remain extremely complex and no gradual evolutionary improvement can automatically be assumed.

Notes

1. Douglass C. North, *Institutions, Institutional Change, and Economic Performance* (New York, 1990), p. vii.

2. I highly recommend the following books for their perspective and objectivity: David Hackett Fisher, *Historians Fallacies: Toward a Logic of Historical Thought* (New York: Harper Torchbooks, 1970); Charles Kindleberger, *Manias, Panics, and Crashes: A History of Financial Crises* (New York: Basic Books, 1978); Douglass C. North, *Institutions, Institutional Change, and Economic Performance* (New York: Cambridge University Press, 1990); George David Smith and Richard Sylla, "Capital Markets" in *Encyclopedia of the United States in the Twentieth Century* (New York: Scribner's Sons, 1996), Vol. III, pp. 1209-41; John Kenneth Galbraith, *A Short History of Financial Euphoria* (New York: Whittle Books, 1993); and Alexander Pope's classic, *An Essay on Criticism.*

3. My field of interest is financial institutions. I am not an economist, bank stock analyst, or public policy official. My views and analysis are based on years of experience as a participant, observer, and student of the financial markets. While working for an American investment bank, I moved to Asia in 1981. Since then I have been deeply and continuously involved on a transactional and organizational basis with JFIs. After twenty years as a participant in the investment banking arena, I left the corporate world to pursue other related interests. In 1988 I became an advisor to a major JFI, realizing that the dangerously flawed JFIs presented an opportunity and a challenge. I had understood for years that the JFIs were squandering Japan's savings and wealth through their misallocation of capital and their

inability to create adjustments within the economy. The result would be an increasingly heavy burden on the Japanese economy, a burden that would slow Japan's momentum. For the next three years, I dissected every aspect of the JFIs overseas business and much of the domestic activity as well, making numerous recommendations.

4. Eugene R. Dattel, *The Sun That Never Rose: The Inside Story of Japan's Failed Attempt at Global Financial Dominance* (Chicago: Probus, 1994), especially Chapter 5.

5. Dattel, Chapter 8.

6. Ibid., Chapter 6.

7. Ibid., Chapter 7.

8. Ibid., p. 248. Here I discuss some categories of skills and types of intelligence that fit certain functions within the financial services industry.

9. Ibid., p. 198.

10. Joseph Stiglitz, "How to Fix the Asian Economies." *New York Times*, October 31, 1997, p. A27.

11. Louise Lucas, "Cruel Irony Thwarts Asian Ambition," *Financial Times*, July 13, 1998, p. 18.

12. Donald Tsang,, "Bonds Can Free Asia's Economy," *Wall Street Journal*, July 22, 1998, p. A14.

13. It is extremely important to revisit and analyze the misadventures of the Japan literature to determine motivation, sensationalist style, and/or faulty methodology. In this category I would include: Daniel Burstein, *Yen! Japan's Financial Empire and Its Threat to America* (New York: Simon and Schuster, 1988); Jeffrey E. Garten, *A Cold Peace: America, Japan, Germany, and the Struggle for Supremacy* (New York: Times Books, 1992); Clyde V. Prestowitz, Jr., *Trading Places: How America Allowed Japan to Take the Lead* (Tokyo: Charles E. Tuttle, 1988); Bill Emmott, *The Sun Also Sets: Why Japan Will Not Be Number One* (New York: Simon and Schuster, 1989); and Daniel Burstein, *Turning the Tables: A Machiavellian Strategy for Dealing with Japan* (New York: Simon and Schuster, 1993).

References

Adams, T. C. F. *Japanese Securities Markets: A Historical Survey.* Tokyo: 1953.
———. *A Financial History of Modern Japan.* Tokyo: 1964.
Burstein, Daniel. *Turning the Tables: A Machiavellian Strategy for Dealing with Japan.* New York: Simon and Schuster, 1993.
Burstein, Daniel. *Yen! Japan's Financial Empire and Its Threat to America.* New York: Simon and Schuster, 1988.
Crichton, Michael. *Rising Sun.* New York: Alfred A. Knopf, 1992.
Dattel, Eugene R. *The Sun That Never Rose: The Inside Story of Japan's Failed Attempt at Global Financial Dominance.* Chicago: Probus, 1994.
Emmott, Bill. *The Sun Also Sets: Why Japan Will Not Be Number One.* New York: Simon and Schuster, 1989.
Feldman, Robert Alan. "The Golden Goose and the Silver Box: Productivity, Aging, and Japan's Economic Future." Japanese Economic/Market Analysis, Salomom Brothers, June 12, 1996.
Fingleton, Eammon. "Japan's Invisible Leviathan." *Foreign Affairs* (March/April 1995).

Fisher, David Hackett. *Historians Fallacies: Toward a Logic of Historical Thought.* New York: Harper Torchbooks, 1970.

Galbraith, John Kenneth. *A Short History of Financial Euphoria.* New York: Whittle Books, 1993.

Garten, Jeffrey E. *A Cold Peace: America, Japan, Germany, and the Struggle for Supremacy.* New York: Times Books, 1992.

Kennedy, Paul. *Preparing for the Twenty-first Century.* New York: Random House, 1992.

Kindleberger, Charles. *Manias, Panics, and Crashes: A History of Financial Crises.* New York: Basic Books, 1978.

Landes, David S. *The Wealth and Poverty of Nations: Why Some Nations Are So Rich and Some So Poor.* New York: W. W. Norton, 1998.

Martin, Neil. "Monstrous Possibility." *Barron's* (May 25, 1998), p. 20.

North, Douglass C. *Institutions, Institutional Change, and Economic Performance.* New York: Cambridge University Press, 1990.

Prestowitz, Clyde V., Jr. *Trading Places: How America Allowed Japan to Take the Lead.* Tokyo: Charles E. Tuttle, 1988.

Sakakibara, Eisuke. *Beyond Capitalism: The Japanese Model of Market Economics.* Lanham, MD: University Press of America, 1993.

"Shipbreaker's Ball." *Forbes* (March 9, 1998), p. 104.

Smith, George David, and Richard Sylla. "Capital Markets" in *Encyclopedia of the United States in the Twentieth Century.* New York: Scribner's Sons, 1996. Vol. III, pp. 1209-241.

Thurow, Lester C. *The Future of Capitalism: How Today's Economic Forces Shape Tomorrow's World.* New York: Penguin Books, 1996.

Thurow, Lester C. *Head to Head: The Coming Economic Battle Among Japan, Europe, and America.* New York: Warner Books, 1992.

Vega, Joseph de la. *Confusion de Confusiones.* Cambridge, MA: Harvard Business School, Research Center in Entrepreneurial History, 1957.

4

China and the Asian Financial Contagion

Nicholas R. Lardy

China appears relatively unscathed by the Asian financial contagion. From mid-year 1997 through the summer of 1998 the value of the *renminbi* vis-à-vis the U.S. dollar was unchanged.[1] In real terms the Chinese economy also has fared far better than any other economy in Asia. Economic growth, while slower than the blistering pace in the immediate prior years, was 8.8 percent in 1997 and 7.0 percent in the first half of 1998. Exports grew over 20 percent in 1997, contributing to an unprecedented US$40.3 billion surplus on the trade account. While the pace of export growth dipped to only 7 percent in the first seven months of 1998, the trade surplus was US$26.7 billion, one-fourth more than in the first seven months of 1997.[2] In 1997 foreign direct investment rose for the seventh consecutive year, to reach US$45.3 billion, and China raised an additional US$12 billion in debt and equity offerings on international markets. Despite the economic crisis in the countries that are the principal source China's foreign direct investment, inflows of FDI in the first half were a robust US$20.5 billion, off only 1 percent from the pace in the first half of 1997. Official holdings of foreign exchange reserves rose sharply in 1997, reaching US$139.9 billion by year-end, second in size only to those of Japan.[3] In the first half of 1998 these holdings were almost unchanged. Compared to the plummeting currency values, sharp declines in real output, and stagnant or even declining exports in much of the rest of Asia, China's economic performance through the middle of 1998 might be regarded as nothing short of stunning.

Why was China not engulfed in the first year of the Asian financial contagion? Why does China, despite the positives just summarized, remain vulnerable to the Asian financial contagion? What actions has the Chinese government taken to avoid the adverse consequences of the crisis? What are the potential implications of these actions?

China's Financial Fundamentals

China shares many of the same characteristics that contributed to the financial crises in Korea, Thailand, and Indonesia. These include, most notably, a bank-dominated financial system, weak central bank regulation and supervision of banks, excessive growth of lending, and a large build-up of nonperforming loans.

Bank-Dominated Financial Systems

Even in a region in which banks dominate financial systems, China stands out. Banks account for fully nine-tenths of all financial intermediation between savers and investors in China, a ratio that exceeds that found in almost all other Asian countries. Only in Latin America can one find financial systems in which banks control an even higher share of all financial assets than in China.[4]

Bank-dominated financial systems, where markets for corporate equity and debt are very small, tend to share several closely related problems. First, the lack of well-developed capital markets creates a high potential for systematic underpricing of loans by banks. That, in turn, contributes to the excessive growth of credit, a problem discussed below. More generally, in bank-dominated financial systems, capital markets do not provide sufficient competition for banks, contributing to lower efficiency of financial intermediation. Third, it is easier for politicians to influence the pattern of bank lending than to determine which borrowers get access to funds raised through capital markets.

Weak Central Bank Regulation and Supervision

China's financial and banking system, like some others in Asia, suffers from weak central bank supervision and prudential regulation of banks. Banks, for example, are not subject to independent audits of their financial performance. Indeed, three of China's four largest banks do not even report their financial results on a consolidated basis, meaning that losses can be buried in subsidiary firms whose financial results are not incorporated with those of the parent bank. Classification of nonperforming loans by banks is based on standards that are more lenient than those commonly used internationally, impairing the value of these data as a means of measuring bank performance. China's system of setting aside reserves for nonperforming loans is also flawed, since the magnitude of reserves that banks are required to set aside is not linked directly to the quality of each bank's loan portfolio but rather is set at an arbitrary low percentage of total loans.

More alarmingly, financial losses caused by fraud, corruption, and other lending irregularities in Chinese banks seem greater than those associated with crony capitalism in Indonesia or by corrupt Korean bank lending practices that were used to channel hundreds of millions of U.S. dollars into the pockets of Korea's highest leaders. The People's Bank of China, China's central bank, in 1996 acknowledged that some banks had lent funds "without recording them in their account books," and that some nonbank financial institutions created "false assets" to cover up the "black holes" in their balance sheets caused by large financial losses. Ominously, the central bank admitted that the number of serious financial crimes was on the rise and that the manner in which such crimes were committed was making them more and more difficult to detect.[5] Since these astonishing admissions, the situation seems to have worsened. An editorial appearing in November 1997 in *People's Daily,* the Chinese Communist Party newspaper, admitted that "financial criminal activities are rampant."[6]

Whether in China or elsewhere in the region, the common element leading to fraud and corruption in lending is inadequate regulation and supervision of banks by central banks and the lack of sufficient central bank independence. In large measure that, in turn, reflects the extreme reluctance of political leaders, especially at the provincial and local level, to relinquish their power to direct loans funds to specific industries and firms.

Excessive Growth of Lending

China shares with several countries in the Asian region an excessive build-up of domestic credit. From the beginning of reform in 1978 through the end of 1997, credit outstanding by all financial institutions grew from RMB 190 billion to RMB 7.5 trillion. Credit outstanding as a percent of gross domestic product almost doubled, from about 53 percent in 1978 to 100 percent in 1997. As shown in Figure 4.1, the build up of credit in China is almost as rapid as that in South Korea and Thailand just prior to the onset of their financial crises in 1997. It has been less rapid, but sustained over a longer period of time, than in Mexico, where bank credit to the private sector shot up from 13 percent of gross domestic product in 1988 to 36 percent in 1994, when the Mexican financial crisis began.[7]

The judgement that credit expansion in China has been excessive is based on several criteria. First, the build-up of excessive bank credit is mirrored by an extraordinary deterioration in the balance sheets of state-owned enterprises, which have been the chief recipients of bank credit. At the outset of reform, state-owned industrial firms had only modest liabilities to banks since their fixed investment traditionally was financed from the government budget and firms were under no obligation to repay these grants. The budget was even the source of much of their working capital funds. They borrowed from banks only to finance that portion of their working capital that was not financed from the budget. Consequently, their balance sheets were quite strong, as reflected in a debt:equity ratio of 12 percent, a level about one-fourth one might expect to find for firms in a market-oriented economy. Because of an extraordinarily rapid increase in their borrowing, by year-end 1994 the debt:equity ratio of these firms was 375 percent. The rapid build-up of debt has not been restricted to state-owned industrial firms. By year-end 1995

FIGURE 4.1 Domestic Credit (1978–1996)

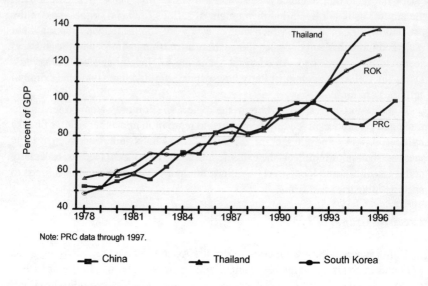

Note: PRC data through 1997.

the debt to equity ratio of all state-owned firms, including commercial and other establishments as well as manufacturing firms, was in excess of 500 percent.[8]

This extraordinary deterioration in the balance sheets of state-owned firms has several important implications.[9] First, a significant portion of China's state-owned firms are insolvent: i.e., the value of their liabilities far exceeds the value of their assets. Second, it suggests that many firms are not able to cover their operating costs with the income they receive from the sale of their output. Their balance sheets have been deteriorating not only because they have been borrowing heavily to finance expansion of their plant and equipment but also because they have been borrowing to pay for inputs, wages, taxes, and, all too frequently, growing inventories of unsold and unsaleable goods.[10] This evidence of operating losses is important because even insolvent firms may be able to improve their balance sheets over time if they have operating profits and their lenders are willing to allow them to continue to operate.

Third, enterprises in China are so highly leveraged that an economic slowdown could create liquidity problems for banks. The average state-owned enterprise in China in 1995 was even more highly leveraged than the Korean chaebol, which even prior to the Asian financial crisis were notorious for their high gearing ratios of from 300 to 400 percent.[11] One shortcoming of such a high debt:equity ratio is that in an economic downturn the earnings of these firms can easily fall below the level necessary simply to pay interest on their heavy debts, subjecting them to the possibility of bankruptcy if their lenders are unwilling to rollover their loans.

A second indicator of an excessive growth of domestic credit and over-investment is excess capacity in many industries. This is evident not only in Thailand, Indonesia, and Korea, but also in China. A major industrial census showed that the rate of capacity utilization in 1995 was less than 60 percent for more than 900 major industrial products.[12] As reflected in the Table 4.1 below, Chinese industries with excess capacity include automobiles, home appliances and other consumer goods, machine tools, steel, and certain chemical products. The incidence of low rates of capacity utilization for so many products cannot be explained by the business cycle since the Chinese economy was experiencing robust economic growth, not a recession, in the years leading up to the census.[13]

The underlying problem in China, as well as the other countries in the region undergoing financial crises beginning in 1997, was that too many firms were motivated by the goal of expanding capacity rather than maximizing profits. That is certainly one explanation why firms in many industries continued to expand, even as the rate of return on assets fell, all too frequently below the levels at which they could even pay interest on their outstanding debt.

One outstanding example of excess investment in China is the automobile industry. In the mid- and late-1980s more than 120 vehicle manufacturers were established in China. This was an astonishingly large number given the initially tiny market for vehicles and the economies of scale that are characteristic of the automotive sector. Production of vehicles of all types, including passenger cars as well as trucks, tripled from about a half-million in 1990 to 1.6 million in 1997. Most of the 120 manufacturers, however, have production levels that are too low to take advantage of the scale economies that exist in the industry. The thirteen largest firms in China produce 91 percent of the vehicles, meaning that the average number of vehicles produced by the remaining firms in 1997 was only 1,300.[14] Capital invested per vehicle produced by the large number of small producers was three times the average of the top thirteen producers. Undoubtedly, labor and other non-capital costs per vehicle also were substantially higher than in the largest producers. But even the largest firms in the industry, with average annual output of 112,000 vehicles, produced less than half the number of vehicles required to take advantage of economies of scale that characterize the industry.

The Chinese government has sought, since at least 1994 when it promulgated an automotive industrial policy, to engineer a consolidation in the industry.[15] But dozens of provincial and local level governments have resisted fiercely, each determined to maintain a presence in what the central government has identified as a pillar industry. Some of these localities have fostered their own producers by imposing restrictions within their jurisdictions on the sale and licensing of vehicles produced elsewhere. They have been abetted by a highly restrictive national auto import policy. After several cuts, tariff rates on imported sedans are still as high as

TABLE 4.1   Capacity Utilization in Chinese Industry, 1995

INDUSTRY	PERCENT
Photographic film	13.3
Movie film	25.5
Color televisions	46.1
Telephone sets	51.4
Video recorders	40.3
Soap	42.2
Household air conditioners	33.5
Metal cutting machine tools	46.2
Cold rolled steel	53.0
Refractory materials	26.2
Chemical pesticides	41.6
Internal combustion engines	43.9
Motor vehicles	44.3

Source: State Statistical Bureau, *China Statistical Yearbook 1997* (Beijing: China Statistical Publishing House, 1997), pp. 454-55.

100 percent and imports are also subject to quotas and other restrictions.[16] In a more market-oriented economy, with more efficient intermediation of capital and less restrictive trade practices, it is highly unlikely that 120 vehicle producers could have been established over a period of almost a decade. If they somehow had been created, it is even more unlikely that they would have had ongoing access to funds, not only to cover their operating losses and thus sustain their existence, but even to continue to expand their fixed assets.

A third indicator of excess lending has been the creation of asset bubbles, particularly in the property market. In the wake of Deng Xiaoping's famous "southern tour" in 1992, investment surged. That stimulated property development on a massive scale throughout China.[17] Although China's financial institutions do not publish, and may not even compile, data on their total lending for property development, there is no doubt that banks and other financial institutions are heavily exposed to real estate lending.

By the mid-1990s it became clear that there had been massive overbuilding. The cities of Beijing, Shanghai, and Shenzhen appear to have the greatest absolute concentrations of unleased space, but there is a significant problem of overbuilding in many smaller cities, ranging from Haikou on Hainan Island to Beihai in Guangxi, and in county-level towns as well.[18]

In Beijing, Shanghai, and Shenzhen there are millions of square feet of un-occupied luxury villas and townhouses and even larger amounts of vacant first-class office space. Moreover, the anticipated additions to the stock of space over the next few years exceed by a several-fold multiple the rate of take up of space in the past few years. For example, based on projects under construction in 1997, the additions to new office space in Beijing in the year 2000 could total 14 million square feet, compared to additions that averaged under one million square feet between 1990 and 1995.[19] Pudong, designated as Shanghai's new financial and manufacturing center in 1991, is even more over-built. The total stock of office space in mid-year 1997 stood at 13.5 million square feet, an astounding five times the 2.7 million square feet at year-end 1994. But 70 percent of this space in the latter part of 1997 was vacant. Buildings under construction in Pudong in 1997 will take the total available office space to 26 million square feet by year-end 1999. Vacancy rates are not quite as high in other districts of the city, but the anticipated additions to the supply of new office space there in 1998 and 1999 exceed the anticipated additions in Pudong. By the year 2000 total office space in Shanghai, almost entirely built in the 1990s, is expected to match that in Hong Kong, built over four decades.[20]

Vacant office space in Shenzhen in late 1997 was the equivalent of three years of take up. An additional 22.6 million square feet was under construction and scheduled to be completed in 1998–2000. Over supply was expected to last for ten years.[21]

By mid-1997 office rental rates had already declined substantially—by almost 50 percent in downtown Shanghai, over 40 percent in Pudong, and by 40 percent or more in Beijing—and were forecast to fall by as much as 70 percent before bottoming out.[22] In retrospect, the repeated boast of Shanghai's mayor that one-fifth of the world's construction cranes were at work in Shanghai should have been seen as a premonition of overbuilding and a coming collapse of property prices rather than an auspicious sign reflecting the city's economic resurgence following the creation of the Pudong Development Area in 1991.

Build-up of Nonperforming Loans

A fourth vulnerability that China shares with other Asian countries undergoing financial crises is a huge build-up of nonperforming loans. In international practice, nonperforming loans are loans on which either an interest or principal payment is 90 or 180 days past due—an important indicator of the health of a banking system. Ultimately, the borrowers of loans that become nonperforming may default, requiring the lender to absorb the loss either from loan loss reserves or from the bank's own capital.

According to statements of high officials, including People's Bank of China Governor Dai Xianglong, the share of nonperforming loans in the portfolios of the four largest state-owned banks has increased steadily in recent years—from 20 percent at year-end 1994, to 22 percent at year-end 1995, and then 25 percent at year-end 1997.[23] By year-end 1997 the ratio of nonperforming loans in China was substantially higher than in South Korea or Thailand prior to the onset of their financial crises.[24]

Once a currency crisis has begun, of course, the share of nonperforming loans is likely to rise sharply. Declining values of domestic currency vis-à-vis the U.S. dollar pose a higher burden of debt repayment for firms that have borrowed in dollars and have not hedged against the possibility of a depreciation of the domestic currency. In Korea, for example, by November 1997 the Ministry of Finance acknowledged that the share of nonperforming loans held by Korean banks had increased sharply to 18.5 percent.[25]

Since China's external debt is relatively modest in comparison with Asian countries undergoing currency crises, devaluation of the Chinese currency is less likely in the short run; and thus this source of escalation of nonperforming loans is not an immediate policy concern. China's system for classifying nonperforming loans, however, falls short of international standards in several important respects. Thus, the system is likely to track poorly the share of loans that, in fact, is nonperforming.[26] Thus, in reality the share of nonperforming loans held by Chinese banks may be much higher than the official s cited above.

The Sources of Chinese Insulation

These international comparisons raise several closely related questions. Why hasn't China already experienced a banking crisis? Is a crisis inevitable? If so, what form might it take?

There are five reasons that China in the short run did not experience a crisis like that of Mexico in 1994–1995 or that of several Southeast Asian countries and Korea beginning in 1997. First, and most important, the Chinese currency is not convertible for capital account transactions. This means that Chinese savers who are concerned about the viability of the country's financial institutions do not have the option of legally converting their *renminbi* deposits and then purchasing foreign currency-denominated financial assets. It also means that foreigners are much less likely to open *renminbi*-denominated bank accounts or purchase *renminbi*-denominated shares on China's domestic stock exchanges. Indeed, nonresidents legally are precluded from purchasing so-called A shares, the shares bought and sold for local currency on the Shanghai and Shenzhen stock markets. They must buy foreign currency-denominated B shares that are priced independently from the A shares of the same underlying company. If foreign sentiment on the value of B shares turns negative, there are no adverse consequences for the value of the Chinese currency. Would-be sellers, in effect, cannot exit the market unless they find a foreign buyer who will pay dollars for their shares.

This contrasts sharply with Southeast Asian markets in the summer and fall of 1997. Foreign portfolio managers all rushed for the exits simultaneously, contributing to a sharp decline in local currency share prices. And, when they then sold the *baht* and other local currencies they had gained from the sale of their shares for dollars, they contributed to the plummet of currency values in these countries. Within a matter of weeks the foreign currency values of shares listed in these markets had fallen 50 percent or more.

The absence of capital account convertibility also means that speculators, either foreign or Chinese, have no way to act on the belief that the *renminbi* is overvalued and likely to depreciate. In countries with capital account convertibility these individuals would borrow domestic currency, sell it for foreign exchange with the expectation that they would profit from an ensuing depreciation that would allow them to repurchase the domestic currency at a lower price. These funds would then be used to repay the initial loan, leaving a profit proportionate to the depreciation.[27] Alternatively, they could simply sell domestic currency in the forward market in the expectation that prior to the time the contract matured the currency would have depreciated, again allowing them to buy it more cheaply to deliver when the contract matured.

But China's foreign exchange market is not open to those who wish to purchase foreign exchange for capital account transactions. Only buyers with a demonstrated need related to trade, tourism, repatriation of profits derived from a prior direct investment, or repayment of a previously approved foreign currency loan are allowed to purchase foreign exchange. That thwarts would-be speculators from buying foreign exchange to sell in the spot market. Similarly, the forward market for foreign exchange in China is extremely limited, so the would-be speculator would not be able to take the short position in Chinese domestic currency described above.[28] Even domestic firms that have foreign currency-denominated loans are not allowed to purchase foreign exchange to repay their loans until their loan is actually due.[29] That prevents an acceleration of demand for foreign exchange on the part of those that have such loans outstanding.

Second, China's capital inflows predominantly take the form of foreign direct investment. In 1996, for example, China was the recipient of US$56 billion in foreign capital. But the largest component, US$42.5 billion, was direct investment.[30] Cumulatively, by mid-1997 foreign direct investment in place stood at over US$200 billion, almost twice the level of China's officially reported foreign borrowing.[31] In contrast, in other countries experiencing financial and banking crises, this ratio of direct investment to financial investment is invariably reversed. At year-end 1996 in Korea, for example, cumulative foreign direct investment of US$12.491 billion was only one-ninth the level of officially reported outstanding foreign borrowing of US$110 billion.[32] Even in Thailand, which has a much more open foreign investment climate than Korea, cumulative foreign direct investment at year-end 1996 was only one-fifth of the level of external borrowing.[33] Direct investors differ fundamentally from financial investors since they invest with a long time horizon and their investments are illiquid. Financial investments, such as lending, bank deposits, stocks, and bonds, are frequently of short duration and can be reversed quickly if the investors reevaluate the risk of lending to a particular country. Some financial assets can be sold in the market immediately. Lenders can wind down their exposure over somewhat longer periods by refusing to roll over loans when they come due.

Third, little of China's borrowing is short term. For example, at year-end 1996 almost 90 percent of China's officially reported external debt was medium and long term.[34] By contrast, at the time of Korea's financial crisis in late 1997, US$66 billion, or 60 percent of its total external debt of US$110 billion, was short term.[35] When lenders grew reluctant to roll-over this short-term lending, a financial crisis was almost inevitable.

Fourth, in contrast to Korea, Thailand, and several other countries in Southeast Asia that experienced currency crises beginning in 1997, China in the mid-1990s experienced record trade surpluses. Its trade surpluses were US$16.69 billion, US$12.3 billion, and US$40.2 billion in 1995, 1996, and 1997, respectively.[36] Thus China was not dependent on continued foreign capital inflows to finance a trade deficit.

Finally, at the end of 1997 China had amassed US$139.9 billion in foreign exchange reserves, enough to finance almost a full year of imports.[37]

In short, the absence of capital account convertibility, the nature of China's capital inflows, and strong trade and foreign exchange reserve positions mean that a banking crisis is unlikely to be precipitated by a change in the sentiment of foreign lenders, foreign or domestic speculators, or domestic firms that have outstanding foreign currency-denominated liabilities.

China's Continued Vulnerability

China's short-term insulation does not mean, however, that China has been immune to the adverse consequences of a weak financial system characterized by a rapid build up of nonperforming loans to state-owned enterprises. The real consequences have been twofold. First is the inescapable cost of the poor domestic lending decisions that banks have made and are continuing to make. This is reflected in the long-term, continuous decline in the rate of return on real assets in state-owned industrial firms.[38] Since bank loans financing these investments have been financed almost entirely by household deposits in the banking system, the cost of these poor lending and investment decisions ultimately will be borne by the population, either through a collapse of the banking system or through higher taxes that will be necessary if the government opts to finance a rescue of the banking system.

Second, China now faces a higher cost of raising money on international capital markets. The higher costs stem both from an increasing perception that China suffers from some of the same underlying economic problems evident elsewhere in the region and from the collapse of the prices of Chinese securities. Moody's in January 1998 downgraded the outlook for nine Chinese banks to negative.[39] In February 1998 they downgraded the outlook for China's foreign currency debt from stable to negative.[40] Standard and Poor's followed in July, changing the outlook on China's long-term foreign currency, sovereign-credit, and senior unsecured-debt rating from positive to negative.[41] Even prior to these downgrades, the margins on Chinese sovereign debt trading in the secondary market had widened compared with pre-crisis levels.[42] As a result, the Minister of Finance announced that China would postpone, until the second half of 1998, a planned sovereign bond offering.[43]

The terms of China's access to international equity markets also has changed dramatically. Like in the rest of Asia, the prices of Chinese securities available for purchase by foreigners have fallen sharply.[44] For example, the index of prices of "Red Chip" stocks by year-end 1997 was down about 60 percent compared to pre-crisis peaks in August. And in the first quarter of 1997, when prices recovered by one-quarter or more on many depressed Asian markets, Red Chips, through March 22, were down an additional 3 percent.[45] Thus, even though the *renminbi* and Hong Kong dollar have been stable vis-à-vis the U.S. dollar, in dollar terms foreign investors buying "Red Chips" at their peaks would have lost almost two-thirds of their investment by late March 1998. H shares fell by almost as much, about 60 percent, from their peaks in late August 1997 through the third week of March.

The result of these developments is that China and Chinese companies are paying more to raise money internationally. The higher spreads of sovereign debt have already been mentioned. New Chinese equity offerings in the first part of 1998 were priced at a much, much lower multiple of earnings than issues that came to market prior to the crisis. For example, the price earnings ratio for the listing of Yanzhou Coal in March was at only seven times estimated 1998 earnings, a multiple only about half that of other Chinese companies trading in Hong Kong.[46] As a result of the much less favorable terms available, the amount of equity raised by Chinese firms on international markets in the first half of 1998 was only a few hundred million dollars, compared with US$7.5 billion for all of 1997.

The limited ability of foreign speculators and lenders to contribute to or even precipitate a crisis seems, at least superficially, to be to China's advantage compared to countries with capital account convertibility. Particularly in light of the

Asian financial contagion, the insulation provided by China's more closed international financial system seems attractive. In reality it is a two-edged sword.

On the one hand, it could work to China's advantage by providing the time necessary to recapitalize and commercialize the banking system and to eliminate the preferred access of state-owned firms to bank loans. Bank recapitalization will be costly in economic terms because of its fiscal implications. Subjecting state-owned enterprises to hard budget constraints also will be costly politically. But the renewed commitment of the Party at the 15th Congress to resolve problems of state-owned enterprises and the urgency with which the highest levels of China's leadership are now addressing the problems of the banking and financial sector provide some grounds for optimism. If the program of reform outlined below is carried out expeditiously, China would emerge with a more efficient financial system and would be more likely to maintain high rates of domestic savings. This combination would sustain China's strong growth performance.

On the other hand, if the leadership delays undertaking these fundamental reforms, the possibility of a domestic financial crisis greatly increases for several reasons. First, slowing growth is likely to expose dramatically the underlying weakness of the domestic financial system. Slower growth, whether originating from purely domestic sources or, as outlined below, from changing relative currency values, is cutting into the operating profits of many state-owned companies. For example, in the first quarter of 1998, when the rate of growth of gross domestic product slowed to 7.2 percent, the earnings before interest and taxes on assets of state-owned enterprises fell to only 5 percent.[47] That is less than the interest rate of 6.9 percent on one-year working capital loans, the most common loan banks provide. Given the extraordinarily high average gearing ratio of state firms, the declining rate of return on assets increases significantly the share of firms that are unable to pay interest on their debt to banks. That is further undermining the financial position of China's major banks. Their solvency problem could become a liquidity problem.

Second, major currency depreciations in Southeast Asia and Korea beginning in 1997 can be expected simultaneously to reduce further the rate of growth of Chinese exports and eventually to increase the growth of imports. China's trade surplus will almost certainly shrink significantly from the historic peak level of 1997. Because China's service account includes increasingly large profit remittances associated with the large stock of foreign direct investment already in place, a shrinking trade surplus could lead to a current account deficit. If strong inflows of foreign direct investment continued, a modest current account deficit would be easily sustainable.

But by mid-1998 it seemed almost certain that foreign direct investment inflows would begin to decline, perhaps sharply. Contracts for future foreign direct investment fell sharply in 1996 and 1997, portending a future slowdown in actual foreign direct investment. The likelihood of a decline was reinforced by the Asian currency crisis. The sharp decline in the value of other Asian currencies vis-à-vis the *renminbi* inevitably made China a somewhat less attractive location for export-oriented foreign direct investment. And slower growth in Asia, the source of the lion's share of foreign direct investment inflows into China, is likely to curtain investment by firms in the region, not only in their home countries but in China as well. Finally, foreign direct investment could fall sharply if those Chinese firms and individuals who have been able to avoid currency controls and move tens of billions of dollars offshore annually would elect to keep these funds offshore rather than bringing them back in as "foreign investment." In effect, China's controls on capital have been very leaky. As long as the firms and individuals controlling these funds have confidence in the currency, they elect to bring a large share of them back into China. Once this confidence is lost, capital flight will increase dramatically.

If a large current account deficit emerged as foreign direct investment declined and capital flight increased, China would have to draw down its foreign exchange reserves, step up its external borrowing, or devalue its currency. The first of these alternatives could be used to postpone, but only temporarily, the need to adjust to China's changed international competitive position. Increased borrowing could serve the same function, but again would not provide a permanent solution since it would become increasingly difficult for China to expand its borrowing, given the combination of its already large external debt and heightened lender sensitivity to the risks of lending to firms and financial institutions with large foreign currency exposures. Devaluation, the last alternative, would pose difficulties for many Chinese banks and firms, given their large foreign currency-denominated debt.[48]

Even if a crisis could be avoided, delaying fundamental reform would be costly since the longer the banks continue to support state-owned enterprises that will not be viable in a more marketized economy when banks are commercialized, the larger will be either the size of the ultimately required bank recapitalization or the financial losses imposed on depositors.

A banking crisis in China is most likely to be precipitated when domestic savers lose confidence in the government's implicit guarantee of the value of their deposits in banks. This loss of confidence could be triggered either by a growth slowdown that weakened the domestic banking system or by the prospect of a major devaluation in response to an emerging current account deficit, a sharp fall in inward foreign direct investment, and increasing capital flight. If households in large numbers attempt to withdraw their savings, the insolvency problem of several of China's largest banks could become a liquidity problem. At that point the central bank would face two alternatives. It could serve the traditional role of central banks as lender of last resort and supply funds to banks to meet the demand for withdrawals. This was not unheard of over the past two decades, when the central bank extended loans to individual provincial branches of state banks to solve liquidity problems.[49] But if the central bank lends money to banks on a large scale to meet a demand for withdrawals throughout China, the resulting burgeoning increase in the money supply could be highly inflationary.

Thus the second, more likely, alternative is that the banks would sharply limit customer withdrawals. That would almost certainly undermine confidence in the banking system and lead to a dramatic reduction in the flow of funds into savings deposits and to greater capital flight. Anticipating rising inflation, households likely would try to convert part of their increased holdings of currency into goods, again creating an inflationary spiral. In short, a banking crisis in China is most likely to be reflected in an inflationary spiral—whether or not the central bank lends funds to state-owned banks, a collapse of credit, and thus a major recession.

The Chinese Policy Response

The Chinese government recognizes the risk associated with delaying further fundamental reforms. On November 17, 1997, China's State Council convened an unprecedented high level National Financial Work Conference in Beijing to discuss the problems of China's financial and banking system. The meeting was held against the backdrop of financial crises in three Asian countries—Thailand, Indonesia, and Korea—that had sought massive international financial assistance coordinated by the International Monetary Fund. Indeed, in an unprecedented move, China contributed US$1 billion to the IMF-led bailout of Thailand in 1997. Participants in the Beijing meeting included not only central bank officials at the national and provincial level, officials from both the headquarters and major provincial branches of all of China's state-owned banks, insurance companies, and many nonbank financial institutions, but also all provincial governors and provincial-level finance officials. The meeting was addressed by President Jiang Zemin, Premier Li Peng, and Vice-premier Zhu Rongji, the latter widely regarded as China's economic czar. Several other members of the Standing Committee of the Politburo of the Central Committee of the Chinese Communist Party also were present.

The meeting focused on similarities between China's weak financial system and those elsewhere in Asia and steps that should be taken to overhaul the country's financial system. In Thailand, Indonesia, Korea, as well as China, excessive bank lending financed excess investment across a broad range of industries. Firms in these and other sectors borrowed excessively to finance rates of expansion that were not sustainable. The parallel roles of the governments in Thailand, Indonesia, Korea, as well as China, in encouraging these lending booms were remarkable, as was the resulting vulnerability of firms that had benefitted from the ability to borrow without limit to a downturn in economic growth. A downturn in economic growth, against the background of massive excess capacity, posed a deflationary threat that left highly leveraged firms unable to maintain payments on their massive debts to banks and other financial institutions.

In each of these countries financial systems were heavily bank-dominated. The lack of well-developed capital markets made it possible for bank loans to be systematically underpriced over the long run, encouraging excess borrowing and capital formation on the part of firms with preferred access to credit—state-owned firms in China, the chaebol in Korea, those well connected to the government in Indonesia and Thailand—while leaving the rest of the economy starved for funds.

Finally, central banks in these countries were weak and did not exercise adequate prudential supervision over commercial lending. In Korea, for example, the central bank was formally subordinate to the Ministry of Finance. The latter focused on providing continuous flows of funds to major industrial groups and effectively precluded the central bank from exercising effective supervision. A key condition of the IMF bailout was legislation making the Korean Central Bank an independent entity. These countries face a shared challenge in their need not only to reform their financial systems but to restructure their productive sectors as well. In Korea increased competition is needed to curb the market power of the chaebol. China's lack of competition is evident not in the domination of the economy by a few large firms, but the birth and survival, through access to bank credit on soft terms, of many small local producers that are grossly inefficient.

In the cases of Thailand, Indonesia, and Korea, the IMF is providing the incentive for needed restructuring—both financial and real. Insolvent financial institutions have been closed—dozens of finance companies in Thailand; sixteen of 240 banks in Indonesia, including several owned by relatives or close associates of President Suharto; and many merchant banks in Korea. The IMF-led bailout in Korea is conditioned on substantial long-term financial reform undergirded by a requirement to open up its financial sector to external competition. That is likely to insure that domestic institutions will pay more attention to the quality of their borrowers' projects and less to government signals on whom to lend to. Otherwise, these institutions would be unable to compete with new foreign financial institutions that will be able to offer higher rates to depositors because they earn more on their outstanding loan portfolios. In Thailand the reforms allow foreign financial institutions to buy majority stakes in domestic banks for the first time.

Because China's currency is not convertible for capital account transactions and because its trade account is at least temporarily quite strong, China temporarily has been insulated from a currency crisis and is not subject to an IMF-imposed restructuring program. There can be little doubt, however, that Premier Zhu Rongji believes that a restructuring program for banks and their principal borrowers, state-owned enterprises, is urgently needed. Commentary in China's leading financial newspaper—published jointly by the central bank and several of China's largest financial institutions—immediately after the financial conference suggested that the problem of an increasing share of nonperforming loans was endemic. According to the paper, "A considerable amount of loans extended by banks are disappearing like stones dropped into the sea; principal and interest is difficult to recover; thus the nonperforming assets of these banks is increasing."[50]

The rate of increase in lending by banks and other financial institutions in 1997 was 17 percent, twice the rate of nominal growth of gross domestic product.[51] The pattern continued in the first half of 1998 when loans outstanding from financial institutions grew by 15.6 percent while the economy expanded by only 7.2 percent.[52] The continued increase in the ratio of loans outstanding to gross domestic product strongly suggests a further expansion of enterprise losses and inventories.[53] Some Chinese manufacturers are sitting on mountains of unsold inventories.[54] The exposure of Chinese banks to a rapidly weakening property sector is on a par with Thailand.

In the wake of the November 1997 financial conference the government announced a series of important steps to reduce the risks that the Asian financial contagion would spread to China. Among the most important of these steps was a reorganization of the local branches of the People's Bank along regional lines in order to reduce political interference in lending decisions at the local level. The initial experiment in creating new supra-provincial branches of the People's Bank is underway in south China where previous provincial branches in Guangdong, Jiangxi, Guangxi, and Hainan are being consolidated to form a single regional office in Guangdong's provincial capital, Guangzhou. The goal of the reorganization remains the same as that of several earlier reforms promoted by Vice-Premier Zhu Rongji—finally ending the common practice of provincial governors and party officials influencing the flow of lending in their regions. Mr. Zhu has been widely quoted as stating, "the power of provincial governors and mayors to command local bank presidents is abolished as of 1998."[55]

A second major step is a planned capital injection of RMB 270 billion into the four largest state-owned banks. This injection, which will basically double the capital of the four largest banks, is a prerequisite to the commercialization of the banking system. Its relatively large size is perhaps a reflection that the leadership believes that the process of commercialization is well begun.

The central government also has committed more funds to finance the write-off of enterprise bad debts. This program began in 1996 with an allocation of RMB 20 billion to write-off bad debts to banks of enterprises that were being restructured. In 1997 the funds earmarked for this purpose were RMB 30 billion. In 1998 the amount was increased to RMB 50 billion with further increases to follow in 1999 and 2000.[56] These funds are generally allocated to assist in the merger of two or more state-owned firms, thus their use is tied to enterprise restructurings.

In addition to stepped up write-offs of bad debt, the authorities announced several other steps designed to encourage banks to operate on a more commercial basis. Perhaps the most important is that the central bank is to allow banks greater flexibility in setting interest rates on loans. The long-standing practice of the central bank setting uniform lending rates for each loan category precluded banks from pricing loans according to risk. Under the plan, banks in 1998 will be given increased authority to set lending rates and will be encouraged to take risk into account when setting rates for specific borrowers.[57] To further encourage commercial banking behavior, reportedly the presidents of banks where nonperforming assets increase will be fired. The system of mandatory lending quotas, which has placed a ceiling on total lending and required loans to specific projects, is also to be phased out in 1998. The precise implications of this remain to be seen since a system of "guidance quotas for lending" is to remain in place.

In the wake of the meeting the Chinese central bank also tightened supervision and regulation of both banks and nonbank financial institutions. The central bank has closed dozens of unauthorized financial institutions, in some cases providing billions of RMB to prevent individual depositors from losing their savings.[58] One element of the enhanced supervision and regulation of banks is a new scheme for classifying nonperforming loans, which will come into effect by the end of 1998.[59] This will move China from its rather lax system of loan classification to a system more closely aligned with international standards. Most importantly, classification will be based partly on risk rather than exclusively on payment status.

Finally, the State Administration of Exchange Control has been charged with the responsibility of insuring both that all international commercial borrowing by domestic institutions is approved in advance and that borrowed amounts do not exceed certain multiples of the borrowers' net assets and foreign exchange earnings.[60] If followed rigorously, these new regulations would limit the ability of non-financial firms without foreign currency earnings to incur additional foreign exchange risk. They are also designed to limit offshore borrowing by subsidiaries or affiliates of Chinese firms operating abroad. In some cases the proceeds from such borrowing enter China as the "foreign" contribution to a joint venture. Thus they are reported in Chinese statistics as foreign direct investment, whereas they are actually foreign currency-denominated debt. There is growing recognition on the part of the State Planning Commission and other parts of central government bureaucracy that China has a large "hidden foreign debt" and that China runs the risk that its foreign debt statistics are inaccurate and that the authorities may lose control of the country's total foreign currency debt exposure.[61] The Chinese authorities want to avoid the Korean situation in which the country's actual foreign debt turned out to be far in excess of the officially reported total, largely because of borrowing by foreign subsidiaries of Korean companies.

Implications

If China is able to implement the series of reform measures summarized above, it will constitute a major breakthrough. It would mean that China would be able to find solutions that have eluded the leadership for two full decades. Success would mean it was more likely that China would restore its competitive position in Asia through reforms that would increase productivity via internally generated efficiencies, rather than through a competitive devaluation of its currency that could set off another round of currency devaluations in the region. Successful implementation of the program would help to restore China's favorable access to international capital markets and indirectly contribute importantly to the viability of pegging the

Hong Kong dollar to the U.S. dollar. All of these developments would contribute significantly to the recovery from the Asian financial crisis.

On the other hand, the failure of the regime to implement on a timely basis the reform agenda outlined above dramatically increases the probability of a domestic banking crisis and a sharp economic recession. Delayed or incomplete implementation of the reforms means financial intermediation would continue to be marked by the inefficiencies already apparent, contributing to the slowdown of economic growth that also is already apparent. That would further weaken the financial performance of state-owned enterprises which, in turn, increases the pressures on an already fragile banking system.

Despite the consensus in favor of accelerated economic reforms that was apparent at the National People's Congress in the spring of 1998, implementation appears to have lagged. Premier Zhu Rongji's bold program to restructure firms and impose commercial discipline on state-owned banks was badly undermined in June 1998, when the People's Bank and the State Economic and Trade Commission instructed the banks to expand their lending to money-losing state-owned enterprises.[62] Only time will reveal to outsiders whether developments like this reflect merely mid-course adjustments or more fundamental problems in reform implementation. If it is the latter we should anticipate a banking crisis, a possible sharp devaluation of the Chinese currency, and a more prolonged Asian financial crisis.

Notes

1. The nominal exchange rate actually appreciated very slightly from 8.29 *renminbi* per dollar at the end of June 1997 to 8.28 *renminbi* per dollar on August 14, 1998.

2. The surplus was up despite slower growth of exports because the growth of imports was down considerably compared to the pace of 1997.

3. State Statistical Bureau, *1997 Economic Statistical Communique*, March 4, 1998, in Foreign Broadcast Information Service, China Daily Report, March 12, 1998.

4. Argentina, Brazil, and Venezuela have financial systems that are more bank-dominated than China. The share of assets controlled by banks in Colombia and Mexico is comparable to that in China. For other countries in the region, the relative role of banks is less than in China. Morris Goldstein and Philip Turner, *Banking Crises in Emerging Economies: Origins and Policy Options*, Economic Papers No. 46 (Basle: Bank for International Settlements, 1996), p. 19. Bank for International Settlements, *66th Annual Report* (Basle: 1996), pp. 120, 126.

5. *Almanac of China's Finance and Banking 1996* (Beijing: China Financial Publishing House, 1996), p. 30.

6. Editorial, "Strive to Usher in Financial Reform and Develop a New Situation," *Renmin ribao (People's Daily)*, November 21, 1997.

7. Stephen Fidler, "More time and money needed," Mexico Survey, *Financial Times*, December 6, 1996, p. 4.

8. Debt:equity ratios calculated from data in Nicholas R. Lardy, *China's Unfinished Economic Revolution* (Washington, DC: Brookings Institution Press, 1998), p. 41.

9. The deterioration is probably greater than that suggested by the official data. Since the depreciation rates used by Chinese firms are too low, the depreciated value of plant and equipment, the single largest component of enterprise assets, is probably overstated. Since equity is equal to assets less liabilities, equity is overstated. Enterprises value inventories at full price rather than market value, also resulting in an overstatement of assets and equity.

10. Dai Jianming, "Enterprises Cannot Rely on Loosening the Money Supply to Solve Their Problems," *Jinrong shibao (Financial News)*, September 6, 1996, p. 1.

11. John Burton, "Seoul fires warning shot over chaebol," *Financial Times*, January 22, 1998, p. 6.

12. State Statistical Bureau, *Communique of the State Statistical Bureau of the People's Republic of China and the Third National Industrial Census Office on the Third National Industrial Census* (Beijing: China Statistical Publishing House, February 1997), p. 21.

13. Gross domestic product expanded by 13.5, 12.6, and 10.2 percent in 1993, 1994, and 1995, respectively. State Statistical Bureau, *A Statistical Survey of China 1996* (Beijing: Statistical Publishing House, 1996), p. 8.

14. New China News Agency, "Vice Minister on Making Auto Industry More Competitive," November 28, 1997, in Foreign Broadcast Information Service, China Daily Report, No. 334, 1997.

15. *Government Policies on the Automotive Industry*, issued by the State Planning Commission on February 19, 1994, approved by the State Council, and published on July 3, 1994 (Beijing: 1994).

16. As of October 1, 1997, tariff rates on sedans were reduced from an initial level of 120 percent to 100 percent or from an initial level of 100 percent to 80 percent, depending on engine size. Shen Bin, "Car sales slack despite interest and tariff cuts," *China Daily Business Weekly*, December 22, 1997, p. 2. Prior to the tariff cuts that began in the mid-1990s, tariff rates on imported autos were as high as 200 percent.

17. Investment jumped by more than half, from RMB 786 billion in 1992 to RMB 1,245 billion in 1993. State Statistical Bureau, *A Statistical Survey of China 1996* (Beijing: Statistical Publishing House, 1996), p. 28.

18. In numerous small county-level towns it is very common "for just one small real estate company to hold non-performing loans worth tens of millions of yuan." Jasper Becker, "Crisis feared in property sector," *South China Morning Post*, December 3, 1997. Mr. Becker's source is a lengthy article in the Chinese newspaper *Economic Information Daily*. In 1996 China had 18,200 towns that were designated as county level.

19. Peter Churchouse, "China: Property," Asia/Pacific Investment Research (Hong Kong: Morgan Stanley Dean Witter, September 10, 1997), pp. 1, 3.

20. Yu Wong, "Shanghai faces a towering overcapacity of office space," *Asian Wall Street Journal Weekly*, October 3, 1997, p. 6.

21. Jasper Becker, "Crisis feared in property sector," *South China Morning Post*, December 3, 1997.

22. Peter Churchouse, "China: Property," p. 3. James Harding, "Shanghai real estate market down 50%," *Financial Times*, October 10, 1997, p. 6. For example, in Beijing the average rent for prime office space fell from US$70 to US$75 per square meter per month in 1995 to as low as US$25 to US$35 in late 1997. Yu Wong, "Developers Build in Beijing, Vying for 'Downtown' Mantle," *Wall Street Journal Interactive Edition*, December 5, 1997.

23. Nicholas R. Lardy, *China's Unfinished Economic Revolution*, pp. 119-122, 206.

24. Nonperforming loans at year-end 1996 in Thailand were 13 percent. James Kynge, "Malaysian banking faces pain, not failure," *Financial Times,* October 8, 1997, p. 6. At mid-year 1997 reported nonperforming loans of the eight largest commercial banks in Korea were roughly 6 percent. J.P. Morgan, *Asia Credit Outlook* (Hong Kong and New York: February 20, 1998), p. 5.

25. Peter Montagnon, "Banks 'face years of losses and cuts,'" *Financial Times,* November 23, 1997, p. 8.

26. For example, banks are required to accrue interest on loans for up two years, meaning that if the interest on a loan is not paid the bank adds the interest to the outstanding principle and treats the addition to the loan as interest income. In most countries, by contrast, banks are required to classify a loan as nonperforming if any scheduled payment of interest or principle is ninety days overdue.

27. Less any interest premium they had to pay to borrow the domestic currency compared to the interest they earned on their temporary holdings of foreign exchange.

28. Beginning in mid-1997 the Bank of China began offering forward foreign currency contracts of up to six months. But the bank will only enter into these contracts with firms that can demonstrate a contractual, trade-related commitment to pay dollars in the future. Thus, a Chinese company with a contract to pay U.S. dollars for imports to be delivered in three months could purchase U.S. dollars for forward delivery. Illegal forward trading by unauthorized financial institutions is frequently reported, but the magnitude of this trading is likely to be limited.

29. The purchase of foreign exchange by Chinese firms and institutions to repay foreign loans requires the approval of the State Administration of Exchange Control. People's Bank of China, "Regulations on the Management of the Settlement, Sale, and Payment of Foreign Exchange," June 20, 1996, *China Economic News,* No. 34 (September 9, 1996), p. 30.

30. International Monetary Fund, *People's Republic of China--Recent Economic Developments,* Country Report 97/21 (Washington, DC: September 1997), pp. 88-89.

31. As of August 1997 cumulative actually utilized foreign direct investment stood at US$204.4 billion. Guo Xin," China's foreign trade blossoms," *China Daily,* November 4, 1997, p. 4. Officially reported external debt at mid-year 1997 was US$118.64.

32. Conference on Trade and Development, *World Investment Report 1997: Transnational Corporations, Market Structure and Competition Policy* (United Nations: 1997), p. 316. Note that the external debt excludes in excess of $50 billion borrowed by Korean subsidiaries operating abroad. Including this borrowing the ratio of borrowing to foreign direct investment is almost thirteen times.

33. Cumulative foreign direct investment stood at US$19.589 billion. Conference on Trade and Development, *World Investment Report 1997,* p. 316. External borrowing stood at US$98.368 billion. J.P. Morgan, *Emerging markets: Economic Indicators,* November 7, 1997, p. 18.

34. International Monetary Fund, *People's Republic of China--Recent Economic Developments,* p. 91.

35. Andrew Pollack, "Package of Loans Worth $55 billion Is Set for Korea," *New York Times,* December 4, 1997, pp. 1, 4.

36. State Statistical Bureau, *Chinese Statistical Abstract 1996* (Beijing: Statistical Publishing House, 1996), p. 105.

37. Tian Li, "Another Steadily Evolving Year: A Review of the Financial Situation in 1997," *Renmin ribao (Haiwai ban) (People's Daily Overseas Edition),* January 13, 1998, p. 2.

38. Nicholas R. Lardy, *China's Unfinished Economic Revolution,* pp. 47-48.

39. Christian Brakman, "China's Problems Deep-Seated, Moody's Analyst Says," *Wall Street Journal Interactive Edition,* January 14, 1998.

40. "Moody's Questions Plans to Recapitalize China Banks," *Wall Street Journal Interactive Edition,* March 12, 1998.

41. "S&P Reaffirms China Ratings, Lowers Outlook to Negative," *Wall Street Journal Interactive Edition,* July 17, 1998.

42. Edward Luce and Alexander Stevenson, "Hong Kong contagion hits China," *Financial Times,* October 24, 1997, p. 22.

43. "Impact of Financial Storm Makes Ministry of Finance Put Off Issuing Bonds Overseas," *Ming Pao,* March 6, 1998, p. A 15, in Foreign Broadcast Information Service, China Daily Report, March 6, 1998.

44. Foreigners may purchase B shares on the Shanghai and Shenzhen stock exchanges, shares priced in foreign exchange which domestic residents may not legally buy; H shares on the Hong Kong stock exchange, listed shares of mainland companies; and so-called Red Chips, shares of Hong Kong listed companies that are majority-owned by Chinese companies.

45. Sara Webb, "Among Most-Favored Emerging Markets, China is Last Year's News; Poland and Africa Come Up," *Wall Street Journal,* March 23, 1998, p. C12.

46. Erik Guyot, "Yanzhou Coal's IPO Shows Shift in Investors' Appetite," *Asian Wall Street Journal Interactive Edition,* March 27, 1998.

47. In the first quarter of 1997 the return on assets prior to interest and taxes was 7 percent. China Economic Performance Monitoring Center, "Indicators for Performance of State-Owned Enterprises in First Quarter '98," in *China Economic News,* June 1, 1998, p. 13.

48. At year-end 1997, external debt was officially reported to be US$130.96 billion. The Bank for International Settlements and other independent sources estimate that China's external debt is about one-fourth larger than the official , with most of the difference in short-term debt. For example, JP Morgan estimated China's total foreign debt at year-end 1997 was US$161.5 billion, of which US$38.8 was short-term, with a maturity of less than one year. Joan Zheng, "China Reaches for a Homegrown Path Forward," *Global Data Watch* (New York: Morgan Guaranty Trust Company, July 24, 1998), p. 8.

49. Paul Bowles and Gordon White, "Contradictions in China's financial reform: the relationship between banks and enterprises," *Cambridge Journal of Economics,* Vol. 13, No. 4 (1989), p. 489.

50. This is confirmed in Ye Yaozhong, "Raise Credit Quality by Deepening Reform," *Jinrong shibao (Financial News),* November 20, 1997, p. 2.

51. Loans outstanding grew from RMB 6.4 trillion to RMB 7.5 trillion in 1997, an increase of 16.7 percent. Nicholas R. Lardy, *China's Unfinished Economic Revolution,* p. 78. Gross domestic product grew at the rate of 8.8 percent in 1997 according to the State Statistical Bureau. See note 1.

52. *Jinrong shibao (Financial News),* July 14, 1998, p. 1.

53. The alternative hypothesis is that state banks in 1997 finally succeeded in directing a dramatically higher share of their loans to more credit-worthy borrowers. Presumably,

many of these would be in the non-state sector and would use such funds for investment. But for the first time in a decade the rate of investment in the first eight months of 1997 in non-state industry fell below that of state-owned industry. That is not consistent with the hypothesis. Tony Walker, "A new and testing phase," *Financial Times China Survey,* December 8, 1997, p. II.

54. Craig S. Smith, "Asia's Vast Inventories Threaten to Make Downturn More Painful," *Wall Street Journal,* November 21, 1997, p. A9, A11. Mr. Smith presents data for seven Chinese companies that in 1996 had ratios of unsold inventory to sales ranging from 9.3 to 80.6 percent. For these firms the average ratio of inventory to sales almost doubled compared to 1995.

55. "Central Authorities Forbid Local Governments to Interfere in Banks' Loan-Granting Power," *Mingbao,* January 11, 1998, p. A8, in Foreign Broadcast Information Service, China Daily Report, No.012, 1998. Tsao Hsiao, "Jiang, Li, and Zhu's New Ideas for Banking Reform," *Ching Pao (Mirror),* January 1, 1998, pp. 32-36, in Foreign Broadcast Information Service, China Daily Report, No.015, 1998.

56. Wang Lihong, "Bad loans only 5% of bank credits," *China Daily,* January 17, 1998, p. 3. Ye Hongyan, "Recognizing the Current Crisis of Bad Debt in China's Financial Structure," *Ta Kung Pao,* January 20, 1998.

57. Craig S. Smith, "China Banks Get Freer Hand," *Asian Wall Street Journal Weekly Edition,* February 5, 1998, p. 6. Sun Shangwu, "Financial reform outlined," *China Daily,* February 23, 1998, p. 1.

58. Mark O'Neill, "Funny money leaves central bank feeling distinctly unamused," *South China Morning Post (Business Post),* February 8, 1998, p. 3.

59. Wang Wei, "Five-Grade Credit System to Come Into Force Late This Year, Zhu Rongji Says No To Double-Track System and Transition," *Sing Tao Jih Pao,* February 26, 1998, p. B5, in Foreign Broadcast Information Service, China Daily Report, No.057, 1998. "China increases control over central bank branches amidst Asia crisis," Agence France-Presse via ClariNet, January 21, 1998.

60. New China News Agency, "Procedures for International Borrowing Implemented," January 3, 1998, in Foreign Broadcast Information Service, China Daily Report, No. 008, 1998. For example, the procedures limit the sum of borrowing and foreign exchange guarantees extended by a firm to an amount not to exceed their foreign exchange earnings of the previous year.

61. "Place 'Hidden Foreign Debt' Under Foreign Debt Control," *Jingji daobao (Economic Reporter),* December 1, 1997, in Foreign Broadcast Information Service, China Daily Report, No. 346, 1997.

62. Wang Baoqing, "Points on Supporting Money-Losing Enterprises to Cultivate Winning Increased Profits," *Jinrong shibao (Financial News),* June 25, 1998, p. 1.

5

Domestic Follies, Investment Crises: East Asian Lessons for India

Surjit S. Bhalla

Introduction

This chapter is about the genesis of the East Asian crisis and its implications for the future of East Asia and India. The financial explosion of East Asia raises several questions: Why did it happen? How could it, especially the contagion, occur? The chapter will explore answers to these questions and address the problems and prospects of India, a major Asian country which escaped the crisis. The fact that, even in 1997, India was essentially a closed economy, with dealings in foreign exchange strictly controlled, helped to avert the crisis. However, there were crises of India's own making, especially with regard to the explosion of a nuclear device in May 1998.

While most analyses of the East Asian financial crisis have centered on parallels with the Mexican devaluation of 1994, the closest parallel actually was the Plaza agreement undertaken to stop the undervaluation of the Japanese yen. This deal was hammered out under the leadership of the U.S. government in September 1985. Its purposes were to devalue the dollar in general and to revalue the yen in particular. The Bretton Woods fixed exchange rate system had been dismantled more than a decade earlier. Yet the yen remained strangely fixed (the yen/$ exchange rate was 260 yen just before Plaza in 1985, and it was the same five years earlier) and undervalued, in a floating rate world. Japan also continued to run up huge trade surpluses, a factor which had not gone unnoticed in American corporate and political circles.

Replace Japan with China in the above paragraph and the parallels become striking. China was also running huge trade surpluses, also rapidly growing, also rapidly approaching East Asian productivity levels, and also continuously operating an undervalued currency. The competitors hurt in this instance by a mercantilist policy were the East Asian neighbors of China, the very same set of countries that took part in the Asian crisis. Indeed, a suggestion which comes out of the analysis is that East Asian policymakers welcomed the Thai crisis because it allowed them to get out of the straitjacket of fixed exchange rates and, like the United States with Japan a decade earlier, allowed them to be competitive once again.

The crisis would have occurred even without Chinese undervaluation. (Its timing, however, would have been much later). An essential component of the crisis was the operation of a fixed exchange rate regime in the context of large scale private capital flows—a phenomenon of the 1990s. A fixed exchange rate regime leads to wrong incentives for lending and wrong investments. Since these flows accelerated in 1993, the timing of the crisis had to be after that year. Mexico fell first in 1994. The first years of faltering East Asian export growth rates, both in absolute and relative terms, occurred post-1995. This dates the crisis in 1996 or after.

What follows is an *ex-post* analysis, but *ex-post* with a difference. The emphasis is always on what happened, and the logical test of the counter-factual—i.e., what would have happened in a floating exchange rate world, what would have happened if China had not persistently undervalued its currency? The true test of any analysis is whether it fits the data *ex-ante*, and whether it fits the description of the counter-factual.

The chapter is organized into several sections. The first part of the study examines the causes of the crisis: managed exchange rates, undervalued currencies, crony capitalism, asset bubbles, Japanese devaluation, and capital account liberalization. A model of capital flows is developed which outlines the incentives for both flows into, and out of, emerging markets. All this model requires is the assumption that capital will tend to seek its highest level, irrespective of national boundaries—an innocuous assumption for the 1990s. This very simple return maximization model also underlines the critical importance of hedging costs (considered zero in a managed exchange rate world) in affecting flows and crises.

Some popular explanations of the crisis are explained here as well. That identification is a serious issue is illustrated by the various recommendations that have hit the marketplace. Sachs (1998), for example, argues that "the problem is not the lack of capital mobility, but the problems of capital mobility in under-regulated financial systems. Within emerging markets, and *within the international system generally*, there is a substantial case for tightened prudential policies to make it harder for markets to create crises through wild swings of euphoria and panic" (Sachs 1998:1 italics added). This chapter reaches a somewhat different conclusion— i.e., there is no need to change the international monitoring system and, domestically, instead of under-regulation, the problem is more the operation of a fixed exchange rate regime. Market euphoria and panic had little to do with the generation of the crisis.

Other arguments examined include the usual suspects in the foreign exchange (FX) literature: e.g., large current account deficits, and/or large fiscal deficits, are the core fundamentals responsible for a financial crisis. This argument did not work in the case of Mexico in 1994. Mexico did have a large current account deficit (about 7 percent), but it had responsible fiscal policy, and fiscal surpluses, in each of the three preceding years. Evidence suggests that the *surest method of ensuring eventual financial market disaster is to have responsible fiscal policy and a managed exchange rate.*

Various aspects about China's mercantilist policy are also discussed, and how the Chinese policy of undervaluation of the yuan led to the crisis in East Asia. The role of the international system (read U.S. political leadership and American business interests) in allowing China to devalue its currency, despite burgeoning trade surpluses, is examined. Also examined is the question of whether China needed to devalue in the early 1990s. Objections to the important contributory role of the Chinese devaluation are analyzed and found wanting.

The second part of this study examines various aspects of the Indian economy. Why did India miss the crisis (its exchange rate is completely controlled, like China's)? Does the new party in power, the Bharatiya Janata Party, represent a new era (it does in non-economic matters)? The favorable future of economic reforms is examined, as is the lack of importance of political instability in affecting economic reforms. The overall prospects for the future are examined, as well as an assessment made of the repercussions of India's atomic explosions.

Genesis of the Crisis

The 1990s were witness to a boom in private capital flows to emerging markets. From nascent levels (around $25-50 billion) in the early years, such flows accelerated to over $200 billion in each of the last four years and were close to $300 billion at the time of the crisis in mid-1997. This was, and is, a perfect example of globalization—capital seeking highest returns. Some countries allowed entry in a completely controlled manner (China, India) while others (Thailand, Malaysia, Indonesia, Chile) had varying degrees of controls. The restrictions on outflows also varied among countries. What was common to all the emerging markets is that none of them had a floating or market determined exchange rate. Central banks intervened, and intervened often, to restrict movements in exchange rates. Most, if not all, the central banks had either an implicit or explicit band, that is, lines in the sand which were not allowed to be crossed. (As events of 1997 showed, lines in the sand only serve to ensure that the dust storm which follows is a blinding one.) All participants—domestic central bankers, international central bankers, and private bankers—knew about the bands and their so-called sanctity.

Model of Capital Flows

One model of capital flows is as follows. Capital flows into a country originate via the decisions of an investment trader based outside the country. Capital flows can be towards three different kinds of investments: equity, debt, and direct investment. The investor is faced with a menu of possibilities in the assets of different countries. An important consideration is the nature of the exchange rate regime. What matters for the investor is whether he or she should hedge exposure. Large gains can be made most of the time if the currency exposure is left unhedged. This model can be expressed in the following equation:

$$\text{Capital Inflow} = f(Re^*, Rd^*, Ri^*) - Hc$$

In the above equation, f refers to the "function of", while R refers to the relative rate of return between the emerging and developed market. Lower case e, d, and i refer to the three sectors of equity, debt, and direct investment. Clearly, the higher any of the returns, the larger the capital inflow. Hc refers to hedging costs which, until recently, were assumed by most actors to be close to zero. (In some cases such as India and China, the actors were not even allowed to legally hedge their exposure.) The market value of Hc is given by the expected difference in inflation rates in a floating exchange rate world and is expected to range between 3-6 percent. The upper end of this range is close to the higher expected relative return in an emerging market investment. If an equivalent amount has to go for hedging costs, then there will be little incentive for investment. Thus, hedging costs play a crucial arbitrage and limiting role. The more realistic the hedging costs, the less the net capital inflow into debt and other assets.

With zero hedging costs, the two almost perpetual gain sectors are debt and direct investment. The former because inflation, and nominal interest rates, are higher in emerging economies; the latter because of "catch-up" possibilities which result in higher productivity growth and higher return to fixed investment.

In a managed fixed exchange rate regime, there is considerable incentive to not indulge in hedging. There are several reasons. First, the currency might appreciate, in nominal terms, as indeed it did in many developing countries during 1991 to 1996.[1] Second, even though the exchange rate might depreciate, it might depreciate less than interest rate differentials with the United States. Third, most investment bankers felt that they would be able to exit before any large discrete devaluation, the experience of Mexico 1994 notwithstanding.[2]

The *counter-factual* is a floating exchange rate regime. In such an environment, the exchange rate will quickly appreciate (or depreciate) in response to profitability perceptions. These are likely to be of a continuous rather than a discrete nature. Hence, not only is volatility contained, but so are excessive and problematic capital flows. For example, as more capital flows in, the more the exchange rate appreciates and the less excess returns the last entrant obtains. A self-regulating system does not need bureaucratic or central bank control.[3] With a managed exchange rate the inward capital flows can be limitless. With floating exchange rates, the possibility of currency appreciation restrains capital inflows.

Explanations for the Crisis

Crony Capitalism and Non-Performing Assets of Banks

Analysts have identified causes of the crisis which are really subsets of a managed exchange rate regime. The example of crony capitalism is one such derived primary cause. The access to rents—i.e., cheaper foreign credit—is rationed by the government to preferred customers (cronies). Hence, cronyism helps obtain rents. If exchange rates are floating, the rents also float away.

Now consider the example of non-performing assets, or banking sector problems. Suddenly, in late 1997, academic economists and bureaucrats at international organizations were touting their latest find: non-performing assets in East Asia were large and were the cause of the crisis. This was a surprise, since the conventional wisdom was that the much more developed financial sector, and realistic interest rates, were causes of the East Asian miracle (World Bank 1993, and almost any research document published prior to June 1997). How do nonperforming assets occur? When bad investments occur. How do bad investments occur? When the returns to investments are not high. What happens if foreign borrowing rates are almost 3 to 5 percent less than risk-free domestic deposits? Excess borrowing occurs which results in excess investments which results in an excess of non-performing assets. In other words, the banking sector problems in East Asia were an *outcome* of the managed exchange rate regime and therefore not a *cause* of the crisis.

What has been described above can be termed *ex-post*. The investments were unprofitable and that is why there were problems. But the questions remain: Why were these investments suddenly unprofitable? Why were these problems not seen beforehand? Why did everybody wait for an explosion?

Identification of factors that could predict the crisis is a difficult exercise after the event, and a near impossible exercise before the fact. The first attack on the baht took place at the time of the Mexican devaluation in 1994. It depreciated by 5 percent within hours. Why? The reasoning was that, like Mexico, Thailand was also running large deficits on the current account (at 6 percent and close to the 7 percent deficit of Mexico in 1994). Thai authorities intervened and just as quickly (within hours) the Thai baht appreciated by 5 percent and settled down to its pre-crisis value of 25 baht per U.S. dollar. The market followed, with the reasoning that Thailand's large deficits were different since they were being used to finance investment rather than consumption.

It was not that the markets were wrong to forego their attack on the baht in 1994. Their reasoning was correct *at that time*. After all, if the rate of return to investment is higher than the cost of borrowing, one should undertake the investment. Which raises the question to a higher level: When did the rate of return on investment collapse?

Equity and Property Markets

The leading indicator of the economy in both developed and developing markets is the stock market. This is not to suggest that the stock market is always right. Most of the time it is not clear what the leading indicator is saying: Is it discounting one month ahead or one year ahead? Or is it in a bubble stage with the true value unknown? These caveats apply to all markets, from fish to fowl. The point simply is that the stock market is the best barometer of the health of the economy; policymakers and investors should constantly have it on their radar screen, especially in developing countries where the policymakers "control" the workings of other financial markets in interest rates and exchange rates.[4] This makes the stock market the residual shock absorber.

Perhaps because of this acknowledged role of the stock market, the first conventional wisdom culprit cause of the crisis was an "asset bubble" (Sachs 1998; Krugman 1998; among various others). The evidence does not support this glib conclusion. Table 5.1 reports two indices for various stock markets: stock index in dollars and a "fair value" index. The fair value is based on the assumption that the *nominal* index should rise with growth in *nominal* income, and with productivity growth. This fair value computation is not being offered as being definitive but rather as a guide.

The indices do not suggest that there was a stock market bubble in East Asia during 1996–1997. There is considerable evidence to suggest the existence of such a bubble four years earlier in 1993. (In that year, in response to the jump in foreign capital inflows, all countries zoomed to their multi-year peak). In end 1996 and/or June 1997, the dollar based indices with *1990 equal to a 100* were as follows: Indonesia at 135, Korea at 79, Malaysia at 236, Philippines at 397, Singapore at 210, Taiwan at 195, and Thailand at 111. Excepting the Philippines, the "best" bubble was Malaysia with stock market prices twice those six and a half years earlier. The Malaysian economy, like the rest of East Asia, was growing at an average of 7+ GDP growth rate during this period. According to a "fair" value index, the Malaysian stock market was trading at a 17 percent *discount* in June 1997, the Philippines at a premium of 60 percent and Thailand and Korea both at discounts exceeding 60 percent! Little, rather no evidence of a stock market bubble. Indeed, the stock market was giving more than adequate notice that something was wrong with the investments that were being undertaken in these economies.

In contrast, the property market in all the East Asian economies (and in India) was in the midst of a property asset bubble. According to So and Kanatunga (1998), in both Hong Kong and Singapore property lending (as a percent of total loans) had zoomed to 35 percent. The capital value index of real estate in major cities was at its peak in all the East Asian economies in June 1997. However, while this bubble was present, it was so in only the capital cities of these economies and could not possibly have absorbed the billions of dollars of excess borrowing. As

TABLE 5.1   Stock Market Indices, 1990–1998 (in U.S. dollars)

	1991	1992	1993	1994	1995
India	116.6	142.3	166.6	177.5	125.4
Premium/Discount in percent	*44.4*	*52.8*	*83.6*	*61.8*	*8.5*
China	277.2	623.9	577.3	378.5	331.0
	141.8	*395.6*	*282.9*	*85.9*	*23.1*
Hong Kong	142.5	183.6	396.9	273.1	336.1
	19.4	*29.3*	*137.5*	*41.0*	*50.4*
Indonesia	57.7	58.3	121.9	96.8	101.8
	-49.8	*-55.4*	*-26.9*	*-49.4*	*-54.7*
Korea	84.1	87.1	105.1	122.2	106.7
	-28.3	*-32.5*	*-26.7*	*-29.9*	*-49.4*
Malaysia	109.5	136.4	272.2	210.1	216.6
	-4.8	*-2.9*	*75.4*	*7.4*	*-8.0*
Philippines	157.7	184.8	431.3	426.8	368.2
	29.7	*32.0*	*208.5*	*128.0*	*85.3*
Singapore	138.2	140.1	228.1	232.7	242.6
	13.2	*4.6*	*37.3*	*5.6*	*-7.8*
Taiwan	98.7	71.4	133.4	162.1	113.2
	-18.6	*-49.3*	*-11.2*	*-7.1*	*-40.4*
Thailand	117.0	158.9	313.0	271.9	264.7
	-1.7	*16.0*	*96.9*	*42.7*	*18.3*

indicated above, these billions are unlikely to have gone into the stock market. Which leaves the remainder, fixed investment, as the only outlet.[5]

The Perverse Role of Fiscal Surpluses

Instead of fiscal deficits, the East Asian economies were running surpluses (Table 5.2). This is indeed fortunate. If they had been running deficits, everyone would have identified the culprit and the emerging economies would still have been left with bad exchange rate policies! Indeed, Bhalla (1997a) makes the point that possibly the *worst* policy for a developing country is good fiscal policy and man-

TABLE 5.1   (continued)

	1996	1997a	1997	1998
India	121.9	168.3	134.0	108.1
Premium/Discount in percent	*-9.8*	*15.3*	*-7.2*	*-24.9*
China	550.9	754.5	723.4	808.8
	66.4	*115.4*	*94.6*	*107.5*
Hong Kong	448.7	506.0	357.0	284.5
	77.2	*91.1*	*28.4*	*1.5*
Indonesia	122.3	135.0	33.7	13.9
	-53.5	*-51.1*	*-75.1*	*-76.4*
Korea	72.2	78.9	24.7	20.3
	-67.4	*-64.4*	*-82.9*	*-86.6*
Malaysia	270.8	235.9	80.8	60.8
	1.5	*-17.1*	*-59.0*	*-67.6*
Philippines	448.5	396.6	173.2	158.6
	92.4	*60.3*	*-0.1*	*-10.3*
Singapore	239.5	210.2	137.4	95.4
	-20.2	*-32.6*	*-51.8*	*-67.5*
Taiwan	151.1	194.7	150.1	131.4
	-28.9	*-13.3*	*-26.8*	*-35.6*
Thailand	168.6	110.2	40.4	33.0
	-33.7	*-59.5*	*-73.4*	*-81.2*

Note: The figures represent a country's stock market index (in U.S. dollars), set to December 1990 = 100. All figures are of as end-December, expect 1997a and 1998, which are as of June 30, 1997 and 1998, respectively. The second row (in italics) for each country expresses the percentage deviation of the actual stock index to the predicted index value, which is obtained as follows: Predicted Index = Base Index + Nominal GDP Growth + 0.5 (Real GDP Growth).
Source: O[x]us Research & Investments Database.

aged exchange rates. This occurs because of the signaling effect. Foreign investors and yuppie traders need to make quick, and hopefully not very taxing, decisions on where to invest. The menu is the world, and the senior management will not approve of investments in "irresponsible" economies.[6]

TABLE 5.2: Key Macro Variables for Asia, 1985–1996

	Avg. 85-89	1990	1991	1992	1993	1994	1995	1996
GDP Growth %								
China	9.5	3.7	9.1	13.6	13.0	12.2	10.2	9.7
India	6.1	5.4	0.8	5.3	6.2	7.8	7.0	7.5
ASEAN-4	5.3	7.9	6.1	5.7	6.3	7.2	7.5	6.6
ASEAN-7	6.2	7.8	6.8	5.8	6.7	7.6	7.6	6.6
CPI Inflation %								
China	13.3	2.1	4.0	7.0	29.5	25.5	17.1	8.3
India	7.8	13.7	13.1	8.0	8.6	9.5	10.1	9.4
ASEAN-4	4.9	9.0	8.0	5.3	6.6	6.7	6.7	6.4
ASEAN-7	4.0	7.7	6.9	4.4	5.7	5.4	5.4	4.9
Current Acc't Deficit (%GDP)								
China	-1.7	3.1	3.3	1.3	-1.9	1.3	0.2	0.9
India	-2.2	-3.2	-0.4	-1.8	-0.5	-1.1	-1.8	-1.0
ASEAN-4	-0.7	-4.9	-5.6	-3.4	-4.2	-4.6	-5.8	-5.4
ASEAN-7	0.9	-0.7	-1.1	0.1	-0.9	-0.1	-0.8	-1.0
Fiscal Deficit (% GDP)								
China		-1.9	-2.3	-2.2	-2.0	-1.9	-1.6	-0.9
India	-8.4	-8.3	-5.9	-5.7	-7.4	-6.1	-5.4	-5.2
ASEAN-4	-2.6	0.0	0.7	0.5	0.7	2.9	0.8	1.6
ASEAN-7	-1.1	1.7	1.7	2.4	3.2	1.5	0.2	0.5
Total Debt / Export (%)								
China	79.9	91.4	86.3	85.6	94.1	80.2	77.3	71.3
India	286.6	320.1	316.0	336.0	290.6	253.8	201.2	170.8
ASEAN-4	189.5	150.4	150.7	139.5	133.7	124.5	110.5	120.5
Total Debt / GNP (%)								
China	11.3	15.6	16.0	17.3	19.9	18.6	17.2	16.0
India	22.3	27.8	32.1	33.7	36.4	34.2	28.2	25.6
ASEAN-4	62.9	51.5	53.8	50.5	50.6	49.1	46.5	49.9
Short-term / Total Debt (%)								
China	24.7	16.8	17.9	19.0	17.8	17.4	18.9	19.7
India	10.4	10.2	8.3	7.0	3.9	4.2	5.4	7.5
ASEAN-4	15.8	17.9	19.4	22.5	23.0	20.6	21.9	28.4

Notes: All figures are end-of-period data. ASEAN-4 includes Indonesia, Malaysia, the Philippines, and Thailand. ASEAN-7 includes the above countries plus Korea, Singapore, and Taiwan. ASEAN-7 debt figures are not reported due to lack of data for Korea, Singapore, and Taiwan.

Sources: IMF International Financial Statistics; World Bank Debt Tables; O[x]us Research & Investments Database.

The best indicator of an economy's health is the fiscal deficit. Why? Because the World Bank, the IMF, and Greenspan say so—and they obviously know better. How can it be wrong to invest in a country which has 8 percent growth and fiscal surpluses? Nobody has ever lost a job on a lemming investment. Hence, the flood of money into East Asia, aided and abetted by the guarantee that things cannot go wrong—i.e., a managed exchange rate. The more the fiscal surplus, the better the economy, the more capital came in, and the exchange rate became more overvalued. A virtuous cycle became a vicious cycle. Hence, the over-capacity, the decline in the rate of return to investment, and the crisis.[7]

Returns on Physical Investment

The puzzle of the timing of the crisis (why the second half of 1997 and not earlier?) turns to identification of the signals pertaining to the decline in rates of return to physical investment. The 1990s not only marked the explosion of the flow of private capital to developing countries, but also the creation of a large amount of capacity in the world market. The new decade brought about reforms in several major developing economies (Brazil, China, India) and was also witness to the emergence of a new set of reformers in Eastern Europe. All these countries brought, at the same time, large amounts of educated manpower to the world trading table. Capital, technology, and firms no longer were required to stay within national boundaries. More efficient, competitive production was the hallmark of the new world order. This has likely been the principal reason why the death of inflation occurred, not because of "tight" and/or "appropriate" monetary policies in countries as diverse as the United States, Germany, or India.

The brave new world required lean and mean competitive machines. Profit margins were significantly reduced, as capital sought investment opportunities in Thailand, India, Vietnam, or Chile. The new virtuous cycle was in full operation. Foreign investment was welcome, domestic markets were cleaned up, fiscal deficits were reduced, and Moody's and S&P became the new arbiters of where capital should go.

Given this competitive environment, where was the "edge"? Most emerging markets, and particularly those in East Asia, could not follow the old mercantilist model of an undervalued currency. Most of these countries were relatively open to foreign capital, so devaluation could no longer be achieved by fiat. Further, any such devaluation would have been met by an extremely hostile response from foreign investors and international banks.

In the context of this boom in worldwide capacity and production, China decided to make growth its first priority and an undervalued currency its primary instrument. This was a natural course to follow, especially given the time-tested Japanese (later Korea, Singapore, Taiwan, Malaysia, Indonesia, Thailand) nature of this policy. Exports started to obtain favorable treatment via the operation of a dual exchange rate regime which started in 1987 but gained currency in the early 1990s.

Did Capital Account Liberalization Cause the Problem?

The East Asian crisis was a financial crisis, and one involving foreign capital inflows and outflows. This fact has led several economists to conclude that unregulated inflows were the problem. Hence, they should be regulated (Sachs 1998), or capital account liberalization (CAL) has no gains for developing economies (Stiglitz 1998). Indeed, Stiglitz argues that CAL increases risk and does not increase growth.

There are several problems with the Sachs-Stiglitz conclusions. First, as discussed earlier, excessive short-term foreign borrowing was the result of a managed exchange rate system and would not have occurred with floating exchange rates. Thus, the only regulation needed is one pertaining to the un-fixing of exchange rates. Second, there is no evidence to support the contention that CAL increases risk, despite Stiglitz's claims that "the statement that capital account liberalization increases risk is uncontroversial" (Stiglitz 1998:17). In the 1990s real interest rates were both lower, and with lower volatility, than corresponding rates in the less CAL 1980s (Bhalla 1997f). Further, and contrary to Feldstein and Bacchetta (1991) contention, advent of CAL has meant that savings rates and investment rates are no longer correlated in the 1990s (also Bhalla 1997f).[8] Fourth, economic growth in the 1990s was significantly above those observed in the 1980s. Fifth, several IMF studies (e.g. Mathieson and Rojas-Suarez (1993), Quirk and Evans (1995) document the positive effects of CAL on growth. Sixth, several other studies (e.g., World Bank 1991, 1993; Bhalla 1992) have also reached similar positive conclusions about capital account liberalization. If all of the above is not accepted, then as Bhalla (1997f) argues, a necessary and sufficient condition for full capital account liberalization is a floating exchange rate regime, or currency board regimes as in Argentina and Hong Kong. If this definition is adopted, then it follows that the managed exchange rate regimes of East Asia were economies *without* appropriate CAL; hence, the presence of CAL cannot be a cause for the crisis.

Did Japan's Devaluation Cause the Crisis?

Table 5.3 examines the IMF (1997) preferred hypothesis: that is, the yen devaluation of nearly 40 percent between mid-June 1995 and end-June 1997 was responsible for the crisis. Apparently, the view is that the yen devaluation mattered, but not China's devaluation—an inconsistency also enthusiastically endorsed by the *Economist* (1998)! Japanese exports and trade surpluses peaked in 1995. In 1997 they were barely above 1995 levels, even though the yen had devalued. It is interesting to note that the IMF mentions the yen devaluation as a contributory

TABLE 5.3   No Evidence that Japanese Devaluation
Caused the East Asian Crisis

	1990	1991	1992	1993	1994	1995	1996	1997
Japan Exports (US $ billion)								
World	309.5	335.8	363.7	388.2	426.7	480.1	457.2	459.2
Ind. Countries	183.4	189.8	198.3	200.2	216.1	229.3	212.8	220.5
U.S.	93.1	95.0	99.5	110.4	122.5	127.2	118.0	121.3
Japan Imports (US $ billion)								
World	207.6	210.3	207.0	213.7	244.6	299.4	316.6	307.2
Ind. Countries	102.1	100.2	97.9	98.1	111.9	134.5	138.6	133.9
U.S.	48.6	48.1	47.8	48.0	53.5	64.3	67.5	67.2
Trade Balance (US $ billion)								
World	101.9	125.6	156.8	174.5	182.1	180.7	140.7	151.9
Ind. Countries	81.3	89.6	100.3	102.1	104.2	94.8	74.2	86.7
U.S.	44.5	46.9	51.7	62.5	69.0	62.9	50.4	54.2
Exchange Rate (vs. US dollar)	134	125	125	112	100	104	116	130
GDP Growth %	5.0	3.9	1.0	0.1	0.5	0.9	3.6	-0.2
CPI Inflation %	3.8	2.7	1.2	1.0	0.7	-0.1	0.1	0.1

Notes: Values for 1997 are obtained by doubling the cumulative value for the first two quarters (i.e., until June 1997). All figures for trade are from recipient country data.
Sources: O[x]us Research and Investments Database; Direction of Trade Statistics (DOTS), IMF, 1997 Yearbook; June 1998 quarterly.

cause with no evidence from exports data. Nor does the IMF acknowledge the possibility of Chinese devaluation with significant data about Chinese exports and trade surpluses. (See below and Tables 5.4 through 5.7.) The World Bank (1998) in its official response to the crisis goes one step further. Nowhere in the text does it even mention the large Chinese devaluation! Indeed, it does not even mention overvaluation as a significant cause of the crisis.

Mercantilist Policy of China

Apart from managed exchange rates, there is one additional cause for the East Asian financial crisis: the large (54 percent) devaluation in China from end-1990 to end-1993. This was in addition to a 220 percent devaluation from 1980 to 1990.

The World Bank had this to say in its glowing China 2020 report published in mid-1997: "Perhaps most important, the government maintained a realistic exchange rate policy. It almost halved the exchange rate at the outset of reforms and devalued the currency on four later occasions" (World Bank 1997:10).

Devaluation by a large economy plays through as follows. With broadly similar economic structures (educated labor force, foreign technology, foreign capital, and foreign management), and excess global capacity, pricing becomes an all-powerful weapon.[9] There are two methods to compete unfairly on price: dump or undervalue the currency. The former runs the risk of being caught by your trading partners. So does the latter via the method of competitive devaluation.

Various mechanisms to identify and punish dumping are in place. Unfortunately, the structure does not allow vigilance over undervaluation. An overvalued currency leads to self-correction, large current account deficits which need to be financed. Trade surpluses, however, are self-correcting only if the domestic political system allows representation, or if IMF plays its appointed role.[10] Workers and consumers lose out with an undervalued currency with the gainer being the mercantilist state. In a democratic system there will be demands for a revaluation of the currency, an outlet not available in communist regimes like China. However, the postwar experience of Japan has shown that a democratic polity is only a necessary and not sufficient condition for providing checks and balances to mercantilism.

Could the IMF and World Bank have acted to stop China's mercantilist march? The former did not have the clout (because the United States was in control), and it was not in the World Bank's interest to act against its biggest client. The United States, for economic and political reasons, was in a help-China mode. In the 1992 campaign Bill Clinton stated that he would take China to task over human rights abuses. After the election, all was forgotten. Most favored nation status was renewed each year, human rights abuses were forgiven, and the Democratic Party became China's biggest supporter (and apparently vice-versa). China's huge trade surpluses are apparently "no problem." but Japan's surpluses signify deep-rooted structural problems.

Several factors about Japan in the mid-1980s are relevant for what happened in China in the 1990s. Most importantly, the political dimension needs to be recognized—i.e., whose side are U.S. policymakers on? This question is also equivalent to asking: What is the view of U.S. business? It is unlikely that the leading member of the regulatory bodies (IMF and World Bank) would ever take a step going against its own large business interests. A simple rule which follows from the above is that transgressions are possible for small countries. If large countries are involved, then such violations can only occur with the implicit, if not explicit, concurrence of the United States of America.

What evidence is there to support the contention that China was not playing by the rules and, to the detriment of others, was operating a mercantilist policy of undervaluation of the yuan?[11] The fair or appropriate value of a currency is a controversial issue. But most agree that one of the consequences of undervaluation is a persistent trade surplus; that of overvaluation, a persistent trade deficit.

Policymakers need short-hand methods to manage their currencies. A convenient procedure is to chose an "equilibrium year" and then adjust the exchange rate for inflation differences. This is called the purchasing power parity (PPP) adjustment. Most economists stop at a PPP rate. However, just as important a calculation is one involving an adjustment for differences in productivity growth. Most often, such differences are minor and even out over the long-run. Therefore, stopping at a PPP adjustment is somewhat justified.

However, productivity growth in China has been unusual. According to IMF economists Hu and Khan, Chinese productivity growth has averaged 3.7 percent per annum for the reform period 1979–1994, and 5.4 percent for the period 1990–1994. For trade, what matters are differences in productivity growth between countries.

As the Hu and Khan paper indicates, productivity growth is not easy to measure. This may mean that measurement is difficult, but it in no way implies that productivity effects are irrelevant. Establishing whether China pursued an under-valued exchange rate policy requires that calculations of productivity growth be done for a large set of countries. One short-cut is to assume that productivity growth is equal to the growth in per capita income of the developed economies and equal to half the per capita growth in developing countries. This method tracks the Chinese productivity growth reasonably well.[12]

The next problem is the choice of a base year. The particular year chosen affects the *absolute* level of undervaluation but does not affect *changes* in such valuations. Table 5.4 reports currency valuations since 1990, and Figure 5.1 plots these for various years (with 1980=100). Table 5.4 also reports valuations according to the incorrect method of only adjusting for inflation differences.

The evidence presented in Table 5.4 and Figure 5.1 confirms what China's competitors have known all along: sweat shops and lack of political representation do make a difference. Between 1980 and 1990 China gained in competitiveness (relative to ASEAN economies) by over 50 percent. In three short years (1990 to 1992), by actively devaluing its currency, China gained in competitiveness by an additional 40 percent relative to the ASEAN 7. Gains in "competitiveness" is the correct way to evaluate whether a country is playing by the rules of the game. (In a floating exchange rate world, the market "rewards" gains via an appreciation of the currency, thus limiting perpetual gains and perpetual surpluses.)

TABLE 5.4   Evolution of Exchange Rates in Asia

	1990	1991	1992	1993	1994	1995
Currency Overvaluation Inflatation- and Productivity-Adjustments: Correct Method						
China	-7.2	-18.3	-41.1	-31.5	-14.5	-1.9
India	28.2	13.3	20.2	14.2	23.3	22.1
ASEAN-4	-8.1	2.7	9.9	13.4	21.8	24.3
ASEAN-7	-7.2	2.7	8.2	11.3	19.0	21.4
Japan	2.3	13.3	17.3	29.1	39.1	37.6
Change in Currency Overvaluation Since 1990						
China		-11.1	-33.9	-24.3	-7.3	5.3
India		-14.9	-8.0	-14.0	-4.9	-6.1
ASEAN-4		10.8	18.0	21.5	29.9	32.4
ASEAN-7		9.9	15.4	18.5	26.2	28.6
Japan		11.0	15.0	26.8	36.8	35.3
Currency Overvaluation. Only Inflation-Adjustments: Incorrect Method						
China	-6.2	-11.2	-26.6	-14.5	2.4	15.8
India	30.4	9.4	12.4	0.8	7.0	2.9
ASEAN-4	-1.9	2.5	5.9	5.8	12.7	13.8
ASEAN-7	-1.1	3.1	4.7	4.6	10.8	11.9
Japan	6.5	12.6	11.4	19.2	26.5	21.5
Annual Per Capita Income Growth (percent)						
China	2.3	7.8	12.5	11.9	11.2	9.2
India	3.4	-1.6	3.2	2.0	2.2	4.1
ASEAN-4	6.4	3.5	3.6	4.2	5.2	5.4
ASEAN-7	6.3	4.7	4.0	5.1	5.9	5.9
Japan	4.7	3.6	0.7	-0.2	0.2	0.7
Annual Consumer Price Inflation (percent)						
China	2.1	4.0	7.0	29.5	25.5	17.1
India	13.7	13.1	8.0	8.6	9.5	10.1
ASEAN-4	9.0	8.0	5.3	6.6	6.7	6.7
ASEAN-7	7.7	6.9	4.4	5.7	5.4	5.4
Japan	3.8	2.7	1.2	1.0	0.7	-0.1

Notes: ASEAN-4 includes Indonesia, Malaysia, the Philippines, and Thailand. ASEAN-7 includes the above countries plus Korea, Singapore, and Taiwan. All currency overvaluation figures are with base 1980 = 100. A positive sign indicates overvaluation.

TABLE 5.4   (continued)

	1996	June 1997	1997	June 1998
Currency Overvaluation Inflatation- and Productivity-Adjustments: Correct Method				
China	0.1	-4.0	-3.5	-7.2
India	26.6	31.8	25.9	27.1
ASEAN-4	26.9	30.7	-25.1	-42.7
ASEAN-7	22.4	24.2	-19.8	-27.7
Japan	30.0	32.7	23.8	21.5
Change in Currency Overvaluation Since 1990				
China	7.3	3.2	3.7	0
India	-1.6	3.6	-2.3	-1.1
ASEAN-4	35.0	38.8	-17.0	-34.6
ASEAN-7	29.6	31.4	-12.6	-20.5
Japan	27.7	30.4	21.5	19.2
Currency Overvaluation. Only Inflation-Adjustments: Incorrect Method				
China	19.9	17.7	18.0	15.4
India	6.4	10.8	3.2	2.8
ASEAN-4	15.2	17.4	-47.5	-77.3
ASEAN-7	11.4	11.9	-39.0	-55.1
Japan	9.5	9.6	-2.4	-10.9
Annual Per Capita Income Growth (percent)				
China	8.7	7.1	7.1	5.8
India	4.7	2.4	2.4	2.4
ASEAN-4	4.6	2.4	2.4	-3.7
ASEAN-7	4.8	3.4	3.4	-1.7
Japan	3.2	-0.7	-0.7	-4.2
Annual Consumer Price Inflation (percent)				
China	8.3	8.3	-0.1	-1.3
India	9.4	9.4	8.3	10.5
ASEAN-4	6.4	6.4	6.0	21.8
ASEAN-7	4.9	4.9	4.6	13.7
Japan	0.1	0.1	1.6	0.5

Sources: IMF International Financial Statistics; O[x]us Research & Investments Database.

FIGURE 5.1 Undervaluation (Competitiveness), December 1980–June 1998: O/V (Base = 1980)

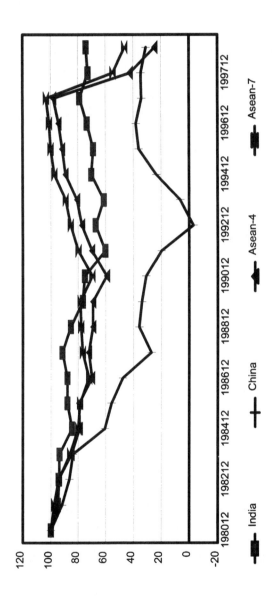

Notes: Dates are indicated in year-month; that is, 198012 represents December 1980. The graph indicates the level of overvaluation for each region since 1980. Changes in the overvaluation indices are independent of base-year selection. Hence, reading the movement from 1990 to 1994, for example, correctly identifies the change in competitiveness.

Did China Need a Devaluation from 1990–1993?

Before discussing the consequences of the Chinese devaluation, an earlier question needs to be addressed: did the Chinese economy require the stimulus of a devaluation in 1990–1993? According to figures reported in Table 5.5, the answer seems an overwhelming no. During the preceding five years (1985 to 1989), the Chinese economy grew at an average growth rate of 9.5 percent per annum with inflation at a high 14 percent. Inflation then collapsed to a 4 percent rate during 1991–1993, while economic growth remained high at 9 percent. Adjusted for productivity differentials (see Table 5.5), the yuan was undervalued by about 25 percent during this time-period. Trade surpluses were reflecting this undervaluation. Surpluses had exactly doubled from $40 billion per year during 1985–1989 to an average of $80 billion during 1990–1993. It is doubtful that any IMF or World Bank economist would have advocated an expansionary devaluation with these statistics in 1990.

Was China's Devaluation Important?

The most talked about issue in international financial markets during the last several months has been the question of a Chinese yuan devaluation: Will they or won't they? From the Chinese premier to the U.S. president, the answer is the same —no, not now anyway. But the threat lingers.[13]

Some early commentators (e.g., Bergsten 1997, Bhalla 1997, Makin 1977, and the *Economist*) had identified the 50 percent Chinese devaluation of January 1, 1994, as a major contributory cause to the East Asian devaluations of 1997. This contention was not left unchallenged, and the IMF in its *World Economic Outlook* of December 1997 stated:

> It has been argued by some observers that the devaluation of the Chinese yuan at the beginning of 1994 also had a significant adverse effect on the competitiveness of Southeast Asian economies. . . . *The yuan's devaluation therefore had a much smaller impact on these countries international competitiveness than the depreciation of the yen during 1995–1997* (IMF 1997:7, n. 4; italics added).

While rejecting the China devaluation hypothesis, the IMF offers the hypothesis that the devaluation of the yen from mid-1995 onwards may have been responsible for the East Asian crisis. It should be emphasized that the IMF report does not provide any evidence for either contention.

The final blow against the Chinese devaluation thesis was delivered by three U.S. economists at the International Division of the Federal Reserve Board of the United States. In a study entitled "Was China the First Domino? Assessing Links between China and the Rest of Emerging Asia," authors Fernald, Edison, and Loungani (1998) contended that "the devaluation was not economically important:

TABLE 5.5   China's Economy at a Glance

	Average 1985-89	1990	1991	1992	1993
GDP Growth (%)	9.5	3.7	9.1	13.6	13.0
Inflation (%)	14.1	2.1	4.0	7.0	29.5
Exchange Rates (yuan / US dollar)					
Official	3.53	5.22	5.43	5.75	5.8
Parallel	4.53	5.88	6.25	7.69	9.1
Weighted Parallel	4.23	5.68	6.01	7.11	8.1
Correct "Fair" Currency					
Overvaluation	12.4	-7.2	-18.3	-41.1	-31.5
Correct "Fair" Exchange Rate	4.8	5.3	5.1	5.04	6.2
Incorrect "Fair" Currency O/V	12.4	-6.2	-11.2	-26.6	-14.5
Incorrect "Fair" Exchange Rate	4.8	5.3	5.4	5.6	7.1
Trade (Recipient Country Data) in U.S. $ billion)					
Exports		88.7	112.9	137.4	157.7
Imports		49.1	61.8	82.1	108.3
Trade Balance		39.7	51.1	55.3	49.4
Trade (Chinese Data)					
Exports	39.6	62.9	71.9	85.5	91.6
Imports	48.6	53.9	63.9	81.8	103.6
Trade Balance	-9.0	9.0	8.1	3.6	-11.9
Trade with Industrialised Countries					
Exports		44.7	56.9	70.7	81.8
Imports		21.1	26.0	23.0	44.3
Trade Balance		23.6	31.0	47.7	37.6
Trade with United States					
Exports		16.3	20.3	27.4	31.2
Imports		4.8	6.3	7.5	8.8
Trade Balance		11.5	14.0	19.9	22.4

Notes: Values for 1997 are as of end of June 1997. All other figures are end-year figures. All trade figures are based on recipient country data unless otherwise stated, and all are in U.S. billion dollars. Incorrect "Fair" Exchange Rate adjusts for inflation difference, while Correct "Fair" Exchange Rate corrects for both inflation and productivity differences.

Sources: Direction of Trade Statistics, IMF, 1997 yearbook; June 1998 quarterly; O[x]us Research & Investments Database.

TABLE 5.5   (continued)

	1994	1995	1996	1997
GDP Growth (%)	12.2	10.2	9.7	8.1
Inflation (%)	25.5	17.1	8.3	8.3
Exchange Rates (yuan / US dollar)				
Official	8.45	8.32	8.3	8.3
Parallel	8.45	8.32	8.3	8.3
Weighted Parallel	8.45	8.32	8.3	8.3
Correct "Fair" Currency				
Overvaluation	-14.5	-1.9	0.1	-4.0
Correct "Fair" Exchange Rate	7.4	8.2	8.3	7.9
Incorrect "Fair" Currency O/V	2.4	15.8	19.9	17.7
Incorrect "Fair" Exchange Rate	8.7	9.9	10.4	10.1
Trade (Recipient Country Data) in U.S. $ billion)				
Exports	192.7	234.0	254.5	262.8
Imports	120.6	146.1	157.6	151.6
Trade Balance	72.1	87.9	96.9	111.2
Trade (Chinese Data)				
Exports	120.8	148.9	151.1	162.0
Imports	115.6	132.1	138.8	125.6
Trade Balance	5.2	16.8	12.3	36.4
Trade with Industrialised Countries				
Exports	104.2	125.7	139.2	144.4
Imports	49.0	58.8	58.6	52.7
Trade Balance	55.2	66.9	80.6	91.7
Trade with United States				
Exports	41.4	48.5	54.4	56.9
Imports	9.3	11.7	12.0	11.6
Trade Balance	32.1	36.8	42.4	45.2

the more relevant exchange rate was a floating rate that was not devalued, and high Chinese inflation has led to a very sharp real *appreciation* of the currency" (emphasis added). Note that the authors (hereafter referred to as FEL) make the popular mistake of ignoring the role of productivity differences in assessing real appreciation. While this was by no means the official view of the U.S. government, the study gained respectability both because of its solidly academic nature and perhaps also by its close association to the U.S. Fed and Greenspan. While rejecting the Chinese devaluation thesis, the authors do not provide an explanation for why the East Asian crisis occurred.

Table 5.5 provides some background data on the Chinese economy in the 1990s. Three exchange rates are reported: the official exchange rate, the theoretical parallel exchange rate for exporters, and a weighted exchange rate which reflects the *actual* exchange rate faced by exporters. The differences in the latter two rates reflects the operation of the dual exchange rate system whereby exporters were allowed to keep approximately 70-80 percent of export proceeds.

This table substantiates a valid point made by IMF (1997) and FEL (1998): i.e., that the devaluation on January 1, 1994, was not actually equal to the nominal 50 percent devaluation (from 5.8 yuan to 8.7 yuan) but rather a smaller 7 percent (8.1 to 8.7 yuan). (Note that the table reports end-period data while the devaluation took place on January 1, 1994, when the exchange rate changed from 5.8 to 8.7 yuan.) Although valid, this point is trivial and pertains to the specification of the exact date of the devaluation. In addition, there are major problems with the (trivial but correct) technical objection. First, the Chinese devaluation was not a one-time affair but rather a continuous process over the preceding few years, a point noted by FEL as well (see Mehran et al. 1996). If the occasion of devaluation is shifted from January 1, 1994, to just six months earlier, then the effective exporter devaluation was 16 percent. If shifted to mid-1992, the devaluation for exporters was a high 35 percent. Since the discussion is about the loss in competitiveness of Asian economies post-1993, the exact timing of when prior to January 1, 1994, is of relatively little consequence.

While the free falling Indonesian rupiah makes these thirty something devaluations insignificant, it should be emphasized that such devaluation magnitudes historically are high. India devalued by only 20 percent in 1991, and that was considered far-reaching. Further, as shown in Table 5.2, this Chinese devaluation was in the context of either stable or appreciating exchange rates in Southeast Asia. Thus, the IMF-FEL argument that the devaluation via unification of China's exchange rate was insignificant is in gross error.

There are other problems with the argument that the Chinese devaluation is insignificant. Both the IMF and FEL are completely silent on the effects of the Chinese devaluation on Chinese imports and its trade surplus. For imports, the official devaluation of 50 percent was equal to the actual devaluation, with predictable effects. Proper beggar-thy-neighbor policies entail an increase in trade surplus which comes about not only through large gains in exports but also via smaller growth in imports. And as shown in Table 5.5, import growth collapsed and trade surpluses zoomed in China in the post-1993 devaluation period.

Left unanswered by the two defenders (IMF and FEL) of the thesis that the Chinese devaluation was irrelevant for the East Asian crisis is yet another question. There is the somewhat surprising claim that devaluation had no effect on China's competitors. This claim is substantiated by noting that the East Asian economies did not lose much market share. The relevant question is not whether East Asian economies maintained their market share, but what would have happened to their market share if China had not devalued. And few people (economists or otherwise) argue that China's emergence as a major world player did not affect the profit and volume of its competitors imports.

In any case, Table 5.6 reports on trade data for China and its competitors. As argued correctly by FEL, the preferred data to be used is recipient country data reported in IMF's Direction of Trade Statistics. In its presentation of data, however, FEL make a gross error. They argue that "it makes economic sense to combine China and Hong Kong trade data (even before the handover) because it is conceptually difficult to differentiate between the contributions of Chinese and Hong Kong firms" (FEL: 7). FEL also cite Krugman (1997) to support their absurd reasoning: "Krugman also argues that we should combine China and Hong Kong, on the grounds that conceptually, it is like separating the trade statistics for New York city and the rest of the United States." The FEL-Krugman argument is less than convincing. Even for data after the June 1997 handover, it is not clear that the trade statistics for China and Hong Kong should be combined. The two regions have different exchange rate regimes, different costs, different tax structures, and different comparative advantages.

Did China Receive Most Favored Exporter Status?

Table 5.6 reports the annualized growth rates for exports for various countries and regions for the periods 1990–1995 and 1995–1997. (Trade growth started slowing in 1995; hence the use of that year as a cut-off point. The results are indifferent to the choice of the cut-off year. Since the crisis is dated after June 1997, the 1997 data is taken for the first two quarters only.) For the whole period 1990–1997, Chinese exports to industrialized countries grew at an average rate of 15.5 percent per annum, in contrast to the 13.5 percent growth registered by the ASEAN-4 countries and the 11.4 percent growth of the ASEAN-7. The period 1995–1997 saw a decline in world trade growth; all regions were affected. China's exports to the United States grew by 8 percent during these two years, ASEAN-7 registered a growth rate of less than 1 percent, and Japanese exports declined by 2.4 percent.

Data on imports show that Chinese devaluation and Chinese policy were hurting exporters in the rest of the world. Chinese imports from industrialized countries declined by 6 percent during 1995–1997. In contrast, ASEAN-7 countries increased their imports by 1.4 percent. The net effect of a devaluation, or a mercantilist policy, shows up in trade surpluses. Since the 1985 Plaza agreement, U.S. policymakers have been obsessed with the large trade surpluses that mercantilist Japan has been able to enjoy.

TABLE 5.6   Trade Between Various Countries

	Exports			Imports		
	1990	Change 1990-95	Change 1995-97	1990	Change 1990-95	Change 1995-97
Exports to and Imports from Industrialised Countries						
China	44.7	20.7	6.9	21.1	20.5	-5.5
Greater China	70.0	15.9	5.0	53.4	17.5	-1.9
India	12.3	10.4	5.9	13.5	7.9	0.5
ASEAN-4	62.3	13.6	5.6	52.0	15.4	5.5
ASEAN-7	179.0	9.9	2.6	162.4	13.4	1.4
Japan	183.4	4.5	-1.9	102.1	5.5	-0.2
Exports to and Imports from the United States						
China	16.3	21.8	7.9	4.8	17.9	-0.5
Greater China	26.2	16.3	5.3	11.6	16.0	1.1
India	3.4	11.5	8.3	2.5	5.6	5.6
ASEAN-4	18.4	18.0	2.7	10.8	15.9	11.3
ASEAN-7	71.7	10.2	0.7	44.8	12.6	5.1
Japan	93.1	6.2	-2.4	48.6	5.6	2.2

Notes: Change is in percentage points; all other figures are in U.S. billion dollars. Greater China includes mainland China and Hong Kong. All figures are from recepient country data. ASEAN-4 includes Indonesia, Malaysia, the Philippines, and Thailand. ASEAN-7 includes ASEAN-4 countries plus Korea, Singapore, and Taiwan.

However, the political economy of U.S-China relations dictated that the United States actually encourage the development of equally large trade surpluses for China. In 1997 China's trade surplus with the world was $111 billion in comparison to Japan's $150 billion. Chinese trade, at $415 billion, was a little more than half of Japan's $770 billion. In 1990 China's trade surplus was only $40 billion compared to Japan's $100 billion. In striking contrast, China's trade surplus with the United States in 1997 was almost equal to the so-called horrendous figure for Japan—$45 billion vs. $54 billion. The ASEAN-7 countries, with almost a third higher volume of trade, registered only a quarter of the surplus ($32 billion) enjoyed by China. Stated differently, China's trade surplus with the United States was twice that of the ASEAN-7 countries in 1997. These figures suggest that the IMF-FEL conclusion about the irrelevance of Chinese devaluation may be questionable.

TABLE 5.6   (continued)

	Trade Balance 1990	Trade Balance 1990-95 Avg.	Trade Balance 1995-97 Avg.
Trade Balance			
China	39.7	59.2	98.6
Greater China	7.8	-7.7	-13.5
India	-2.0	0.1	0.4
ASEAN-4	8.0	11.3	12.7
ASEAN-7	19.3	19.3	19.5
Japan	101.9	153.6	157.8
Trade Balance with Industrialised Countries			
China	23.6	43.7	79.7
Greater China	16.7	20.7	39.9
India	-1.1	1.4	1.9
ASEAN-4	10.3	12.6	12.2
ASEAN-7	16.6	-0.5	-17.9
Japan	81.3	95.4	85.2
Trade Balance with the United States			
China	11.5	22.8	41.5
Greater China	14.6	23.0	37.1
India	0.9	2.1	3.2
ASEAN-4	7.6	13.9	20.2
ASEAN-7	26.9	29.0	32.6
Japan	44.5	56.2	55.8

Chinese Devaluation and Competitiveness: Crisis Foretold?

If Chinese devaluation was important, then one can surmise that the East Asian economies would want to regain their competitiveness with devaluations with regard to the yuan. Table 5.7 presents data on different estimates of currency overvaluation for various countries in June 1997. Also reported is a column on expected competitive devaluation. The results are revealing. The actual devaluation that occurred is close to that predicted for most countries. Only Indonesia, where politics induced capital flight and panic, and the Philippines are off predicted targets. The fair value for Thailand is 37, for Taiwan 35, for Malaysia 3.7, and for Korea 1061. The fact that the actual exchange rates today are close to these levels suggests that domestic policymakers in the East Asian economies were aware of how much they were hurt by the Chinese devaluation. Through the crisis, did they

TABLE 5.7   Chinese Devaluation and Competitiveness: Crisis Foretold

	Exchange Rate 1990	Exch. Rate June 1997	Exch. Rate June 1998	Fair Value, June 1997			Percent devaluation expected in June 1997	Percent devaluation actual June 98 / June 97
				Inflation (PPP) Adjusted	Inflation & Productivity Adjusted	Adjusted for China under-valuation 1991-1993		
India	18.1	35.8	42.4	40.1	52.5	57.8	61.4	18.4
Indonesia	1901	2431	14500	2722	3069	3376	38.9	496.5
Philippines	28	26.4	41.8	37.8	54.1	59.5	125.8	58.6
Malaysia	2.7	2.5	4.1	2.9	3.4	3.7	47.7	64.2
Thailand	25.3	24.9	42.2	29.5	33.2	36.5	46.7	69.5
Korea	716	886	1373	854	965	1061	19.8	55
Singapore	1.7	1.4	1.7	1.7	1.9	2.1	49.2	18.2
Taiwan	27.2	27.8	34.4	27.7	31.8	35	25.9	23.8
Japan	134	114	139	127	170		48.6	21.2

Notes: Exchange Rates are end-period values. Adjustment for China's 1991-1993 undervaluation assumes that the yuan was undervalued by 10 percent during these years, relative to the East Asian economies. In reality, its relative undervaluation was close to 20-40 percent during this period (see Table 4.3).

Sources: IMF International Financial Statistics; O[x]us Research & Investments Database.

conduct their own Plaza agreement? The Taiwanese government, in announcing that it was loosening its stranglehold on the Taiwanese dollar in late 1997, cited "competitiveness" as a major element in their changed outlook.

Why Did the East Asian Economies React via a Crisis?

What are policymakers (especially of export-oriented economies) to do when they are competed out of markets by their big neighbor? They can complain to the international authorities about a genuine non-level playing field, but for political reasons (the U.S.-China bond) this was not possible. The other alternative was to devalue. But this would have met with wrath from foreign investors, or from other neighbors, about not playing by the rules. So the policymakers looked for a convenient excuse (provided by the genuine Thai baht problem) to let go and stop managing overvalued and stable exchange rates, willfully choosing volatility and depreciation today for prosperity tomorrow. The miracle of good Southeast Asian policymaking continues to be pragmatic, respecting not dictating market forces.

It is this response to an unfair China and to an equally myopic United States that may have been the driving force behind the readjustment of Asian currencies in 1997. Simply put, if China would not revalue, the rest of the currencies would devalue. It would have been a lot simpler if China had played by the rules and perhaps grown at only 9 percent per annum rather than 13 percent.

India and the Crisis of 1997

Why Did India Escape the Crisis?

India and the rest of South Asia escaped the crisis of 1997, but they were not left untouched. There were several factors which made this reality predictable. After examining why India was able to avoid a currency crisis, this part of the paper considers the new political environment in India, the future of economic reforms, the implications of India's nuclear explosions, and future growth prospects.

At the time the crisis started in Thailand in early July 1997, the position of the Indian economy was as follows: economic growth had averaged above 7 percent in each of the previous three years , inflation had declined to the 4-6 percent range, and exports in the previous three years had grown at an average rate of more than 15 percent per annum (Table 5.8). The rupee was strong at Rs. 35.7 for the past several months, with the Reserve Bank of India continuously intervening to buy dollars.[14] The budget, usually presented on the last day of February and an important policy document containing policies for the fiscal year, had lifted spirits by drastically cutting income tax rates (to a maximum of 30 percent) and corporate tax rates (down to a maximum of 35 percent). Expectations about India finally be-

TABLE 5.8   Indian Economy at a Glance

	Average 1985-89	1990	1991	1992	1993
Macro Variables					
GDP-growth	6.1	5.4	0.8	5.3	6.2
Inflation-CPI	7.8	13.7	13.1	8.0	8.6
Inflation-WPI	6.5	10.3	13.7	10.1	8.4
Fiscal Deficit (% GDP)	-8.4	-8.3	-5.9	-5.7	-7.4
Current A/c Deficit (% GDP)	-2.2	-3.2	-0.4	-1.8	-0.5
Savings / GDP	20.8	24.3	22.9	22.0	22.7
Investment / GDP	23.6	27.7	23.4	23.9	23.3
Money Supply (M3) Growth	17.7	15.1	19.3	15.7	18.4
Trade and Debt					
Export Growth	10.4	13.4	-1.7	10.8	10.2
Import Growth	6.2	15.1	-13.6	15.5	-3.5
World Export Growth	10.4	13.8	3.0	7.3	-0.2
Total Debt / Export					
Total Debt / GNP					
Short-term / Total Debt					
Capital Flows					
Foreign Institutional Investment Inflows (US $ billion)			0.0	0.0	2.05
Foreign Direct Investment Inflows (US $ billion)			0.13	0.32	0.59
Exchange Rates					
Correct "Fair" Currency O/V		28.2	13.3	20.2	14.2
Correct "Fair" Exchange Rate		25.2	29.8	32.9	36.6
Incorrect "Fair" Currency O/V		30.4	9.4	12.4	0.8
Incorrect "Fair" Exchange Rate		26.0	28.5	29.9	31.6
Exchange Rate	14.0	18.1	25.8	26.2	31.4
Stock Market					
Stock Index (Sensex)	784	1275	2125	2630	3689
Stock Index ($)	55.5	70.5	82.2	100.4	117.6
Ratio (Predicted / Actual)		0.0	44.4	52.8	83.6

Notes: All values are end-of-period data. 1998 figures are as of June 1998. Incorrect "Fair" Exchange Rate adjusts for inflation differences, while Correct "Fair" Exchange Rate corrects for both inflation and productivity differences. Predicted Stock Index for years after the base period (end-December 1990) is obtained as follows: Predicted Index = Base Index + Nominal GDP Growth + 0.5 (Real GDP Growth). All are percentage changes unless otherwise stated.

TABLE 5.8   (continued)

	1994	1995	1996	1997	1998
Macro Variables					
GDP-growth	7.8	7.0	7.5	5.0	
Inflation-CPI	9.5	10.1	9.4	8.3	
Inflation-WPI	10.9	7.7	6.4	5.0	8.0
Fiscal Deficit (% GDP)	-6.1	-5.4	-5.2	-6.1	
Current A/c Deficit (% GDP)	-1.1	-1.8	-1.0	-1.5	
Savings / GDP	25.6	25.3	26.1		
Investment / GDP	26.9	27.1	27.3		
Money Supply (M3) Growth	22.3	13.7	15.9	17.2	17.5
Trade and Debt					
Export Growth	16.3	22.7	7.4	2.6	
Import Growth	17.9	28.6	8.3	8.0	
World Export Growth	13.8	20.3	3.4	3.9	
Total Debt / Export	253.8	201.2	170.8		
Total Debt / GNP	34.2	28.2	25.6		
Short-term / Total Debt	4.2	5.4	7.5		
Capital Flows					
Foreign Institutional Investment					
Inflows (US $ billion)	1.74	2.07	1.95	1.0	
Foreign Direct Investment					
Inflows (US $ billion)	1.31	2.13	2.7	3.0	
Exchange Rates					
Correct "Fair" Currency O/V	23.3	22.1	26.6	25.9	27.1
Correct "Fair" Exchange Rate	40.9	45.2	48.9	52.9	58.1
Incorrect "Fair" Currency O/V	7.0	2.9	6.4	3.2	2.8
Incorrect "Fair" Exchange Rate	33.7	36.2	38.3	40.5	43.6
Exchange Rate	31.4	35.2	35.9	39.2	42.4
Stock Market					
Stock Index (Sensex)	3927	3110	3085	3707	3231
Stock Index ($)	125.2	88.4	86.0	94.5	76.3
Ratio (Predicted / Actual)	61.8	8.5	-9.8	-7.2	-24.9

Sources: Various.

coming a magnet for both foreign and domestic investment were crystallizing. The assumption was that India would be a safe haven relative to East Asia.

The status quo in India continued (as it did in East Asia excluding Thailand) until well after the early July 1997 Thai devaluation. The stock market peaked at 4600 in August, falling back to 3200 at the end of end July 1998. The Indian stock market was mildly affected by the extension of the Asian Crisis in November 1997, and the rupee depreciated by a paltry 10 percent by end-December. The stock market ended 1997 at 3700, up more than 20 percent for the year. There was little evidence of any contagion from East Asia, where declines in currency and stock markets were closer to 50 percent.

Exchange Rate Non-Market in India

There are several reasons why India avoided the crisis. However, all the explanations have a common thread: India is still, in 1998, one of the more closed economies in the world, and its exchange rate is heavily controlled by the government. Indeed, the closest parallel to the Indian exchange rate regime is that prevailing in China.[15] Any change in the exchange rate only takes place if the government wants it so. A speculative run is simply not possible.

That the Indian exchange rate is market determined is a myth perpetrated by the Indian government. The reality is that there is nothing market about the Indian rupee. Flows outward on capital account are not allowed, period. For example, the Foreign Institutional Investors have invested more than $9 billion as portfolio investments in India, but these investments are not allowed to be hedged. Debt investments total less than a billion dollars and have only recently been allowed to be hedged. External corporate borrowings are controlled (rationed) by the Ministry of Finance. Outflows by domestic residents are not allowed—indeed (and this law is undergoing change), any illegal foreign exchange transactions are considered a criminal offense!

Thus, the foreign exchange market operates exclusively on the basis of current account transactions. There are a number of small current account players, and a few big players. All the latter happen to be part of the government—commodity importers, oil importers, and other state monopolies. The largest bank—State Bank of India—is 55 percent owned by the government. By allocating or delaying its purchases and by instructing the banks when to enter or not enter the market, the central bank is able to control all movements in the exchange rate. With hardly any players, and foreign exchange dealers not allowed to speculate even for a micro-second (the dealer has to match a buyer with a seller for each transaction), the central bank is in complete control. The rupee moves only when dictated by the authorities to do so. Hence, the *ex-ante* and conventional wisdom notion that the rupee would be unaffected by the crisis turned out to be correct.

The exchange rate has been the holiest of sacred cows in superstitious India. This is another reason why India was unlikely to be affected by the dollar storm in East Asia. The intellectual climate was (and is) in favor of a artificially strong currency. Mr. Chidambaram, ordinarily a reform-oriented Finance Minister, was vehemently against any devaluation of the currency because he felt such changes would induce loss in elections.[16] Further, in striking contrast to the East Asian economies and other export engines, the debate in India, in 1997 and today, is whether exchange rates matter in affecting exports.[17]

It is naïve, however, to think that the Indian markets and economy are unaffected by external developments. While interest rates and foreign exchange are heavily controlled, both are increasingly becoming less so. Further, the all important stock market (capitalization of $125 billion) has become the residual shock absorber in the system. This also shows up in data on volatility. Until June 1997, the Indian market had the highest volatility and the lowest returns among most emerging markets (Bhalla 1998a). If investors believe the rupee is going to depreciate, they first sell the stock market since hedging of currency exposure is prohibited.

Are Movements in the Controlled India
Exchange Rate Predictable?

The rupee has changed in value, but it has done so because government officials wanted it to move in a specific direction and of specific magnitude. The reaction function of the authorities is known: it is to keep the rupee at the same real exchange rate as it was in March 1993, when the dual exchange rate was removed and the rupee unified. The data contained in Table 5.8 and Figure 5.2 suggests that the management of the exchange rate in India since 1991 has been reasonably predictable. At no time has the government allowed the real exchange rate (adjusted only for inflation differential with the United States and not for any productivity differentials) to exceed 15 percent. Generally, it has been kept within a narrow plus or minus 5 percent band. (Note that all calculations are on a PPP basis via the United States, with the average 1993 value as the base. This is close to the official view which uses March 1993 as the reference). It also is the case, however, that the government has not been too keen to undervalue the currency a la the Japanese and Chinese models of growth.

While the valuation at present vis-à-vis the U.S. dollar is equal to the rate predicted by inflation adjustments, it is another matter whether Indian exports can compete in a market severely affected by the East Asian devaluations. Further, whether the authorities are convinced about the importance of productivity changes affecting currency values remains to be seen. According to Table 5.8, the Indian rupee is at present 25 percent overvalued, using the "correct" method of adjusting exchange rates for both inflation and productivity growth. However, if a synthetic consumer price index is used to adjust the outdated CPI index, the rupee's fair value is close to 44.

FIGURE 5.2 Indian Rupee Exchange Rate, January 1993–June 1998

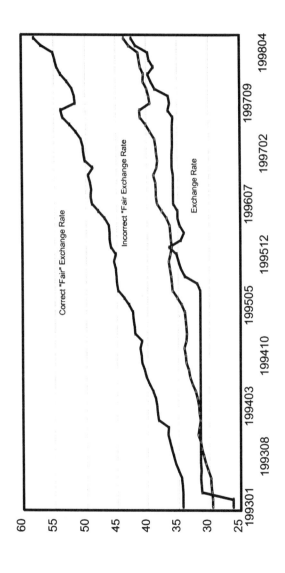

Notes: Dates are indicated in year-month; that is, 199301 represents January 1993. Incorrect "Fair" Exchange Rate adjusts for inflation differences, while Correct "Fair" Exchange Rate corrects for both inflation and productivity differences.

Indian Stock Market: Going Nowhere for Seven Years

One of the striking features of the Indian stock market is that it literally has gone nowhere during the last seven years in dollar terms and the last six in nominal local currency terms. The end of year data reported in Table 5.1 tells this rather unusual story. After the financial crisis, East Asian stock markets collapsed. The Indian debacle seems part of an continuous process. What makes this performance unusual is that genuine economic reforms have taken place since 1991: the economy is a lot more open, and the growth rate seems to have entered a new structural higher level. Yet even in nominal terms the market is moribund. Why?

Part of the explanation has to be the over-regulated nature of the Indian stock market. As part of its economic reforms, the government set up the Securities and Exchange Board of India (SEBI) in 1993. This watch-dog has brought about some good, such as greater disclosure, and a lot of bad. The rules enacted seem to specialize in actions that are particularly anti-market and anti-performance. For example, the largest mutual fund, United Trust of India, is owned by the government and is allowed to guarantee returns on an absolute basis—e.g., you can invest in an equity mutual fund and be guaranteed 14 percent return per year. Last year, another government owned fund operated by Canara Bank went bust and had to be bailed out with taxpayers' money. Yet the regulator (SEBI) insists that guaranteed returns are here to stay because the Indian people desire it! Notions of moral hazard (why perform if the government is guaranteed to provide a bailout?) are not unknown in India. A second example of mindless regulation is even more in cuckoo land: portfolio managers are *prohibited* from charging fees based on performance!

The above examples are just the tip of an iceberg, but they illustrate why confidence in the stock market and in mutual funds is low. From mobilizing more than 20 percent of household savings in 1991, the mutual fund industry has mobilized less than 5 percent in each of the last three years. The investor has left the market, which is contrary to the experience of most, if not all, stock markets in the world in the 1990s—at least until the East Asian crisis!

Economic Reforms: Past Is Future

Indian economic reforms came of age in response to the foreign exchange crisis of 1990–1991. An economist and non-politician, Dr. Manmohan Singh, was appointed as Finance Minister. Dr. Singh instituted far-reaching, and for India radical, economic reforms. This was not necessarily an easy task since opposition to economic reforms had been well entrenched in democratic India. Reforms have been slow, not because of the lack of will or knowledge, but more because leftist politicians in India, and other rent-seeking policymakers, have continued to stall reforms. One of the lasting legacies of Manmohan Singh's tenure as Finance

Minister was the bringing to prominence of technocrats in the Ministry of Finance and the Reserve Bank of India. This "team of excellence," headed by Oxford educated Montek Singh Ahluwalia, has been effectively in charge of policymaking since 1991, first with Manmohan Singh (Congress) and later with P. Chidambaram (Congress and then United Front) as Finance Minister and now (to date) working under the new Bharatiya Janata Party Finance Minister, Mr. Yashwant Sinha.

This feature of economic reforms in India is common to that observed in most developing economies today—Western educated technocrats, above suspicion, politics, and corruption, guiding policymaking with a rational market touch. The role of the team in providing Indian politicians with a rational market framework should not be underestimated. Nor should the profound changing of the mind-set that has taken place be ignored. The presence of the team has ensured that the abundant political instability in India has not been able to have too profound a negative effect on the economy.

Does the Bharatiya Janata Party (BJP) Represent a New Era?

The 1998 elections resulted in a truly non-Congress government at the helm of affairs for the first time since independence in 1947. India has had other non-Congress governments in the past—1977 to 1980, 1989 to 1990, and 1995 to 1997. But on all three occasions, the government in power was just the Congress with another name, not another face. The Bharatiya Janata Party (BJP) won the most recent elections in February 1998. In many ways it is the antithesis of Congress. Their victory is also not likely to be a one-shot event. Indeed, the political equation has changed from the Congress being the dominant party fighting a disunited opposition, to the BJP being the center-of-gravity fighting against a disunited Congress-led opposition. The days of the present BJP government may be numbered, but the future will definitely have the BJP as a major player.

All this is not necessarily good news for those who believe in either social or economic liberalism. The BJP has been on a collision course with Indian Muslims (who number over 100 million, or about 12 percent of the population) since its inception; their raison d'être has been Hindutva, or Hindu Raj (Hindu rule). In a country that prides itself on secularism, this rabble rousing has not been music to the ears for many Indians, regardless of religion.

The correct description of the BJP is that it is a fundamentalist party. Not unlike the Taliban, it believes in cultural and religious purity. In Delhi University, the BJP-led students union has banned the on-campus drinking of Pepsi and Coke. A recent ordinance banning the wearing of skirts by schoolgirls has fortunately been overturned. Their are ongoing attempts to cleanse TV of "bad" Western influences. Government-run schools in the largest state in the country, Uttar Pradesh, are required begin roll call with patriotic songs. Political correctness is mandatory for being appointed a scholar at the Indian Council for Historical Research. The list is endless.

Apart from social and religious fundamentalism, the BJP has offered a new version of economic correctness—*swadeshi* policies. Swadeshi means "of the home country," and this policy intends that domestic industry should be favored and foreign industry excluded. It is a fact that the illiberal economic policies of the Congress from 1947 to 1990 also favored the rent-seeking import substitution "in the name of the poor" model. But India did change course in 1991, and it is troublesome that in the internet 1990s there is advocacy for the bullock cart age and a step back to confused de rigiste policies. For example, the BJP slogan is "computer chips, yes; potato chips, no." No recognition is given to the fact that production of potato chips leads to greater employment of the poor than computer chips, or that both may be in India's comparative advantage. It is this extremism in all areas that makes the BJP a right wing party with a difference. It is correct to call it a Hindu fundamentalist party, with little difference with Christian or Muslim fundamentalist parties elsewhere in the world.

All this might suggest that the Indian economy, and polity, is doomed under BJP raj. This would be incorrect and unduly pessimistic. For even within the BJP, and ostensibly from the Prime Minister Mr. Atal Behari Vajpayee downwards, there are large non-fundamentalist elements. The tension between the two wings is not unlike that found within the pro- and anti-choice elements within the Republican Party in the United States or, until recently, between the socialist and liberal elements within England's Labour Party.

It was this Jekyll and Hyde behavior that was manifested in the utterly confused premier BJP budget presented on June 1, 1998. India has the highest nominal tariffs (average tariff equal to 40 percent) in the world. These were increased by a further 8 percent, and later, in response to almost universal criticism, retracted to "only" a 4 percent increase! The budget was also the first Indian policy document to call openly for privatization of government enterprises and for the opening up of the insurance sector. There were other Jekyll-Hyde signatures as well. All in all, it was a thoroughly confused budget which faithfully reflected the fundamentalist-reform constituencies of the BJP.

Whose budget document was it? It is unlikely that the Ministry of Finance was in charge. The same team of excellence has been involved in seven prior budgets, and done so under three governments, without any glaring inconsistencies. More than likely the budget was made in the Home Ministry under Mr. L. K. Advani, the fundamental representative of the extreme Hindu-nationalist faction within the BJP.

The fact that the premier BJP budget was met with stinging criticism suggests that the reform process is now entrenched in the Indian psyche. There was a clear dichotomy in the reception—applause for the reform components and extreme condemnation for the anti-reform elements. The liberal team of excellence is still in place, though no one knows for how long. And the anti-reform budget makers have been pushed, perhaps only temporarily, into the background. This suggests that economic reforms in India will continue, with or without the BJP.

India Goes Nuclear

Only two months after it assumed power, the BJP government exploded an atomic bomb on May 11, 1998, following with two more blasts on May 13. This came as a shock to almost all Indians. What was even more shocking was the fact that no Indian political party criticized the blasts. Ever the calculators, the political opposition felt the explosions would be politically popular. Only after the wearing off of the initial euphoria did the opposition begin to criticize the timing of the blasts, not asking the important question of why the blasts in the first place.

Why did the BJP explode the bomb? Several explanations abound, but the most satisfactory one remains that it was part of their agenda, part of their manifesto, and part of their vision of what constitutes a strong India. Also, this explosion served to demarcate BJP politically from the now reformist and liberal Congress, further emphasizing the signature of BJP as a nationalist Hindu party. The fact that the major short-term loser was the BJP's enemy, a Muslim Pakistan, was an additional plus. However, by forcing Pakistan to also explode the bomb, the BJP may have revealed naïveté—two unequal nations, India and Pakistan, are now more equal than before. An unintended side benefit of BJP machismo may well be a more nuclear free-world as both India and Pakistan sign the Comprehensive Test Ban Treaty over the next few months.

Economic Sanctions: Do They Work?

The explosion of the bombs automatically brought into force the U.S. Glenn Amendment—the unilateral imposition of economic sanctions by the United States. The use of such sanctions is a several decades-old policy of the United States. Researchers at the International Institute of Economics (Hufbauer et al. 1998), have provided a detailed study of the effects of economic sanctions. They conclude in an executive summary published on the Internet in January 1998:

> Of 115 cases of economic sanctions between World War I and 1990, we judged 34 percent to be at least partially successful. These cases include instances of multilateral sanctions and they include sanctioners other than the United States. The objective is to provide as comprehensive an analysis of sanctions as possible. Comparing the economic and political circumstances across these episodes, we found that sanctions tend to be most effective when:
> - The goal is relatively modest.
> - The target is much smaller than the country imposing sanctions.

- The sender and target are friendly toward one another and conduct substantial trade.
- The sanctions are imposed quickly and decisively to maximize impact.
- The sender avoids high costs to itself.

There is an important caveat to this general story. Economic sanctions proved far more useful in contributing to foreign policy goals prior to 1973, when they had a 44 percent success rate. Of 59 cases initiated between 1973 and 1990, only 14 (24 percent) resulted in at least a partial success even though the number of cases involving modest policy goals soared. Among other things, this can be attributed to the declining dominance in the world economy of the United States, which has been by far the most frequent user of economic sanctions (77 of 115 cases).

The authors also suggest that sanctions can only achieve limited goals, are generally ineffective if other countries do not go along ("without significant co-operation from its allies, a sender country stands little chance of achieving success in cases involving high policy goals"), are most effective if the targeted country is politically and/or economically weak, and if the costs to the sanctioned country are high (upwards of 2.5 percent of GDP).

A cursory examination of the data would suggest that U.S. economic sanctions are unlikely to succeed in India. India is a large country, has political stability and a relatively robust economy, and possesses friends such as Russia and England who are willing to counter the United States. Moreover, the sanctions exact only minimal economic costs, at most $3 billion or about 1 percent of GDP. Even the $3 billion figure is an overestimate of the cost since India has a large body of rich emigrants who are expected to send remittances via purchases of attractively priced bonds.[18]

An equally cursory examination of data for Pakistan would suggest the opposite: sanctions should bite. Prior to atomic explosions in May, Pakistan had foreign exchange reserves of only a few weeks of imports. Close to $10 billion dollars were held in non-resident Pakistani accounts. Today, Pakistan is technically at default on these obligations since it has suspended all repayments.

So will sanctions work? The preliminary, and perhaps hasty, conclusion is that they already have worked in the case of Pakistan. The economic collapse of Pakistan was hastened, and made inevitable, by the imposition of sanctions. Negotiations are presently underway, and it would be surprising if Pakistan does not sign the CTBT in the next few months. Until that happens, arguments of symmetry would suggest that economic sanctions will be lifted vis-à-vis India.

Thus, with regard to India, there is what economists call an identification problem. Sanctions were not expected to bite, and they are biting even less because the Pakistan economy is in the doldrums. Attempts to salvage it will mean a Nelson's eye towards sanctions on the part of the United States and the international organizations it influences such as the World Bank and the International

Monetary Fund. The true test of the efficacy of sanctions on India would occur if Pakistan signs the CTBT and India does not.

What are the chances that India will not sign or at minimum accept a *de facto* agreement to the terms of the CTBT? Small. Presently, the political opposition is arguing that it would be anti-national to sign the CTBT. This is the biggest indicator that sanctions are working, even in India. The opposition realizes that the surest way for the government to fall is if BJP refuses to sign the CTBT and plunges India into likely economic chaos. Will BJP fall for the bait? Unlikely.

The world today is more against nuclear experiments than it was even four years ago when China exploded a nuclear device. It is quite likely that sentiment among investors would sour if India were not to sign the CTBT. The expected rate of return to investments will likely fall, and there is likely to be a significant outflow of capital, notwithstanding any high cost NRI contributions. Once sentiment turns, and both domestic and internationally owned capital outflow starts, there is relatively little that the Indian government can do to change the tide. It is unlikely that India will not sign the CTBT. If it does not, the hypothesis of the sanctions hurting will be tested.

Political Instability Does Not Matter

The conventional wisdom is that political instability is bad for the economy. In its most recent survey of investment houses, *Asia Pacific Consensus Forecasts* (July 13, 1998) reports that the most unfavorable factor affecting the economic prospects of India was "political uncertainty," followed by international sanctions and the Asian crisis. There is a different, more compelling view. Political instability is actually *good* for economic reform. The contention is that lack of political dominance means that politicians in power will make the extra reform in order to fight for marginal votes in a future election. And if political stability is present, the politicians are unlikely to make the effort because of their inherent shortsightedness.

There are four pieces of evidence to support this unconventional view. First, the Narasimha Rao–Manmohan Singh reforms were undertaken by a minority government amidst considerable political and economic uncertainty in 1991. Second, once Narasimha Rao got comfortable with a majority, the reforms stopped. Third, the United Front (UF) government undertook significant reforms with the political disadvantage of two prime ministers in eighteen months (1995–1997). Among the reform achievements of the UF were: tax reform with a reduction in the maximum rate on personal taxes to only 30 percent; rationalization of the pricing of the important oil sector; movement, albeit painfully slow, towards privatization of the bloated and inefficient state sector; deregulation of interest rates such that only rates of fifteen days and below are now regulated by the central bank; and movement towards capital account convertibility starting with the opening up of gold imports.

The previous section documented the Jekyll and Hyde nature of the BJP government on the issue of economic reforms. It was also noted that while regression is present, in net terms the economic reforms are moving forward and in some important areas (privatization, opening of the insurance sector) are even accelerating. The BJP leads an eighteen-party coalition; by most definitions, the future of this government is highly uncertain. Yet reforms are continuing. This is the fourth piece of evidence supporting the argument that political instability does not hurt economic reforms or economic growth.

It is an open question whether the BJP government will last. What can be said with relative certainty is that implementation of economic reforms will not be a causal factor in its demise. Indeed, such reforms may be its only asset. The leading opposition party, Congress, openly supports speedy economic reforms. Thus, the future prospects for the Indian economy are extremely good, even though dark political uncertainty may cloud one's vision.

Medium-Term Prospects for the Indian Economy

In each of the last three years (1994–1996), the Indian economy registered a growth rate above 7 percent. Last year (1997–1998) economic growth slowed to only a 5.1 percent rate. The question arises—is India headed back to a floundering growth rate of 4-5 percent, or can 7 percent and higher be expected and sustained?

The relevant benchmark for growth rates is the *potential* growth rate. In Bhalla (1997c) a model is developed which relates the provision of economic freedom with economic growth in a large cross-section of countries. This model extends the estimates contained in Bhalla (1992), where it was argued that the determining factor for explaining differences in growth rates in developing countries was the provision of freedom in each country. Freedom was separated into its two components (economic and political) and it was observed that economic freedom was the more important variable.

Some of the more important variables affecting economic growth are those representing the state of the financial market: black market premium on the currency, which reflects the extent to which capital account liberalization is present in the economy, and the level of real interest rates in an economy (too low real interest rates are just as bad as too high real interest rates). Also important are variables representing the openness of the economy, such as magnitude of import tax rates. These variables are contained, among several others, in Gwartney-Lawson-Block, *Economic Freedom in the World, 1975–1995*. Bhalla (1997c) uses some of these components to construct a sub-index of economic freedom without endogenous variables like money supply growth and fiscal deficits. Regression results verify that healthy financial markets (and economic freedom) positively affect economic growth. If India were to undertake the financial sector reforms proposed in RBI (1997), a document which lays out the "roadmap" for capital account convertibility over the next three years, then the annual growth rate would, according to the estimated model, increase by 1.2 percent a year. In other words, if the pre-reform base is 6.5 percent, this would mean a potential growth rate of 7.7 percent per year.

Needed: Financial Sector Reforms

One of the important lessons from the East Asian crisis is the significance of the health of the financial sector. As was noted, a wrong view of exchange rate markets led to the miracle economies losing their tiger status, albeit temporarily. It is not an exaggeration to claim that the financial markets in India are the most ignored sector. Prominent policymakers seem blissfully unaware of the dangers of managing exchange rates and wanting large doses of foreign capital; of not recognizing that a primary reason for the Indian economy not taking off, and reverting back to growth recession, is the abnormally high level of real interest rates (upwards of 10 percent). Further, that the stock market is generally a good, and leading, indicator of the problems facing the economy and the financial sector. That without a financial crisis, stock market values in India are no different than they were in 1991 is a shocking and disturbing statistic.

Some of the priorities of the Indian government are as follows: a large need for infrastructure financing; the inflow of foreign equity capital; lower cost for domestic corporates; and a more flexible exchange rate regime, with hedging costs borne by firms and individuals and not subsidized by the government. Possible remedies include: deregulation of the banking sector; its privatization; movement towards open market operations; and competition in fund management. Further, mergers of banks should be allowed. The goal should be to allow capital to seek its highest level, both domestically and abroad.

There is an all important hurdle to economic and financial sector reforms in India. It is the judicial sector. Notions of good corporate governance have not yet reached the judiciary. It is widely, perhaps universally, viewed as extremely corrupt. Cases languish in courts for years; stay orders stay stayed forever. Lenders of money cannot recollect, which is one reason why real borrowing rates for non-blue chip institutions and individuals is upwards of 15 percent. The future of judicial reforms is uncertain, but it cannot get worse.

Conclusions

What caused the East Asian crisis of 1997? Chinese exchange rate and associated trade policies were found to have been a major contributory factor of the crisis, along with the misguided managed exchange rate policies of East Asian economies. Several alternative hypothesis for the crisis (from Japanese devaluation to asset bubbles) were also examined and found wanting. *A simple application of competitive exchange rate behavior was not only able to forecast the crisis but also to come close to the magnitude of devaluation that actually did occur* (excepting, of course, Indonesia and the normal over-kill that occurs with structural adjustment of exchange rate policies).

The other major objective of this paper was the documentation of the political economy of the mercantilist exchange rate policies followed by China. The close association of the United States and other industrialized countries, along with multilateral institutions like the IMF and the World Bank, with Chinese economic policies made mercantilism possible and the East Asian crisis inevitable.

Several implications for exchange rate policies in developing countries follow from the analysis of the crisis. First, the movement towards capital account convertibility in developing countries is inexorable and inevitable, notwithstanding the spirited opposition of the World Bank's chief economist, Stiglitz (1998), and as quoted in Meuhring (1998). Most Asian, Latin American, and Eastern European nations have their currencies significantly more convertible today than in June 1997, the date prior to the onset of the crisis. Even India is now more open on the capital account than it was a year ago. Second—and regardless of the evidence provided in this paper or elsewhere—the stark reality is that financial markets, and policymakers around the world including China and the United States, take for granted that the Chinese devaluation of end-1993 was important in generating the crisis of 1997. The common belief is that the East Asian crisis would take a significant turn for the worse if the Chinese were to devalue anytime soon. Not only does this study agree with major policy wonks and financial markets, but it also contends that prior to June 1997, the Chinese yuan was significantly *undervalued* with respect to the dollar and the East Asian economies. Today, the yuan is still undervalued, but by only 5 percent. Consequently, there is little economic reason for the Chinese yuan to devalue in the near future.

This forecast of "no devaluation" of the Chinese yuan incorporates political realities. (The Hong Kong peg is a different issue, and the Chinese may under the guise of exchange rate unification again devalue the Hong Kong dollar to the dollar-yuan rate of 8.3 from the 7.75 HKD/US at present.) International politics, particularly those involving the United States, are an important force in determining exchange rate policies in developing countries. And it is precisely an extension of this politics which leads to the conclusion that China will not devalue as a quid-pro-quo to the United States for allowing it to pursue a mercantilist policy in the 1990s.

Other implications also follow from this forecast. Without a Chinese devaluation, the East Asian economies will be able to recover faster and the world will move towards a more level playing field. Capital account convertibility will accelerate, and bring with it reduced real interest rates and higher growth in developing countries. And all without the imposition of old-new schemes to control capital flows (Tobin tax) and without new global institutions to supplant or replace the IMF.

A large part of the analysis centers around the proposition that the regime of fixed, quasi-fixed, managed, or fuzzy-logic exchange rate regimes was at the core of the problem. If a flexible exchange rate regime had been in place, problems would still occur—they always do. Nevertheless, under such a regime, problems would have been sorted out on a continuous basis by the markets. And policy-makers would have countered the problem with market-friendly responses. In other words, problems would not have converted themselves into crisis.

This two-cause hypothesis is an *ex-post* one, and one that does not exclude other contributory factors. Property price booms played a role, as did nepotism, over-borrowing, and excessive bureaucratic control. However, note that the impact of each of the above contributory causes (they are actually *effects* of bad policies) would have been lessened, if not non-existent, if exchange rates were flexibly market determined.

One way to understand the consequences of the East Asian crisis is to examine the reasons certain countries did not catch the flu. India did not catch the flu because it had not been allowed to breathe the air of free capital. Foreign exchange controls were extreme, and the government was in complete control. Another reason for India being relatively unaffected is because the economic fundamentals were sound. Ever since the rejection of the anachronistic, closed, and over-regulated regime, India has been on an upward trajectory. Politics have taken a back seat as the lasting legacy of the reforms initiated by former Finance Minister and technocrat, Mr. Manmohan Singh. This phenomenon is not unique to India. During the last decade, most developing countries have allowed technocracy to overrule bad politicians. Indeed, if one looks at the economic technocrats in most countries, one can obtain a reasonably accurate estimate of the growth rate and reforms. The reward in India has been steady and high growth of over 7 percent per annum for the last three years (excluding last year's 5.1 percent) and 6.5 percent for the last six years. With population growth at 2 percent, per capita income growth has recorded a continuous growth of over 4.5 percent per annum—reasonably good given that the economy had basked in the glory of a 3.5 percent Hindu aggregate and a 1 percent per capita growth rate for most of the forty-year period between 1950 and 1990.

This good economic performance has been achieved in spite of considerable political uncertainty. Evidence was offered to suggest that such uncertainty is not problematic for growth; indeed, political uncertainty may actually speed the process of economic reform by making politicians answer the demands of the people. This hypothesis finds support in both directions—i.e., stable governments are found to get comfortable and reform less, while unstable governments get uncomfortable and reform more.

Notes

I would like to thank Montek Ahluwalia, Karl Jackson, T.N. Srinivasan, and Arvind Virmani for comments and discussion. Comments by SAIS seminar participants, as well as those attending an ICRIER seminar on "Exchange Rates and Chinese Competitiveness" were extremely useful. I am thankful for excellent research assistance of Arindom Mookerjee and Suraj Saigal.

1. For example, the Malaysian ringgit appreciated by 10 percent during 1991–1992; the Korean won by 5 percent during 1994–1995; and the Philippine peso by over 10 percent from 1993 to 1996.

2. A managed exchange rate does not mean that there is zero risk. Soon after the Mexican crisis, Wall Street firms (along with the IMF) set up research cells to monitor and forecast event risk. Several models of exchange rate collapse were estimated, yet they all individually, and collectively, failed to forecast the godzilla of all collapses.

3. This self-regulation aspect is important in the context of the present debate on restricting capital flows or imposing a Tobin tax. These regulations are only necessary if a managed exchange rate is considered preferable, a policy which has few takers after the East Asian crisis.

4. Finance ministers, in India and elsewhere, are fond of saying that they do not lose sleep over the workings of the stock market. There is also Paul Samuelson's famous line about the stock market having forecast nine of the last six recessions.

5. A portion of short-term loans (less than one year) also likely ended up more in fixed investment than in the property market. Unless the bank sat on the inflows, the only outlets were construction activity, real estate "speculation," and physical investment.

6. It is a moot question whether senior managers know more or less than yuppie traders about what the determinants of growth are in an emerging economy. What is clear is that both are heavily influenced by the latest fashion (literally) on Wall Street.

7. Where is the next crisis? History maybe repeating itself with capital flowing into Brazil with 46 percent short-term rates and a managed exchange rate.

8. The Feldstein argument is that one measure of capital integration across economies is the amount of correlation between domestic savings and domestic investment. If correlation is large, then the capital account is relatively closed. If the correlation is small, then the capital account is relatively open. After controlling for co-integration, it is observed that the Feldstein conclusion of high correlation is rejected. Indeed, the hypothesis that the correlation became zero in the 1990s cannot be rejected. This means that capital account liberalization allows capital to seek the highest return—something that is consistent with higher, not lower, growth.

9. In Bhalla (1998b) a model of export growth in developing countries was estimated for the period 1980–1996. Preliminary results suggest that the elasticity of exports with respect to relative prices increased, and the elasticity with respect to world income declined, for the time-period 1990 to 1996 compared to the earlier period 1980–1989. This econometric evidence is consistent with the conventional view that pricing became all important in the 1990s.

10. The IMF failed to act with regard to Japan's trade surpluses, and it failed again with China's surpluses. Both failures had the same rationale: the United States wished otherwise.

11. The definition of mercantilism, as offered by Webster's, fits China's exchange rate policy: "An economic system developing during the decay of feudalism to unify and increase the power and especially the monetary wealth of a nation by strict governmental regulation of the entire national economy usually through policies designed to secure an accumulation of bullion, a favorable balance of trade, the development of agriculture and manufactures, and the establishment of foreign trading monopolies."

12. According to Hu-Khan, the productivity growth for the 1979–1994 period was 3.7; it was 5.8 percent for the latest five-year period, 1990–1994. Half the GDP per capita growth yields 4 percent for 1979–1994, and 4.5 per cent for the 1990–1994 period.

13. This suggests that the "China devaluation was not important" commentators just don't get it. If all market participants agree that the devaluation was super important, of what relevance is an academic debate?

14. Bhalla (1997b) argued at the end of July 1997 that the Indian currency was the strongest currency in the world and did not deserve the honor. The rupee began to depreciate three weeks later.

15. But there are important differences as documented earlier. Most importantly, the Chinese have persistently believed in undervaluing their currency, something not possible in a more politically open economy like India.

16. It is another story, and a matter of record, that Mr. Chidambaram's party, the United Front, lost the elections that took place in March 1998. Exports have also fallen precipitously to a growth rate of less than 5 percent for the second consecutive year.

17. This is not that outlandish, especially when compared to the editorials in the *Wall Street Journal*. Recall that just after the Mexican devaluation of end 1994, the *Journal* consistently argued that the pre-devaluation exchange rate was appropriate, especially since Mexican exports were growing at above 15 percent per annum.

18. Five-year bonds priced at 250 basis points over corresponding U.S. treasuries are just being issued by the government-owned State Bank of India. Only non-resident Indians are allowed to purchase these bonds; the targeted volume is $2 billion, though they are likely to garner over $5 billion.

References

Alesina, Alberto et. al. 1992. "Political Instability and Economic Growth." *NBER Working Paper*. No. 4173. Boston.

Bank of Thailand. 1997. "Thailand, The Right Medicine for Recovery." Advertisement in *World Magazines* (October).

Barro, Robert J. 1991. "Economic Growth in a Cross Section of Countries." *Quarterly Journal Of Economics* (May): 407-43.

Barro, Robert J., and Jong-Wha Lee. 1993. "International Comparisons of Educational Attainment." *Journal of Monetary Economics* (December).

Barro, Robert J., and Sala-i-Martin. 1990. "Economic Growth and Convergence Across the United States." *NBER Working Paper*. July.

C. Fred Bergsten. 1997. "The Asian Monetary Crisis: Proposed Remedies," prepared remarks to the U.S. House of Representatives Committee on Banking and Financial Services, November 13.

Bhalla, Surjit S. 1992. "Freedom and Economic Growth: A Virtuous Cycle?" In *Democracy's Victory and Crisis: Nobel Symposium 1994*, ed . Axel Hadenius. New York: Cambridge University Press, 1997.

——. 1994. "Update on Mexico," Deutsche Bank. December 19.

——. 1995. "China and the Yuan: Medium Term Prospects," Deutsche Bank. April 12.

——. 1997a. "When will the Thai baht float? Waiting for Godot, Armageddon or the inevitable?" Paper presented at conference on "Investing and Trading in Emerging Market Currencies," in New York, June 19-20.

——. 1997b. "Exports Burn while Delhi Fiddles." *Economic Times* (July 28).

——. 1997c. "Economic Freedom and Growth Miracles : India is Next." Paper prepared for panel discussion on "South Asia: The Next Miracle?" at World Bank - IMF Annual Meeting in Hong Kong.

——. 1997d. "Money Markets and Madness." *Economic Times* (November 3).

——. 1997e. "The BJP Choice—Is it Right?" *Business Standard* (November 21).

——. 1997f. "Eureka: KAC and the Laws of Flotation." Paper prepared for World Bank conference on "India: A financial Sector for the 21st Century," in Goa, India, December.

——. 1998a. "What Ails the Indian Stock Market?" Speech given at Fourth Annual Seminar on the Mutual Fund Industry, UTI Institute of Capital Markets & Association of Mutual Funds in Mumbai, India, July.

——. 1998b. "Exchange Rates and Chinese Competitiveness: Implications for Emerging Economies." Paper presented at ICRIER in New Delhi, India, July 25.

Developing Trends. 1997a. Oxus Research and Investments. New Delhi, India. Vol. 1, No. 1 (January 6).

——. 1997b. "Rupee and Indian Exports - Facts and Fancy." Oxus Research and Investments. New Delhi, India. Vol. 1., Nos. 5 and 6 (September 2).

Dornbusch, Rudiger, and Alejandro Werner. 1994. "Mexico: Stabilization, Reform, and No Growth." *BPEA* 1: 253-97.

Economist. 1997. "China's Currency: Sign of Success." December 13.

——. 1998. "Frozen Miracle—A survey of East Asian Economies." March 7.

Elliott, Kimberly Ann. 1997. "Evidence on the Costs and Benefits of Economic Sanctions." Prepared remarks to the U.S. House of Representatives Commitee on Ways and Means, Subcommittee on Trade, October.

Fernald, John, Hali Edison, and Prakash Loungani. 1998. "Was China the First Domino? Assessing Links between China and the Rest of Emerging Asia." Board of Governors of the Federal Reserve System, International Finance Discussion Paper No. 604, March 1998. Referenced in text as FEL.

Feldstein, M., and C. Horioka. 1980. "Domestic Saving and International Capital Flows." *Economic Journal*.

Feldstein, M., and P. Bacchetta. 1991. "National Saving and International Investment." In *The Economics of Saving*, eds. J. Shoven and D. Bernheim. Chicago: University of Chicago Press.

Friedman, Milton. 1962. *Capitalism and Freedom*. Chicago: University of Chicago Press.

Gastil, Raymond D. 1987. *Freedom in the World*. New York: Freedom House.

Gwartney, James, Robert Lawson, and Walter Block. 1996. "Economic Freedom of the World 1975-1995." The Fraser Institute, Canada.

Hayek, Friedrich. 1944. *The Road to Serfdom.* Chicago: University of Chicago Press.

Hu, F. Zuliu, and Mohsin S. Khan. 1997. "Why is China growing so fast?" IMF Staff Papers, Vol. 44, No.1 (March).

Hufbauer, Gary Clyde, Jefferey J. Schott, and Kimberly Ann Elliott. 1990. *Economic Sanctions Reconsidered: History and Current Policy.* 2nd ed. Washington, DC: Institute for International Economics, 1990. Also, Executive Summary, 1998.

International Monetary Fund, 1997. *International Financial Statistics.* CD-ROM. September.

————. 1997. *World Economic Outlook.* September.

————. 1997. *World Economic Outlook.* December.

Jackson, Karl D. 1997. "Thailand: The Crash of '97 and its Aftermath." Draft manuscript. Global Alliances, Inc.

Journal of Monetary Economics. 1993. "Special issue on National Policies and Economic Growth: A World Bank Conference." December.

Khan, Mohsin S., and Carmen M. Reinhart, eds. 1995, *Capital Flows in the APEC Region.* IMF Occasional Paper No. 122. Washington, DC: IMF, March.

Krugman, Paul. 1994. "The Myth of Asia's Miracle," *Foreign Affairs* 73(6): 62-78.

————. 1997. "The East in the Red: A Balanced view of China's Trade." *Slate Magazine,* July 17.

————. 1998. "Will Asia Bounce Back?" Speech for Credit Suisse First Boston, Hong Kong, March.

Makin, John H. 1997. "Two New Paradigms." Washington, DC: American Enterprise Institute, October.

Mathieson, Donald J., and Lilians Rojas-Suarez. 1993. *Liberalization of the Capital Account: Experiences and Issues.* IMF Occasional Paper No. 103. March.

Mehran, H. et al. 1996. *Monetary and Exchange System Reforms in China: An Experiment in Gradualism.* IMF Occasional Paper No. 141. September.

Muehring, Kevin. 1998. "House Divided." *Institutional Investor.* May.

Quirk, Peter J., and Owen Evans. 1995. *Capital Account Convertibility: Review of Experience and Implications for IMF Policies.* IMF Occasional Paper No. 131. October.

RBI. 1997. *Report of the Committee on Capital Account Convertibility.* Chairman: S.S.Tarapore. Mumbai, India: Reserve Bank of India.

Sachs, Jeffrey. 1998. "The Asian Financial Crisis: Lesson for India." Paper presented at National Council for Applied Economic Research, New Delhi, India, January.

Scully, Gerald W. 1998. "The Institutional Framework and Economic Development." *Journal of Political Economy,* Vol. 96, No. 3.

Scully, Gerald W., and Daniel J. Slottje. 1991. "Ranking economic liberty across countries." *Public Choice,* No. 69.

So, John J., and Sanjay Kulatunga. 1998. *The Long Hot Summer.* Hong Kong: Jardine Fleming Securities, April.

Stiglitz, Joseph. 1998, "The East Asian Crisis and Its Implications for India." Commemorative Lecture for the Golden Jubilee Year Celebration of Industrial Finance Corporation of India, New Delhi, May 19.

Tseng, Wanda et al. 1994. *Economic Reform in China: A New Phase.* IMF Occasional Paper No. 114. November.

World Bank. 1991. *World Development Report 1991: The Challenge of Development.* Washington, DC: World Bank.

———. 1993. *The East Asian Miracle: Economic Growth and Public Policy.* Policy Research Report. Washington, DC: World Bank. July.

———. 1994. "Lessons from the East Asian NICs: A Contrarian View." *European Economic Review* 38(3-4): 964-73.

———. 1997. "China 2020: Development Challenges In the New Century." China 2020 Series. Washington, DC: World Bank. September.

———. 1997. *World Development Report 1997: The State in a Changing World.* Washington, DC: World Bank.

———. 1998. *The East Asia Crisis: The World Bank Group's Response.* Discussion Draft. Washington, DC: World Bank. March 24.

6

The Financial Crisis in South Korea:
Anatomy and Policy Imperatives

Hak K. Pyo

Introduction

Contrary to earlier speculation that the current crisis in Southeast Asia would not generate much contagion, the crisis did spread to Northeast Asia. By the end of November 1997, currencies in Korea and Taiwan had declined significantly together with the yen. There had been wide speculation that Hong Kong would delink its currency from the U.S. dollar, a prospect that sent the Hong Kong dollar tumbling and interest rates soaring. During the four months after the breakdown of the Thai currency, stock prices in Hong Kong, Taiwan, and Korea declined as much as 20 to 30 percent of peak values. The Asia crisis circled the globe, hitting Wall Street on October 23, 1997, when the stock markets in Hong Kong and Tokyo also stumbled with the expectation that the slowdown in East Asia would hurt the earnings of U.S. companies that had been selling to the region. The World Bank had joined the International Monetary Fund (IMF) to help solve the currency crisis in East Asia. However, there was a great deal of uncertainty as to how long it would continue and how much slowdown it would generate.

In South Korea, which had often been called the model economy or the front-runner of the "Asian Miracle," seven out of the nation's top thirty conglomerates (*chaebol*), including Kia Motors Group, filed for court-mediated protection or court-ordered receivership by October 1997. (For a summary of the South Korean economy from 1991 to 1997, see Table 6.1.) During the twelve-month period between the end of 1996 and the end of 1997, the average stock price index tumbled from 833.4 to 654.5 and the Korean won weakened against the U.S. dollar from 844.2 won per dollar to 1,415.2 won per dollar, a 67.7 percent depreciation. In fact, there had been a three-year advance signal of trouble in Korean stock market: the stock price index started falling in 1994 from its high of 1,027. In economies, which are capital hungry and have inflexible exchange rates, the stock market is a proxy for the weakness of the currency because it indicates that people are already leaving paper assets for liquid ones.[1] There was widespread speculation that one or two more major conglomerates could file bankruptcy and the won-dollar rate could go beyond the level of 2,000 won per dollar before the year's end. Indeed, the won-dollar rate rose to the level of 2,000 won per dollar at one point during December 1997. The "Asian Miracle" really seemed like a mirage.

Indeed it took less than four months for a financial crisis in Thailand to sweep through East Asia and finally land in South Korea. On August 11, 1997, Thailand was pledged $16 billion in loans in a rescue package led by the IMF and Japan; on October 8, Indonesia asked the IMF for a $10 billion emergency bailout; and finally on December 3, a $57 billion IMF rescue package was unveiled for South Korea. The South Korea bailout was a record package in terms of its magnitude, which was bigger than the $51 billion rescue of Mexico in 1995. It included $21 billion in IMF loans, a $10 billion World Bank loan, a $20 billion back-up loan put up by major industrial nations (including $10 billion by Japan and $5 billion by the United States), and other loans such as one provided by the Asian Development Bank.

The announcement of the IMF-led bailout, however, did not reverse the flight of foreign capital. The investment climate became more pessimistic, even after the presidential election on December 18 in which the opposition party candidate, Kim Dae Jung, was elected by less than a 2 percent margin. The Seoul stock market continued to fall together with the won, which was down at one point to a level of 2,000 won per dollar. It was contrary to the expectation of both the IMF and the U.S. Treasury, which thought that most of the $57 billion may not be even needed if the rescue plan rebuilt the confidence of international banks and global investors in the Korean market. As the meltdown continued, as much as $1 billion per day was flown out of South Korea. With the initiative of Treasury Secretary Rubin, large U.S. banks and major banks in Japan and Europe agreed to help Korean banks and firms avoid default by extending most of the $10 billion short-term loans falling due by early January 1998. It was followed by the IMF's early disbursement of a $2 billion loan, the World Bank's early disbursement of a $3 billion loan, and a commitment by thirteen industrial nations to lend the Bank of Korea an additional $8 billion more quickly than scheduled.

While South Korea managed to avoid sovereign insolvency at last year's end, the financial turmoil continued through the first quarter of 1998. It was reported by *Hankook Ilbo* (December 24, 1997) that a total of $12 billion in debt was coming due in January 1998 and a further $8 billion in February. The *Washington Post* (December 30, 1997) reported that there was about $28 billion in short-term loans due by February 28, 1998. March is the final month of the Japanese fiscal year, therefore, the Japanese banks could call in their loans to South Korea, reported to be around $24 billion. According to the Ministry of Finance and Economy, which released newly compiled statistics of foreign debt on December 30, 1997, South

TABLE 6.1   Major Economic Indicators: Korean Economy (1991–1997)

	1991	1992	1993	1994	1995	1996	1997
Per Capita Income (US $)	6,745	6,988	7,484	8,467	10,037	10,543	9,511
Real GNP Growth (%)	9.1	5.0	5.8	8.4	8.7	6.9	5.5
Gross Savings Rate (%)	36.1	34.9	35.2	35.4	36.2	34.8	34.6
Real Consumption (Private Consumption) (%)	9.3 (9.5)	6.8 (6.6)	5.3 (5.7)	7.0 (7.6)	7.2 (8.3)	6.9 (6.5)	3.5 (3.1)
Real Investment (%)	12.6	-0.8	5.2	11.8	11.7	7.1	-3.5
Nominal Wage (%)	17.0	15.0	12.2	12.7	11.2	11.9	8.1
Consumer Price (%)	9.3	4.5	5.8	5.6	4.7	4.9	6.6
Current Account Deficit (US$ bil.)	-8.7	-4.5	0.4	-4.5	-8.9	-23.7	-8.6
Export Growth (%)	10.5	6.6	7.3	16.8	30.3	3.7	5.0
Import Growth (%)	16.7	0.3	2.5	22.1	32.0	11.3	-3.8
Stock Price Index (1/7/80 = 100)	610.9	678.4	866.2	1027.4	882.9	651.2	376.3

Sources: Korean Ministry of Finance, *Monthly Economy*, April 1998; the Bank of Korea, National Accounts 1996 (preliminary), May 21, 1998.

Korea's total foreign debt outstanding as of December 29, 1997, was $153 billion, composed of $80.2 in billion short-term debt with maturity less than a year and $72.8 billion in long-term debt. The short-term debt was composed of $54.6 billion by banking institutions ($12.9 billion by domestic banks, $15 billion by their branch offices abroad, $9.5 billion by off-shore loans, and $17.2 billion by foreign banks in Korea) and $25.6 billion by domestic firms. Following World Bank guidelines for compiling debt statistics, it did not include corporate overseas loans not guaranteed by domestic banks. According to *Hankook Ilbo* (February 12,

1998), the total amount of corporate short-term foreign debt not subject to debt-restructuring negotiation with creditor banks was estimated to be about $40 billion. It was $24.7 billion as of the end of 1997. The total amount of foreign debt by Korean firms' overseas subsidiaries was reported to be $51.4 billion as of June 30, 1997: of this amount, $22 billion from domestic banks' foreign offices and $29.4 billion from foreign banks.

With such a large amount of debt-overhang, it will be very difficult for South Korea to regain growth momentum unless it succeeds in rescheduling its short-term debts and in going through drastic reform measures as mandated by the IMF. Because the interest rate being charged to the rescheduled short-term loans by creditor banks ranges between LIBOR+2.22 percent and LIBOR+2.75 percent and the current LIBOR rate is about 5.6 percent, an average rate of 8 percent can be assumed. If this is true, then the estimated interest payments to foreign debt in 1998 alone would amount to $20 billion: $12.2 billion by debtor banks, $3.2 billion by firms, and $4.8 billion by the Bank of Korea and other public sectors—assuming that Korea's current loan outstanding is about $60 billion, including IMF loans and government bonds. It is exactly this debt-overhang which has created widespread bankruptcies, massive unemployment, and social unrest with increasing income disparity during the first four months under IMF austerity programs.

According to more recent debt statistics confirmed by both the Korean government and the IMF, the total foreign debt increased by almost three times from $42.8 billion ($18.5 billion short-term and $24.3 billion long-term) at the end of 1992 to $120.8 billion ($51.3 billion short-term and $69.5 billion long-term) as of the end of 1997. During the same five-year period, the amount of Korean assets abroad increased from $31.7 billion to $65.1 billion. Thus, the net foreign liability increased by almost five times from $11.1 billion to $55.7 billion. This astounding increase in both total debt and net liability within one single term of presidency is unprecedented and calls for much more explanation than a simple failure of economic management or a simple model of moral hazzard.

IMF programs designed to solve such a financial crisis usually mandate domestic austerity programs and further liberalization of the financial sector. The stand-by agreement made between the Korean government and the IMF on December 3, 1997, was no exception. It was intended to reduce the current account deficit to below 1 percent of GDP in 1998 and 1999, to contain the inflation rate at or below 5 percent, and to aim at a much slower rate (3 percent) of growth in real GDP in 1998 and move toward a potential recovery in 1999. The core goal of the IMF programs was to reduce domestic credit and money supply drastically so that the domestic banks and finance companies that could not meet the BIS standard would have to close down. South Korea managed to follow these austerity measures as closely as possible during the first four months by forming a tripartite committee among the government, business leaders, and labor unions to build a consensus on the required reform measures.

The overall economic performance seems to be one of overreaction. While there was a $6.9 billion current account surplus during the first two months of 1998, the inflation rate was likely to be around 10 percent and the GDP growth rate could be lower than 3 percent, as massive bankruptcies and unemployment started to spread. Criticisms emerged, from both inside and outside the country, on the validity of the IMF austerity programs.

Against this background, the purpose of this paper is two-fold: first, to analyze the causes of the financial crisis in South Korea; and second, to assess policy imperatives and future prospects. The proposition is advanced that the financial crisis of South Korea was a combined political and economic failure (to some extent, more of a political failure than an economic failure), which could have been prevented if the Korean government was politically strong and economically efficient. A careful reexamination of the drastic changes in global economic fundamentals and domestic social and economic fundamentals provides a relevant anatomy of why the South Korean crisis happened.

After enjoying three decades of its benefits, South Korea is now paying all at once for the cost of late development. However, once a financial crisis of this magnitude with such an astounding amount of short-term debt overhang breaks out, there is almost no other practical alternative except adopting IMF programs. Declaring a debt moratorium, as suggested by Wade and Veneroso (1998), might make more sense in purely economic terms, but it could bring devastating social and political consequences to South Korea—which is still technically at war with North Korea. The best option for the Korean government, which managed to extend the maturity of more than 95 percent of short-term debts to one to three years with its creditor banks within three months after the outbreak of the crisis, seems to be sticking to the IMF programs but adopting much more flexible macroeconomic targets through continuous consultation with the IMF. For example, since the exchange rate has been stabilized at around 1,350 won per dollar at the end of March 1998, the high interest policy imposed by the IMF can be reexamined. The IMF programs, if adopted in an efficient and timely manner, can provide the South Korean economy with a valuable opportunity to overhaul its system, which has been long overdue.

After drawing lessons from the explosion of the financial crisis in South Korea and exploring policy imperatives to preserve growth potentials, two proposals will be outlined to answer the key questions of what changes need to be made in international regimes to deter such a crisis and contain it as soon as possible. I propose the establishment of an International Finance Insurance Corporation as a multinational institution to cover the private risk of short-term international capital flows on a voluntary basis and the creation of a supplementary Asian Monetary Fund within the IMF facilities with Japan playing a due leadership role. The paper concludes with the proposition that it is too premature to discredit the East Asian model entirely.

Dramatic Changes in Economic Fundamentals

In the aftermath of the currency crisis in Southeast Asia, two opposing views have been advanced on the roots of the crisis: one view emphasizes dramatic changes in economic fundamentals and the other attributes the crisis to so-called "sunspots"—the result of self-fulfilling speculative behavior. A consensus is now emerging that some combination of fundamental flaws and self-fulfilling factors must have contributed to the Southeast Asian currency crisis.

In order to identify the roots of the currency crisis and their contagion affecting Asia—including Hong Kong, South Korea, and Taiwan—it is necessary for us to examine some dramatic changes in economic fundamentals around the region. Among many such changes, three developments should be highlighted. First is the continuing depreciation of the yen while Japan's current account surplus accumulates and other trading nations, such as the United States and most East and Southeast Asian nations, are running persistent deficits against Japan. This is the primary disturbing factor in the region, which is heavily dependent on imported intermediate inputs and capital goods from Japan for their export processing. The depreciation of the yen in such a circumstance is like exporting its deflation to other trading partners. South Korea's cumulative trade deficits with Japan since 1965, when bilateral diplomatic relations resumed, reached a total of $138.6 billion by 1997. In 1996 the deficit amount reached $15.7 billion, surpassing the year's total trade deficit by $15.3 billion.

The second development is the rapid integration of commodity and capital markets on a global scale under the World Trade Organization (WTO) system and the resulting change in comparative advantages. In particular, the emergence of China as a new competitor across almost every type of light manufacturing has created rapid, footloose production phenomenon.[2] The inauguration of the WTO system has accelerated the expectation that Southeast Asian manufacturing, based on footloose production with little value-added processing, will lose its competitive edge against China and Vietnam.

The situation in South Korea could be somewhat different because its industrial base is deeper than most Southeast Asian economies and its industrial structure is much more sophisticated than the simple footloose production structure. However, trade liberalization under the WTO system and the accelerated capital market liberalization after the accession to OECD have pushed conglomerates toward excessive diversification and unchecked strategic investments both domestically and abroad. But long before the crisis, Korean conglomerates were already too heavily leveraged. In 1996 the debt-equity ratios of the top thirty chaebols were between 2.5:1 and 85:1. One of the reasons Taiwan is performing relatively better than Korea and Southeast Asian economies is that its small- and medium-sized industries abstained from making excessive strategic investments. In other words, differing market structure has produced differing reactions to a drastically changing global economic environment.

Another major difference between South Korea and Southeast Asian economies lies in the degree of financial market liberalization and the role of foreign direct investment. In January 1992 foreigners were allowed to invest in Korean stocks subject to a limit of 10 percent of any one company's total outstanding shares to all foreign investors, and 3 percent to a single investor. Since then, both the aggregate ceiling and the individual ceiling rose to the level of 20 percent (15 percent in public corporations) and 5 percent respectively. But the degree of openness in the Korean stock market is relatively low compared with other Southeast Asian economies. The opening up of the bond market has been slower than that of the stock market. In July 1994 foreigners were allowed to directly purchase convertible bonds subject to a 30 percent aggregate ceiling for total foreign investment and a 5 percent individual ceiling. International financial organizations were allowed to issue won-denominated bonds in 1996. Even though the Korean government recently accelerated the bond-market opening measures by allowing foreigners' investment in long-term corporate bonds, the degree and speed of financial market liberalization are relatively insignificant. The delayed liberalization in Korean financial markets and the relatively insignificant foreign direct investment may have contributed to avoiding self-fulfilling currency speculations. But they may have caused further distortions in the domestic financial market by raising effective costs of loans and increasing excess demand for unchecked investment loans.

The third dramatic change in economic fundamentals in East Asia is in the political and institutional relationship between government and private enterprise. The rapid export-led growth in East Asia during the last three decades or so has invited rising wages and income disparity between the capitalists and the laborers and between skilled and unskilled labor. The emergence of the urban middle class produced not only demand for a more democratic regime and for more transparent policy making, but also demand for social welfare, better schooling, and higher environmental standards. The net consequence of such demands is an ever-increasing demand for massive investments in social infrastructure. When it is combined with increasing income and desire for higher standards of living, it results in land speculation and excess investments in non-tradable goods, which puts extra pressure on the wage-inflation spiral.

In the face of rampant speculative investments and increasing demand for social and political transparency, the East Asian regimes—which have acted as quasi-internal organizations—have lagged behind in institutional reforms. The protection of domestic oligopolies and conglomerates became much more difficult due to both domestic and foreign factors. Domestically, there were increasing number of opposing interest groups interfering in the quasi-internal organizational relationships between the bureaucrats and the oligarchies. Internationally, trade liberalization under the WTO system and the integration of advanced capital markets with emerging capital markets made it more difficult to bailout troubled companies and manipulate their exchange rates.

We can learn two lessons from the recent turmoil in the Southeast Asian currency markets and its contagion affecting Northeast Asia. First, the fixed exchange rate regime is more vulnerable to currency speculation when economic fundamentals change drastically or when there are self-fulfilling shifts in speculative behavior. As of October 23, 1997, currencies in the region had declined from the end of 1994 as follows: Japan (18.4 percent), Korea (14.2 percent), Taiwan (13.0 percent), Thailand (34.1 percent), and Singapore (8.2 percent). On the other hand, the Hong Kong dollar and the Chinese yuan appreciated during that period by 0.2 percent and 1.96 percent, respectively. When the 10.4 percent plunge in the Hang Seng Index occurred on October 23, 1997, the Hong Kong government pushed interest rates at astronomical levels; at one point Hong Kong's overnight bank rate was as high as 300 percent. The Thai currency crisis may have been due to a delayed currency realignment following drastic change in economic fundamentals. The self-fulfilling speculative attacks on the Southeast Asian currencies may have contributed to the acceleration of the currency crisis, but it came after a prolonged period of worsening current accounts, accelerating inflation, and mounting government deficits. From the above statistics on changes in exchange rates, it should be noted that both the Hong Kong dollar and Chinese yuan might have been overvalued for some time. They might also be subject to the next round of speculative attacks.

The second lesson to be learned from the recent turmoil is that a country's degree of financial liberalization and market-opening measures must be commensurate with the country's industrial competitiveness. In other words, there must be a balance between the financial sector and the real sector. Otherwise, the country's currency can be subject to speculative attacks when the imbalance between the two sectors begins to widen.

There are two reasons why the Korean won was not subject to a self-fulfilling speculative attack when the Thai crisis occurred. One was due to its relatively flexible exchange rate system based on a major-currency basket. Therefore, when the yen depreciated, the won also depreciated (not as much as the yen but at least by proportion of the weight given to the yen). In an earlier paper (Pyo 1996), I proposed giving more weight to the yen in the currency basket for many currencies in East and Southeast Asia. The second reason was the limited openness of Korea's stock and bond markets. As of November 1997, before the breakout of the financial crisis in December 1997, foreign investment in the Korean stock market and bond market had been limited to below 15 percent and 10 percent, respectively. But the crisis came anyway and had in fact been apparent in the Korean stock market since 1994.

Monopolistic Competition
Across Industries and Market Failure

A distinguishing feature of export-led growth in South Korea is its unique industrial structure and corporate governance. The top thirty conglomerates produce over half of Korea's GNP and the top five conglomerates' share reaches one-third of the country's total production. The business groups called chaebol are quite similar to the Japanese zaibatsu, but they are different in the way the subsidiary companies are governed.

The Korean model of economic development is one of monopolistic competition across industries where the government acts as both competition promoter and project monitor. In the literature of industrial organization, a monopolistic competition is usually defined within an industry. It is frequently characterized by the competition among a limited number of firms producing differentiated products. The existence of monopolistic competition is due to scale economies, entry barriers, and discriminating tastes.

In the case of South Korea, the government deliberately has introduced limited competition by lowering entry-barriers over time and by monitoring market failures by major conglomerates. In other words, the government has played the role of competition promoter; and it supervises through government-controlled banks, which are part of quasi-internal organization. In this regard, the system has promoted monopolistic competition across industries. That is the reason why one observes several automobile manufacturers, airlines, oil refineries, semiconductor manufacturers, and so forth in Korea.

Government policy protected bureaucrats from blame by linking them to one or two conglomerates' interest; at the same time, the government provided big conglomerates with irresistible incentives for horizontal diversification. The phenomenon of "too big to be failed" set in, because big conglomerates themselves became stockholders of many financial institutions. And as we know, moral hazard in financial institutions can erode their competitiveness.

But now the model of monopolistic competition across industries is subject to dramatic change both domestically and internationally. First of all, the so-called Lipset phenomenon, which hypothesizes that economic growth in developing countries usually brings about a movement from authoritarianism to democracy, has arrived in the sociopolitical scene of South Korea (Pyo 1993). The country's success in export-led growth has brought about increasing demand for democracy, and the transition from the authoritarian regime to the democratic one has been rather turbulent. The increasing demand for higher wages and benefits by organized labor—at times through violent disputes and strikes—has produced extra burden on firms seeking to restructure and downsize. But most of all, in the face of increasing domestic and foreign competition, some monopolistic competitors carried out a series of ill-fated preemptive strategic investments. In other words, they were obsessed with increasing market share, not the rate of return on their investments.

The Kia Group expanded its automobile production capacity drastically and, at the same time, pursued unchecked vertical integration (Kia Special Metals Co.) and horizontal diversification into construction and financing business. The New Core Group made strategic investment in retail and large merchandise distribution networks in anticipation of domestic conglomerates' and foreign multinationals' entry into retail business. The slow business in retail sales could not pay off the high cost of borrowed funds, resulting in the company's application for court protection.

Many economists watching the recent financial turmoil in South Korea are disturbed that the economy's macroeconomic indicators do not warrant massive market failures. In the middle of continuing won depreciation and stumbling stock prices, the GNP managed to grow at an annual rate of 5.4 percent during the first half of 1997. But it should be noted that the growth rate was significantly lower than in the previous years: 8.4 percent in 1994, 4.6 percent in 1995, and 7.2 percent in 1996. As a result, conglomerates which had higher debt-equity ratio were squeezed out, and the failure of Hanbo Steel Group and Kia Automobile Group caused an even higher ratio of bad loans in total loans outstanding by both banks and other financial intermediaries. In other words, while macroeconomic indicators were seemingly not terribly bad, there were existing serious macroeconomic problems. According to a report released by Fair Trade Commission, the average debt-equity ratio of the top thirty business groups deteriorated drastically from 386.5 percent in 1996 to 518.9 percent in 1997.

One good sign came from the balance of payments side. The current account deficit during the first half of 1997 was cut drastically to $242 million from $1.305 billion dollars during the corresponding period of 1996. Between the first half of 1996 and the first half of 1997, the growth rate of consumer price index declined from 3.3 percent to 2.4 percent and the nominal wage index in all industries also declined from 9.8 percent to 6.3 percent. Therefore, one could have concluded that the South Korean economy was following a typical pattern of slowing down, but not a drastic one that would bring about massive corporate failures in the immediate future. But in the end, there were further corporate failures in the process of reducing speculative bubbles and restructuring across industries by major conglomerates. In short, there was a fundamental weakness in the management of the microeconomy.

Hyundai Group announced in September 1996, before the bankruptcy of Hanbo Group, its intention to enter into steel manufacturing, which had been monopolized by Pohang Steel Co. Considering global market trends toward privatization and deregulation, it was difficult for the government to discourage the entry but it managed to do so. This was another pattern of oligopolistic competition in the steel industry. Many Korean firms in the automobile industry and semiconductor industry tried to put themselves in strategic positions in the global market. They still seem to view that there is increasing demand for their products from emerging markets and transition economies. They regard their products as not necessarily top quality products but as reasonably priced, competitive ones in such markets. Their success or failure will depend on their income-generating capacities, since they have to pay back the interest and principal of loans borrowed from domestic and foreign banks. This game of high-yield and high-risk in strategic markets will determine the substantiality of export-led growth in South Korea.

IMF Programs and Policy Imperatives

There are two issues at hand at this point about the IMF-led South Korea bailout. One is an imminent issue of following up the debt restructuring plan concluded recently between the Korean government and creditor banks. Since there were not enough official resources available from IMF, World Bank, and G-7 countries combined that could replace all the loans coming due, it was inevitable for private creditor banks to come up with a global consensus. Even though banks from different countries have different interests at stake, it is doubtful any bank will pull the plug on the eleventh largest country of the world. The Asian crisis needs to be stopped in Korea. Otherwise, there is no guarantee it will not spill over to Japan, China, and ultimately to Europe and the United States.

Unlike the bailout of Latin debts in the 1980s, in which banks were required to reduce interest charges, none of the banks owed money from Korea is expected to incur such losses because they will receive higher interest rates on the loans being rolled over to compensate for their high risk. In addition, South Korea has a good track record in paying off loans from the IMF, World Bank, and commercial banks in the 1980s. On August 25, 1997, the Korean Minister of Finance and Economy announced the Korean government will ensure the payment of foreign debt liabilities by Korean financial institutions. The new government will honor the announcement and that is why it considers swapping short-term debt with longer-term loans backed by government guarantee. In such a loan restructuring program, it will be most important not to ruin the country's repayment capacity. Excessively high interest rates above the international standard will erode the credibility of the entire package and prolong the vicious circle of debt. In this regard, it would be desirable for the Japanese banks to play a more active role by restructuring their outstanding loans to South Korea: their loan amount is the largest among G-7 countries and they still have the lowest domestic interest rate. It would be self-defeating if Japanese banks tried to rescue their domestic bad loan problem by calling in loans to South Korea.

The second, more long-term issue deals with preserving IMF conditions imposed on South Korea. In the aftermath of the December 3 bailout, there have been criticisms on the validity or sustainability of such conditions. They include Stiglitz (1997), Sachs (1997), and Wade and Veneroso (1998). Arguing that macroeconomic management in many troubled Asian countries is basically sound, they believe IMF conditions are too deflationary. This could ultimately lead to massive social unrest. But in my judgment, their macroeconomic soundness has been overvalued. The built-in interest groups opposed to currency realignment continued their rent-seeking game by monopolizing information on development plans and by maintaining cheap credit lines through government-controlled banks. They sought to pursue higher growth rates at the cost of repressed prices, wages, and interest rates. The resulting domestic distortions brought about currency misalignment, speculative bubbles, and debt overhang. The lack of large amounts of fiscal deficit in many Asian countries can be a misleading indicator of fiscal soundness. The welfare content of their fiscal policies is low if we deduct defense budget from the total budget and if we factor in the frequent subsidies to farmers and local governments.

In this regard, discrediting the entire IMF programs is not warranted. However, there seems to be two improvements that can be made in regards to the implementation of such programs. One is the fact that it does not necessarily have to follow a big-bang approach applied to transitional economies, because these countries have had long history of their own market mechanisms, however imperfect they are. Therefore, there has to be some respect for their endogenous systems. The other is the need for sequencing various reform programs imposed by IMF. For example, in case of South Korea, I think that it would have been more desirable if the first three months could be spent primarily dealing with foreign exchange market. After restoring some confidence in exchange rate by supporting the country's foreign reserve, the IMF reform program could touch upon bank supervision, banking regulations, the role of the central bank, etc., which often require rewriting laws and rules. For example, the mandate for local banks in South Korea to meet the BIS standards within three to six months seems to be too harsh and unrealistic considering the fact that they were governed by different rules over the past four decades. Other macroeconomic guidelines will have to be compatible with the country's intended debt repayment schedule and domestic consumption demand needs not be overly suppressed because the bulk of import demand comes from investment demand rather than consumption demand in many East Asian countries. A timely adjustment was made by IMF recently in cooperation with the Korean government about macro economic targets reflecting the turmoil after the announcement of the December 3 rescue package: allowing a more flexible budget target, reducing the target growth rate of GDP, and increasing inflation target together with the growth rate of money supply.

Regarding a reform package on corporate governance, there has to be more transparency and improvement in accounting practices. But conglomerates should not be discredited entirely because they were sources of comparative advantage in the past, as much as they are current liabilities to their nation. With relatively poor resources and limited technology, they had to maximize economies of scale by diversifying and overextending because they did not possess the power of vertically integrated multinational enterprises. They also had to face a domestic market less than one-tenth of the size enjoyed by Japanese firms. Pyo (1997) describes the success model of Korean development as "monopolistic competition across industries," where the government promoted competition and monitored performance. Dissolving chaebols in Korea will not solve the debt crisis, and it may cripple permanently its debt servicing capacity and momentum for sustainable future growth. Dissolving the conglomerates may also endanger property rights, a core principle allowing entrepreneurship for export-led growth.

Warning System and a
Supplementary Regional Arrangement

From the recent profile of resolving the financial crisis in East Asia, we can learn two lessons: the importance of maintaining a workable early warning system and the need for creating a supplementary regional arrangement. Both of these lessons need to be considered further.

Warning System for Currency Crisis

One of the reasons South Koreans have been so frustrated with the outbreak of the current financial crisis is because, up until the very end of November 1997, there had been no warning from either the government or the private sector —including the news media—on the impending crisis. Even though the Southeast Asian currency crisis started from early August 1997, the Korean government announced repeatedly that there would be little spill-over to Korea and that its economic fundamentals remained sound. Such announcements were made repeatedly by the Deputy Prime Minister of Finance and Economy and the president of the Bank of Korea during the October Annual IMF-World Bank Meeting in Hong Kong. The improvement in the balance of payments during the year's second quarter may have invited optimism among policymakers, leading them to ignore the stock of short-term debt and the possibility of a run on the stock market and foreign exchange market. To some extent, the failure of catching early warning signals by international investors and institutions should also be noted, even though the IMF reportedly started warning Korean authorities after the major turbulence in stock markets of Hong Kong, Seoul, and Tokyo on October 23.

In retrospect, the failure of predicting and detecting both the timing and the magnitude of contagion effects from Southeast Asian markets to South Korea within and outside the country raises a serious issue. Even though there have been voluminous studies on the range of indicators that may provide warning for currency crisis—as surveyed in Kaminsky, Lizondo, and Reinhart (1997) and Boughton (1997)—neither models based on "economic fundamentals" nor models based on "sunspots" succeeded in predicting the contagion to Northeast Asia. A combination of the two approaches—known as the "signals" approach proposed by Kaminsky, Lizondo, and Reinhart (1997)—suggests such variables as output, exports, deviations of the real exchange rate from trend, equity prices, and the ratio of broad money to gross intentional reserves may have promise. But this approach has not yet been institutionalized or widely used by policy authorities. Looking back at the profile of the South Korean crisis, it would have been difficult to predict the crisis based solely on these indicators. The sudden drop in equity prices preceded the currency crisis but almost simultaneously, leaving little time for policy authorities and investors to react. But we must note that the Korean stock market index continued to fall from the peak of 1,027 in 1994, to 882 in 1995, and 651 in 1996. It was a failure of Korean policy authorities to ignore such a continued downfall in the stock price for over a three-year time-span.

As pointed out in Pyo (1997), the Korean exchange rate system had maintained a major currency-basket system with a narrow band so that when yen was depreciated, won was also depreciated—not as much as yen, but at least by the proportion of the weight given to yen. When the baht crisis broke out and other dollar-pegged Southeast Asian currencies started to fall, it must have been comforting to the Korean authorities to have maintained such a partially flexible exchange rate system. But as it turned out in the aftermath of the Southeast Asian crisis, such a partially flexible exchange rate system was not sufficient to stabilize the foreign exchange market.

What is more important than whether there is a fixed exchange rate system or a flexible exchange rate system is whether—as evidenced in the relatively strong external positions and sustained growth performance in China, Hong Kong, Taiwan, and Singapore during the current East Asia turmoil—the country's absolute magnitude of short-term foreign debt can be managed with existing usable foreign reserves in face of a massive potential calling-in of short-term loans and a run on foreign investment in local stock and bond market. As of December 3, 1997, when the $57 billion IMF rescue plan was formally announced in Seoul, the Korean stock market and bond market were opened to foreign investment only up to 15 percent and 10 percent, respectively. It must have been equally comforting to the Korean authorities to have such a relatively low degree of openness, possibly misleading them to remain optimistic over the ability of maintaining stability in both the exchange and stock markets. What mattered most was not the relative magnitude of openness and relative indicators such as debt-GDP ratio or the ratio of broad money to gross international reserves, but the term structure of debt and the size of short-term debt.

In summary, the painful experience of the monetary crisis in East Asia calls for an institutionalized system of predicting and detecting such crisis well ahead of time so that both international institutions and the region's respective governments can be prepared and better coordinated. Such system must be based on a modified "signals" approach in which due attention is paid to the absolute amount of short-term foreign debt and foreign investments in domestic stock and bond markets, in addition to the conventional indicators. In other words, what counts at the time of a currency crisis is the sustainability of exchange and stock markets in face of a sudden simultaneous exodus of foreign investments and a continuous calling-in of the short-term loans. We have to pay more attention to the direction of private debt and portfolio investment statistics. For this reason, there should be an institutionalized system of monitoring short-term flows of capital. A system like the Tobin-tax needs to be explored more seriously, a point stressed by Wade and Veneroso (1998).

Personally, I favor a system of voluntary loan insurance in which both lenders and borrowers pay a proportional amount as a partial insurance coverage when it becomes default. This would allow the international institution to compile such statistics. For example, an International Capital Insurance Corporation—similar to International Finance Corporation of the World Bank—could be created jointly by the World Bank and International Monetary Fund.

A Supplementary Regional Arrangement

While there is a momentum of restoring stability in the currency markets of East Asia, the crisis is far from being over. The situation in Indonesia is still volatile due to its political uncertainty, and Thailand is also clouded as massive bankruptcies and unemployment start to spread. The situation in South Korea will critically depend on two outcomes: (1) the debt-rescheduling negotiation with its creditor banks, and (2) the progress in domestic reform programs such as a more flexible lay-off system and restructuring the chaebol system. Depending on the outcome of each country's stability, there could be a new round of currency depreciation in Asia and elsewhere. It will be important to hold the line at the present level of exchange rates.

Under these circumstances, a series of questions have been forwarded about adequacy and sufficiency of IMF-led rescue plans and IMF-mandated reform programs. However, there seems to be no better alternative to the IMF playing the role of monitoring and managing the currency crisis. Japan's proposal for Asia-only facility, an "Asian Monetary Fund" (AMF), was rejected by many countries. Instead, Bergsten (1997) proposed that APEC serve a supplementary facility, noting that IMF credits to any individual country are limited by that country's quota at the Fund—even the unprecedented multiples for Mexico (700 percent of quota) and Thailand (500 percent of quota) produced only one-quarter and one-third of the amounts needed. The $21 billion second bailout effort for South Korea by G-7 countries and the IMF at the end of last year, despite the record amount of the IMF's commitment in the December 3 rescue package ($57 billion), is further evidence of insufficiency of funds. An additional increase in the IMF quota is not likely in the near future, considering objections by the U.S. congress and European countries.

During the debate surrounding the proposed AMF last fall, the IMF reportedly proposed that a regional grouping be created and staffed by its new office in Tokyo. An intermediate solution between the AMF proposal and the IMF's own proposal would be feasible. A supplementary facility can be created within IMF and operated by the Tokyo office in conjunction with the main IMF arrangement. Japan would be a major donor country, but other industrial member countries could join Japan. Such a supplementary facility would enhance the credibility of IMF programs without coming into conflict with the main IMF lending arrangement. Since Japan is still the largest creditor nation in the world and the dominant one in Asia, Japan should be given a more active leadership role in creating such a facility.

Longer Term Prospects

As a front-runner among newly industrializing economies, the South Korean economy is entering a difficult period. First, its new domestic sociopolitical environment makes it difficult for the government to play its traditional role of promoting competition and monitoring market failure. Second, increased foreign competition in the domestic market makes domestic monopolistic competitors' financial structure more vulnerable. Third, in transition to a full market economy, there could be a prolonged period of political instability, a lack of prompt decision making, and an erosion of industrial competitiveness.

For example, the failure of the Hanbo Steel Group was not only a big economic incident but also a tremendous political shock. The ensuing political scandal has almost paralyzed the financial system. The government has come up with temporary measures, such as the Anti-bankruptcy Accord among financial creditors and the Cooperative Loan System, to salvage major conglomerates. But the efficiency of such temporary measures has been questioned by financial institutions. On the other hand, the financial markets are too imperfect for the government to hand off in a short period of time. At present, the Financial Reform Bill—which plans to consolidate various financial supervisory boards into a single unified one and to introduce a more independent central banking system—is pending for deliberation in the National Assembly. Even if the bill is passed, it will take several years to establish new rules of the game.

Under drastically changing sociopolitical conditions at home and global competition abroad, the most important policy agenda is how to introduce an efficient conflict management system. The efficacy of a cabinet system is doubtful, because it will inherently invite more distributive politics than conflict management. A presidential system with more delegated powers to cabinet members would be desirable in guiding the economy from a high-growth path to a more sustainable medium-growth path.

Even though there remains a great deal of uncertainty about the extent and duration of the currency crisis and the stock market turmoil in East Asia, the region still possesses a great deal of potential for further sustained growth and for maintaining a competitive edge against other regions in the world. The emergence of a strong China could be a liability for some economies, but it can be turned into an asset for the region as a whole. South Korea is one of major beneficiaries because, while some industries lost comparative advantage against Chinese industries, others have found an important new market. Many economies in East Asia are still saving at a level above 30 percent and are investing in R&D and educational facilities. There is less likelihood of regional military and religious conflicts. There is a tremendous demand in the region for quality products.

What happens to the South Korean economy has important implications for the future development of East Asia, since the pattern of Korean industrialization will be duplicated by other developing economies, including China. It is also important for the balance of power in Northeast Asia and regional security. Most important of all, a sustainable export-led growth in South Korea will increase the likelihood of a peaceful unification of the Korean Peninsula. As history tells us, economic prosperity in East Asia, including South Korea, will ultimately depend on each society's political capacity and maturity for conflict management in the transition from government intervention to a full-fledged market economy. Continued corruption without political and institutional reform will erode the comparative advantages of a country, while steady progress in such reform puts the economy onto the right track. In this regard, the partial success and partial failure of President Kim to implement political and economic reform in South Korea will provide important lessons for policymakers in East Asia.

Even though there have been arguments suggesting the "East Asian Miracle" is over, it may be premature to discredit the East Asian Model entirely; as yet, there is no better alternative model of development. Viewed from the history of capitalism, there has been no linear progression in the path from underdevelopment to development. Therefore, the current stagnation in Japan and South Korea can be regarded as a self-correcting phase after the unprecedented period of rapid growth during last three decades—at growth rates well above the norms of both OECD and developing countries. Both Japan and South Korea have to restructure their financial sectors to accommodate the current trend of integrating world capital markets. South Korea will have to pay the cost of late development because it could not maintain a prolonged period of balance of payments surplus, as Japan did in the early 1980s before being opened to foreign investment.

It is interesting to note that the period of economic downturn in many East and Southeast Asian countries coincides with the period of weak yen, and the period of economic upturn coincides with the period of yen appreciation. That is the reason developing countries in East Asia should either peg their currencies to yen or at least give more weight to yen in their currency baskets (Pyo 1996). Their economic integration with the Japanese economy usually is deeper than what is normally reflected in bilateral trade weights. In addition, as found by Pyo, Kim, and Cheong (1996) using a computable general equilibrium model, the welfare consequences of WTO impacts can be larger than originally thought. For example, it has invited a preemptive investment run by many conglomerates in the non-tradable sector, thereby contributing to reinforcing bubbles but at the same time aggravating their debt-equity ratio. The recent model of moral hazard by Krugman (1998) suggests all of these are the costs of late development.

Considering the current magnitude of outstanding corporate domestic and foreign debt, South Korea will have to go through a painful process of restructuring both the industrial sector and financial institutions. Unemployment will result on an unprecedented scale. I would predict that it might take at least three years before South Korea can resume a sustainable medium growth path of maintaining 5-7 percent growth rate again, because the average corporate debt-equity ratio needs to be reduced from the current level of 7:1 or 6:1 to the level of 3:1 or 2:1 to restore foreign investors' confidence. But it will take both time and effort in domestic reforms in many areas. Any premature attempt to short-cut this process will only hurt the country's long-term competitiveness. By implementing the IMF mandates, South Korea has to overhaul a system long overdue for correction. The overhaul came in a difficult way and the entire Korean population has had to swallow hard, but South Koreans have succeeded in alleviating absolute poverty in the past and the current struggle with debt overhang is nothing compared to past struggles. In this regard, the more democratic social and political environment created in the past few years will be the biggest asset for the current restructuring and social transformation. South Korea's development will find its own course of navigation through several years of financial turmoil and industrial restructuring.

Notes

I am indebted to Karl Jackson and participants at SAIS Policy Talk Seminar on April 23, 1998, for helpful comments on an earlier draft.

1. I owe this point to Professor Karl Jackson.

2. The manufactures in question are mostly finished consumer goods; clothing, footwear, and electronics predominant. The production processes typically involve the simple assembly of imported raw materials. Because no extensive or highly specialized capital

goods or labor skills are required, these activities are easily expanded in any country where they prove profitable (Caves, Frankel, and Jones 1996:185).

References

Bergsten, C. Fred. 1997. "The Asian Monetary Crisis: Proposed Remedies." Statement before the Committee on Banking and Financial Services, U.S. House of Representatives, November 13.

Boughton, James M. 1997. "From Suez to Tequila: The IMF as Crisis Manager." IMF Working Paper No. 97/90.

Caves, Richard E., Jeffrey A. Frankel, and Ronald W. Jones. 1996. *World Trade and Payments.* 7th ed. New York: Harper Collins.

IMF Survey. 1997. International Monetary Fund (August 18).

Kaminsky, G., S. Lizondo, and C. M. Reinhart. 1997. "Leading Indicators of Currency Crisis." IMF Working Paper No. 97/79.

Krugman, Paul. 1998. "What happened to Asia?" Mimeograph from Paul Krugman home page (January).

Pyo, Hak K. 1997. "Is Export-Led Growth in South Korea Sustainable?" Paper presented at East Asian seminars of East Asian Institute, Columbia University, and Asia Society meetings in Washington D.C., November.

———. 1996. "Sustainability of Export Growth in East and Southeast Asia." Paper prepared for Asian Development Outlook Conference, Asian Development Bank, Manila, November.

———. 1993. "The Transition in the Political Economy of South Korean Development." *Journal of Northeast Asian Studies* (Winter).

Pyo, Hak K., K. H. Kim, and I. Cheong. 1996. "Foreign Import Restrictions, WTO Commitments, and Welfare Effects: The Case of Republic of Korea." *Asian Development Review,* Vol. 14, No. 2. Asian Development Bank.

Sachs, Jeffrey. 1997. "The Wrong Medicine for Asia." *New York Times* (November 4).

Stiglitz, Joseph. 1997. "How to Fix the Asian Economies." *New York Times* (October 31).

Wade, Robert, and Frank Veneroso. 1998. "The Asian Financial Crisis: The High Debt Model and Unrecognized Risk of the IMF Strategy." Working Paper No. 128 (February 14). New York: Russell Sage Foundation.

7

Thailand: From Economic Miracle to Economic Crisis

Richard F. Doner and Ansil Ramsay

Introduction

Thailand has had one of the best records of economic growth of any country in the world since 1960. Between 1985 and 1995 it was the world's fastest growing economy, hailed by several authors as the next Asian NIC. This growth came to an abrupt halt in 1997, and by 1998 Thailand was in the midst of the worst economic crisis in its modern history. Growth rates for 1998 were expected to be minus 5.5 percent, and possibly worse. Business failures and layoffs threw thousands out of work, and unemployment was expected to rise to more than 2.5 million persons by the end of the year (Vatchara 1998:B12).

How did a country which had been so successful in the past get into such difficulties? Our broad answer is that state and private sector institutional arrangements which supported rapid growth in recent decades have proved inadequate to meet the challenges of increasing industrial competition from other newly developing countries and rapid financial liberalization in the late 1990s. The first section of the chapter sketches out the main features of Thai institutional arrangements that led to rapid growth after 1960. The second section explores why these institutional arrangements have not been adequate to meet the challenge of increasing industrial competition from other developing countries. The third section examines why the institutional arrangements led to economic failure in 1998, and the final section examines the prospects for the restoration of sustained growth in the future.

Explaining Past Growth

In broad terms economic growth requires movement through a continuum of increasingly difficult adjustment challenges. At one end is a country's capacity to maintain profitability in existing sectors despite cyclical changes such as domestic or global market gluts. A second stage is the capacity for structural change through diversification by transferring resources to new sectors, industries, or products. Such diversification includes a wide range of structural shifts. These include movement from a monocultural economy to one based on the cultivation and export of several commodities; from cultivation and export of raw materials to their processing and export; from agriculture and mining to manufacturing; from simple assembly of finished consumer goods to manufacture of upstream capital and intermediate inputs; from one industrial sector to several; from manufacture for domestic consumers to production for exports; from export to one market to export for a greater number of more demanding export markets. At the most difficult end of the growth continuum is the capacity to develop global competitiveness in new and higher value-added activities. Here the objective is not simply to shift into and expand exports in new sectors, but to increase local capacity for product development. By the early 1990s the Thai economy had expanded rapidly up this ladder. There was considerable diversification of agriculture, the economy as a whole had shifted from agriculture to services, manufacturing activities had become more diversified, and manufactured goods had risen from 6 percent of Thai exports in 1965 to 65 percent in 1990 (Doner and Ramsay 1996:4-6).

The origins of this growth can be located in a set of institutional arrangements that grew out of political conflicts in Thailand in the late 1950s. Field Marshal Sarit Thanarat came to power in 1958 and implemented a strategy of maintaining power that changed institutional arrangements in ways that helped him politically as well as creating conditions for economic growth. To undercut the power of opponents whose main bases of power were in state enterprises Sarit turned to the private sector. Having no clear economic policies of his own, but desiring rapid economic growth to enhance his legitimacy, Sarit gave control of macroeconomic agencies to technocrats who were allowed considerable leeway in policy making. Officials such as Dr. Puey Ungphakorn used this power to promote macroeconomic stability and to gain control over the budgetary process. Many line ministries such as industry, commerce, and agriculture, on the other hand, remained heavily politicized and were used for patronage purposes. The implicit agreement between technocrats and government leaders was that "technocrats would not encroach on the sectoral and microeconomic mismanagement which benefits the political masters, while the latter would allow the technocrats to keep control over the macroeconomy" (Christensen and Ammar 1993:7).

Observers of these arrangements in the 1960s gave Thailand little chance for economic success. The most-cited academic analyst, Fred Riggs, for example, assumed that ethnic Chinese were "pariah entrepreneurs," the presumption being that these entrepreneurs could make little contribution to economic policy and growth. But as Ruth McVey points out, the institutional arrangements of the Sarit years "have less the aspect of a developmental bog than of a container for fundamental transformation, a chrysalis in whose apparently confused interior the change from one sort of socioeconomic order to another was taking place" (McVey 1992: 22).

They led to rapid economic growth because they created an economic environment for profitable private investment. One central aspect of this favorable economic environment was macroeconomic stability. Under the technocrats' guidance Thailand achieved remarkably low rates of inflation, realistic exchange rates, cautious fiscal policies, and hard budget constraints for private enterprises. A second aspect was ensuring politically vulnerable ethnic Chinese entrepreneurs that their property and earnings would not be confiscated. Entrepreneurs could do this in two ways. One was by finding patrons in the military and upper reaches of the civilian bureaucracy. Officials were willing to protect entrepreneurs because they discovered that it was more profitable to nurture and protect entrepreneurs than squeeze them dry. Their connections with private business firms also gave them safe landing places in case they lost out in the political struggles (McVey 1992:23). A second way entrepreneurs could protect their property rights was by creating joint ventures with foreign firms attracted to Thailand by its promising investment climate. As the domestic firms grew in size they became less dependent upon patronage for protection and growth, but this protection was critical for the early years of commercial and industrial growth.

The institutional arrangements introduced by Sarit also created incentives for firms to plan well and operate efficiently. This was done, first, through refusing to use state funds to bail out firms which got into difficulties. Second, competitive clientelism encouraged competition among firms and discouraged monopolies. Competition among patrons in the state elite eager to obtain extra-bureaucratic funds helped facilitate a constant flow of new private sector entrants into markets because intra-elite rivalries insured that aspiring entrepreneurs could always find patrons. Patrons in a range of agencies could satisfy particular groups of supporters because powers to grant licenses and permits were scattered throughout the bureaucracy. Five departments in three ministries influenced access to industrial permits and licenses. As a result, firms prohibited from expansion due to excess capacity by the Industry Ministry were able to expand under Board of Investment (BoI) incentives. Firms that thought they would gain privileged market positions through BoI measures found themselves competing with firms supported by officials in other ministries (Doner and Ramsay 1997:253). The argument here is not that clientelism or corruption is efficient in general. It is rather that the particular type of clientelism in Thailand tended to expand rather than restrict new opportunities for entrepreneurs. It is worth emphasizing that these arrangements had their roots in the 1950s. As Ammar Siamwalla has noted, the 1950s was "a formative period during which the two elites, military/political and business, starting from a position of animosity, were forging an alliance and developing a system of payoffs which would be perfected in the following period" (Ammar 1997:5).

The Sarit regime also established a Board of Investment (BoI) with the power to grant a wide range of incentives for investment in Thailand. In the early 1960s "the most important single authority given to the BoI was the power to guarantee that the government would not nationalize a promoted firm or undertake any new activity that would compete with such a firm" (Muscat 1994:104). The BoI could also grant firms a wide range of tax and tariff exemptions to encourage investment. These incentives, along with the economic environment created by the institutional arrangements discussed above, led to the rapid growth of import substituting industries in Thailand in the 1960s.

In the early 1970s in response to balance of payments problems caused by the import substituting industries and by declining prices for raw material exports, the BoI began to offer an array of export incentives to firms. These included rebates on import taxes, bonded warehouses, streamlined customs procedures, tax and tariff exemptions, and cuts in electricity costs. It is important to emphasize that there were no significant changes in the existing, protectionist trade incentives. Overall tariff levels actually increased during the 1970s and 1980s, even as the government proclaimed its shift to export promotion. Nominal tariffs rose from 35 percent to 30-55 percent during the 1970s, with the highest rates on consumer goods, and vehicles and textiles having the highest effective rates. By 1985 the effective rate of protection for Thai manufacturing was 52 percent, nearly twice that of the Philippines, Malaysia, and Korea. Efforts to restructure tariffs during the latter 1980s foundered on the opposition of private firms in import-competing industries, their allies in the Ministries of Industry and Commerce, and a Ministry of Finance reluctance to lose revenues generated by tariffs (Nipon and Fuller 1997:479-80; Christensen et. al. 1993:10; and Doner and Anek 1994).

Dspite these increases in protection, exports grew rapidly due to a combination of shifting comparative advantage, astute economic policies, and institutional arrangements. First, Thai producers of low-wage manufactured goods faced excess capacity problems in the 1970s and 1980s as a result of aggressive promotion by the BoI, smuggling in some sectors (especially consumer electronics), and a general inability of the Thai government to impede new entrants. Pushed to export by this overcapacity, Thai firms turned out to have very strong comparative advantages in labor-intensive products (Narongchai, Dapice, and Flatters 1991:xiv; Muscat 1994: 152).[1] As the currencies of Asian NICs rose and they began to shift into less labor-intensive exports, Thailand turned out to be well placed to pick up some of the labor-intensive product demand that was too expensive for the NICs to produce (Narongchai, Dapice, and Flatters 1991:xiv). The devaluation of the baht in 1984, coupled with the rise in the value of other major currencies in the aftermath of the Plaza Accords in 1985, gave Thai exports a major cost advantage over several other Asian exporters. Finally, the BoI's tax and tariff incentive packages (noted above), combined with low labor costs, were highly effective in attracting electronics multinationals such as Data General, Seagate, and Minibea.

Also contributing to consistent export growth, even in the context of anti-export bias in the trade regime, were Thai state and private sector institutions with the capacity to resolve a number of collective action problems which accompanied the growth of industrial exports. Individuals and small groups of individuals in state agencies helped overcome collective action problems in such important exports as rice, sugar, garments, and automobile parts. The Board of Trade and the Commerce Ministry helped rice exporters work together to set prices, share quotas, maintain rice export quality, and share risks (Doner and Ramsay 1997:260). Given the importance of rice exports (and related export tax revenues) for the Thai economy, this was a key contribution to economic growth. A deputy minister of industry helped sugarcane growers and sugar millers resolve major conflicts over sugarcane pricing in the mid-1980s, and officials in the Sugar Office of the Ministry of Industry helped sugarcane growers and millers shift to a new way of pricing sugarcane in the early 1990s which promised higher productivity (Ramsay 1987; Ramsay, interviews in Bangkok, 1992). The Thai Garment Manufacturers' Association played a key role in assigning garment export quotas (Doner and Ramsay 1996).

State officials typically worked with private sector institutions to resolve collective action problems, especially in important export sectors. The NESDB, led by Dr. Snoh Unakul, worked closely with the tourist industry to make tourism into one of the country's leading export earners during the economic difficulties of the 1980s (Muscat 1994:197-98). The Thai Textile Manufacturers' Association played a critical role in resolving an overproduction crisis during the 1970s and early 1980s and helping firms in the industry make the transition to export-oriented growth. The Bangkok Bank was another institution that contributed to the resolution of collective action problems in agricultural exports and textile industry. In addition to organizing the rice export trade, the bank helped to shift resources from agriculture to industry as the largest provider of credit to textile firms and a key player in linking firms with newly trained textile engineers (Doner and Ramsay 1996). Large conglomerates such as Saha Union and Siam Cement also played important roles in conjunction with government agencies. Siam Cement, in conjunction with the Board of Investments, was especially important in projects to promote the local production of diesel engines and cathode ray tubes.[2]

There was, however, one significant weakness running through these collective action efforts: none of them devoted consistent attention and resources to technological upgrading. As discussed below, the country relied on cheap labor in industries such as garments and toys, and foreign investment in industries such as hard disk drives, for its exports while allowing most domestic-oriented producers to enjoy the fruits of protection.

Thai Institutions and Increasing Industrial Competition

Between 1988 and 1995 Thailand's exports grew at a rate of 28 percent per year, but in 1996 this growth rate slowed to zero. Several cyclical factors contributed to the drop in export growth including a slowing of world trade, lower world demand for electronic products, appreciation of the baht, and high domestic inflation and interest rates. The most important factors, however, were structural: (1) increased wages in the labor intensive industries which include many of Thailand's most successful export industries, and (2) increased competition in these industries from other developing countries (Thammavit 1996:9; Warr 1997:328).[3] Between 1982 and 1994 Thai "real wages increased by 70 percent." "The implication of rising real wages is a loss of competitiveness in the labor intensive export oriented industries that have been the basis of much of Thailand's growth over the past decade" (Warr 1997:328-30). This is clearly the case in textiles, which was the major export-earning sector between 1986 and 1990 (see Table 7.1).

While a number of factors influence competitiveness in addition to wages, labor rates do play a major role in a number of highly labor intensive industries, and these are the industries which suffered the most in the export slowdown in 1996, as can be seen in Table 7.2.

While there was a slowdown in exports in several categories in 1996, the biggest drops were concentrated in the lower wage, labor intensive exports that had been the major sources of export growth from the mid-1980s to the early 1990s. There was less of a drop in integrated circuits (ICs), computer parts, televisions and television parts, and air conditioners and parts. Overall, exports of labor-intensive manufactured exports declined approximately 14.6 percent through the first eleven months in 1996 (Chalongphob 1997). In summary, Thailand's lack of industrial upgrading began to catch up with it in 1996.

Economists typically attribute inefficiency to protectionism and politically powerful import-competing sectors. But the story is more complicated. For one thing, protection has not impeded efficiency in South Korea or Taiwan. For another, due to the involvement of the country's large banks in the export of raw materials and low-wage goods, Thailand did not have the kind of import-competing coalition seen in many parts of Latin America. Instead, three related factors help to account for the country's weakness in higher value added products: institutional and political features of key governmental agencies; a trade regime that super-imposed export promotion on protection; and ineffective and half-hearted efforts at technology development. These in turn led to dualistic production structures whereby locally owned firms did expand but lacked linkages to the more demanding and foreign-dominated production of higher value added goods for export.

TABLE 7.1 Wages of Textile Laborers in Major Manufacturing
and Exporting Countries (US dollar per hour)

	1990	1994	Avaerage Increase (%)
Japan	13.96	25.26	16.0
Taiwan	4.56	5.98	7.0
Hong Kong	3.05	4.40	9.6
South Korea	3.22	4.00	5.6
Singapore	2.83	na	na
Malaysia	0.86	na	na
Thailand	*0.92*	*1.41*	*11.3*
Philippines	0.67	0.95	9.1
India	0.72	0.58	-5.3
China	0.37	0.48	6.7
Indonesia	0.25	0.46	16.5
Pakistan	0.39	0.45	16.5
Sri Lanka	0.24	0.42	15.0
Vietnam	na	0.39	na

Source: Sombat 1997:29.

Government Agencies

Several of the institutional arrangements put in place by the Sarit regime and discussed above, while contributing to rapid growth between 1960 and 1995, have acted as fetters upon industrial upgrading. One is the insulation of major macroeconomic ministries, and the Finance Ministry in particular, from line agencies and from the private sector. As designer of the country's tariff policies, the Ministry of Finance is especially important for industrial upgrading. The minis-

TABLE 7.2   Commodity Structure of Thailand's Export Slowdown

	1994	1995	1996
Total exports (million baht)	1,137,602	1,406,310	1,401,392
Growth rate (percent)	20.9	23.6	-0.35+
Growth Rate by Major Commodity:			
Textiles	4.5	22.1	-4.4
Garments	12.4	1.3	-21.9
Shoes and parts	40.5	37.0	-40.9
Gems and jewelry	8.3	11.5	8.4
Integrated circuits	27.5	28.4	3.4
Computers and parts	44.9	38.7	31.3
Air conditioners and parts	62.1	49.6	33.6
Televisions and parts	26.2	12.7	14.1
Plastic products	-29.1	102.2	51.4
Rice	18.9	24.1	8.4
Sugar	41.2	67.2	11.7
Frozen shrimp	29.9	2.3	-17.8
Canned seafood	24.7	4.1	-0.3
Tapioca products	-13.6	-2.8	16.7
Rubber	43.3	46.5	1.4

Sources: adapted from Warr 1997:320, citing *Bangkok Post Year-End Economic Review,* December 1996.

try's insulation protected it from rent seeking and politicization that has plagued other less developed countries. On the downside, officials in the Finance Ministry have developed little knowledge of, or interest in, particular industrial sectors.[4] For them the overriding importance of import duties has been to strengthen the state's financial position, even if short-term revenue needs protected inefficient domestic producers. As noted earlier, import tariffs rose substantially in the 1970s and 1980s, and efforts to restructure the tariffs were strongly opposed by the firms who benefited from them and their supporters in the Ministries of Industry and Commerce. The Ministry of Finance agreed to lower them only in the early 1990s when substantial budget surpluses were on hand. And even these reductions were offset by a cascading tariff structure and a business tax system that encouraged vertical integration rather than the growth of local suppliers (Doner 1998).[5] The Board of Investment both contributed to and offset this protectionism. On the one hand, the BoI has made use of its power to grant temporary protection through measures such as surcharges. On the other hand, the board has led the way in providing a wide range of countervailing export incentives, as noted earlier.

Trade and Investment Regime

The result of this mixture was a regime aptly labeled "export-oriented protectionism" (Nipon and Fuller 1997:480). That is, the BoI simply grafted export-oriented measures on to continued protection for local firms producing for the domestic market. Any attempts to link local firms with more export- or quality-oriented foreign firms were undermined not only by the cascading tariff structure and business tax systems noted above, but also by the BoI's lack of knowledge about particular industries. There was also an almost total absence of incentives for technology transfer from foreign investors to local firms. There was a significant liberalization of the trade regime beginning with reduction in protection for final goods and some inputs in 1990. But this has prompted final assemblers to demand similar reductions in tariffs for raw materials and intermediate inputs. The result has been a series of upstream-downstream conflicts over tariffs between steel producers vs. steel users, petrochemical producers vs. autoparts, electronics, and textile firms, sugar millers vs. consumers, and packaging manufacturers vs. suppliers of paper and ink.[6]

Technology Development

The preceding factors have contributed to difficulties in establishing public or collective institutions to resolve collective action problems and to promote technology transfer and diffusion of technical knowledge. One of the best examples of this is the effort to establish a National Textile Institute. For years, Thai textile producers have been aware that rising wage rates will make it necessary to move into higher value-added products requiring more advanced machines and workers with greater technical skills. In the mid-1980s a career official in the Ministry of Industry proposed the creation of a National Textile Institute to help the industry deal with these issues. Efforts to create the institute foundered for the next ten years over issues of whether the institute should be publicly or privately controlled, the reluctance of the Finance Ministry to provide government funds for sector-specific support, conflicts among large and small firms in the textile industry, and opposition from legislators. Rural-based legislators challenged giving money to create an institute that would help rich textile magnates when Thai farmers needed so much help (Doner and Ramsay 1996:34-35). The Textile Institute was finally established in 1996, but it has accomplished relatively little because of conflicts over how it will be funded that have been exacerbated by the economic crisis that began in 1997 (Rochana 1998:11; Ramsay, interviews in Bangkok, 1998). Similar problems have plagued other sectors. Only recently have officials discussed the promotion of training in automotive engineering and despite several private sector initiatives, not much has occurred. Similarly, despite the electronics industry's long-standing importance, only in 1997 did a local university float the idea of a national electronics institute (Doner and Brimble 1998).

These sectoral weaknesses mirror the ineffectiveness of broader initiatives in vendor development as well as technology transfer and human resource development. In 1991 officials within the BOI initiated a kind of vendor development program to encourage technology diffusion and subcontracting linkages between MNCs and local suppliers. The BOI Unit for Industrial Linkage Development program (BUILD) first developed a database of local firms in areas such as metal working, tool and die making, PCBA and plastic injection molding, and then attempted to match these firms up with the specific needs of MNC assemblers. Despite positive responses from long-established firms such as Minibea, the program basically faded, even after it was upgraded to a "National Supplier Development Program" involving all major agencies responsible for small- and medium-enterprise development. Unlike Malaysia's Vendor Development Program, the Thai effort lacked solid political and administrative support. Indeed, most of the initiative and resources for the program came not from the BoI but from a consultant under contract to the board. By 1997 the program was basically dormant (Doner and Brimble 1998).[7] The picture in technology transfer and human resource development is similarly discouraging.[8]

Dualistic Production Structures

Owing to these policies and institutions, Thailand has a distinctly dualistic industrial structure in manufacturing sectors. On the one hand, Thailand is acknowledged to have a relatively deep base of supporting industries in metalworking, plastic parts, tool and die production, and electrical and electronics components.[9] Yet these local firms are largely without linkage to the dynamic export sectors, especially in higher value-added products. The auto, textile and garment, and electronics industries illustrate these problems. The auto industry has enjoyed extensive protection since the 1970s. The resulting indigenous parts producers, along with the country's booming domestic market, have contributed to Thailand becoming Southeast Asia's acknowledged automotive production base and the site of significant investment by auto multinationals in the 1990s. But with a small number of exceptions, locally owned firms remain relegated to "commodity" or "universal" components requiring little high technology and producing for the domestic market. Overall, the original equipment manufacture (OEM) sector is dominated by Japanese affiliated firms. Out of 225 OEM parts producers, 90 percent are either joint venture with foreign technology owners or involved in technical licensing agreements with foreign firms. As of 1997, only seven parts firms exported in large volumes and these were all Japanese-affiliated firms (Brooker 1997: Part V).

The production structure of the textile and garment complex is divided between the upstream and midstream sectors which produce fiber, yarn, and fabric on the one hand, and downstream garment producers on the other hand. Many of the upstream and midstream firms developed as import substitution industries and suffer from high costs and old machinery. They produce fabric which can be sold domestically, or low quality gray cloth for exports. This cloth is not suitable for use by Thailand's export-oriented garment manufacturers who must import much of the cloth they use for garments. As a result, Thailand loses significant amounts of value added to foreign textile makers, garment producers are unable to react quickly to changing market trends, and Thailand is hard pressed to meet low-wage competition by moving into higher value-added goods. In the words of a recent *Bangkok Bank* report, the textile industry's "upstream products cannot sufficiently satisfy the demand of the downstream industries both in quality and variety" (Sombat 1997; Nipon and Pawadee 1997).

The situation is electronics is even most strikingly dualistic. In electronic components, foreign firms dominate export-oriented IC and ball bearing production, and PCB firms are divided between a large number of local firms producing low-end products for the domestic market and a smaller group of firms, the strongest of which are foreign dominated, producing for export. In the computer hardware and peripheral sector, technologically advanced foreign firms such as Read-Rite and Seagate produce for export alongside a smaller number of weaker Thai firms importing CKD parts to produce personal computers for the domestic market. The story is largely the same in consumer electronics where large foreign producers such as JVC and Samsung produce for export, while technologically weaker local firms sell to the domestic market. Only in the smallest sector, industrial electronics, do local firms exhibit strong technical capacities (Nipon and Pawadee 1997; Doner and Brimble 1998).

These weaknesses made it difficult for Thailand to move to higher value-added production and left its labor-intensive exports increasingly vulnerable to competition from other countries. It was this vulnerability, coupled with slowed world trade in 1996, appreciation of the baht, and high domestic inflation rates that caused a slowing of Thailand's rapid economic growth in 1996. At the end of 1996 there was concern in Thailand about poor export performance and a large current account deficit which had reached a worryingly high 8 percent of GDP. Despite these difficulties, a number of analysts in Thailand were optimistic about the prospects for 1997. The new Chavalit Yongchaiyudh government promised to be more effective in dealing with economic issues than the former Banharn Silpa-archa government, and projections of expanding world trade suggested a renewal of export growth (Thammavit 1996:11). The export stagnation, however, had "triggered a warning sign to international creditors," who saw a growing accumulation of serious problems that export stagnation threatened to make even worse (Mingsarn 1998:8). These included a current account deficit of 8 percent, huge over investment in real estate and other low yielding sectors of the economy, and high levels of nonperforming loans that threatened the solvency of many commercial banks and finance companies. As these weaknesses became apparent, foreign speculators began attacks on the baht in November 1996 and investors began pulling investments out of Thailand. The Bank of Thailand's defense of the baht nearly exhausted foreign reserves, and the Bank was forced to allow the baht to float on July 2, 1997. It promptly began dropping in value. In August 1997 Thailand was forced to go to the IMF for help, and by 1998 Thailand was deep in the worst economic crisis in its modern history. The next section examines how institutional arrangements led to these problems and an economic crash.

Thai Institutions and Financial Liberalization

Ironically, the economic crash had its origins in changes in global capital markets that were expected to benefit Thailand. These changes made large amounts of investment funds available which could have been used to upgrade firms' export capacities, improve infrastructure, and improve the training and education of the workforce. This did not happen. Instead, the inflow of funds, and the way they were used, led to economic disaster. There are several main causes for the disaster: (1) policy mistakes made by the Bank of Thailand as it proceeded with financial liberalization; (2) implicit guarantees by Thai governments and the Bank of Thailand that commercial banks would not be allowed to fail; (3) institutional weaknesses within the Finance Ministry and central bank; and (4) an electoral system that encourages non-programmatic parties and unstable governments.

Policies

The first reason for the financial disaster was the way in which the Bank of Thailand proceeded with financial liberalization in efforts to attract investment funds from global capital markets to Thailand. It took several steps, which taken together contributed directly to the disaster: making it easier for foreign funds to flow into Thailand, maintaining a high domestic interest rates, and keeping the baht pegged to the dollar. The decisions were made by a very small number of persons who were not prepared to deal with the complexities of liberalization. First, during the 1970s, the government promoted the growth of finance companies as a way to stimulate competition within a finance sector dominated by a small number of powerful commercial banks (Doner and Unger 1993). At the minimum, this increased the number of financial firms to be monitored by government officials. Monitoring was also made more difficult by steps to make it easier for foreign investment funds to flow into Thailand. In 1990 Thailand accepted the International Monetary Fund's Article VIII which removed all controls on foreign exchange transactions in the current account. In 1993 the Bangkok International Banking Facilities (BIBF) were created in an effort to increase the flow of funds into Thailand needed to sustain rapid economic growth and to make Thailand a regional financial center. Forty-two licenses were granted to Thai and foreign commercial banks allowing them to engage in a number of foreign exchange activities. The most significant was taking "deposits and loans from abroad and extending loans in the form of foreign currencies to . . . local markets" (Thanisr 1992:8). "Most of the business generated by the BIBF was to facilitate lending by foreigners to Thai firms, with the banks in the facility acting as intermediaries" (Ammar 1997).

The second policy leading toward disaster was maintaining high interest rates as a way to try to limit aggregate demand and keep inflation low, even though economists had known for a long time that monetary policy was futile with fixed exchange rates and open capital accounts.[10] High domestic interest rates made it much cheaper for Thai businesses to borrow foreign loans at lower costs than they could borrow domestically.[11] The forty-two BIBF license holders could borrow dollars and "still make a clean profit relending the dollars to local customers at lower rates than those of baht loans," because the interest rates on these dollar loans was 4-6 percent lower than baht loans (Bello 1997b). The Bank of Thailand's effort to slow down an overheated economy by raising interest rates in 1995 caused foreign borrowing to grow even more rapidly (Phatra Research Institute 1997). By the end of 1996, $31.2 billion had been loaned, or "almost a half of total private foreign debt." These were mainly short-term loans and most were not hedged against currency fluctuations (Ammar 1997).

The third step in the series of policy mistakes was to keep the baht pegged to a basket of currencies with the dollar weighted at 80 percent of the total. As the dollar rose in value in the mid-1990s, Thai exports became less competitive, contributing to the export difficulties discussed in section two of the chapter. The other, more immediately harmful effect was to lead borrowers to assume that the government "would never leave them holding the bag under devaluation pressure" (Passell 1997b:D2). Local firms thought they could safely borrow dollars, convert them into baht, and then pay off debts at the same exchange rate at which they had borrowed them. Foreign investors believed they could invest in the Thai stock market or in government bonds with the assurance that their investments could be changed into baht and back into dollars with little or no risk (Kirida 1997).

Guarantees and Moral Hazards

If these funds had been used productively, the previous three steps by the Bank of Thailand would not have had such disastrous effects. But much of the capital flowing intoThailand was not used productively. Much of it went into real estate and low-yielding commercial and industrial projects. Thai firms' incremental output to capital ratio dropped from 0.5 in mid-1987 to approximately 0.25 in 1996, and return on assets of all non-financial companies listed on the Thai stock market dropped from 7.5 percent in 1991 to 2.3 percent in 1996 (Phatra Thanakit 1997a:6-8). One of the central puzzles in trying to explain what went wrong in Thailand is why so much of this capital was misallocated. There are three tentative answers to this puzzle.

The first is that capital flowed into real estate because real estate could be used as collateral for bank loans. Most businesses in Thailand continue to be family owned businesses and depend heavily upon bank borrowing for the capital needed to expand. Financial institutions provide loans more readily when land or real estate is put up as collateral. Normally, of course, the amount of loans provided is less than the value of the collateral. But when land prices were rising rapidly, as during the boom years of 1988–1995, the investment in land and real estate paid off additionally in terms of the ability to float more debt. Part of the increased debt was used to purchase even more land, which drove prices up further, and so on (Ammar 1997). All of the money did not go into real estate, of course, nor was the family structure of Thai firms the only reason for misallocation of investments.

A second reason for the pattern of misallocation of capital by entrepreneurs was that the prolonged economic boom and large inflows of foreign funds had contributed to inflation, which made it more "attractive to produce for domestic consumption because prices could be raised without fear of foreign competition" (Phatra Research Institute 1997b:7). This meant that more money went into protected sectors such as property, petrochemicals, and steel.

A third answer lies in the Thai banking system itself. Why did Thai banks and finance companies continue to make loans under the above conditions? Paul Krugman suggests that the problem began with commercial banks and other financial institutions

> whose liabilities were perceived as having implicit government guarantee, but were essentially unregulated and therefore subject to severe moral hazard problems. The excessive risky lending of these institutions created inflation—not of goods but of asset prices. The overpricing of assets was sustained by a sort of circular process, in which the proliferation of risky lending drove up the prices of risky assets, making

the financial condition of the intermediaries seem sounder than it was (Krugman 1998).[12]

This problem was made worse by globalization of financial markets. If the Thai banks and financial companies had been limited to capital available only in Thailand, the problem would not have become as severe as it did. Access to global capital markets allowed the asset bubble to grow much larger than it would have otherwise (Krugman 1998).

Thai commercial banks have been politically powerful for decades, serving Thai politicians in the Sarit era and after as a critical source of funds and financing the commodity exports and industrial growth which have been so important to the Thai economy and tax base (Doner and Unger 1993:100, 118).[13] This combination of economic and political influence assured that the fifteen Thai-owned commercial banks would not be allowed to fail. When three Thai banks ran into troubles between 1983 and 1986, the government bailed them out with over ten billion baht in soft loans and two billion baht in working capital (Doner and Unger 1993:115; Unger 1989:18).[14] At the time the World Bank warned that Thailand had too much of a tendency

> to protect the solvency and stability of existing banks and financial institutions, rather than to promote efficiency and competition broadly among all categories of institutions, or providing for orderly exit or reorganization of financial firms that become insolvent. As regulatory policies move toward greater freedom of entry and exit . . . Thai authorities will need to vigorously implement the power to force individual institutions to reorganize or disappear when necessary without damaging the confidence and stability in the financial system as a whole (cited in Unger 1989).

This advice was not followed. Bankers and finance companies continued to be encouraged to finance risky projects "in the expectation that they would enjoy the profits, if any, while the government would cover serious losses" ("Why did Asia crash?" 1998:66). A study by the Research Department of the Bangkok Bank found that through early 1997 "experience has thus far shown that whenever financial institutions struggled to survive the authorities intervened to assist them to remain solvent especially through the Financial Institutions Development Fund" ("Financial Institution Crisis" 1997). When the Bangkok Bank of Commerce (BBC) got into financial troubles in 1994 and 1995, and a run on the bank began, the Bank of Thailand supported it with nearly $7 billion from the Bank's Financial Institution Development Fund (Ammar 1997). The bank was supported even though it had violated several central bank orders and had engaged in fraudulent behavior. Most of the bank's bad loans had been made to politicians from the Chat Thai political party, who had gotten the loans without sufficient collateral and used them in a scheme to buy land (Parista 1996:18-19). Problems in several finance companies and smaller banks in 1996 followed difficulties at the BBC. Senior officials from the Bank of Thailand reassured depositors that all deposits were guaranteed, and most significantly for the argument made by Paul Krugman: "There was also talk of the guarantee being extended to the creditors of the finance companies as well" (Ammar 1997; see also Handley 1997b).

Such guarantees can work, and the cycle of asset inflation can continue, as long as the central bank is willing to provide bailouts and is capable of doing so. Providing bailouts became increasingly difficult for the Bank of Thailand in 1997. In addition to supporting troubled banks and finance companies locally, defenses of the baht from attacks by foreign speculators in November 1966 and February and May 1997 were extremely expensive. The FIDF lent out more than a trillion baht trying to shore up weak finance companies (Ammar and Orapin 1998:15)

An alternative to defending the baht would have been to devalue, but the Bank of Thailand rejected this alternative. The main reason seems to have been that the bank assumed that the problems were short term ones and could be overcome without devaluation (Ammar 1997:66-67). In addition, from the bank's perspective there is rarely ever a good time to devalue. When the economy is stable, there is no need to devalue. When the economy is unsettled, it is not a time to devalue because devaluation might cause greater instability. Even if the bank had decided it was necessary to devalue, it would have been very difficult politically to do so. The bank, and other macroeconomic agencies, did not have the political autonomy they had enjoyed in earlier decades. Devaluing the baht in late 1996 or early 1997 would have left numerous firms and banks in serious financial difficulties because they would have had to pay back foreign currency loans in devalued baht. These politically influential companies could have put substantial pressure on a weak government not to devalue.

By July the Bank of Thailand had essentially exhausted the foreign exchange reserve defending the baht and was forced to announce a "managed float" of the baht on July 2. The baht began to sink rapidly in value, and as this happened the full consequences of large-scale foreign borrowing began to take hold. In the summer of 1997 Thailand's economy was "a disaster waiting to happen." Firms' debt dependence had grown rapidly in the 1990s. "[A]mong the listed non-financial companies . . . average debt/equity ratio rose from 1.58 to 1.98 between 1994 and 1996, [and] their interest cover (earnings before tax and interest payments divided by liability) fell from 14.2 to 10.7 percent" (Ammar 1997). Non-bank companies in the private sector had $63 billion of debt at the end of 1996, and $29.2 billion was due in less than a year (Ammar 1997). Businesses had built up a debt pyramid which depended upon continued rapid economic growth, but the slowing of exports in 1996 was a signal that the rapid growth of the past ten years was not likely to continue. Also ominous was oversupply in the automotive, housing, steel bar, and petrochemical industries (Phatra Thanakit 1997a:11). Large numbers of firms had borrowed dollars and had to pay back the loans in dollars. Yet their revenues were in baht. To make matters worse, most of the funds borrowed from abroad were unhedged. Firms had assumed there was no reason to pay the hedging fees because they were lulled into believing that the value of the baht would remain stable vis-a-vis the dollar. As these borrowers scrambled to convert baht into dollars before the value of the baht declined further in value, they pushed the baht further down by their actions. Firms could not repay loans to finance companies and banks, which led to losses for the finance companies and banks, beginning "a downward spiral of asset deflation and disintermediation" (Krugman 1998).[15]

In August 1997 Thailand was forced to go to the International Monetary Fund for help. The IMF organized a $17.2 billion package that included standby credits of $4 billion. Of this amount, $14.5 billion came from contributions from other Asian countries and $2.7 billion came from structural adjustment loans from the World Bank and the Asian Development Bank (Soonruth and Chiratas 1997; Handley 1997b).[16]

Institutional Weaknesses and New Tasks

Central to Thailand's financial meltdown has been a combination of what Ammar Siamwalla calls the "decline of the technocracy" and new challenges posed by liberalization policies.[17] The technocracy can be divided into those officials responsible for fiscal policy, housed largely in the Finance Ministry, and those responsible for monetary policy, housed in the Bank of Thailand. As Ammar notes, both the quality and autonomy of fiscal policy officials have declined; however, the country's economic boom has masked this decline, until this past year. The problems of the central bank, the agency responsible for exchange rates and bank supervision, are more critical for our purposes.

According to Ammar, the BoT's management structure became outmoded and its relationship to the Finance Ministry more problematic as the ministry became more politicized. With regard to management structure: concentration of power in the hands of the governor made sense when the objective was to shield the bank from the military and when there was a clear gap in authority and seniority between upper and lower levels of the bank's hierarchy. But with extensive overseas training programs, the governor has become only one among equals. Competition among staff pursuing lifetime careers resulted in factionalism, a failure to make effective use of the bank's personnel, and a severe deterioration in the bank's ethos of dedication to the public interest (Ammar 1997; Nukul Commission Report; and Vatchara and Thanong 1998).

Although Ammar does not mention this, the central bank also seems to have been quite unprepared for the herd mentality, the demand for transparency, and the quick release of data resulting from expansion and globalization of financial services. Bank officials were clearly unprepared for the innovations brought by new capitalists to the country's stock exchange. For example, in a process termed "chain listing," entrepreneurs would float a new firm on the market and then follow that up "by listing a subsidiary or related companies, with share prices bolstered in each successive flotation, through a book-keeping exercise where assets and profits are 'transferred' from one company in the group to the one being listed" (Handley 1997:100). BoT officials were also resistant to exchanging information with the traders and analysts whose growth accompanied the expansion of the country's stock exchange. In one telling case, the Finance Minister, on the advice of the central bank governor, fired a deputy governor and former head of the Security and Exchange Commission for sharing confidential information with commercial banks. The National Intelligence Agency based the evidence used to back this accusation on wiretaps. This level of suspicion is in marked contrast with the historically close ties between the BoT and the Thai Bankers' Association prior to liberalization.

Electoral Rules, Parties, and Coalitions

The financial difficulties during the summer and fall of 1997 highlighted shortcomings of Thailand's parliamentary politics. As long as macroeconomic agencies had firm control over monetary and fiscal policy and the baht was firmly pegged to the dollar, government instability had relatively little effect upon the performance of the economy. This has now changed. Now that the baht is no longer pegged to the dollar there is a direct connection between Thailand's domestic politics and international confidence in its currency. In October 1997 Standard and Poor's downgraded Thailand's sovereign long-term currency rating from A- to BBB, citing political confusion as a reason: "Patronage-based politics has impaired the ability of technocrats to manage ongoing financial stress, while Thailand's fragmented political landscape offers little prospect of cohesive governance in the near term" (cited in Parista 1997; Soonruth and Chiratas 1997). Even with the new Chuan Leekpai government in place, credit rating agencies continued to criticize Thai politics. In December Moody's investor services dropped the sovereign debt rating to just above junk bond status and Thomson BankWatch Asia downgraded Thailand's sovereign risk rating to "BBB minus," citing "continued weak governance" which "has failed to inspire confidence, provide for greater stability or lead to any reversal in capital outflows" (BankWatch 1997).

There are several ways in which the political system undermined the capacity to address Thailand's problems and the confidence of foreign investors.[18] First, during most of Thai history since 1932 parties have either been banned or, when permitted, have been closed off from central national policy issues which remained in the hands of military leaders or technocrats. They have had no say in the formulation of budgets; much of the struggle on fiscal policy has focused not on the size of the budget or taxes but on budgetary allocation (Ammar and Orapin 1998). Politicians have been left to scramble for seats in the cabinet, where control of line ministries and agencies gives access to the allocation of quotas, licenses, contracts, and ministerial and departmental funds. The agriculture, commerce, communications, and industry ministries are some of the most sought after ministries because they control so many quotas and licenses. These can be used for the benefit of the politicians who head these agencies to maintain patronage networks and win votes. Political parties are basically "vehicles for seizing control over ministerial resources" (Christensen 1991; Doner and Unger 1993:108).[19]

The second key weakness was the electoral system. Under the constitution in effect when the Chuan Leekpai came into power in 1997, the 200-member Senate was appointed by the Prime Minister. The lower house was composed of 393 members of parliament (MPs) from multimember (usually two or three) constituencies based on a ratio of one MP to 150,000 people. Provincial constituencies supply approximately 80 percent of the seats, with one-third of votes coming from the Northeast region alone. Such a system encouraged patronage-based rather than policy-based parties. Part of the reason for this is simply that highly represented rural voters are not as concerned or exposed to the broad policy issues familiar to Bangkok voters. "Policy issues have sometimes been salient, but outside Bangkok these are typically issues of direct local concern: should another bridge over the Mekong river be built in Nakhon Phanom or Mukdahan" (Surin and McCargo 1998:135).

But this problem was itself in part a function of the kinds of parties encouraged by electoral rules. Because the multimember system allowed voters to support candidates on an individual rather than party basis, it encouraged competition between candidates of the same party. The result was not the development of party programs, but rather high-cost campaigning. Politicians maintained their own personal networks of support based on local business networks capable of managing these constituencies (Pasuk and Baker 1998:31). In order to continue to win office, a politician had to maintain these networks and the support of locally influential persons who helped hold them together. Many of these were local businesspersons, officials, or powerful local leaders involved in an array of legal and illegal activities known as *chao pho*. Maintaining such networks required constant funding, and the principal source of such funds was cabinet positions. As the economy grew, cabinet positions generated considerable amounts of corruption money to be funneled back to constituents in the provinces and to factional supporters appointed to the Senate or named as unpaid cabinet advisors. They also generated quotas, concessions licenses, and public works contracts useful in strengthening politicians' factional base.[20]

This system also encouraged cabinet instability. Party loyalty was irrelevant for many members of political parties. If an MP had a better chance of getting a cabinet seat by abandoning his or her party and joining another political party, he or she would do so. Most parties today are best understood as loose factions of politicians who readily leave the party and join another party which has a better chance of getting into the cabinet (Ockey 1994:255). While there are exceptions such as the Democrats, new parties are continually forming and splitting apart. Formation of Thai cabinets is an intricate exercise in allocating numbers of seats and cabinet positions. Democratically elected Thai cabinets are always unstable coalitions of several parties prone to fission and collapse. One of the main goals of political parties not included in a cabinet is to bring about the collapse of the cabinet in hopes that in the next reshuffle of cabinet positions they can become members of the cabinet (Ockey 1994:265).

This is an institutional arrangement with serious flaws in a new era of floating baht and economic crisis. First, there is no guarantee that competent persons will become prime minister or will head key macroeconomic agencies. This was clearly the case in the Banharn Silpa-archa government (July 1995–November 1996). Banharn himself was seen "as a wheeler dealer with ties to shady businessmen and politicians," and his finance minister was a university academic who had considerable expertise in international trade law but was widely viewed as out of his depth as finance minister (Murray 1996:372-73). In contrast, Prime Minister Chuan Leekpai was widely respected for his integrity and competence, and he had extremely capable persons as Finance Minister (Tarrin Nimmanahaeminda) and Commerce Minister (Supachai Panitchpakdi). However, it is easy to forget just how narrowly this government won office in 1997. Its accession to office depended upon the support of twelve members of the Prachakon Thai Party who broke ranks with their leader to support Chuan as Prime Minister ("Chuan set to be new PM," *Bangkok Post*, November 8, 1997).

Second, it leads to unstable, insecure governments and instability in key ministries. One of the main reasons economic stability did not return after the IMF package was announced in August 1997 was doubt as to whether the Chavalit government would adhere to the plan with the IMF. For example, it gave confusing policy signals over how fifty-eight suspended finance companies would be treated (Soonruth and Chiratas 1997). Since Thailand returned to civilian rule in September 1992, there have been four major government changes. The longest lived administration was the Chuan Leekpai government which survived two years, seven months, and twenty-seven days between September 1992 and May 1995 (Murray 1996:362). New elections in July 1995 brought Banharn Silpa-archa into the prime ministership. Another round of elections in November 1996 led to the prime ministership of Chavalit Yongchaiyut, who in turn stepped down from office in November 1997 to be replaced by Chuan Leekpai. Each of these governments was a multiparty coalition, which made it very difficult for finance ministers to take politically unpopular decisions. Amnuay Viravan resigned as finance minister in June 1997 because of conflicts within the Chavalit cabinet over raising excise taxes. His successor, Thanong Bidaya, quit in October after the government rescinded a fuel tax hike it had agreed to three days earlier as part of IMF conditions for running a budget surplus in 1998 ("Thanong to quit in reshuffle,"

Bangkok Post, October 20, 1997). Thanong was in turn replaced by Kosit Panpiemrat, who was in turn replaced by Tarrin Nimmanahaeminda in November in the new Chuan Leekpai cabinet. In short, in the middle of Thailand's worst financial crisis in decades, when expertise and stability was most needed in the finance ministry position, Thailand went through four finance ministers in six months.[21] It was fortunate in late 1997 to have an exceptionally capable finance minister in Tarrin Nimmanahaeminda, and a highly respected prime minister in Chuan Leekpai, but the rules of the game did not guarantee that either would have a long tenure in office or that they would be replaced by persons of equal integrity and competence.[22] One of the key challenges facing Thailand is finding a way of changing the rules of the game to insure effective leadership capable of finding the political support necessary to promote industrial upgrading and financial reform.

Prospects for the Future

The central thesis of the paper has been that state and private sector institutional arrangements that supported rapid economic growth in the past are inadequate to meet the challenges of increased industrial competition and financial liberalization Thailand now faces. The main implication for the future is that these institutional arrangements must be changed in ways that are more supportive of industrial upgrading and sound financial practices. In this section we begin with changes in the financial sector because the need for changes here is most pressing and because, for all of the difficulty involved, change here is likely to be easier than changes in upgrading industry and improving governance. We then turn to changes needed to support industrial upgrading and the creation of political arrangements supportive of industrial upgrading and financial reform.

Financial Institutions

Institutional change is "most likely when there is an increase in the effectiveness of individuals seeking change and a decrease in the blocking power of persons whose interests are served by the current institutional arrangements" (Levi 1990:407). The economic crash dramatically increased the effectiveness of persons seeking change in the Thai financial system and weakened the blocking power of the banking families and business groups that benefited from past institutional arrangements. Thailand's financial vulnerability increased the leverage of the IMF, foreign banks, and reformers in Thailand such as Tarrin. Thailand had to have the $17.2 billion package assembled by the IMF to get through its financial crisis. The leverage provided by these funds allowed the IMF to break the domestic political logjam and push for substantial change in the financial sector. Between November 1997 and August 1998, the government closed fifty-six finance companies and began disposing of their assets, took over four failing commercial banks, tightened standards for nonperforming loans and provisioning, and initiated reforms in the Bank of Thailand. The government was able to push these reforms along despite the considerable costs they imposed upon shareholders in the failed finance companies and the failing commercial banks. Major banking families who controlled the four banks taken over by the government, such as the Tejaphaibuls and Wanglees, have lost control of their banks and suffered major financial losses in the process.

In addition to closing or taking over failing financial institutions, the government has strengthened regulations for continuing institutions. In the past banks did not have to put loans in the nonperforming category until interest had not been paid for six months. Now loans will be deemed nonperforming after only three months of non-payment of interest. Tighter provisioning against bad debts and capital adequacy regulations have also been put into place.

Finance companies and commercial banks have not been the only targets of reform. The Bank of Thailand has been severely criticized for its failed defense of the baht which nearly exhausted Thailand's foreign exchange reserves, and for its lax oversight of the Financial Institution Development Fund (FIDF). The FIDF spent over a trillion baht (approximately $25 billion at exchange rates in April 1998) supporting ailing finance companies and commercial banks. To place the costs of this expenditure in perspective, in 1998 interest on the expenditure was over 100 billion baht, compared with total budget expenditures of 800 billion baht (Ammar and Orapin 1998:16). The Bank of Thailand was the subject of a major investigation by a commission headed by former Bank of Thailand Governor Nukul Prachuabmoh. The Nukul Commission recommended substantial changes to strengthen the management of the Bank, reduce factionalism, and increase its autonomy from political interference (Vatikiotis 1998; Nukul Commission Report 1998). The publication of the commission's report, along with massive criticism of the Bank's management in the press, resulted in the resignation of Chaiyawat Wibulsaswadi as governor and his replacement by Chatumongol Sonakul in May 1998.

In a related set of changes, the Ministry of Finance has also announced plans to deal with the central problem of preventing banks and finance companies from making risky loans with the assurance that shareholders will bailed out by the government if the loans result in losses. Two decrees amending the Commercial Banking Act and Finance Companies Act enable the Bank of Thailand "to write down the value of shares and thus make shareholders pay for the losses" caused by poor management decisions ("Joint Statement" 1997).

If Paul Krugman's argument is correct, the most important change of all in the financial sector would be for Thai authorities to move toward a "sink or swim" type of policy in their treatment of troubled financial institutions" ("Financial Institution Crisis" 1997). The present Thai government is not willing to go this far. Prime

Minister Chuan Leekpai said in an interview in January 1998, "the government will not allow banks to go under, and will guarantee depositors" ("We Accept Hardship" 1998). It remains to be seen whether the government can maintain this policy. The Chair of the Thai Bankers Association, Banthoon Lamsan of the Thai Farmers Bank, has said that some, if not all, of the four banks taken over by the government will have to be closed and their assets liquidated (Woo 1998).

In the long run these changes will produce a much stronger financial system in Thailand with better bank management and better supervision of banks. Major issues still remain, however. These include selling off the assets of the closed finance companies, deciding how much of the costs of the bailout bill will be paid by taxpayers, recapitalization of banks, and providing liquidity to cash starved businesses. Assets of the finance companies are being sold off, but the process is going very slowly. Nonperforming loans are estimated to peak at 35 percent of outstanding loans, and local banks were estimated to need $20 billion to deal with these nonperforming loans (Soonruth 1998).

By the summer of 1998 the most serious problem had become providing liquidity for cash starved businesses. Businesses were finding it difficult to borrow money, partly because of the high interest rates required by the IMF, but also because of the reluctance of commercial banks to loan money to them. The banks were reluctant to loan the money because of fears that companies might not be able to repay the loans. Banks were already facing high levels of nonperforming loans and were afraid to make additional loans because of a shrinking Thai economy and unfavorable economic conditions elsewhere in Asia. In the words of one observer, "a vicious cycle has set in whereby a progressively weakening real sector has sent nonperforming loans soaring, thus further diminishing the financial sector's ability to support the real sector" (Chet 1998).

This dilemma began to create tensions within the Thai cabinet midway through 1998. Finance Minister Tarrin Nimmanahaeminda continued to argue for maintaining high interest rates and sticking closely to IMF policies. Other ministers, most notably the Commerce Minister Supachai Panitchpakdi, argued for modifications in the policies including injecting more money into the economy, lower interest rates, and a weaker baht to help businesses (Piyanart 1998). This debate is likely to continue within the government as the firms continues to struggle, and as businesspeople and others put increasing pressure on the government to do something about the liquidity crisis.

Industrial Upgrading

Upgrading Thai industrial competitiveness is less immediately pressing than resolving the liquidity crisis, but unless this occurs Thailand will not be able to sustain economic growth in the long run no matter how successful the reforms in the financial sector. As Banthoon Lamsan, the Chief Executive Officer of the Thai

Farmers Bank and Chair of the Thai Bankers Association puts it, recapitalization and increased liquidity are not panaceas. If companies get more money and produce "low quality, non-competitive goods and services, no amount of liquidity will save businesses" (Woo 1998).

One of the consequences of the financial crisis is that it is likely to make the need for greater export competitiveness seem less pressing. The fall in the value of the baht increased Thai export competitiveness in some commodities and industrial goods such as garments, textiles, and shoes. After zero growth in 1996, exports grew by approximately 10 percent in 1997 with the help of a dramatically weaker baht. Garments were being written off as a sunset industry for Thailand in 1996, but in the first nine months of 1997 garment exports grew by 7 percent in contrast with a 21 percent decline in 1996.[23] Thai garment and textile exports were projected to rise by 15 percent in 1998 (Woranuj 1997). In the short run these exports will help Thailand get through an extremely difficult economic situation, but in the longer run it is necessary to upgrade the quality of garment and textile exports, as well as other traditional exports, and move into newer, higher value-added exports.

Fortunately, Thailand has already begun to do this to some extent. Exports of medium-high technology products such as computer parts and electronics began to accelerate after 1990. Between 1990 and 1995 exports of these products grew at 30 percent per year while exports of labor intensive exports grew at only 14 percent per year. "By 1995, exports of medium-high technology products were about 40 percent larger than that for labor intensive products" (Chalongphob 1997). The falling value of the baht also helped increase exports of automobiles, autoparts, electrical and electronic products in 1997 (Thammavit 1997). The problem with these exports is that for most of these products Thailand

is simply an assembly base. The technological development, design and brand name of these products are predominantly foreign. Thus, similar to the case with labor intensive exports products, the current comparative advantage of Thailand in medium-high technology products is based on low assembly cost (Chalongphob 1997).

Thailand is losing its cost advantage in low cost garments and textiles, and will also lose its comparative advantage in medium-high technology products as other countries' workers become able to perform the work at lower costs (ibid). In the next ten to fifteen years Thailand should be able to keep its comparative advantage in medium to high technology product assembly and exports, but it must be prepared for the next stage when the multinationals who manufacture most of these products move production bases to other countries.

Increasing value-added requires human resource development (education, vocational training, etc). In 1997 nearly 80 percent of Thai workers had only a primary education or less (Thammavit 1997), and Thailand had the lowest ratio of science and technology graduates per 10,000 population of any country in Asia (Schlossstein 1991:163). Also important are vendor development and general technology diffusion. These gaps are obvious. The more challenging question involves the institutional channels and political will through which Thailand might improve in these areas. Since this is a huge question, we will simply note the following considerations:

Fewer Policy Instruments and Greater Challenges. Given impending WTO membership and IMF-induced financial constraints, the Thai government will influence industrial growth with fewer instruments of direct protection and subsidization. Policy emphasis now has to be on helping local firms to succeed in regional and global markets by identifying new market opportunities and by promoting real upgrading.

Government as Catalyst and Public-Private Sector Linkages. Despite the above-noted constraints, the government still has critical roles to play in the provision, direct or indirect, of public goods and positive externalities. Government linkage to and support for various kinds of "collective service providers" can be critical. Such providers can be entirely private, collective, or quasi-public. Indeed, a key part of any upgrading policies must be a strengthening of existing private sector and quasi-public organizations. Thailand has many trading companies, business associations, suppliers' clubs, technical universities, vocational schools, and institutes (e.g., the Food Processing Institute, Thai Petrochemical Institute, Textile Institute, Thai-German Institute, Thai-Japan Institute).

Consider the example of private trading companies, collective associations, and government in the success of Taiwan's auto parts firms in export production, where exports account for 80 percent of Taiwan firms' parts production. A few large trading firms were established to handle export and market development for small parts producers. In addition, the Taiwanese Transportation Vehicle Manufacturers Association helped member firms to find markets, established links with overseas after-market associations, and invested in quality standards to reassure overseas clients. Finally, government officials supported these efforts and encouraged technology transfers with foreign joint venture partners.

As noted earlier, the Thai government has in fact performed these kinds of functions in certain kinds of agricultural exports where standards and market development were key to the country's financial stability. Whether this kind of capacity is possible for industrial products, given the long period of protection and the difficulty of breaking into more demanding export networks for manufactured goods, is in part a function of political arrangements.

Electoral Rules and Parties

Finally, in addition to the changes needed in the financial sector and upgrading industrial competitiveness, Thailand needs to change the ways in which politicians compete for office so that there is a greater probability of stable governments which can address problems of financial reform and industrial upgrading effectively. Before turning to an examination of how this might be done, it is important to note that even with all their flaws parliamentary institutions have advantages over more authoritarian institutions. The great advantage of the parliamentary system in Thailand is that it allowed a relatively easy change of government from one that was clearly not effective to one that was. In contrast, Indonesia, with an authoritarian political arrangement and a single leader who had been in power since the late 1960s, had no way of making the change as smoothly. There is a great deal to be said for parliamentary government in these circumstances ("Stand down, Suharto," *The Economist*, January 17, 1998). And for all the criticisms that have been made of Thai politicians, when all is said and done they approved the new constitution in 1997. The issue is how to keep parliamentary institutions while strengthening them.

One of the major obstacles to parliamentary reform was that rural network politicians, who are the social force most strongly supportive of parliamentary government, were also the social force most resistant to changes aimed at strengthening political parties and reducing the importance of money politics.[24] Access to parliament gives them an avenue not only to wealth, but also to power and status which they were denied in Thailand's highly centralized, authoritarian governments of the 1950s through the 1970s (Anderson 1990). They strongly opposed changes in electoral laws and other proposed constitutional changes that would have weakened their power. The economic crisis weakened their resistance by revealing the necessity for more competent and stable governments. With the strong backing of "the King, the army, the Bangkok business elite, and the middle class," a new constitution was approved by parliament in September 1997 (Jackson 1998:53).

The new constitution addresses major weaknesses of Thailand's electoral and parliamentary politics. To encourage political parties to recruit political leaders with national views and who address national issues in their campaign the new constitution has a requirement that 100 members of the new 500-member parliament will be elected nationally from party lists. For these MPs the entire country will be one constituency. The parties are likely to run the members of their party they wish to be cabinet ministers on the lists, and these candidates will have to address national issues in their campaigns (Ammar 1997). Another provision aimed at improving the educational quality of MPs and also closing out a number of provincial entrepreneurs is a requirement that all MPs must hold at least a bachelor's degree. To eliminate some of the undesirable consequences of the past multiple-member constituencies they will be replaced by 400 single-seat constituencies. The new constitution also requires MPs who become ministers to give up their MP status. This provision is designed to strengthen cabinet stability by making it much harder for MPs to move easily from parliament membership to cabinet and back again. To prevent the switching of party memberships which has been a constant feature of Thai elections politicians must be members of a party for at least ninety days before voting day. The increased size of the new lower house will make it more difficult for smaller parties to have much influence, thus causing the creation of larger parties or at least a drop in the number of tiny parties which are essentially the election machine of a single politician. These parties will also be penalized by a provision which requires parties to win at least 5 percent of the popular vote before they can win any seats from their party lists. The constitution also creates an Election Commission to oversee elections, a responsibility previously administered by the Interior Ministry and one frequently used in the past to manipulate elections in provincial areas. While it is unrealistic to expect that these provisions will make dramatic changes in Thai politics in the next few years, they do increase the probability of more competent leadership and more stable governments.

Two problems remain despite the new constitution. First, some of the major forces in Thai politics and society are skeptical of parliamentary democracy, and even those who are supportive can turn quickly against incumbent governments. Those who are skeptical include large numbers of civil servants and military officers, metropolitan business people, and technocrats.[25] There is more support for parliamentary institutions and democracy among the Bangkok middle class, but the depth of this support is questionable. Finally, large numbers of urban workers seem to accept the basic parliamentary framework but are largely excluded from influence in it (Pasuk and Baker 1997).[26] A worsening of the present economic difficulties, coupled with government instability would increase demands for dispensing with normal parliamentary politics in favor of some kind of unelected, interim government similar to those headed by Anand Panyarachun in 1991 and 1992.

It is not clear how long the middle class and workers will support the Chuan-led government as the economic slump continues and large numbers of person lose their jobs. In September 1992 when Chuan first became prime minister, large numbers of middle class citizens and members of the press supported him. But "a little over two-and-a-half years later the same groups were disenchanted with the government and relieved when the House was dissolved" (Murray 1996). Worker protests have been limited so far, but the Chuan government was strongly criticized for the way police handled a rowdy crowd of strikers at the Thai Summit Auto Parts Company in January 1998 (Sopon 1998). The government is also having to deal with threats of rallies of poor farmers from the Northeast in Bangkok.[27] These protests provide opportunities for other political parties to criticize the Chuan government. It is vulnerable to such criticism because of a reputation from the first Chuan administration (1992–1995) of lack of concern for the poor (Sorrayuth 1998; "Democrat disdain for the poor . . ." 1998). The government is attempting to respond to poor farmers and urban workers who have been laid off and are returning to their rural homes by setting aside funds to finance job creation in rural communities (Nussara 1998).[28] It has also negotiated with the World Bank for loans to create jobs for workers left unemployed (Chiratas and Wichit 1998).

A second problem is that the new rules still leave rural network politicians with considerable power. Any political party intent on pressing forward with the kinds of reforms we have discussed in this paper will still need "to form strategic alliances with old-style faction bosses who [can] deliver upcountry parliamentary seats" (McCargo 1997:130-31; Surin and McCargo 1997:142). Their presence in governments will make it more difficult to address the problems discussed. One likely consequence is continuing factionalism that will contribute to unstable governments. Another is that many of these politicians are unlikely to support initiatives to upgrade industries. Many of the industries that would benefit from upgrading are in Bangkok or in areas immediately around Bangkok. There is no payoff for rural network politicians for supporting such reforms. Upgrading Bangkok-based firms brings no resources into most of their provinces, and some of them have opposed support for Bangkok-based firms in the past on the grounds that such support is helping rich capitalists when more money should be allocated to the provinces. Finally, as long as they control line ministries and use them for patronage purposes it will be difficult to use these ministries in efforts to restructure and upgrade manufacturing.[29]

While the constitutional changes are useful steps toward better governance, further improvements depend upon changing provinces in ways that weaken the influence of rural network politicians and increase support for parliamentary democracy. The first Chuan government began substantial efforts in this direction by pursuing economic decentralization policies aimed at increasing investment in the provinces in order to promote provincial growth, alleviate poverty, and slow urban migration (Parichart 1997:254). A renewal of this policy could have substantial political benefits in addition to the economic and social benefits that it would bring. A good deal of the power of rural network politicians is based upon local monopolies (Pasuk and Baker 1997:30). Economic development in the provinces has the potential for breaking up these monopolies through the growth of new businesses, and increasing urbanization is likely to create greater support for parliamentary democracy (LoGerfo 1996). Growth and more effective social welfare policies will also weaken the conditions facilitating "machine politics" (Ockey 1994:252).

Notes

1. Some have criticized the BoI for the aimlessness and promiscuity of its promotion policies (Ammar 1975:38). One clear goal of the BoI, however, was to generate enough investment in Thailand to saturate the domestic economy and force firms to begin exporting (Doner, Bangkok interview).

2. The best discussion of Siam Cement's role in consumer electronics is found in Felker (1998).

3. Sanjaya Lall cautions that rising wages "may not be the whole explanation" for the decline in growth of these sectors. One reason for caution is that wages had been rising for several years. They do not explain the sudden drop in labor intensive exports in 1996.

4. This began to change when Tarrin Nimmanahaeminda was Finance Minister in Prime Minister Chuan Leekpai's first government between 1992 and 1995. We shall return to the significance of this point in the final section of the paper.

5. The cascading tariff structure refers to one in which the highest rates of protection are on final goods. This has encouraged local firms to concentrate in final assembly for two reasons: they enjoy the highest level of protection, and they avoid paying the duties on imported inputs required if they produced parts and components. And in many industries, including electronics, knocked-down assembly kits paid lower tariffs than individual components, further discouraging local assembly firms from unpackaging their kits and obtaining parts locally. This section draws upon research done for the Data Storage Globalization Project supported by the Sloan Foundation (Doner and Brimble 1998). The business tax was replaced by a VAT in 1992, but there have been delays in VAT rebates for indirect exporters and reports of widespread fraudulent export claims to obtain VAT funds.

6. Wichit Sirithaveeporn, "Petrochemicals/Import Tariff Reductions: Ministers Split Over Proposals," *Bangkok Post*, November 24, 1997; "Major Producers to Relocate if Import Duty Is Not Restructured," *Business Day* (Bangkok), December 17, 1997; and "Thailand to Raise Structural Steel Imports Duty," *Xinhua*, January 11, 1998.

7. This section draws upon research for the Data Storage Industry Globalization Project supported by the Sloan Foundation.

8. For an overall analysis of the problem, see Brooker (1996). For an excellent analysis of Thai technology institutions, see Felker (1997:149-55).

9. See JICA (1994) on the depth of the Thai supply base. For an overview of the policies impeding the upgrading of the supply base, see FIAS (1991).

10. Ammar Siamwalla, personal communication, June 2, 1998.

11. The closer link between foreign and domestic markets was expected to narrow the gap between domestic and foreign interest rates, but this did not happen (Ammar 1997).

12. This practice was followed in other Asian countries which experienced economic crashes in 1997, and it is a key part of the explanation of why the currency crisis which began in Thailand spread to several other East and Southeast Asian countries ("Why did Asia crash?" 1997).

13. The sixth largest bank is the Thai Military Bank. Its military connections have protected it from the Bank of Thailand and minority shareholders, despite numerous problems and substantial numbers of nonperforming loans (Handley 1997b).

14. The government also rescued thirty-two finance companies, but fifteen other finance companies were allowed to collapse (Doner and Unger 1993:115).

15. Krugman suggests that this theory helps explain why the crisis spread to other Asian countries. The countries caught up in the crisis share a boom-bust cycle in asset prices along with "banks and finance companies that lent on overly risky projects" on the assumption they would be bailed out by governments ("Why did Asia crash?" 1997).

16. The failure of the United States to help Thailand more in its time of crisis has been a point of resentment in Thailand and has been the subject of much discussion and letters to editors.

17. Ammar (1997), from which this discussion draws heavily.

18. A new constitution was adopted in September 1997 and was designed to address many of the weaknesses discussed here. We will turn to a discussion of the new constitution and its possible consequences in the final section of this chapter.

19. Not all of politicians' behavior can be explained by this quest for cabinet seats and resources (see McCargo 1997:118).

20. There are times when politicians behave in ways which undermine their chances for cabinet seats (see McCargo 1997:118).

21. To be fair, this rate of turnover in the finance ministry position was unusual, caused in part by personality conflicts between finance ministers and the prime minister rather than structural problems. Other ministers were more stable during this period. Also the number of political parties has declined since the first open elections in Thailand in the mid-1970s, albeit slowly.

22. Ammar Siamwalla notes that since the Ministry of Finance deals with national policy issues, and therefore presumably non-divisible goods, most politicians have been happy to cede that ministry to technocrats. However, given the ways in which politicians have become involved in the stock exchange and commercial banks, the value of this insulation has lessened.

23. Garments and textiles do not have to be sunset industries as countries develop. Italy, Germany, the United States, and France are among the top ten clothing exporters in the world.

24. The term "rural network politician" is from Robertson (1996).

25. The present Royal Thai Army Commander-in-Chief, General Chetta Thanajaro, strongly supported the new constitution, and the military has accepted a cut in its budget from 18 percent to 10 percent of the national budget (Vatikiotis, Tasker, and Thayer 1998:22-23). The military has also accepted Chuan as the first civilian defense minister.

26. See the excellent article by Handley in Hewison (1997) for an argument that the Bangkok middle class is not nearly as supportive of democratic politics as many assert. A further problem in discussing this issue is the definition of the "middle class" and finding reliable and valid data on its attitudes.

27. Two of the organizations threatening farmers' protests are the Assembly of the Poor and the Federation of Small-time Northeastern Farmers. Both argue that the public, and poor farmers, should not be taxed to help pay foreign debts generated by rich urban business people and by incompetence in the Bank of Thailand. Significantly, "it's the first time that poor farmers have pressed aggressively on national policies rather than immediate issues affecting their daily lives." Protests are likely to center on increases in the VAT and oil tax increases (Sorrayuth 1998).

28. In the longer run the government will have to pay greater attention to job training for labor.

29. It is misleading to blame these problems solely on provincially-based politicians. Fragmentation of parties and rampant rent-seeking were prevalent in the 1970s well before the rural network politicians and *chao phos* rose to prominence.

References

Ammar Siamwalla. 1997. "Can a Developing Democracy Manage Its Macroeconomy? The Case of Thailand." In *Thailand's Boom and Bust*. Bangkok: Thailand Development Research Institute.

———. 1997. "The Thai Economy: Fifty Years of Expansion." In *Thailand's Boom and Bust*. Bangkok: Thailand Development Research Institute.

———. 1975. "Stability, Growth, and Distribution in the Thai Economy." In *Finance, Trade and Economic Development in Thailand: Essays in Honour of Khunying Suparb Yossundara*, ed. Prateep Sondysuvan. Bangkok: Sompong Press.

Ammar Siamwalla, and Orapin Sobchokchai. 1998. "Responding to the Thai Economic Economic Crisis." Paper prepared for the United Nations Development Programme (UNDP Bangkok), High-Level Consultative Meeting on "Policy Response to the Economic Crisis and Social Impact in Thailand," Bangkok, May 22, 1998.

Anderson, Benedict. 1990. "Murder and Progress in Modern Siam." *New Left Review* (May/June).

Anek Laothamatas. 1996. "A Tale of Two Democracies: Conflicting Perceptions of Elections and Democracy in Thailand." In *The Politics of Elections in Southeast Asia*, ed. R. H. Taylor. Washington, DC: Woodrow Wilson Center Press.

Arom Suwansapap. 1996. "Japanese Investment in Thailand." *Bangkok Bank Monthly Review* (August): 8-13.

"Banking and Finance: Clouds threaten a rich harvest." 1990. *Bangkok Post Year-End Economic Review* (December 31):36-38.

"Banking and Finance: Profits come down to earth." 1991. *Bangkok Post Year-End Economic Review* (December 31).

"BankWatch downgrades Thailand's sovereign risk." 1997. *Bangkok Post* (December 5).

Bello, Walden. 1997a. "Addicted to Foreign Capital." *The Nation* (December 3).

———. 1997b. "'Fast Track' Capitalism." *The Nation* (December 4).

———. 1997c. "Shadow of Gloom Lengthens." *The Nation* (December 5).

Benjamas Rojvanit, and Patira Suksthien. 1992. "Bangkok International Banking Facilities." *Bangkok Bank Monthly Review* (November): 8-14.

Brooker Group. 1997. "Automotive Industry Export Promotion Project: Thailand Industry Overview." Bangkok: Unpublished manuscript.

———. 1996. "Modalities of University-Industry Cooperation in the APEC Region." Bangkok: APEC Research Project. Prepared for the Thai Ministry of University Affairs.

Chalongphob Sussangkarn. 1998. "Thailand's Debt Crisis and Economic Outlook." *Bangkok Post* (February 8). http://www.bangkokpost.net/today/080298_Perspective02.html.

———. 1993. "Thailand: Looking Ahead to 2020 in Light of Global and Regional Changes." *TDRI Quarterly Review* 12:2 (June): 3-13.

Chatrudee Theparat. 1997. "Govt needs B16b to plug hole after excise flip-flop." *Bangkok Post* (October 27).

Chet Chaovisidha. 1998. "Vicious cycle sets in motion an ever-weakening real sector." *Bankok Post* (July 1).

Chiratas Nivatpumin, and Wichit Sirithaveeporn. 1998. "Govt seeks new loan to create jobs upcountry." *Bangkok Post* (February 1). http://www.bangkokpost.net/today/010298_News05.html.

Christensen, Scott. 1991. "The Politics of Democratization in Thailand: State and Society Since 1932." Bangkok: Thailand Development Research Institute Background Paper.

Christensen, Scott, and Ammar Siamwalla. 1993. "Beyond Patronage: Tasks for the Thai State." Bangkok: Thailand Development Research Institute.

Christensen, Scott, David Dollar, Ammar Siamwalla, and Pakorn Vichyanond. 1993. "Thailand: The Institutional and Political Underpinnings of Growth." Washington, DC: The World Bank.

Cholada Ingsrisawong. 1997. "Thais will lose control of banking business." *Bangkok Post* (December 29).
    http://www.bangkokpost.net/291297/291297_Business01.html.

"Democrat disdain for the poor has potential to topple Chuan." 1998. *The Nation.*
    http://www.bangkokpost.net/today/310198_News22.html.

Doner, Richard F., and Anek Laothamatas. 1994. "Thailand: Economic and Political Gradualism." In *Voting for Reform: Democracy, Poltitical Liberalization, and Economic Adjustment*, ed. Stephan Haggard and Steven B. Webb. New York: Oxford University Press.

Doner, Richard F., and Peter Brimble. 1998. "Thailand's Hard Disc Drive Industry." Working paper, Information Storage Industry Center, University of California, San Diego.

Doner, Richard F., and Gary Hawes. 1995. "The Political Economy of Growth in Southeast and Northeast Asia." In *The Changing Political Economy of the Third World*, ed. Manochehr Dorraj. Boulder, CO: Lynne Reinner Publishers.

Doner, Richard F., and Ansil Ramsay. 1997a. "Competitive Clientelism and Economic Governance: The Case of Thailand." In *Business and the State in Developing Countries*, ed. Sylvia Maxfield and Ben Ross Schneider. Ithaca, NY: Cornell University Press.

——— . 1997b. "Rents, Collective Action, and Economic Development in Thailand (revised)." Paper presented at the Conference on Rents and Development in Southeast Asia, Kuala Lumpur, Malaysia, August 27-28, 1996.

——— . 1996. "Clientelism and Economic Development in Thailand." Paper prepared for the annual meeting of the Association for Asian Studies, Honolulu, Hawaii, April 11-14, 1996.

Doner, Richard F., and Daniel Unger. 1993. "The Politics of Finance in Thai Economic Development." In *The Politics of Finance in Developing Countries*, ed. Stephan Haggard et. al. Ithaca, NY: Cornell University Press.

Ehito Kimura. 1998. "The New Unequal Treaties." *Bangkok Post* (January 22).
    http://www.bangkokpost.net/today/220198_News24.html.

"Exploding a popular myth." 1991. *Bangkok Post Year-End Economic Review* (December 31).

Felker, Gregory. 1997. The Politics of Technology Development—State, Business, and Multinationals in Malaysia and Thailand. Ph.D. diss., Woodrow Wilson School, Princeton University.

"Financial Institution Crisis: from Japan, Korea, to Thailand." 1997. Research Department Bangkok Bank PCL.
    http://www. bbl.co.th./research/jun_pr1.htm.

Goad, G. Pierre. 1997. "Government, Not Hedge Funds, to Blame For Asia's Woes, IMF's Camdessus Says." *Wall Street Journal* (December 3): A17.

Haggard, Stephan. 1998. "Asia and Pacific Asian Financial Crisis." Testimony before the Subcommittee on Asia and the Pacific, Committee on International Relations, U.S. House of Representatives (February 4). Internet, lexis-nexis.

Handley, Paul. 1997a. "More of the same? Politics and business, 1987–96." In *Political Change in Thailand: Democracy and Participation*, ed. Kevin Hewison. New York: Routledge.

———. 1997b. "Bangkok's long road to recovery." *Institutional Investor* (September). Internet, lexis-nexis.

Hauss, Charles. 1994. *Comparative Politics: Domestic Responses to Global Challenges.* New York: West Publishing Company.

Hewison, Kevin, ed. 1997. *Political Change in Thailand: Democracy and Participation.* New York: Routledge.

———. 1996. "Emerging Social Forces in Thailand: New Political and Economic Roles." In *The New Rich in Asia: Mobile phones, McDonalds and Middle-Class Revolution*, ed. Richard Robison and David S. G. Goodman. New York: Routledge.

———. 1989. *Bankers and Bureaucrats: Capital and the Role of the State in Thailand.* New Haven: Southeast Asia Studies, Yale University.

Janssen, Peter. 1996. "Banking and finance: Banks underpin economic success." *Banking and Finance* (June).
http://web3.asia1.com.sg/timesnet/data/ab/docs/ab1021.html.

Kirida Baopichitr. 1997. "Thailand's Road to Economic Crisis: A Brief Overview." *The Nation* (December 12).

Kitti Withchuroj. 1993. "The Thai Textile Industry." *Bangkok Bank Monthly Review* (February): 33-36.

Krugman, Paul. 1998. "What Happened to Asia?"
http://web.mit.edu/krugman/www/DISINTER.html.

Lall, Sanjaya. 1998. "Thailand's Manufacturing Competitiveness: A Premliminary Overview." Paper prepared for conference on Thailand's Dynamic Economic Recovery and Competitiveness, Bangkok, May 20-21.

Levi, Margaret. 1990. "A Logic of Institutional Change." In *The Limits of Rationality*, ed. Karen Schweers and Margaret Levi. Chicago: University of Chicago Press.

LoGerfo, Jim. 1996. "Attitudes Toward Democracy Among Bangkok and Rural Northern Thais." *Asian Survey* (September): 904-23.

"Major Producers to Relocate if Import Duty is not Restructured." 1997. *Business Day* (November 17).

Maneerungsee, Woranuj. 1998. "Millers may be stockpiling up to ten million 100-kilo sacks." *Bangkok Post* (January 20).
http://www.bangkokpost.net/today/200198_Business02.html.

———. 1997. "Trading our way to success." *Bangkok Post* (January 20).
http://www.bangkokpost.net/today/200198_Business02.html.

McCargo, Ducan. 1997. "Thailand's Political Parties: Real, Authentic, and Actual." In *Political Change in Thailand: Democracy and Participation*, ed. Kevin Hewison. New York: Routledge.

McVey, Ruth. 1992. "The Materialization of the Southeast Asian Entrepreneur." In *Southeast Asian Capitalists*, ed. Ruth McVey. Ithaca, NY: Southeast Asia Program, Cornell University.

Mingsarn Kaosa-ard. 1998. "Economic Development and Institutional Failures in Thailand." *TDRI Quarterly Review* 13, 1 (March): 3-11.

Murray, David. 1996. "The 1995 National Elections in Thailand: A Step Backward for Democracy?" *Asian Survey* 36:4 (April): 361-75.

Muscat, Robert J. 1994. *The Fifth Tiger: A Study of Thai Development Policy.* Armonk, NY: M.E. Sharpe.

Mydans, Seth. 1997. "Economists Cheer Thailand's Tough Action on Ailing Finance Companies." *New York Times* (December 9).

Nabli, Mustapha, and Jeffrey Nugent. 1993. "The New Institutional Economics and Its Applicability to Development." *World Development* 17(9): 1333-1347.

Narongchai Akrasanee, David Dapice, and Frank Flatters. 1991. *Thailand's Export-Led Growth: Retrospect and Prospects.* Bangkok: Thailand Development Research Institute.

Nimit Nontapunthawat. 1997. "The Thai Economy: Where Is It Going After the Current Crisis?" *Bangkok Bank Monthly Review* (November-December): 15-23.

Nipon Paoponsakorn, and Belinda Fuller. 1997. "Thailand's Development Experience from the Economic System Perspective: Open Politics and Industrial Activism." In *East Asian Development Experience: Economic System Approach and Its Applicability*, ed. Toru Yanagihara and Susumu Sambommatsu. Tokyo: Institute of Developing Economies.

Nipon Paopongsakorn, and Pawadee Tonguthai. 1998. "Technological Capability Building and the Sustainability of Export Success in Thailand's Textiles and Electronic Industies." In *Technological Capabilities and Export Success in Asia*, ed. Dieter Ernst, Tom Ganiatsos, and Lynne Mytelka. New York: Routlege.

The Nukul Commission Report: Analysis and Evaluation of the Facts Behind Thailand's Economic Crisis. 1998. *The Nation.* Translated from *Raingan phon kanwikhro lae winitchai khothetching kiawkab sathankan wikrit thang sethakit* (Report of the Results of Analysis and Evaluation of the Facts Behind Thailand's Economic Crisis). 1998. Bangkok: Thailand Development Research Institute.

Nuntawan Polkwamdee. 1997. "Banking and Finance: Lesson on greed and laxity." *Bangkok Post Year-End Economic Review.* http://www.bangkokpost.net/ecoreview97/review9709.html.

Nussara Yenprasert. 1998. "Bt10 bn set for job-creation." *The Nation* (January 31). http://www.nationmultimedia.com/news/bus3.html.

Ockey, James. 1994. "Political Parties, Factions, and Corruption in Thailand." *Modern Asian Studies* 28(2): 251-77.

Pana Janviroj. 1997. "Central Bank Fails Globalization Test." *The Nation* (August 18): A4.

Parichart Chotiya. 1997. "The changing role of provincial business in the Thai political economy." In *Political Change in Thailand: Democracy and Participation*, ed. Kevin Hewison. New York: Routledge.

Parista Yuthmanop, Cholada Ingsrisawang, and Wichit Sirithaveeporn. 1998. "Bank of Thailand takes over three banks." *Bangkok Post* (February 7).

Parista Yuthmanop. 1997. "Recovery efforts return to square one." *Bangkok Post* (October 28).

——— . 1996. "Banking and Finance: Public faith severely shaken." *Bangkok Post Year-End Economic Review*: 18-20.

Pasuk Phongpaichit, and Chris Baker. 1997. "Power in Transition: Thailand in the 1990s." In *Political Change in Thailand: Democracy and Participation*, ed. Kevin Hewison. New York: Routledge.

Pasuk Phongpaichit, and Sungsidh Piriyarangsan. 1996. *Corruption and Democracy in Thailand*. Chiang Mai, Thailand: Silkworm Books.

Pattnapong Chantranontwong. 1996. "Politics: Plenty of big rats to smell." *Bangkok Post Year-End Economic Review*: 54-55.

"Petrochemicals/Import Tariff Reductions: Ministries Split Over Proposal." 1997. *Bangkok Post* (November 24).

Pimjai Siripotiprapan. 1997. "The IMF and Thailand's Economic Rehabilitation." *Bangkok Bank Monthly Review* (October): 7-10.

Piyanart Srivalo. 1998. "Ministers clash over economic steps." *The Nation* (June 16).

Pontusson, Jonas. 1995. "From Comparative Public Policy to Political Economy: Putting Political Institutions in Their Place and Taking Interests Seriously." *Comparative Political Studies* 28:1 (April): 117-47.

Ramsay, Ansil. 1987. "The Political Economy of Sugar in Thailand." *Pacific Affairs* 60:2 (Summer): 248-78.

Robertson, Philip S., Jr. 1996. "The Rise of the Rural Network Politician: Will Thailand's New Elite Endure?" *Asian Survey* 36:9 (September): 924-41.

Rochana Kosiyanon. 1998. "By the Way." *Textile Digest* 5:55 (March-April): 11.

Rosenberger, Leif Roderick. 1997. "Southeast Asia's Currency Crisis: A Diagnosis and Prescription." *Contemporary Southeast Asia* 19:3 (December): 223-51.

Sombat Champathong. 1997a. "The World Textile Industry and Thailand's Potential." *Bangkok Bank Monthly Review* (January): 11-20.

———. 1997b. "The Textile Industry." *Bangkok Bank Monthly Review* (June): 22-31.

Soonruth Bunyamee. 1998. "Tejapaibuls likely big losers." *Bangkok Post* (January 27). http://www.bangkokpost.net/today/270198_Business01.html.

Soonruth Bunyamee, and Parista Yuthamanop. 1998. "'Thai approach' to debt urged." *Bangkok Post* (June 30).

Soonruth Bunyamee, and Chiratas Nivatupumin. 1997. "Banking and Finance: The Year They Sank the Baht." *Bangkok Post Year-End Economic Review*. http://www.bangkokpost.net/ecoreview97/review 9704. html.

Sopon Onkara. 1998. "Labour time-bomb ticks away under government." *The Nation* (January 28). http://www.nationmultimedia.com/news.e2901.html.

Sorrayuth Suthassanachinda. 1998. "Chavalit displays worrying sign by forecasting unrest." *The Nation* (January 31). http://www.nationmultimedia.com/news/pol2.html.

Suchada Khokhachaikiet. 1997. "Integrated Circuits: Emphasis on Developing Technology and Export Potential." *Thai Farmers Research Center, Co.* 2 (September).

Suchit Bunbongkarn. 1990. "The Role of Major Political Forces in the Thai Political Process." In *U.S.-Thailand Relations in a New International Era*, ed. Clark D. Neher and Wiwat Mungkandi. Berkeley: Institute of East Asian Studies, University of California, Berkeley.

———. 1988. "Contemporary Thai Political Development." In *Thailand-U.S. Relations: Changing Political, Strategic, and Economic Factors*, ed. Ansil Ramsay and Wiwat Mungkandi. Berkeley: Institute of East Asian Studies, University of California, Berkeley.

Surin Maisrikrod, and Duncan McCargo. 1997. "Electoral Politics: Commercialisation and Exclusion." In *Political Change in Thailand: Democracy and Participation*, ed. Kevin Hewison. New York: Routledge.

"Thailand to Raise Structural Steel Imports Duty." 1998. *Xinhua* (January 11).

Thammavit Terdudomtham. 1997. "The Economy: The bubble finally burst." *Bangkok Post Year-End Economic Review.*
http://www.bangkokpost.net/ecoreview97/9701.html.

———. 1996. "The Economy: Analysts Taken By Surprise," *Bangkok Post Year-End Economic Review*: 9-11.

Thanisr Chaturonkul. 1992. "BIBF: Essence and Impacts." *Bangkok Bank Monthly Review* (September): 7-9.

Unger, Danny. 1989. "Regulatory State or Developmental State? The State and Commercial Banks in Thailand." Paper prepared for the annual meeting of the American Political Science Association, Atlanta, Georgia, August 31-September 3.

Vatchara Charoonsantikul. 1998. "Decisiveness needed to head off second crisis." *The Nation* (June 16).

Vatchara Charoonsantikul, and Thanong Khanthong. 1998. "Rerngchai's men let him Down." *The Nation* (March 23). Part 2 in a special series on the baht defense.

———. 1998. "Market forces played havoc with currency." *The Nation* (March 24). Part 3 in a special series on the baht defense.

———. 1998. "Amnuay's resignation triggered chaos in financial market." *The Nation* (March 25). Part 4 in a special series on the baht defense.

———. 1998. "Chaiyawat's silence cost the nation dear." *The Nation* (March 26). Part 5 in a special series on the baht defense.

———. 1998. "Amnuay had little to do with BOT's baht defense." *The Nation* (March 27). Part 6 in a special series on the baht defense.

———. 1998. "Tarrin, Olarn were unaware of swap contract deals." *The Nation* (March 31). Part 9 in a special series on the baht defense.

———. 1998. "Phaiboon's role in baht's defense." *The Nation* (April 2). Part 11 in a special series on the baht defense.

———. 1998. "Nukul report may change views." *The Nation* (April 3). Final part in a special series on the baht defense.

Vatikiotis, Michael. 1998. "Anatomy of a Crisis." *Far Eastern Economic Review* (May 21): Internet edition.

Vatikiotis, Michael, Rodney Tasker, and Nate Thayer. 1998. "Military Affairs: New Rules, Same Game." *Far Eastern Economic Review* (January 29): 22-23.

Virawan, Amnuay. 1998. "East Asia after the bubble burst." *Bangkok Post* (February 6). http://www.bangkokpost.net/today/060298_News30.html.

Walters, Sir Alan. 1997. "What went wrong: The baht, the bank, and the blame," *Bangkok Post Internet Edition* (November 11).

Warr, Peter G. 1997. "The Thai Economy: From Boom to Gloom?" *Southeast Asian Affairs.* Singapore: Institute of Southeast Asian Studies.

Watsaya Limthammahisom. 1997a. "Financial Crisis in Japan, South Korea, and Thailand: A Comparison." *Bangkok Bank Monthly Review* (August): 10-19.

———. 1997b. "ASEAN at 30: The End of the Economic Miracle?" *Bangkok Bank Monthly Review* (October): 11-21.

———. "Thai Industries: Where Are They Heading?" 1997c. *Bangkok Bank Monthly Review* (November-December): 11-14.

"We Accept Hardship: Thailand's prime minister gives a sober assessment of the economy." 1998. *Asiaweek* (January 16).

Weena Thongsamai. 1993. '"Real Estate Business." *Bangkok Bank Monthly Review* (December): 20-22.

"Why did Asia crash?" 1998. *The Economist* (January 10): 66.

Wichit Sirithaveeporn. 1997. "Scrapping oil tax will leave state short of target." *Bangkok Post* (October 20).

Woo, K. I. 1998. "Banthoon—telling it like it is." *The Nation* (June 15): B8.

8

Indonesia's Crisis and Future Prospects

Ross H. McLeod

Background

In the first half of 1997, the Indonesian economy seemed to be performing very well. Growth had averaged about 8 percent per annum (p.a.) since the late 1980s, inflation had fallen from the average of 9 percent p.a. achieved over the previous sixteen years to under 6 percent, the budget continued to be conservatively managed, the exchange rate maintained its slow and controlled depreciation of about 4 percent p.a., and the balance of payments was so strong that international reserves—already high—were increasing rapidly. Although foreign debt was relatively high as well, for some time most of the growth therein had been generated by the private sector, which appeared to be having no trouble meeting its repayment commitments. At the macroeconomic level, then, there was little sign of the turmoil that was to emerge in the second half of the year.

With the benefit of hindsight, however, it would appear that investment and financing decisions had become too much driven by the euphoria engendered by years of largely uninterrupted expansion, and too little driven by careful analyses of business prospects and risks. In other words, Indonesia seems to have been in the advanced stage of an economic boom, in which growth momentum depended increasingly on continued optimism on the part of investors and financiers.

In less heady times, bankers and funds managers sensibly adopt the attitude that they need to be persuaded to part with funds by way of well-researched business proposals, offers of solid security, and a willingness on the part of applicants to put a substantial amount of their own funds at risk in the venture to be financed. When an economy has been racing ahead for years on end, however, there is a strong tendency for those same bankers and financiers to become aggressive salesmen, almost begging businesses to take funds off their hands. All too often, collateral is in the form of real estate, valued on the basis of extrapolated recent upward trends in property prices, and projects are financed on very high gearing ratios. History shows that when large risk exposures accumulate in this manner, optimism can turn to pessimism in the blink of an eye, and deep recession can take the place of booming growth within months. Such was Indonesia's fate in the second half of 1997.

Start of the Crisis

The rupiah began to come under speculative attack shortly after the float of the Thai baht on 2 July. The government reacted almost immediately by widening its exchange rate intervention band but, after a short hiatus, there was further heavy speculation. It was decided to float the currency from 14 August. By contrast with Thailand, not much loss of international reserves was involved, since the government had determined quickly that it would not play the speculators' game. There was an immediate depreciation followed by considerable volatility, and then a steady slide that became quite rapid in early October.

The government reacted almost immediately to the depreciation by imposing a severe liquidity squeeze in order to raise interest rates and attract capital back into the country—a strategy it had employed to defeat currency speculators in 1984, 1987, and 1991 (Binhadi and Meek 1992:115), and that it had promised never to repeat because of its disruptive effects (Boediono 1994:124). But whereas on these earlier occasions the squeeze did not last long, this time it lasted for many weeks rather than a few days, and was more severe.[1]

In retrospect, it can be argued that this was a mistake. Perhaps it was worthwhile to experiment yet again with a sudden monetary shock to try to stabilise the exchange rate, although it must be said that implementing such a shock when there is a clear intention to defend the existing exchange rate is very different from doing so having just announced the decision to float the currency. But when the experiment did not have the desired impact immediately, it should have been abandoned. Firms that had foreign currency borrowings were already very hard hit by the unexpected devaluation of the rupiah, and the last thing they needed to add to these concerns was a very considerable and lasting increase in their domestic borrowing costs. This strategy showed that the government had by no means fully embraced the idea of allowing markets to determine the value of the currency. On the contrary, it still sought to control the exchange rate, but rather than intervening directly in the market for foreign exchange, it chose to do so indirectly through the money market.

Although the liquidity squeeze may have slowed the rupiah's fall, it failed clearly to return the currency to its earlier level. Accordingly, the government decided that further belt-tightening was necessary in the form of a cutback of government spending. In September 1997 it announced a list of major infrastructure projects that would be cancelled, postponed, or reviewed. To some extent this did not actually involve expenditure reduction: some of the largest postponed projects were those which were not part of the current budget, nor were they likely to proceed in the near future, if ever. These included three overly ambitious bridges to connect Java with Madura and Sumatra, and Sumatra with Malaysia. Ironically, the list was dominated by toll road construction projects, which almost certainly have very high social rates of return (notwithstanding concerns about non-transparency in the selection of contractors and the financial relationships between the operators and the government's own toll road company), given the inadequacy of Indonesia's existing road network. As a result of severe monetary tightening and the spending cuts, the construction and property development sectors in particular were hard hit. Regular workers started being laid off, while those who ordinarily sought work on a daily basis began to find no one to employ them.

With their reserves having been cut drastically, the banking system had little choice but to raise interest rates so high as to make it virtually impossible to write new business. Doubts quickly emerged about the banks' soundness in light of their heavy exposure to the property sector, which had already been a cause for concern because of the likelihood that its rapid expansion would outstrip demand. By this time significant declines in the value of companies listed on the stock exchange had also been posted.

A government announcement that it would seek IMF assistance effectively halted the slide in the rupiah's value, and the currency settled at roughly Rp3,600 per dollar—up from Rp2,430 before the crisis began. An IMF assistance package was eventually announced at the end of October, after difficult and protracted negotiations. This brought about an immediate recovery of the rupiah in first days of November, but very soon there was a resumption of the slide, which again became rapid in early December. Concerns about the President's health came to dominate market sentiment after he decided, on medical advice, not to attend two overseas meetings to which he had been committed. This caused the rupiah to slump to around Rp6,000 per dollar before recovering to around Rp5,000 as the President began to be seen carrying out his normal duties. By late December the rupiah was fluctuating in a wide range around Rp5,000-6,000 per dollar.

The First IMF Package

The first IMF package remained surprisingly unclear as to details, even two months after the package was announced. A large amount of funds had been provided, estimated as anywhere from $18-41 billion. This contained commitments from the IMF, the World Bank, and the Asian Development Bank totalling $18 billion, supplemented by additional amounts from several countries, foremost amongst which was Singapore, whose astonishing pledge of $10 billion matched that of the IMF. But there seemed quite a bit of smoke and mirrors involved: the size of the initial package was said to be $23 billion, but this turned out to involve no less than $5 billion of Indonesia's own funds![2] It also appears that some of the World Bank and ADB pledges were simply amounts that would have been loaned to Indonesia in any case, in the normal course of events.

In return for these funding commitments, Indonesia agreed to undertake various microeconomic policy reforms and to maintain an austere macroeconomic environment focused on achieving a budget surplus of 1 percent of GDP. Careful monetary policy was also required, but what this meant in practice—indeed, whether there was any concrete target for growth of the monetary aggregates at all—was not made known.

What Were the Funds For?

Attention centred initially on whether agreement could be reached with the IMF, what conditions would be attached, and in particular how large the package would be. Nobody seemed interested in asking what the funds would be used for. It is an obvious understatement to say that the question is relevant, but there was virtually no public discussion on this most fundamental aspect.

One possibility was to use the funds for intervention in the foreign exchange market to stabilise the rupiah, and this seems to have occurred to a limited extent. But this would conflict with the August 1997 decision to allow the currency to float; it would amount to getting into the fight with speculators that the government wisely avoided in July and August; and it could result in a large increase in Indonesia's indebtedness. High indebtedness, of course,wais one of the factors widely blamed for the fall of the rupiah in the first place.

A second possibility would be to use some of the funds to bail out troubled banks and real sector companies, especially those heavily exposed to speculative property developments. The possibility of using the funds "to supply liquidity" to private firms was aired in November by leading businessman and Chairman of the Indonesian Chamber of Commerce and Industry, Aburizal Bakrie, who was accompanying the President on a state visit to South Africa (*Kompas*, 22 November 1997); indeed, it was stated as though it had become government policy, even though Mr. Bakrie was not a government official.[3]

Using the funds in this way would have been most unpopular, because it would be seen as, and would be, yet another example of special privileges for those already fabulously wealthy at the expense of the general public. Not surprisingly in view of these considerations, there was a strong outcry against Mr. Bakrie's interpretation of government policy, and the idea was apparently shelved. Indeed, the then Minister of Finance stated on several occasions that the government had no intention of bailing out private sector firms (*Pilar*, 17 December 1997).

The most likely explanation for the government wanting to acquire such a large volume of funds was to bluff the speculators and to dispel the general lack of confidence in the rupiah. That is, if it could portray itself as having access to, say, $60 billion (taking into account Indonesia's considerable foreign reserves), it might have hoped that speculators would not dare to sell rupiahs on such a scale as to cause these funds to run out, and that those who previously feared losses from holding rupiahs would not now feel the need to do so. But again, this view was in conflict with the obvious reluctance of the government to get involved in large battles with speculators and its desire to decrease rather than increase its outstanding debt. Moreover, the IMF funds were to be released over many months in relatively small tranches, and the supplementary bilateral funds were available only on a stand-by basis for use if necessary after the IMF funds had been fully committed.

It was therefore not surprising that the government's bluff was quickly called, and the first IMF package failed to stabilise the currency. Apparently the speculators and the doubters did not believe that Indonesia would significantly increase its indebtedness in order to defend the rupiah or that the agreement with the IMF would permit this to happen. Thus, the provision of stand-by loans by the IMF and some neighbouring countries turned out to be an impotent gesture, at least for the time being.

Arguably the President was aware of this, and he did not see much need to adhere closely to what the IMF was trying to impose on Indonesia. Early on, he seemed to signal his unhappiness with budget tightening and appeared to be backtracking on this. For example, he was reported as having reaffirmed the government's commitment to a balanced budget (which in the Indonesian context must be interpreted as spending being covered by domestic revenues plus foreign borrowings), without referring to the agreement with the IMF to run a small surplus. Certain infrastructure projects previously cancelled or postponed were quietly reinstated, and plans were announced to provide make-work programs (such as street cleaning and the like) for labourers thrown out of work by the current cutbacks in construction projects.

The Microeconomic Reforms: Background

Notwithstanding Indonesia's exemplary record of macroeconomic management and performance, concerns had been voiced frequently prior to the crisis about a range of microeconomic issues. Before turning to the details of the microeconomic reform component of the IMF package, it will be useful to discuss these concerns.

Although the general level of tariffs and the incidence of quantitative import restrictions had been reduced significantly over the previous decade or so (Fane and Condon 1996), a few industries still enjoyed very high levels of protection through tariffs or quantitative import controls. Running in parallel with these concerns about trade policy were other concerns about the government's strategy for industrial development and, in particular, the role of Soeharto's longest serving minister, the Minister for Research and Technology and Head of the Agency for Management of Strategic Industries, Dr. B. J. Habibie. Dr. Habibie was an engineer by training, but he had strong views on the appropriate path of economic development. This involved state enterprise-led technological leap-frogging—jumping straight into large scale activities involving high technology, such as the manufacture of aircraft, ships, and motor cars, power generation using nuclear fuel, exploitation of the almost impossibly difficult Natuna gas reserves, construction of enormous bridges to link various Indonesian islands, and so on. For the previous year or two, most prominent among these enterprises had been the attempt to design, construct, and market a jet propelled passenger aircraft.

Although at least some Indonesians shared these visions, few came from the ranks of trained economists, most of whom saw such activities as inappropriate to current circumstances. These circumstances are characterised by a severe shortage of individuals with high level skills in fields such as engineering, science, management, marketing, information technology, and so on, alongside an abundance of relatively unskilled labour. Raising the productivity, and therefore the incomes, of the latter depends crucially on combining it with capital and these high level skills, which is not feasible in high technology activities since they have little use for unskilled labour. Perhaps because of these concerns, Habibie's room to move became more and more constrained during the term of the Sixth Development Cabinet (1993–1998). The nuclear power option was shelved for the foreseeable future because of cost and environmental considerations; development of Natuna was stymied by the lack of customers willing to pay a high enough price for gas to make the project economically viable; bridge projects were put on hold for want of institutions willing to fund them; and the jet aircraft project was hampered by its private sector status, there being few potential shareholders willing to put their funds at risk in such an ambitious undertaking. Thus Dr. Habibie was increasingly seen—wrongly, as it turned out—as a spent force on the economic landscape (McLeod 1997:5-6).

Of much greater concern than trade policy and industry policy, in relation to the public's perception of how the economy was being managed, has been the prevalence of special treatment for a relatively small number of conglomerates owned by members of the first family and their close associates. To a growing extent over a long period of time, firms within these conglomerates walked on red carpets strewn with delicate flowers, not having to compete for prime government contracts, being granted more or less exclusive access to important new areas of economic activity (in fields as diverse as television broadcasting, satellite communications, air passenger transport, construction and operation of toll roads, power generation facilities, and so on), having ready access to cheap funds from the state banks, and being able to borrow heavily from their own banks in contravention of regulations on the permissible levels of concentration of loans on firms linked by management and ownership.

If all that were not enough, one first family member had been put in the position of sole legal middleman between peasant clove farmers and the cigarette factories that provide their major market (Tarmidi 1996:103-106), and had been designated the sole producer of an Indonesian "national" car (that turned out to be designed in, and for the foreseeable future fully imported from, Korea), thus qualifying for very large tax concessions not available to other car producers (Manning and Jayasuriya 1996:18-21). A third generation first family member enjoyed a monopoly on the distribution of fertiliser pellets to the peasant farming community, backed by state-sponsored coercion intended to force farmers to use these pellets rather than the granulated fertilisers they preferred. A firm owned by the same individual also briefly enjoyed a monopoly on the sale of tax stickers to be affixed to bottles of beer sold in Bali. Although each sticker cost Rp600, the revenue turned over to the provincial government that authorised the monopoly was only Rp200 (Bird 1996:25-26). A proposal that all of Indonesia's primary schoolchildren would henceforth have to purchase their school shoes from a company associated with the same presidential grandson apparently was scotched before it became operational, such was the extent of public outrage.

Perhaps the most significant recent event to crystallise attitudes on the part of the general public, the intellectual and business elite, and the foreign investment community regarding the direction in which government had been heading was the so-called Busang saga. Busang was the site of what was reported to be perhaps the world's largest known gold deposit, "discovered" by the little-known Canadian exploration company, Bre-X. The value of Bre-X shares soared to fantastic heights on what was shown subsequently to be an elaborate hoax, there being virtually no gold at all at this location (Feridhanusetyawan 1997:29-30).

Before the hoax was discovered, however, a most unedifying squabble ensued between members of the first family, who saw the opportunity to gain free access to the expected enormous cash flow from Busang by virtue of their political influence over the government processes by which permission to exploit the deposit would be granted. In what can only be described as expropriation pure and simple, Bre-X was forced to accept an arrangement which saw a significant share of this expected cash flow diverted to companies and foundations associated with the first family and one of the President's closest business associates, Mr. Bob Hasan. A small share was also diverted to the Indonesian government itself.

Besides the behaviour of the first family and its business associates, there had been many other concerns about the way the country was being run. One such was the increasing tendency for government financial operations to be undertaken outside the formal budget. Payments by forestry companies into a reafforestation fund, for example, had been tapped to support Minister Habibie's aircraft manufacturing activities. A new tax surcharge of 2 percent had been imposed on post-tax incomes above a relatively modest level, to be paid to a new special purpose foundation headed by the President, and administered by the owners of some of the biggest conglomerates in the country. The funds collected in this manner were to be used to make very low interest loans to the poorest members of the population but, being outside the budget, their disposition effectively escaped parliamentary scrutiny (McLeod 1997:25-29).

This is not to imply that the public could rely on parliamentarians to protect its interests. Towards the end of 1997 a scandal erupted involving the passage of labour legislation through parliament. It was discovered that a large number of parliamentarians—whose job, of course, is to analyse, debate, and perhaps modify or even reject legislation submitted to it by the government—had been accommodated at luxury hotels in Jakarta during their "deliberations" on this legislation, at a cost in excess of $1 million. The public sense of revulsion was heightened by suggestions that this was by no means an isolated occurrence, and by the fact that the costs had been met by unsuspecting Indonesian workers covered by the government's social security program known as Jamsostek, whose accumulated contributions were tapped for this purpose (McLeod 1993).[4]

There had been many other episodes, fairly extensively documented in the media, that added to the growing perception that the government served the interests of a narrow elite rather than the public at large. In the banking field, for example, a large private bank, Bank Summa, failed in 1992; but none of its shareholders or senior managers had been held accountable for the high level of insider lending, mainly directed to speculative property development, that led to the banks' demise (MacIntyre and Syahrir 1993:12-16). The state bank, Bapindo, lost an enormous sum in 1994, after making large loans to the so-called Golden Key Group, without even the benefit of written contracts, much less adequate security (Pangestu and Azis 1994:3-4). One of the companies in this group was partly owned by a first family member, who sold his interest after the loans had been drawn. The loans were supposedly to finance the construction of three petrochemicals factories, notwithstanding the fact that the principal shareholder, one Eddy Tansil, had no previous experience in this field. This proved no obstacle to at least one, and possibly two, influential former high ranking government ministers lobbying the bank strongly to provide the loans. Several serving and former directors of the bank, and the borrower, ended up in jail, but Tansil bribed his way out early in 1997 and has not been heard of since.

To these unhappy instances could be added many others, some more political than economic, such as the closure of the respected weekly journal *Tempo* in 1994; the torture, murder, and mutilation of the young labour activist Marsinah in 1993; the murder of a journalist who had made startling allegations about huge sums of money changing hands in connection with the appointment of a local government chief in Yogyakarta 1995; the clumsily orchestrated ouster of Mrs. Megawati

Sukarnoputri as leader of the Indonesian Democratic Party in 1996; and countless cases of callous eviction of the poor from their homes and land, with little or no compensation, to make way for modern sector developments. All of these stories should be seen in the context of an almost universal lack of confidence in the legal system because of its susceptibility to bribery and vulnerability to political interference.

It is beyond the scope of this essay to catalogue episodes of this nature. Suffice it to say that they had come to be regarded as commonplace. If the abuses of power for financial ends could have been quarantined, their impact would have been considerably less; but in practice there was a demonstration effect, the result of which was that corrupt practices came to infect most aspects of public life. If parliamentarians needed to be bribed in order to smooth the passage of government legislation, it can hardly come as a surprise that police officers seemed far more concerned to extract bribes from motorists guilty of minor road law infringements than to make traffic flow freely.[5]

The argument that these microeconomic concerns were responsible for the financial crisis is not clear cut, however, real though they were. There was no obvious break in the general direction of policy in 1997 to which we can attribute the precipitate loss of confidence in the rupiah, which leaves the many proponents of this view in the uncomfortable position of saying that policies that were tolerable to investors in July had suddenly become intolerable by August. It must be appreciated that the concerns discussed above had been part and parcel of the economic and political scene for as long as anyone could remember. Investors were aware of the risks involved in doing business in Indonesia, and the term "high cost economy"—a euphemism for the deadweight cost businesses have to bear in dealing with the bureaucracy at all levels—had become a cliche. These costs were built into firms' product pricing (and thus were passed on to their customers), while the risks were balanced by expected returns that were higher than would be acceptable if the risks were less. If the microeconomic environment was perceived to be deteriorating over time, why was this not simply reflected in a progressive increase in the risk premium demanded by investors?

On the other hand, one has to bear in mind the comments above about the vulnerability of the long-booming economy to a sudden loss of confidence. Past speculative bubbles have often burst when investors became concerned about price risk in relation to equities and property, but a sudden new awareness of exchange rate risk in relation to foreign borrowings can have an analogous impact. It is argued below that this was exactly what happened as a result of the unexpected decline of the baht in July—in combination with the existence of a large volume of unhedged foreign debt and foreign portfolio investment.

One only has to glance over the investment advice newsletters regularly published by stockbrokers, merchant banks, and the like to realise that recommendations to buy, hold, or sell are constantly being revised in response to unfolding events. It is not implausible that events such as the expropriation of Bre-X's shares in Busang would cause buy recommendations in other fields to be changed to hold, and hold recommendations to be changed to sell. Or, that as projections of the supply of new office space, apartments, shopping malls, hotels, and the like became higher and higher relative to projections of demand, sooner or later the time would come when the weight of advice to investors would be to get out of the property sector. When concerns about exchange rate exposure suddenly emerged in July 1997, all of these other concerns—even if still below the surface hitherto—quickly became far more prominent.

In any case, Indonesia very quickly began to succumb to a crisis of confidence, and its prolongation and deepening were surely related to perceptions of the way the Indonesian economy and polity were being managed. At the back of many people's minds was the suspicion that the long wait for a presidential successor, and thus for a more democratic style of government and a lessening of abuses of power for economic gain, may ultimately have been in vain—that the first family would somehow find a way to ensure there would be no diminution of its power and influence in the future. There is little doubt that these concerns are an important explanation for why the crisis became so severe relative to those of other economies in Asia.

The issue of causation is of fundamental importance from the policy point of view. The IMF approach gives the appearance of being premised on the view that poor microeconomic policies were a significant contributor to the crisis, and therefore that microeconomic reform is capable of ending it. But if the extent and nature of microeconomic policy deterioration needed to bring about a currency collapse is essentially arbitrary—which must be the case, given the near simultaneity of the collapses in the highly disparate countries hit by the present epidemic of crises—then it must follow that the extent and nature of reform required to restore investor confidence is also something that cannot be known to the policymakers.

In other words, there is no way of knowing whether any given set of reforms will be capable of ending the crisis, since everything depends on the psychology of investors. The scope for reform in Indonesia is vast. How much would be enough to satisfy the markets, and which areas should be given top priority? If the main concerns were political rather than economic, how could a purely economic reform package be expected to restore stability?

The Microeconomic Reforms: Details

For the sake of argument, let us accept that reforms could contribute to restoring stability. How far did the reforms announced in the first package go? At first glance, the package may have seemed impressive (as government media releases are supposed to do), but more sober analysis suggests that its contribution was likely to be modest. One component of the package involved further movement in the direction of trade liberalisation. Tariff reductions were limited to a few items, however, and were to be phased in over a number of years. There was also a freeing up of imports of certain important commodities, including the removal of a monopoly on wheat imports that had been of immense benefit to the giant Salim conglomerate in the past. But this was replaced by one on the distribution of wheat flour, so it is hard to believe that there was any really meaningful change here.

Perhaps the most significant component of the reform package was the commitment to an overhaul of the financial sector, particularly the banking system. This was followed immediately by the closure of sixteen poorly run private banks, including some partly owned by members of the first family. Although Indonesia has no formal deposit insurance scheme, and despite previous official statements that the government would not cover depositors' losses if banks failed, the government undertook to pay out the deposits of these banks up to a limit of Rp20 million per customer. This was accomplished without serious difficulty very shortly after the bank closures, and appears to have required some Rp8.5 trillion from the central bank.[6]

The impact of the closure of these banks was highly significant. There was widespread astonishment when two first family members whose banks were closed immediately commenced legal proceedings against the then Minister of Finance and the then Governor of the central bank. There was no attempt to deny that the banks in question had ignored the legal lending limits set out in BI's prudential regulations, nor, apparently, that their capital had fallen below the permissible minimum relative to risk-weighted assets; on the contrary, such behaviour was argued to be excusable because many other banks had been doing the same things.

Closing this group of banks (none of them really a large player in terms of market share in a total of nearly 240 banks altogether) in the midst of an emerging financial crisis was a risky strategy. On the one hand, it seemed to demonstrate a genuine and tangible commitment to reform in line with the IMF's expectations, especially since it involved an atypical attack on first family interests. On the other hand, it confirmed fears in the market place that prudential supervision of the banks had been lax hitherto and raised fears that some, perhaps many, other banks (and their depositors) might meet a similar fate. Matters were not helped by unconfirmed but widespread rumours that a list of forty banks actually had been under consideration for closure, before the smaller group of sixteen was decided upon. In turn, these rumours forced the government to state categorically that no more banks would be closed—a promise that obviously could not be interpreted to mean forever, thus leaving open the question as to how long it would remain valid. The public was not entirely persuaded by this reassurance, and the private banks as a group had to battle subsequently to maintain their liquidity in the face of the government's monetary squeeze and their customers' preference either to hold cash or to shift their deposits to state-owned, foreign, and offshore banks. In the event, the promise was indeed broken within three months.

Most people believed their savings to be safe with the state banks, not because they were well managed but because it seemed unthinkable that the government would let any of them fail, despite the fact that their problem loans—or at least so much of them as had been revealed—were far bigger relative to total assets than those at the private banks. For this reason, and because of concern about their poor performance generally, the government had been talking about merging the state banks for some time prior to the crisis. It finally made an announcement on 31 December, presumably as part of its agreement with the IMF, as to how this would proceed.

Four of the banks (Bank Dagang Negara, Bank Bumi Daya, Bank Ekspor Impor Indonesia, and Bapindo) were to be merged into a single bank; the Bank Tabungan Negara (BTN) was to become a subsidiary of one of the others (Bank BNI, the only state bank yet listed on the stock exchange); while the last of the seven, Bank Rakyat Indonesia, was to continue as before. To allow the new management to concentrate on consolidation, existing problem loans of the state banks were to be stripped out and sold to a newly established state enterprise, which would have the job of recovering whatever it could from them. There was no explicit statement as to where the capital for this new entity would be raised, but in later developments the government announced that it was going to issue bonds for this purpose.

The late President Sukarno once tried to merge all of the state banks (including the central bank) into a single unit. The attempt was a dismal failure, and the component parts of the new mega-bank were again made separate after President Soeharto took power. Apparently this salutary lesson on the immense difficulties involved in merging large organisations had been forgotten during the ensuing three decades, with government spokesmen and commentators alike giving the strong impression that merger was the key to solving the state banks' ills. It is not clear how this can be so. The merger of even two reasonably well managed, large firms is rarely easy, and the difficulties will be vastly greater when four institutions, some of which have been quite inefficiently managed, are involved. Nor is there any guarantee that the new bank will not persist with the same kinds of behaviour that generated such high levels of problem loans in the past.

On the contrary, the implicit bail-out of the state banks had the potential to reinforce the moral hazard problem that contributed so heavily to their present difficulties. It should be noted that there has been in existence for several decades a government body (Badan Utang Piutang Negara, BUPN) whose responsibility has been to collect overdue debts to the state—in particular, unpaid loans from the state banks. This body has met with very little success: not, perhaps, because of weaknesses of the legal system—indeed, its very purpose would seem to be to bypass the legal system—but presumably because there has been little pressure on it to perform, and because delinquent borrowers have been more than willing to offer inducements to its officials to drop their cases or indefinitely to delay dealing with them. Its activities have been almost entirely opaque to the public.

It is worth noting that the government could have been putting pressure on the state banks to clean up their own mess simply by forcing them to adhere to the prudential regulations introduced in 1988 and strengthened in 1991. Central amongst these regulations were minimum requirements for capital relative to risk-weighted assets, and any objective evaluation of the state banks' capital in the late 1980s would have shown it to be deficient. If these regulations had been enforced, they would have been obliged, in the absence of any equity injection, to contract and to become efficient and genuinely profitable if they wanted eventually to expand.

All things considered, it seems reasonable to assert that the reform package was disappointing in scope, especially in relation to the major public concerns about the general direction of economic policy outlined earlier. Besides the various shortcomings already discussed, it was noteworthy that the highly controversial national car and national jet projects were not touched. Although neither was really important in the overall scheme of things, both were highly symbolic of a continued attachment to policies that were in part the modern day equivalent of former President Sukarno's preoccupation with building grand monuments, while also reeking of special deals for the favoured few. The clove and fertiliser monopolies also were untouched and, rather than attacking the first family's near monopoly on toll road construction by committing itself to competitive tendering procedures, the government first postponed many of these projects and then rather surreptitiously reinstated them.

Thus, the reform package failed to dispel the perception that it was still a case of "business as usual." Even in the case of the private bank closures, this was so: the President's second son, Mr. Bambang Trihatmodjo, no sooner lost his bank than he was permitted to buy another one—apparently on the grounds that he, personally, had not been responsible for the misdeeds of the bank in which he was a large shareholder. In turn, this was highly reminiscent of the Chandra Asri olefines refinery case. This project was blocked in 1991 by imposing foreign borrowing limitations (an indirect way of trying to stop the project, which was seen to be uneconomic and bound to require subsidisation in some form), but its owners (first family members and their associates) got around these most efficaciously by reincorporating the company as a foreign entity, thus putting it beyond the reach of those limitations.

Macroeconomic Austerity

On the macroeconomic front in November and December of 1997, there was continued weakening and volatility of the currency; and much modern sector activity slowed seriously, if not halting altogether. Indeed, the government's policy of fiscal and monetary tightening was quite counterproductive in Keynesian terms, in circumstances in which agricultural incomes were low (because of drought), investment demand was low (because of uncertainty), consumer demand was low (because of the negative wealth effect of those exposed to currency weakness), and demand for tradeables was very patchy. Belt-tightening policies were imposing avoidable costs on to the poor by increasing unemployment (especially in the construction sector), whereas these costs should really have been confined to foreign investors and the middle and wealthy classes (specifically, owners of firms that had borrowed in foreign currencies).

In normal circumstances the usefulness of Keynesian macroeconomic management concepts in Indonesia is limited. The most fundamental Keynesian concept is that, in circumstances in which aggregate demand is low for some reason, the government can offset this by manipulating its fiscal and monetary policies. Specifically, it can increase its own spending, decrease taxes, and/or expand the money supply. These kinds of fine-tuning policies are difficult to apply in practice in any country, and in Indonesia especially so, because of data limitations that make it difficult to know the level of aggregate demand until after a long lag, logistical and administrative difficulties in making rapid changes to government spending and taxation, and the uncertain magnitude of the impacts of these policy changes on the level of aggregate demand and the time lags involved.

In the circumstances of the second half of 1997, however, the fundamental Keynesian insight was surely relevant. There was no doubt that aggregate demand had fallen considerably, yet the first IMF agreement put pressure on the government to implement policies that would reduce it even further. In other words, the push was for contraction, when it was obvious that expansion was required if Indonesia was to regain its momentum. The IMF view seemed almost to be that Indonesia had gotten itself into exchange rate trouble and needed to be punished for doing so. Or, to use a more familiar metaphor, it had allowed itself to become ill and now needed to swallow bitter medicine before it could be brought back to good health.

The IMF's approach suggested that it was unable to distinguish Indonesia's problems from balance of payments crises suffered by other countries in the past. Almost invariably, those crises had been preceded by a period of relatively high and perhaps accelerating inflation, usually caused by excessive budget deficits financed by central bank money creation. With the exchange rate fixed, inflation quickly eroded competitiveness, the balance of payments went into deficit, and international reserves were steadily eroded. As markets began to perceive what was happening, they began to speculate against the currency, causing reserves to fall even more rapidly. In such circumstances, the IMF typically stepped in and advised the governments in question to devalue immediately to overcome the immediate problem of falling reserves, and then to bring down money supply growth (and therefore inflation) by getting government spending under control and increasing taxes, so as to prevent a recurrence.

This brief description bears no resemblance whatsoever to the Indonesia of mid-1997. Fiscal and monetary policy had been conservatively managed, inflation was moderate and declining, and international reserves were increasing rapidly. Indeed, Indonesia had often been praised by institutions such as the IMF itself for the quality of its macroeconomic management. It is therefore hard to know how anyone could have arrived at the conclusion that fiscal contraction and monetary tightness were needed to cure Indonesia's ills, when fiscal and monetary policies clearly had nothing to do with causing them.

This is a matter of considerable but regrettable irony. Indonesia's economic progress over the last three decades had been very largely attributable to policies guided by the so-called "technocrats"—led by Professors Widjojo Nitisastro and Ali Wardhana—who were extremely well respected as economic policymakers by institutions such as the IMF and the World Bank. Above all, they had maintained a stable macroeconomic background by operating conservative fiscal and monetary policies, and they had kept the economy competitive by always being prepared to adjust the exchange rate as necessary in response to changing circumstances.

But now, with the encouragement of the IMF—presumably with the backing of the World Bank, the Asian Development Bank, and the various governments that had supplemented the IMF package—the technocrats were continuing to implement belt-tightening fiscal and monetary policies that could not fail to deepen the emerging crisis. This was a significant misjudgment that could not quickly be rectified. A new cabinet was to be formed in March 1998, and this would occur against an economic background of a very severe economic slowdown, with extensive job losses and large increases in many sensitive consumer prices. The policy successes of three decades were likely to be overwhelmed in the public consciousness by the negative impact of macroeconomic policies of the preceding seven months, raising serious doubts as to whether the technocrats would be able to retain their positions as trusted advisors to the President on economic policy.

The technocrats lacked any real power base, and to a large extent had relied on institutions like the World Bank and the IMF, and on the foreign investment community, to sing their praises and help keep them in positions of influence. But they did not lack domestic opponents: ministers whose extravagant spending plans they had opposed; first family and associated businesspeople whose constant quest for protection, tax privileges, subsidised inputs, and so on they had frustrated whenever possible; economic nationalists who resented their closeness to Western multilateral institutions and their policies of openness to the world economy and to foreign ideas. All these groups would be only too happy to help push the technocrats from their pedestal after they had been seen to falter. How could the latter defend themselves in the face of a severe slowdown, with millions of workers out of jobs, share prices far lower than previously, and failed banks incurring big losses that now needed to be covered by the government, at the expense of the general public?

Some Non-Economic Concerns

The deterioration of the President's health in December 1997 could not have come at a worse time, so far as the quest to regain financial stability was concerned, because his health was crucial to the near-term economic outlook. A whole generation of Indonesians has known no other national leader, and the evidence of his failing health served to bring home the reality that his departure from office might not be too far into the future. In effect, President Soeharto was the government, such was his power and influence. If he were suddenly no longer around, there would be enormous doubts as to the future direction of economic policy.

An additional cause for uncertainty emerged toward the end of December, with the abrupt removal from office of four directors of the central bank (from a total of seven), just three months before their five-year terms were to end. No explanation was given; moreover, it seemed clear that the Governor had not even been consulted about this move. This was truly an extraordinary action to take in the midst of a severe and worsening financial crisis, and the manner in which it was done could hardly have been less sensitive to market perceptions. Almost immediately, three of the four began to be questioned by the police, who soon revealed that they were investigating losses to the state as large as Rp1.5 trillion—or around $600 million at the old exchange rate. The background to these losses remains unclear, but they may well be related to large, non-transparent loans extended to a number of commercial banks by the central bank since the financial crisis began.[7] Private domestic bank borrowings from the central bank increased by no less than Rp12 trillion in the three months to October 1997, without any official announcement as to their existence, much less their purpose.

By the start of the fasting month around New Year, Jakarta was stricken by a mood of confusion and pessimism. Many prices had risen substantially, although the impact on official price indices was as yet modest. Lay-offs were already occurring on a large scale, and the prospect of further job losses was very real. Many businesses were reluctant to undertake their normal activities for fear that adverse price and exchange rate changes would make these unprofitable, and much investment activity had come to a halt pending clarification of future prospects. People seemed to think it was all too much to comprehend, and resigned themselves to waiting for things to work themselves out. The view was quite strong that matters had moved well outside the realms of economics: nothing much could be explained in pure economic terms, and most predictions were, in truth, pure guesses plucked from thin air.

view to rolling over short-term debts. This indeed seemed the most sensible course of action, and it was important to remove lingering hopes that the government itself would take any responsibility for meeting private sector obligations. Rolling over rather than immediately repaying debts implied a lower demand for foreign exchange, so this also helped to stabilise the rupiah.[9]

Policy Making in Disarray

Putting a brake on capital outflow was an important step, but it was by no means enough to return Indonesia to normality. There was little chance that the corporate sector's foreign borrowings could be repaid with the cost of foreign currency four times higher than had been expected when these loans were taken out. The economy was already in deep recession, and unemployment had exploded to undreamed of levels. Even more important, prices had been rising rapidly, and it was impossible to conceive that the rupiah prices of tradeable goods and services—in particular, basic food essentials, fuel and power, transportation, and so on—could be prevented from rising ultimately by factors of perhaps two or three. This could be expected to cause enormous hardship for the poorer members of society, and it had already led to many outbreaks of violence against ethnic Chinese retailers, who had become scapegoats and targets for working off these frustrations.

The question has been raised as to whether anti-Chinese rioting, especially that which occurred in the weeks prior to the Presidential election in March, was spontaneous or was orchestrated for political purposes. These suspicions were boosted by blatant moves by high-ranking armed forces personnel to inflame anti-Chinese sentiment. Mr. Sofyan Wanandi, one of the most prominent and respected ethnic Chinese business leaders, was interrogated by the police amid great publicity on the basis of the ludicrous suggestion that he had financed a small subversive group intent on undertaking a bombing campaign. The Center for Strategic and International Studies—a highly respected think-tank with which the Wanandi family is closely associated—was picketed and its staff intimidated, by what was undoubtedly a hired mob. Phone calls were made by the leadership of the Army to many of the top conglomerate owners (read: the wealthiest ethnic Chinese), again amid great publicity, urging them to repatriate funds they had allegedly sent abroad.

By February 1988, after four months of active IMF involvement, little had been achieved towards overcoming the crisis. On the contrary, it had become vastly more threatening and no end was in sight. Understandably, perhaps, the President began to look elsewhere for suggestions. He was introduced to the concept of the currency board system, forms of which were already in operation in Hong Kong and a small number of other economies. Under this system, the rupiah would be tied rigidly to the dollar, and the government would have no independent monetary policy at all. The currency board would have to buy or sell dollars at the specified peg rate, regardless of the effect these transactions would have on the money supply. The determination of the peg rate would be crucial: if the dollar were made too expensive, this would result in one-off large increases in domestic prices which would likely aggravate social unrest; if it were made too cheap, there would be a renewed rush to sell rupiah, resulting in a further tightening of monetary conditions and an even more severe crisis for the banks, and perhaps a still more severe slow-down in growth.

On the other hand, the crisis had been brought on initially by widespread concern about the possibility of a large rupiah devaluation, even though the fundamentals did not point in that direction. If the investment community and the general public could be persuaded that the new peg rate would hold—i.e., that there was now no possibility of devaluation—no matter how tight liquidity became or how high interest rates were driven, then there would be no reason to speculate against the rupiah. Liquidity then would not diminish, and interest rates would not rise.

The currency board proposal encountered stern opposition from the IMF, and from much the same group of governments that had complained about the 6 January budget. Nor did there appear to be much support for the idea amongst cabinet ministers. Indeed, the President dismissed the Governor of the central bank, Dr. Soedradjad Djiwandono, just a few weeks before his term of office was due to expire in March 1998, presumably in part because of the latter's opposition to it. Within a short time, however, most parties softened their positions somewhat. For his part, the President spelled out clearly at the beginning of March his frustration with the lack of progress to date in dealing with the crisis—calling for new ideas and continuing to view the establishment of a currency board as an important option—but also noting the importance of continued IMF support.

These comments were made on the first day of the carefully stage-managed, five-yearly session of the People's Consultative Assembly, at which the Assembly reelected the President (unopposed) for a further five-year period. As on previous occasions, the primary focus of the Assembly session was on the choice of a Vice President and the subsequent appointment of ministers to the new cabinet.

It has always been the Soeharto style to keep everyone guessing and to ensure that there are always multiple contenders for positions of power and influence. While this has been one of his great political strengths, helping to explain how he has managed to dominate the political scene for so long, it is by no means desirable from the point of view of the public interest. The real implications of failure to groom a successor or to lay the foundations for the succession process became painfully apparent when the President's health deteriorated in December, and the nation suddenly found itself facing the possibility of a leadership vacuum. Likewise, the reaction of the markets in January 1998 to the news of Minister Habibie's impending election as Vice President—once the President made it known that this was his wish—provided further evidence of fears that Indonesia was still quite unprepared for the looming end of the Soeharto era.

The new cabinet was announced within a few days of the President's reelection. Its composition was notable for several reasons. First, the prospect of a Soeharto dynasty became more real with the elevation of the President's first daughter, Siti Hardiyanti Rukmana—already a highly placed official of the government's Golkar party, and a highly visible and effective campaigner in the 1997 parliamentary elections—to the position of Minister for Social Affairs. Second, for the first time in the history of the New Order, the cabinet would contain an ethnic Chinese Indonesian—Mr. Bob Hasan, one of the President's closest business associates. Third, the waning influence of the technocrats became even more apparent. The central bank governor had already been removed from his post and another director aligned with the technocrats, Dr. Boediono, had also been replaced shortly prior to the Assembly session. The reformist Minister of Finance and technocrat protege, Mr. Mar'ie Mohammad, was now replaced, as was another member of the technocrat camp, former Coordinating Minister for Economics, Finance and Development, Dr. Saleh Afiff.

With these changes it became difficult to believe other than that the government's putative commitment to an astonishingly wide range of important microeconomic policy reforms toward the end of the Sixth Development Cabinet would come to nothing. These reforms were essentially an attack on the privileged position of the first family and its business associates, and on the grandiose visions of the former Minister for Research and Technology. But although their apparent acceptance by the President may have seemed a significant victory for the technocrats and their supporters in the bureaucracy, the danger that they would be nullified became clear with the appointment of new ministers unlikely to have any inclination to implement them, much less to push them even further in the future.

The Role of the IMF

Clearly, the IMF has played a major role in the unfolding crisis. Although well intentioned, it cannot be said that this role has been helpful, for reasons already explained. It attached higher priority to stabilising the rupiah than to keeping resources fully employed. It pushed for the immediate closure of banks, seemingly irrespective of the impact this would have on those that remained. And it insisted on microeconomic reforms that, however desirable in themselves, had little direct relationship with the crisis.[10] When the first package failed to have a favourable impact, it surely was incumbent upon those who framed it to question the initial approach. Instead, the response was to point to the government's failure to abide by its commitments, and then to multiply the list of demands for reform several times over. One is reminded of the obstinate bureaucrat who, upon finding that the first regulation he devised was not working, imposed ten supplementary regulations—without bothering to consider the possibility that the first was simply misguided.

The IMF reform packages amounted to an increasingly vigorous attack on policies that had served the President and his supporters well. They could only have succeeded if the President had been persuaded that they were genuinely necessary for recovery, and ultimately in his own interest. Clearly, he was never persuaded of this. As a consequence, many of the reforms remain to be implemented, and this fact itself has greatly amplified the initial loss of confidence. The lesson to be learned from this, to paraphrase Grenville (1998), is that when the emergency room is full of train crash victims, it makes good sense to give top priority to those in mortal danger, leaving those with minor lacerations for later. To this we might add that the doctor will have better things to do than trying to convince those present that they should give up smoking and drinking to excess.

Future Prospects

There has been a widespread tendency to argue that we have seen the last of the high growth era in Indonesia (and in the other Asian countries that experienced financial upheaval in the latter half of 1997). Although the crisis in Indonesia will certainly result in slower growth for at least a year or two, it seemed at first unduly pessimistic to believe that its consequences would be any worse than this. What had happened? Basically, there had been a sudden, widespread loss of confidence—first in the currency, triggered by the floating of the Thai baht, and then in relation to economic prospects more generally, amplified by a range of misfortunes, policy misjudgments, and concerns about both the present and the future.

The misfortunes included a severe drought and its contribution to a significant decline in agricultural production and a worsening of the impact of forest fires in Indonesia and on its near neighbours; the crash of a domestic flight in August 1997 and an international flight in December 1997, both with heavy loss of life; and the destruction by fire of several floors of a brand new building owned by the central bank, also in December. Concerns about the present and future included ever present governance issues—extensive, high level corruption, increasingly blatant nepotistic practices, the propensity to sacrifice the interests of the general public for the benefit of the economic elite, the absence of a credible legal system, and so on. But none of these things reflected any significant or permanent deterioration in Indonesia's position in the global economy.

It followed from this that the real value of the rupiah should have been expected to recover strongly from the range in which it had found itself, even if the level of capital outflow were to remain high, providing political and social stability could have been maintained. The switch from capital inflow prior to the crisis to capital outflow necessarily was matched by a similar turnaround in the current account, from deficit to surplus.[11] For this to have been achieved, given the great difficulty of increasing exports substantially within the very short time frame in which the turnaround in the capital account occurred (and, to a lesser extent, the similar difficulty of quickly reducing imports), it was necessary for a very large devaluation to occur. But with more time to adjust, the rupiah would not have needed to fall nearly so far to generate a current account surplus to match the new level of capital outflow. To put it another way, if the rupiah were to have remained at, say, 8000 to the dollar, exports should have increased and imports decreased dramatically, generating a balance of payments surplus that, in a floating rate regime, would result in appreciation of the rupiah.

Thus, the point to note is that the huge devaluation of the rupiah that resulted from the sudden turnaround in capital flow could not have been expected to be sustained, even if capital outflow had remained high. But was it realistic to assume that capital outflow would remain so high?

Domestic investors are certainly willing to transfer liquid assets out of the country when there is a speculative opportunity, the prospect of an exchange rate loss, or when the political outlook is threatening. But it is unlikely that they will do this on a continuous basis, for various reasons. Most obvious is that if capital flight was driven initially by the fear of devaluation, then once that devaluation has occurred this fear is no longer relevant. A second reason is that longer-term interest rates offshore will be lower than those available domestically (after adjusting for exchange rate movements) when and if the atmosphere of crisis can be dispelled. The wealthy have some opportunities for redeploying their capital offshore by making direct investments but, again, the returns available to them are unlikely to be as high as when operating on home turf because, for such investments to be successful, it is necessary for them to be monitored, if not managed, personally. Another consideration is that for many small businesses, ownership of financial capital is the means of securing employment for one's own human capital and that of other family members. If financial capital is put offshore, what is to be done with the human capital that stays behind?

These considerations do not apply to foreigners, of course, who can as easily put their funds into many other countries as into Indonesia. But where now? The same new perception of risk applies in many other developing countries as it does in Indonesia. Where could they go to escape the possibility of a similar crisis? Of course, they could turn to Europe, the United States, or perhaps Japan, but the returns available would be small by comparison.

Having said all this, it is necessary to recall the discussion about the vulnerability of the ethnic Chinese community. It is an unfortunate fact of life that social unrest seems inevitably to result in violence toward this ethnic minority, and one of the great failings of the Soeharto era has been the failure to make the Chinese—most of whom have lived in Indonesia for many generations—feel at home. It is often asserted that this 3-4 percent of the population accounts for 70 percent of the country's wealth. The usual implication drawn from this observation (the statistical basis for which, it should be noted, is highly dubious) is that social unrest is almost inevitable given the resentment this arouses. But looked at from a different angle, it is clear that large-scale emigration of the Chinese would deprive the economy of the entrepreneurial skills that have indeed created a very large proportion of the country's wealth. Despite the readiness of leaders and would-be leaders to use the Chinese from time to time as political pawns, however, the prevailing view is that most are well aware of the importance of this group to Indonesia's economic well being. It seems unlikely, therefore—at least for the present—that such emigration will occur.

The point of this lengthy discussion is that the high level of capital outflow that followed the abrupt change in risk perceptions will not continue indefinitely. Indeed, it seems likely that capital inflow eventually will be restored, albeit at a lower level than prior to the crisis, consistent with the higher risk premium. For this reason also, the exchange rate can be expected to appreciate over time from its current level.

In short, in the absence of permanent deterioration in the external trading environment, a sustained highly depreciated rupiah would imply a steady increase in the level of capital outflow; this is quite improbable. Profitable investment opportunities will still exist (subject only to the possibility of sudden deterioration in the quality of government or severe disruption of civil society). With the recent high level of capital outflow driven more by panic than by a reasoned assessment of the realities of the situation, wiser investors eventually will find these opportunities too good to ignore.[12] In the longer term, then, there is no reason why the economy should not return to something similar to its previous growth pattern. The short-term outlook is greatly clouded, however, by political considerations tied up with the presidential succession, which in turn have significant implications for the general direction of economic policy making in the future.

Policy Lessons

Was the extensive liberalisation of the second half of the 1980s a mistake? Although the economy is experiencing severe difficulties at present, it is essential not to forget the immense gains that have been achieved through ongoing economic liberalisation over many years. The rate of growth of output has averaged close to 8 percent p.a., allowing per capita incomes to grow at over 6 percent p.a. since the late 1980s, and permitting very significant progress to be made in eradicating poverty. It is hard to imagine that this could have been achieved without wide-ranging liberalisation, and it would be quite foolish to undo any of the liberalisation that has already been achieved because of the short-term turbulence now being experienced.

Paradoxically, a clear example of the gains from liberalisation can be seen in the banking sector. Although many now blame this sector for the troubles in which Indonesia now finds itself, the fact is that it made great gains in the fourteen years since it began to be deregulated. It should not be forgotten that, before deregulation, banking was dominated by the state banks, which between them accounted for about 80 percent of total banking sector assets. These banks were inefficient and not at all customer-oriented. They showed little interest in retail business—small business and individuals—and typically had very high levels of bad debts, on several occasions having to be rescued by the government.

Since 1983, and especially since 1988 when the sector was thrown open to competition, it expanded enormously relative to the economy itself; and private sector banks, both domestic and foreign, drastically cut the state banks' market share. The accessibility of banks to the wider public increased beyond imagination—as indicated, for example, by the total number of branches (an increase from 1,700 to 6,500 since 1988) and the total number of savings deposit accounts now in existence (an increase from 24 million to 55 million in the same period). Although there are clearly negative aspects to this story in relation to lending operations, the fact is that it is the enormous and totally unexpected fall in the value of the rupiah—something quite outside the banks' control—that is mainly responsible for their current plight. Prior to the rupiah's collapse, there is little doubt that the economy was far better served by its banking system than would have been the case in the absence of this liberalisation.

Time to Revive Laissez-faire: More Liberalisation, Not Less

The story of the banking sector holds true for the economy as a whole. Indonesia's successes in recent years are largely attributable to liberalisation, and its recent troubles to some extent reflect *failure to carry through the principles of liberalisation* to certain key areas. The key to recovery and future success, therefore, is to pursue further liberalisation, not to wind back that which has already been achieved.

The basic principles of market-oriented economic policies (i.e., liberalisation) are the following: (1) reliance on markets rather than government planning to determine resource allocation and demand patterns; (2) determination of prices by market forces rather than by regulation or other forms of intervention; (3) encouraging freedom of both entry and exit, which includes the promotion of competition wherever possible, ensuring that as many firms as is practicable have access to compete in markets, the avoidance of protection and bail-outs for firms of any kind that may get into difficulty, and the encouragement of quick transfer of ownership of failed firms to minimise disruption to their productive activities;

(4) restriction of economic activity by the government to fields that the private sector is not capable of handling, which implies reliance on privately owned firms rather than state enterprises to meet private demands for goods and services, and reliance on privately owned firms to the fullest extent possible in the provision by the government of non-marketed services to the public, using transparent bidding mechanisms; (5) avoidance of promises by governments of what they may not be able to deliver; and finally (6) sharing of complete and accurate information in the possession of the government with the general public.

Government Intervention as Cause of the Crisis

The current crisis reflects a failure to observe some of these principles. For example, the government was not prepared to accept the market outcome in relation to the level of capital inflow. Under *laissez-faire*, higher capital inflow (in response to attractive domestic investment opportunities) tends to cause an exchange rate appreciation. But the government was concerned that this would have a negative impact on exports, and so chose to intervene in the foreign exchange market as a buyer to prevent this appreciation from occurring. To offset the expansionary monetary impact of its intervention, it then had to borrow from the public by way of issuing central bank certificates of deposit.

But this was an unending and ultimately unsustainable process. By becoming a large borrower in the domestic market, the central bank forced private sector borrowers offshore, thus encouraging more capital inflow; it then had to continue to intervene in the foreign exchange market to prevent the rupiah from appreciating..As a result, Indonesia's international reserves increased enormously over time, from just $6 billion in mid-1990 to as much as $29 billion in mid-1997, just before the crisis began to unfold. This amounts to almost a five-fold increase in the space of just seven years. Private sector foreign borrowing was unnecessarily increased by roughly the same amount as a result.

The fact that reserves were healthy and growing, the fact that the government had caused the rupiah to depreciate quite steadily at around 4 percent p.a. over more than a decade, and the fact that the government frequently reiterated its intention to continue this policy, all meant that domestic borrowers and foreign investors were lulled into a false sense of security in relation to the exchange rate risk of shifting capital across the international boundary. No doubt a small exchange rate risk premium was built into interest rates, but few entities thought it worthwhile to go to the trouble to hedge this risk. In retrospect, it is not surprising that there was a rush to buy dollars when the baht depreciated so suddenly in July.

Not only did the government try to override the market outcome, it also failed to inform the public fully as to what was happening by deliberately understating the official figure for foreign exchange reserves—apparently in order to have a hidden reserve should external circumstances take a turn for the worse.[13] Since the markets pay attention to official reserves figures, it is ironic that the government may have contributed to the crisis by not informing the world how large its reserves were, and how rapidly they were growing.[14]

Besides making an explicit promise about the exchange rate that ultimately it could not keep, the government also made implicit promises about the soundness of banks, and again failed to take the people into its confidence. The central bank had an elaborate system and formula for evaluating the soundness of each bank (Habir 1994:177-79), in the interests of depositor protection; yet it quite deliberately refrained from making the banks' soundness "scores" known to depositors.

It was widely known amongst more sophisticated observers—and certainly by officials at the central bank—that many banks flouted the regulations, especially in relation to having too much of their loan portfolios concentrated on particular borrowers, frequently firms owned by the same parties as the banks themselves. The general public may not have had the same awareness, however; and all were encouraged to believe that the government, through the central bank, was monitoring the situation, and doing what was necessary to maintain the safety of deposits belonging to the public. In other words, there was a perception that ultimately the government would protect depositors from loss in the case of bank failures.

The consequence of this was a so-called moral hazard problem: private entities paid little attention to risk and failed to impose the discipline of the market—by withdrawing deposits—on banks that indulged in risky behaviour. The government had a long record of propping up its own banks when their bad loans exhausted their capital, and many members of the public did not really distinguish state-owned from private banks. As a consequence, there was a deterioration of financial discipline: "everybody was doing it," making it even more likely that the government would have to bail out any failures.[15]

The state banks had enormous problems with bad loans, which had been widely publicised. But the perception that the government would not allow one of its own institutions fail meant that there was little reason for their depositors to flee when things began to go wrong in August. As far as the private banks were concerned, there is no doubt that prudential supervision was also ineffective. The central bank had hurriedly introduced a book of almost 600 pages of prudential regulations following the failure of a prominent private bank in 1990, but its very bulk suggested that its authors had little conception of what was important and what was not. A careful reading confirmed this to be the case: as Habir (1994) pointed out, under the new rating system contained therein, even a bank whose capital had become significantly negative could still be rated sufficiently sound to stay in business! In any case, the central bank found it virtually impossible to enforce even these regulations in practice because of the political forces brought to bear whenever powerful interests were threatened.

To point out these weaknesses of prudential supervision does not necessarily imply that the private banks were universally badly managed, however, nor that they were generally exposed to excessive risk. The fact that the majority probably became technically bankrupt as the crisis progressed owes a great deal to the enormous change in the value of the rupiah, far outside the bounds of what anybody could reasonably have predicted. The extent to which bank failures resulted from bad lending decisions on the one hand, and this totally unexpected decline in the currency on the other, will remain a matter for speculation in the absence of detailed research.

Fane (1998) argues that the problem of moral hazard in banking is almost unavoidable. Even if governments insist that there will be no bail-outs of failed financial institutions (as the Indonesian government did), it is virtually impossible to prevent people from believing the opposite (as they appear to have done in Indonesia—and were proven correct in their view subsequently). His suggestions for dealing with this problem include: significant increases in the minimum amount of capital relative to risk assets (so that the leverage of banks would be closer to that of real sector companies, thus ensuring that their owners had more at stake); much greater attention to the prompt recognition of non-performing loans (without which the reported figures for capital are meaningless); and allowing branches of foreign banks full freedom to compete with domestic banks (partly for the salutary impact of their presence on the management of local institutions, but more importantly because the globally diversified portfolios of multinational banks would be much better able to withstand negative shocks). In regard to the latter, it may be noted here that the Indonesian government's policy (until late-1988) of banning the entry of any additional foreign banks and, after the relaxation of that ban, of restricting the operations of foreign banks to just two branches in only seven cities throughout the archipelago, also helped to make the crisis worse than it need have been.

Conclusions

Indonesia's crisis was sparked by a loss of confidence on the part of economic entities that suddenly came to realise the extent to which they were exposed to various kinds of risk. Domestic and foreign investors with rupiah assets financed by unhedged foreign currency liabilities; banks and other lenders who had relied on names and relationships instead of solid collateral, and who had assumed that high growth would continue indefinitely; depositors who trusted the authorities to monitor and supervise banks, and to shore them up if necessary; property developers who deluded themselves into thinking that real estate values could never decline; market players who had come to believe the government immune to major errors of judgment in relation to macroeconomic management; market participants who were conscious of the succession issue, yet chose to imagine that it could be resolved somehow without causing serious disruption—all these had good reason to be concerned about what the future might hold. When they started to think about, and act to protect themselves against, these risks, their concerns became self-fulfilling.

The government's own policies helped create the preconditions for the crisis, and the incoherence of its response to the sudden devaluation of the rupiah made the crisis much more severe than it needed to have been. The lack of a clear and consistent strategy for dealing with the sudden change in sentiment has been due to various factors: genuine confusion as to how to handle a crisis of a kind not previously experienced; divisions within the government between a President reliant on economic policymakers who themselves were increasingly concerned about the privileged position of his family and business associates, and his stubborn support for the high technology visions of former Minister and later Vice President, Habibie; a strong tradition of economic nationalism within the community, reflected in the views of some ministers and their departments; ethnic and religious tensions between the numerically dominant indigenous community and the economically dominant ethnic Chinese; increasingly widespread concern about the President's intentions regarding the succession; a general lack of sympathy for the private sector and for market processes within large sections of the bureaucracy; and so on.

The most crucial policy misjudgment was to forget that the primary economic objective should always be to keep productive resources fully employed. Instead, when the rupiah began its slide, the government panicked and began to regard stabilisation of the rupiah as its primary objective. To this end, it imposed a brutal liquidity squeeze designed to push up interest rates and encourage capital inflow, and it cut back its own spending—partly to prevent the emergence of a budget deficit and partly to reduce its own demand for imports. The collapse of the rupiah had not been brought on by lax monetary or fiscal policy, however, but by a sudden change of investor sentiment. Policy needed to address this problem and to introduce measures that would help restore confidence.

Instead, policies adopted almost universally had the opposite effect. The abrupt decisions to float the currency; to drop the policy of steady money growth (and instead use monetary policy to stabilise the exchange rate); to turn on its head the Keynesian notion of increasing government spending in order to offset the sudden fall in private sector demand; to close down banks in the middle of a crisis; to announce the controversial decision to introduce a currency board without any attempt first to achieve a consensus amongst deeply sceptical ministers—much less the wider community—as to its viability; to remove the entire board of directors of the central bank in stages over a period of only three months; to accept IMF assistance, but then to vacillate in implementing the reforms that were the price of that assistance; to vilify the ethnic Chinese conglomerates for their alleged role in bringing down the rupiah: all these were enormously destructive of business confidence.

By mid-May 1998 it was difficult to view Indonesia's future with any degree of optimism. Its people had been willing to overlook increasingly blatant nepotism, cronyism, and corruption for as long as the system also generated significant material benefits for themselves. But spreading unemployment and huge increases in the prices of goods and services—that can only be expected to continue—have quickly undermined the President's "performance legitimacy." Were the government fully to implement the commitments it made to the IMF, this might pave the way for confidence and capital to return, and it would certainly set a sound basis for strong economic performance in the future. But the chance of this happening seems remote, for it would require the President to sacrifice his own interests and those of his family and associates to those of the nation. At the time of writing, there was little to indicate that he was willing to do so. With the spread of social unrest from the campus to the streets, and the likely continuing descent into violence and the violent suppression of protest, it is hard to see how Indonesia can emerge from its troubles except under new leadership, brought about by whatever means.

Notes

1. The liquidity squeeze was so severe that the authorities then had to exercise regulatory forbearance in relation to the banks' required reserves, if the banks were not to be forced to close their doors immediately. This issue is not at all clear, however: the central bank's monthly report contains no less than three quite different sets of figures for banks' reserves.

2. Presumably these were foreign exchange assets not included in the official reserves figures.

3. Quite possibly, of course, Mr. Bakrie was simply testing the water on behalf of the government.

4. Nor were parliamentarians themselves safe from the opportunistic behaviour of others. Nearing the end of their five-year terms in 1997, members of parliament were presented with "24-carat" gold rings that, when taken to gold dealers for appraisal, turned out—rather like Busang—to have minimal gold content and a disappointingly low resale value.

5. These comments should not be taken to imply that all parliamentarians and all police were similarly motivated, of course.

6. Bank Indonesia's loans to the private sector are shown in its *Weekly Report* as jumping by this amount at the beginning of November, from a very low level previously.

7. An alternative hypothesis is that the dismissals may have been a payback for closure of the sixteen banks mentioned previously.

8. It seemed curious to be focusing on tariff cuts and the removal of import restrictions, given that the main objective of policy making at the time was to induce a strengthening of the rupiah. A greater flow of imports, although desirable of itself, would be expected to *weaken* the currency.

9. There have been allegations, however, that some borrowers quite able to service their loans seem to have seized the opportunity presented by the general atmosphere of financial chaos to cease doing so.

10. Many observers argue that the reforms were necessary in order to restore confidence on the part of the business community. No doubt this is true of some investors, but to assert that it is true in the aggregate would appear to be an article of faith.

11. By definition, the current account balance is equal and opposite to the capital account balance.

12. Good examples of this phenomenon from the Sukarno era are Caltex and Freeport, both of which faced an extremely inhospitable business environment, but took the view that in the long term it would be well worth the risk to persevere with their operations in Indonesia, rather than pull out as many other firms were doing.

13. A strategy that, clearly, turned out to be an abject failure.

14. It does not reflect well on private sector analysts that they unquestioningly accepted the official reserves figures. It was easy to see from the central bank's own balance sheet that these were considerably understated.

15. When the sixteen banks were closed as part of the agreement with the IMF, the government indeed protected most depositors from loss—something it had said in the past that it would not do—thus justifying many peoples' expectations and setting the scene for the future, when it would be difficult if not impossible to convince people that their funds in banks must always be considered to be at risk.

References

Binhadi, and Paul Meek. 1992. "Implementing Monetary Policy." In *The Oil Boom and After: Indonesian Economic Policy and Performance in the Soeharto Era*, ed. Anne Booth. Singapore: OUP: 102-31.

Boediono. 1994. "Problems of implementing monetary policy in Indonesia." In *Indonesia Assessment 1994: Finance as a Key Sector in Indonesia's Economic Development*, ed. Ross H. McLeod. Canberra: Research School of Pacific and Asian Studies, and Singapore: Institute of Southeast Asian Studies: 119-28.

Fane, George. 1994. "Survey of Recent Developments." *Bulletin of Indonesian Economic Studies* 30(1): 3-38.

———. 1998. "The Role of Prudential Regulation." In *East Asia in Crisis: From Being a Miracle to Needing One?* ed. Ross H. McLeod.and Ross Garnaut. London and New York: Routledge: 287-303.

Fane, George, and Tim Condon. 1996. "Trade Reform in Indonesia, 1987-95." *Bulletin of Indonesian Economic Studies* 32(3): 33-54.

Feridhanusetyawan, Tubagus. 1997. "Survey of Recent Developments." *Bulletin of Indonesian Economic Studies* 33(2): 3-39.

Grenville, S. A. 1998. "The Asian Economic Crisis." *Reserve Bank of Australia Bulletin* (April): 9-20.

Habir, Manggi. 1994. "Bank Soundness Requirements: A Commercial Bank Perspective." In *Indonesia Assessment 1994: Finance as a Key Sector in Indonesia's Economic Development*, ed. Ross H. McLeod. Canberra: Research School of Pacific and Asian Studies, and Singapore: Institute of Southeast Asian Studies: 171-85.

MacIntyre, Andrew, and Sjahrir. 1993. "Survey of Recent Developments." *Bulletin of Indonesian Economic Studies* 29(1): 5-33.

McLeod, Ross H. 1993. "Workers Social Security Legislation." In *Indonesia Assessment 1993: Labour: Sharing the Benefits of Growth?* ed. Chris Manning and Joan Hardjono. Political and Social Change Monograph 20. Canberra: Australian National University: 88-107.

———. 1997. "Survey of Recent Developments." *Bulletin of Indonesian Economic Studies* 33(1): 3-43.

Manning, Chris, and Sisira Jayasuriya. 1996. "Survey of Recent Developments." *Bulletin of Indonesian Economic Studies* 32(2): 3-43.

Tarmidi, Lepi. 1996. "Changing Structure and Competition in the *Kretek* Cigarette Industry." *Bulletin of Indonesian Economic Studies* 32(3): 85-107.

9

The Philippines as an Unwitting Participant in the Asian Economic Crisis

Manuel F. Montes

Political and Economic Crisis of Confidence

When the Asian currency crisis erupted in mid-1997, the Philippines was in the midst of a developing political crisis in relation to efforts to amend the constitution to permit Philippine President Fidel Ramos, who enjoyed the aura of a successful presidency, to run for a second term. Supporters of the president initially attempted to amend the constitution through the method of "popular initiative," gathering six million signatures, a million more than required to force a constitutional amendment, within a few weeks in March 1997. Responding to a series of lawsuits which stretched through August 1997 by opponents of constitutional change, the Supreme Court ruled that the enabling law for the popular initiative was legally inadequate.

Supporters of the president also attempted to convene the two houses of Congress into a constituent assembly to amend the constitution. Since the members of the House of Representatives stood to gain by being able to extend their own terms through constitutional amendment, only the Senate resisted the effort. This resistance showed distinct signs of weakening with the possibility of political payoffs in exchange for supporting constitutional change. The seemingly unstoppable legal momentum was halted (1) by the mobilization in the streets of the old anti-dictatorship alliance against Ferdinand Marcos and (2) by the unmistakable correlation between falling currency and stock market values, on the one hand, and progress toward constitutional amendment on the other since mid-July when the peso had been unhinged from its dollar peg following the Thai baht devaluation in 2 July 1997. One day before a large rally of the alliance was held on 21 September 1997—to be led by former president Corazon Aquino and Manila Cardinal Jaime Sin and at a time when indications of the widespread diffusion of the currency crisis in the region were unmistakable—President Ramos made an unequivocal statement that he would not be running for a second term, thus putting an end to the constitutional crisis.

The 1997 Philippine crisis was characterized by a strong and immediate correlation between political uncertainty and economic outcomes. This distinguishes the crisis from the more traditional type of balance of payments crisis, making the phrase "a crisis of confidence" unavoidable. There is a crisis of confidence in local currency denominated assets—an asset crisis—as opposed to a flow crisis, where trade deficits and government deficits force currency values downward to restore equilibrium. The current Asian crisis demonstrates once again that asset crises have no natural equilibrium value, and that currency values can be brought down way out of line with what would be required to bring exports and imports into sustainable balance.

This essay develops the proposition that the Philippines was an unwitting participant to the Asian economic crisis. There are two aspects in which the Philippines was an unwitting victim. First, like the other countries in the region, Philippine authorities exerted great effort in the period before the crisis to attain the elevated rates of growth its neighbors seemed to be achieving. Its liberalization programs prior to the crisis installed the policy infrastructure that made it vulnerable to this type of crisis.

Second, the Philippine financial system and the rates of economic growth the country had achieved did not justify the extent to which it was drawn into the crisis. The international value of the peso has fallen almost as much as the Thai baht. The Philippine experience, and the Malaysian and Singaporean experience as well, throw light on the role of imperfect international capital markets in creating the conditions for and igniting this type of crisis.

The next section discusses how the liberalization process sets the stage for the currency attack in 1997. The extent of the crisis in the Philippines is then explained, demonstrating that the crisis is real, with profound effects on employment, growth, and policy, even though the principal problem is a confidence crisis. The responses of the Philippine authorities and Philippine political forces to the crisis are discussed, as well as prospects for Philippine recovery. A final section sets out the conclusions of the essay.

The "Twin Liberalizations" in the Philippines

The type of crisis that broke out in Thailand, and subsequently in Indonesia, can be thought of as balance of payments crises that have been triggered by accumulated weaknesses in the domestic financial system (Montes 1998). The weaknesses in the financial system are built up in the wake of the "twin liberalizations": the liberalization of the domestic financial system and the opening of the capital account. The Asian crisis shares many features with those that economically devastated the Southern Cone of Latin America (Chile, Argentina, Uruguay) in the early 1980s, the Scandinavian countries (Norway, Sweden, Finland) in the early 1990s, Mexico and Argentina in 1995. Significant private borrowing from abroad, dominated by short-term borrowing, creates a lending boom and a price asset bubble which fatally weakens the economy's financial sector.

During the lending boom, exchange rates tend to be stable or fixed, making borrowers and lenders forget the risk they undertake when lending out, in domestic currency, resources made accessible because of the opening of capital borrowed in foreign currency.[1] The international value of the currency becomes unsustainable because (1) the country's short-term liabilities eventually exceed the resources it has to immediately service these liabilities (its international reserves) and (2) the lending boom builds a mountain of non-performing loans in the banking system, increasing the probability of the non-servicing of external obligations. The balance of payments problem begins with an attack on the sustainability of the currency peg. By analyzing the nature of the twin liberalizations in the Philippines, we can understand how the Philippines erected the policy framework which made it vulnerable to such a boom and subsequent attack.

Domestic Financial Liberalization

Balance-of-payments crises have punctuated Philippine economic growth since 1946 (Montes 1989). The major crises occurred in 1949 (which became the occasion for the establishment of the central bank), in 1962 (which resulted in the dismantling of the quota system in controlling imports), in 1970 (precipitated by government overspending in connection with the reelection campaign of Ferdinand Marcos paving the way for the authoritarian experiment under martial law from 1972 to 1986), and in 1984–1985 (in connection with the international debt crisis). In 1990–1991, there was a balance of payments crisis, smaller by comparison to the earlier major ones, but significant nevertheless, following the post-martial law economic recovery in 1987–1988 and a series of attempts by military factions to overthrow the Aquino government.

The Philippines' 1984–1985 balance-of-payments crisis was actually preceded by a banking crisis that erupted in 1981 when a prominent businessman left the country leaving behind at least $80 million in debt. Other private banks and government corporations had borrowed heavily (or, which is the same thing, had been lent to heavily) from abroad based on government guarantees. The resolution of the crisis required significant work outs of nonperforming loans and also saw a tightening of prudential rules.

The financial reforms the Philippines carried out in response to the crisis dealt with the capital adequacy of banks and restrictions regarding the access to credit of, in the Philippine formulation, "directors, officers, stockholders and related interests" (DOSRI). DOSRI loans could not exceed at any one time the outstanding deposits and book value of paid-in capital of the borrowing bank officer in the lending bank. A limit of 30 percent of the total credit accommodation of the borrowing party was imposed in unsecured credit. Minimum capital requirements for banks have been increased steadily. These reforms express both the Philippine collective memories of the cost of the aggressive behavior of the few fast growing banks in the 1970s, which since have also gone bankrupt, and the acquired distaste for the favoritism in access to foreign loans and to bailouts during the martial law years.

Conservatism also serves to confirm the dominant position of the larger, more established banks and serves as a ready argument against reforms to increase competition in the domestic market and in regard to the entry of more foreign banks.

Before the financial liberalization program in 1983, the Philippines had interest rate restrictions, imposed heavy reserve requirements (above 20 percent of deposits), enforced specialization by function between different kinds of financial companies, and severely restricted entry into the financial system (Montes and Ravalo 1995). Government banks played a large part in the financial system through the Philippine National Bank in the commercial banking sector and the Development Bank of the Philippines in development finance.

The Philippines carried quite an orthodox approach to financial liberalization (Montes and Ravalo 1995). Reserve requirements, theoretically the principal culprit in financial repression, were reduced. The Philippines was probably the first country in Asia, excluding Singapore but including Japan, to remove interest rate restrictions, which it did in 1983. After the removal of controls on interest rates, the Philippine National Bank (which had accounted for about 50 percent of deposits) was privatized; and the entry and scope of operations of foreign banks in the country, but not the new entry of any new banks, was liberalized (Lamberte 1994:11).

The extent of intermediation improved significantly in the 1990s as a result of the reforms and the return of economic stability. The M3/GNP ratio jumped from 27.8 percent in 1990 to 38.6 percent in 1996 and approximately 40 percent in 1997. Interest rates, as represented by the 91-day Treasury bill rate benchmark, declined in 1996 up to the first half of 1997 (Table 9.1).

The textbook nature of the Philippines liberalization program included the removal of restrictions on bank specialization (through the encouragement of the creation of "universal banks") and the fact that it did not contain any specific features to increase competition among banks. Interest rate liberalization of both deposit and lending rates actually resulted in an increase in the loan-to-deposit margins enjoyed by banks (Montes and Ravalo 1995).[2] Banks appeared to collude in not competing for deposits (keeping deposit rates low), while being able to charge what the "market could bear" on the lending side. To be sure, the generous margins helped the banks use their profits to reduce the nonperforming proportions

TABLE 9.1   Selected Monetary Indicators

	91-day Tbill Rate	90-day LIBOR	Bank Lending Rate (a)	Exchange Rate (b)	M3 / GNP	REER
1985	N/A.	8.39	28.20	18.61	24.20	78.97
1990	23.40	8.28	24.30	24.31	27.90	100.00
1991	21.40	5.98	23.50	27.48	27.50	100.90
1992	16.10	3.83	19.40	25.51	27.80	91.02
1993	12.30	3.29	14.60	27.12	32.00	93.57
1994	13.60	4.74	15.00	26.42	35.00	88.02
1995	11.30	6.04	14.60	25.71	38.90	84.63
1996	12.40	5.50	14.80	26.22	38.60	78.40
1997	12.90	5.73	16.23	29.47	39.88(c)	91.41(d)
Jan	10.80	5.57	14.60	26.32		
Feb	10.70	5.50	12.90	26.34		
Mar	10.10	5.61	13.70	26.33		
Apr	10.00	5.82	12.90	26.36		
May	10.90	5.82	13.40	26.37		
Jun	10.50	5.80	13.30	26.38		
Jul	12.20	5.75	15.50	27.67		
Aug	14.20	5.72	18.60	29.33		
Sep	15.30	5.72	18.20	32.39		
Oct	16.50	5.77	20.90	34.46		
Nov	15.90	5.83	15.30	34.52		
Dec	17.70	5.90	25.50	37.20		
1998 Jan	19.00	5.60	28.00	42.70		

Notes: (a) Starting December 1992, monthly rates reflect the annual percentage equivalent of sample commercial banks' actual monthly interest income on their peso-denominated loans to the total outstanding levels of their peso-denominated demand/time loans, bills discounted, mortgage control receivables, restructured loans.

(b) Bankers' Association of the Philippines (BAP) reference rates; weighted average rate under the Philippine Dealing System (PDS) starting 4 August 1992.

(c) Using November 1997 M3.

(4) As of September 1997.

Sources: Bangko Sentral ng Pilipinas (BSP), BAP, *Asian Wall Street Journal*, Reuters Finance and Bullion, and Dow Jones Telerate from December 1996 onwards.

of their assets (Montes and Ravalo1995). Moreover, the Marcos and subsequently the Aquino governments' strategy of nationalizing the foreign debt forced the public sector to borrow heavily from the domestic financial system and helped maintain high lending rates.

Competition policy concerns began to be directly addressed in 1993, when banks were permitted to open branches anywhere as long as they met requirements on capital adequacy, liquidity, profitability, and soundness of management. The entry of foreign banks (in addition to the existing four) was liberalized in 1994 through fully-owned full-service branches (of which only ten banks were allowed), through equity purchase in an existing bank, or through the establishment of a joint venture between foreign and local groups.

Nevertheless, the clubby style of doing business in the banking sector described by Hutchcroft (1993) has appeared to continue. There are advantages and disadvantages of this approach. The club tends to be small and banks are able to monitor each other, especially in regard to possible special treatment from the Central Bank in its regulatory function. This tends to make regulation more even. The smallness of the club gives the Central Bank a convenient channel for communication and influence. However, the smallness of the club has tended to dampen aggressive competitive behavior among the banks and sustain conservative loan behavior.

Entry into the financial system in the Philippines has been restricted, with the entry of four new foreign banks and one local commercial bank since the late 1980s being touted as most significant. The Thai and Indonesian financial liberalization programs saw an explosion of entry into the financial industry. In the case of Indonesia, in response to its 1988 liberalization decree, the total number of banks increased from 124 (with 2,044 branch offices) in 1988 to 158 in 1989. By 1994 there were 244 banks, with 6,090 branch offices (Montes and Abdusalamov 1998).

The advantages and disadvantages of the "clubby" approach are best seen in the controversy publicly aired by the Central Bank governor in late February and early March 1998. By this time, the attacks on the Philippine peso, save those apparently associated with the uncertainties in Indonesia, had abated. The Central Bank governor criticized the banks for keeping loan interest rates high (about 23 percent per year), the persistence of which would certainly weaken the economy and endanger prospects for recovery (*BusinessWorld*, 12 March 1998).

As in the case of the high lending interest rates in the late 1980s discussed above the bankers association had a ready answer as to why lending rates were high: the cost of intermediation (due to reserve requirements and taxes) and the exchange rate risk were still high. In more direct terms, these objections could be explained this way: if banks were more generous in lending, it would provide nonbanking economic actors with the resources to speculate against the currency; the banks would prefer to, in effect, do it themselves and earn higher profits. The controversy was not resolved directly, and the Central Bank did not have the explicit power to force lending rates down, except to threaten to let more foreign banks into the industry.

One other explanation for the high margins has been informally discussed but difficult to document. Banks have been experiencing increasing failures to service loans. As in second half of the 1980s, under conservative banking, higher loans margins permit banks to use new loans to write off potential losses on old ones.

When the 1997 crisis began, the banking system in the Philippines was relatively sound, even though the patterns of growth since 1994 were in the direction of potentially weakening the banking system. The adverb "potentially" speaks to the fact that these trends are observed just as overall Philippine economic growth rates were recovering. If the growth rates remained modest, they might have been sustainable.

Table 9.2 provides the sectoral breakdown of loans outstanding of commercial banks. The total amount of loans outstanding grew by 25.4 percent in 1994, 35.8 percent in 1995, and 51.9 percent in 1996. The first two growth rates are comparable to those seen in Indonesia, Malaysia, and Thailand in the years before the crisis (Montes 1998). The 1996 rate is extremely elevated and corresponds to the period when short-term portfolio flows increased tremendously, as will be explained below. What is worrisome about the trends in Table 9.2 are the relatively strong growth rates in lending to real estate (especially in 1996), transport and communications, and construction. This pattern was also seen in Thailand and Indonesia.

In June 1997, just before the crisis, the Central Bank (whose official name is Bangko Sentral ng Pilipinas and acronym is BSP) issued a directive limiting bank loans to the real estate sector to no more than 20 percent of the bank's total loan portfolio.[3] The BSP also required commercial banks to lend no more than 60 percent of the appraised value of the real estate property in property lending.

Nevertheless, the financial system was still in a relatively healthy state in 1997. Estimates of the profitability of commercial banks had been at around 2 percent of total assets in 1996; the proportion of non-performing loans to total loans was estimated at 4.02 percent (BSP 1998). In the case of Indonesia, by 1995, 5.08 percent of total credit of state-owned banks and 5.82 percent of the total credit of private non-foreign exchange banks were non-performing. Estimates before the crisis for Thailand of the proportion of non-performing loans were in the order of 9 percent (Montes 1998). Comparing these numbers across countries is difficult since countries have different rules for determining when a loan is "non-performing." For the Philippines, the trends in these and other ratios were trending down until 1996, because the larger banks were increasing their capitalization, originating from their conservatism and in preparation for the entry of more foreign banks.

Overall, however, the banking system had not been weakened too much by mid-1997. One can list the reasons: (1) the lending boom had been limited to 1996; (2)

TABLE 9.2   Loans Outstanding of Commercial Banks
             Growth and Distribution

	1994	1995	1996
A. Growth Rate (in percent)			
Agriculture, Fisheries, and Forestry	8.1	19.6	6.4
Mining and Quarrying	-48.1	55.9	9.4
Manufacturing	32.5	33.9	42.5
Electricity, Gas, and Water	25.7	24.7	90.6
Construction	32.3	37.4	74.2
Wholesale and Retail Trade	39.8	37.3	38.1
Transportation, Storage, and Communications	53.8	72.0	53.3
Fin. Institutions, Real Estate, and Bus. Services	37.4	24.8	97.2
Community, Social, and Personal Services	-10.4	61.8	57.6
TOTAL	25.4	35.8	51.9
B. Share (in percent)			
Agriculture, Fisheries, and Forestry	9.2	8.1	5.7
Mining and Quarrying	1.0	1.2	0.9
Manufacturing	34.9	34.4	32.3
Electricity, Gas, and Water	2.4	2.2	2.8
Construction	3.3	3.4	3.9
Wholesale and Retail Trade	17.5	17.7	16.1
Transportation, Storage, and Communications	4.8	6.1	6.1
Fin. Institutions, Real Estate, and Bus. Services	18.3	16.8	21.8
Community, Social, and Personal Services	8.5	10.2	10.5
TOTAL	100.0	100.0	100.0

Source: Commercial Banks Monthy

the inherent conservatism of Philippines banks, especially the bigger ones, because of memories of previous crises; (3) the capitalization programs most banks undertook in the 1990s; (4) the relatively greater experience and efficacy of Central Bank supervision, again as a result of memories of previous crises; and (5) the relatively small amount of short-term capital inflows before the crises.

Opening the Capital Account

The second liberalization was the opening of the capital account. For most items with regard to the opening of the capital account, the Philippines was ahead of Thailand by about one to two years. In order to develop the capital market, the Securities and Exchange Commission promulgated rules in 1989 that permitted the emergence of mutual funds. At the same time, the Central Bank removed requirements from foreign investors to register with the Central Bank prior to making investment in Central Bank approved securities. Duly registered foreign investors were entitled to full and immediate capital repatriation, which operationally meant that an authorized bank could sell and remit the "equivalent foreign exchange representing sales/divestment or dividends/interest." Most of remaining exchange controls in the currency market, including the surrender requirement for export proceeds and prior Central Bank approval for capital repatriation/dividend/interest remittances were dismantled beginning September 1992.

The cumulated liberalization in the financial system, the foreign exchange system, the nascent privatization program, and some reforms in the equity markets had made viable the sourcing of external private funds for domestic relending or domestic portfolio investment.

In 1991, after restrictions on short-term investments had been liberalized, the Philippines liberalized direct foreign investment, removing ownership restrictions on export-oriented enterprises and installing a negative list on domestic areas reserved against foreign participation. The macroeconomic impact of direct foreign investment is more limited than portfolio investment.[4] These inflows also tend to increase the demand for imports for the required capital goods and intermediate inputs, thus offsetting the inflow recorded in the capital account. This means that the impact on domestic liquidity and money supply of foreign investment projects undertaken to install new manufacturing or service activities is small, and monetary authorities do not have to worry as much about their effect on the exchange rate or the money supply.

However, in the early 1990s, as it was in Latin America, debt buybacks and proceeds from asset privatization in 1994 and 1995, both residuals from the crisis of 1984–1985, dominated the direct foreign investment inflows. These kinds of investment projects—since these involve only the sale of already existing operations to foreigners—do have a monetary impact.

These reforms provided the context within which the Philippines began to generate foreign investor interest at the start of the 1990s. The first experience in portfolio inflows occurred in 1989, with the listing of the First Philippine Fund in the New York Stock Exchange. The abortive *coup d'état* of December 1989 and a large earthquake and the eruption of a volcano on the main island of Luzon stopped the portfolio interest temporarily. The restoration of political and social stability during the Ramos administration restarted private investment interest in the Philippines.

As in Thailand and Indonesia (and the Scandinavian economies in the late 1980s and Mexico in the early 1990s), liberalization provided the private sector with access to foreign borrowings, which were available at interest rates lower than could be obtained domestically. Eventually, the share of the private sector in total foreign exchange liabilities increased from 21.4 percent in 1990 to 44.5 percent as of June 1997. Total foreign exchange liabilities increased from $28.5 billion to $44.8 billion in this same period.

As proportions to GDP, Philippine portfolio inflows were much lower than those observed for Thailand and Malaysia. For Malaysia, short-term inflows peaked at 14.1 percent of GDP in 1993. For Thailand, the annual short-term capital inflow estimates are all above 6 percent and peaked at levels of 10 and almost 12 percent (Montes 1998:18, 24). Estimates of the different kinds of short-term capital inflows are discussed in the next section. While the amounts were relatively small, these flows had noticeable impact on the exchange rate; they also had an impact sufficient on domestic interest to generate policy dilemmas.

The most immediate dilemma started in 1992, when the capital inflows were sufficiently strong to help keep the peso strong. At that juncture, the Philippines was completing the first major phase of its import liberalization program. The strengthening of the peso, by reducing protection from imported goods and weakening export incentives, threatened to undermine the import liberalization program. Table 9.1 shows that the real effective exchange rate began to appreciate in 1992 and continued to appreciate until 1997, when the peso devalued during the crisis.

The Central Bank faced the dilemma by attempting to absorb the capital inflows and to prevent the exchange rate from appreciating too strongly (Montes 1997b). Capital inflows had been increasing not only because of the interest differential but also because, in the run-up to the presidential elections of 1992, funds were being brought back to the country for election spending. The Central Bank undertook significant sterilization operations to prevent these inflows from increasing the money supply to meet liquidity ceilings under the IMF program. When the stock of Central Bank bills was exhausted, the national treasury issued its own bills and deposited the proceeds with the Central Bank.

The extent of Philippine sterilization has been significant. From the end of 1991 to the end of 1994, Central Bank purchases of foreign exchange were $7.1 billion, about 3.1 percent of GDP for those years. For the period January to November 1994, Cororaton (1995) reports that the Central Bank incurred a loss of Pesos 4.6 billion, or 0.02 percent of that year's GDP. The amount is rather small in comparison to Gurria's report of 3.1 percent cost for Mexican sterilization.[5]

The government reduced its rescheduling request under the Paris Club and began to pre-pay part of its foreign debt. The government also accelerated the phasedown of providing foreign exchange cover for oil imports. In mid-1993 the Central Bank temporarily halted sterilization operations (Reinhart 1996). Government deposits were moved back to commercial banks and the peso was allowed to appreciate. In July 1994 the Central Bank raised the limit on outward investments sourced from the banking system from $1 million to $3 million. At the same time, restrictions were lifted on the repatriation of investment and related investment earnings funded by debt-to-equity restructuring programs.

The export sector complained loudly about the steady real appreciation of the peso, and academics accused the Central Bank of doing a worse job than Indonesia in managing the exchange rate. Indonesia had been managing a steady real exchange value of the rupiah in line with the difference in its domestic inflation rate (Montes and Abdusalamov 1998), and the U.S. inflation rate while the Philippines seemed to have shown the largest degree of currency appreciation, in comparison with other economies in the region, during the same period (Yap 1998).

Yet Another but Milder Crisis

By the middle of 1997, the Philippine economy was well on a recovery path from its most recent balance-of-payments crisis of 1990–1991. In 1991 the GDP growth rate was negative 0.6 percent (Table 9.3). In 1992, at the start of the Ramos presidency which promised annual GDP growth rates at 8 to 10 percent under a program called "Philippines 2000," the growth rate was a barely positive 0.3 percent.[6] The rate of growth steadily increased to 5 percent by 1996 and was growing at that rate in 1997.

Philippine recovery from the 1990–1991 crisis can be traced to three economic factors. First, the country's participation in the Brady bond debt workout program in 1992 permitted the government to reduce the refinancing of its debt from the domestic market and led to the unmistakable reduction in interest rates in 1992 (Table 9.1). The debt workout plan that had been negotiatiated under the Marcos and the Aquino governments had essentially tranferred to the national government the responsibility to service the foreign debt built up during the Marcos years. With its limited taxing capacity and not being an export-oriented agency, the government had to resort to domestic borrowing to raise the resources for foreign debt service. With the Brady bonds, the government experienced a significant reduction in its debt servicing load.

TABLE 9.3   The Philippines: Main Economic Indicators

	1991	1992	1993	1994
GDP Per Capita (US$, current prices)	726	827	830	956
GDP Growth Rate (%)	-0.6	0.3	2.1	4.4
Inflation Rate	18.7	8.9	7.6	9
Unemployment Rate (Average)	10.5	9.8	9.3	9.5
Daily Real Wage (US$, current prices)	2.82	2.79	2.80	2.83
Share in GDP				
Agriculture	22.7	22.8	22.8	22.4
Industry	34.7	34.4	34.3	34.7
Manufacturing	25.6	25.0	24.7	24.8
Services	42.6	42.8	43.0	42.9
Gross Domestic Investments	20.2	21.3	24	24.1
Gross Domestic Savings	17.2	16.4	15.5	17.8
Government Current Expenditure		16.2	15.9	16.4
Government Capital Expenditure		3.4	2.6	2
Government Surplus	-2.1	-1.2	-1.5	1
Average Nominal Exch. Rate (P/US$)	27.5	25.5	27.1	26.4
Current Account Balance (US $ Millions)	-869	-858	-3016	-2950
Percent of GDP	-1.9	-1.6	-5.5	-4.6
Foreign Exchange Reserves (US $ Millions)	4,470	5,218	5,801	6,995
Months imports	3.3	3.3	3.1	3
Foreign Debt (US $ Millions)	29,956	30,934	34,282	37,079
Percent of GDP	66	58.4	63	57.8
Medium and Long Term Foreign Debt US$mil	25,129	25,678	29,247	31,882

The second factor was recovery from a severe shortage of electrical power supply that occurred in 1991 due to government neglect to replace aging power plants after 1986 in the turnover of power between the Marcos and Aquino governments.[7] The acceleration of investment and installation of short-lived but expensive plants permitted the restoration of power beginning in early 1993. The third factor, not possible without the second, was the achievement of double-digit rates of growth in exports in 1994 and 1995. The steady inflow of direct foreign investment in export enterprises was certainly a key factor in the export recovery. This was indirectly indicated in 1996 when the export growth rate fell to single-digit levels as the Philippines joined other Asian countries in the worldwide slump

TABLE 9.3   (continued)

	1995	1996	1997
GDP Per Capita (US$, current prices)	1,081	1,193	1,186
GDP Growth Rate (%)	4.8	5.7	5.1
Inflation Rate	8.1	8.4	5.1
Unemployment Rate (Average)	9.5	8.5	8.7
Daily Real Wage (US$, current prices)	2.69	2.77	2.39
Share in GDP			
Agriculture	21.5	21.0	20.5
Industry	35.4	35.7	35.9
Manufacturing	25.3	25.3	25.0
Services	43.0	43.4	43.5
Gross Domestic Investments	22.5	23.2	25
Gross Domestic Savings	14.7	19.4	-
Government Current Expenditure	15.2	n/a	n/a
Government Capital Expenditure	2.8	n/a	n/a
Government Surplus	0.6	0.3	0.1(a)
Average Nominal Exch. Rate (P/US$)	25.7	26.2	28.8
Current Account Balance (US $ Millions)	-2575	-3772	-2865(b)
Percent of GDP	-3.5	-4.5	-3.4
Foreign Exchange Reserves (US $ Millions)	7,633	11,620	9,957(c)
Months imports	2.5	3.2	3.6
Foreign Debt (US $ Millions)	37,778	41,875	44,809d
Percent of GDP	51	50	52.6
Medium and Long Term Foreign Debt (US $ mill.)	32,499	34,668	36,261d

Notes: (a) As of December 1997; (b) as of July 1997; (c) as of October 1997; (d) as of June 1997.

in the electronic industry (Montes 1998). A fourth, but non-economic, factor would be the return of political stability under the Ramos government.

Nevertheless, when the Asian crisis began, the Philippines was nowhere near the 8 percent growth rates projected in the Ramos presidency's medium-term development plan.[8] Eight percent growth rates could not be achieved because the Philippine investment rate remained stuck at about 22 percent of GDP (Table 9.3) in the first years of the 1990s, while the Philippines' Southeast Asian neighbors were investing over 30 percent of GDP every year. In alphabetical order, Indonesia was investing an average of 34.1 percent per year, Malaysia 35.1 percent, and Thailand 39.8 percent in the same period (Montes 1998:36, Table 5).

In response to the 1990–1991 crisis, the Aquino administration set in train a comprehensive economic reform program with a key objective of restoring investment confidence in international circles.[9] However, as the investment numbers in Table 9.3 indicate, the Philippines seemed to be suffering from "investment anemia."[10] The investment boom that preceded the Thai and Indonesian crises had not come to pass, but the government and certainly the overwhelming majority of the Philippine population were in prayerful hope for the advent of such a boom (Montes 1998).

In 1996 the boom seemed to have arrived. The tale can be told using Table 9.4, which provides a breakdown of key capital flows from 1990 to September 1997. Philippine trade and current account balances show a clear ratchet up to about 5 percent of GDP after 1993, the start of the recovery and the first full year after the capital liberalization of September 1992. The current account deficits were financed through loans, direct foreign investment, and short-term capital flows.

Between 1990 and 1996, direct foreign investment contributed 1 to 2 percent of GDP; and, as explained in the previous section, the macroeconomic impact of direct foreign investment is quite benign. Medium- and long-term loans contributed between 2 and 5 percent of GDP. A significant part of these resources came from the international finance institutions for use by the government. Since the Philippines had significantly reduced and reformed the state corporate sector, these flows did not have the same potential for harm as they did during the Marcos years.

Of greatest interest are the various categories of short-term capital inflows. Table 9.2 shows three items: (1) short-term capital which is dominated by trade credit accommodations, (2) changes in commercial bank dollar deposits, and (3) portfolio flows which are broken down in the data as flows by residents and non-residents. The total of these short-term flows are quite small, peaking at 2.96 percent of GDP in 1996, the year the boom was starting. Also in 1996 non-resident portfolio inflows peaked at 2.51 percent and increases in dollar deposits increased by 5.03 percent of GDP.

The pattern of resident versus non-resident portfolio flows reveals much about the impact of the capital account opening in the Philippines. The category of "residents" refers to agents based in the Philippines, including non-Philippine nationals such as foreign corporations based in the country; the category of "non-residents" includes Filipino nationals whose funds are based in overseas markets. The opening of the capital account in 1992 was followed by significant outward portfolio flows by residents; the positive net portfolio flows have come from non-residents who seemed to have more faith in Philippine reforms that residents themselves! The capital account liberalization of 1992 has resulted in the noticeable increase in incoming non-resident portfolio investment, as has been the case in other countries. Before 1992, non-resident investment constituted less than 1 percent of GDP; since then, as reflected in Table 9.4, this category has increased to over 2 percent of GDP.

TABLE 9.4   International Capital Flows Data

	1990	1991	1992	1993
Levels (in US million dollars)				
Trade Balance	-4020	-3211	-4695	-6222
Current Account	-2567	-869	-858	-3016
Medium & Long Term Loans, net	674	835	633	2455
FDI, net	528	529	675	864
Short Term Loans, net	19	349	660	-148
Portfolio, net	-56	125	62	-52
Non-residents, net	-52	125	155	897
Residents, net	-4	0	-93	-949
Commercial Banks	603	40	289	-299
All Short Term Capital, net	566	514	1011	-499
Share to GDP (in percent)				
Trade Balance	-9.07	-7.07	-8.86	-11.44
Current Account	-5.79	-1.91	-1.62	-5.55
Medium & Long Term Loans, net	1.52	1.84	1.19	4.52
FDI, net	1.19	1.16	1.27	1.59
Short Term Loans, net	0.04	0.77	1.25	-0.27
Portfolio, net	-0.13	0.28	0.12	-0.1
Non-residents, net	-0.12	0.28	0.29	1.65
Residents, net	-0.01	0	-0.17	-1.75
Commercial Banks	1.36	0.09	0.55	-0.55
All Short Term Capital, net	1.27	1.14	1.92	-0.92

TABLE 9.4   (continued)

	1994	1995	1996	1997(a)
Levels (in US million dollars)				
Trade Balance	-7850	-9844	-11342	-8252
Current Account	-2950	-3297	-3914	-3162
Medium & Long Term Loans, net	1313	1276	2690	3295
FDI, net	1289	1361	1338	1016
Short Term Loans, net	1002	-56	540	386
Portfolio, net	269	248	-170	-3332
Non-residents, net	901	1485	2101	-322
Residents, net	-632	-1237	-2271	-3010
Commercial Banks	674	1574	4211	3010
All Short Term Capital, net	1945	1766	4581	64
Share to GDP (in percent)				
Trade Balance	-12.25	-12.06	-13.54	-12.97
Current Account	-4.6	-4.45	-4.67	-4.97
Medium & Long Term Loans, net	2.05	1.72	3.21	5.18
FDI, net	2.01	1.84	1.6	1.6
Short Term Loans, net	1.56	-0.08	0.64	0.61
Portfolio, net	0.42	0.33	-0.2	-5.24
Non-residents, net	1.41	2.0	2.51	-0.51
Residents, net	-0.99	-1.67	-2.71	-4.73
Commercial Banks	1.05	2.12	5.03	4.73
All Short Term Capital, net	3.03	2.37	5.47	0.1

Note: (a) Includes January through September 1997 only.

Source: BSP, Selected Philippine Economic Indicators.

However, outgoing resident investments have offset these inflows. In 1994, for example, net portfolio inflows were $269 million due to $901 million of non-resident incoming investment netted against $632 million of resident outgoing investment (Table 9.4). From 1994 onwards, the net amount residents have been investing in foreign assets in the portfolio category increased consistently, to $1.2 billion in 1995 and $2.2 billion in 1996. In the first nine months of the crisis year of 1997, residents invested $3 billion in foreign assets in the portfolio category.

Increases in the flows through dollar accounts, represented in Table 9.4 by the rows marked "commercial banks," are likely dominated by residents' asset behavior and offsets the outflows in the portfolio account. In the case of residents, increases in this category represents movement into dollar-denominated deposits away from peso-denominated assets. When the crisis began, it was residents that exhibited the most flighty behavior. This divergence in expectations between residents and non-residents has most often been seen in Mexico (Griffith-Jones 1997). As before the 1980s debt crisis, external inflows are financing resident investments abroad, except that in the case of the Philippines after 1994 the capital inflow category is not loans.

The data suggests that net short-term capital inflows (and their consequent impact in increases in domestic credit) have been small in the Philippines before crises because residents have been carrying the contrary behavior of investing abroad. In the context of the Central Bank's efforts to prevent the peso from strengthening further, these outward investments were helpful. Indonesia through its credit ceiling program had long experience in keeping the rupiah weak, in spite of signficant foreign exchange earnings from oil, by implicitly encouraging such outflows (Montes and Abdusalamov 1998). It appears that the conservatism of Philippine banking plus pessimism of Philippine investors relative to foreign investors had the same type of effect before 1996.

When the Asian crisis began, the problem of dealing with too much inflows immediately reversed into the problem of preventing too much capital from flowing out. As shown in Table 9.4, short-term flows reversed from positive 2.96 percent of GDP in 1996 to minus 0.41 percent for January to September 1997. Residents exhibited a highly elevated minus 5.75 percent of GDP outflow in 1997. For the whole of 1997, for which data is not yet available, it remains to be seen if non-residents joined residents in as much flight.

The Philippines made up for the capital outflows by accelerating medium- and long-term loans (arranged from the IMF and with private commercial banks) which showed a net inflow of 5.18 percent, in effect paying for the resident portfolio outflow.

The impact of the changed investment climate will be severe on the Philippines. Domestic interest rates have been declining since the previous crisis in 1990, but they have now again increased to levels comparable to 1990 crisis levels. Interest differential against international interest rates, measured by the ninety-day LIBOR rate, also has widened (Table 9.1). Current bank lending rates are known to be in the range of 30 percent, comparable to levels in Malaysia and Indonesia. This will cause a severe contraction in investment, which had already peaked at 25 percent in 1997. Investments, which recovered to a growth rate of 15.6 percent in real terms in 1996, grew by only 10 percent in 1997 (Table 9.5). As a proportion of GDP, investment could fall to the level of 20 percent in 1998.

Bank clients will experience difficulties in servicing their loans due to the higher rates of interest and slower growth. This will weaken almost all the banks in the system; and the proportion of non-performing loans will increase, although probably not double as it did in Malaysia because the credit expansion before the crisis was smaller. Two banks faced difficulties in 1997. One bank, which was found to have exceeded limits in lending to insiders, was being rehabilitated by the entry of a foreign partner. In the case of the other bank, the controlling stockholders expressed willingness to infuse more capital.

The lower investment rate implies that the economic growth rate in 1998 will be in the range of 2 to 4 percent, in a year fraught with uncertainty over how soon the Indonesian crisis will stabilize and if China will be swept into the crisis. For 1998, these rates of economic growth would be the envy of Indonesia and Thailand, both of which face negative rates of growth. For the Philippines, which had not yet shared in the region's elevated growth, the 1998 rate would mean a return to the average growth rate during the recovery from the previous crisis. In 1999 the economic growth rate could reach the top end of the 2 to 4 percent range.

Unemployment, which had been declining steadily since 1991 to 8.5 percent in 1996, began to increase in 1997 to 8.7 percent (Table 9.3). The Department of Labor estimated the number of layoffs increased by 43,000 in the first six months of 1998. In the context of 2.5 million already unemployed, this increase is quite modest and is not comparable to the doubling in the numbers of unemployed estimated for Thailand or Korea. Since the economy is still growing, the unemployment rate is expected to rise by only 1 or 2 percent as a result of the economic slowdown. More worrisome is the expected repatriation of workers from Indonesia, Malaysia, and Thailand. This is another factor in which events are not completely under the control of Philippine authorities, but there have no estimates of the potential impact of this development.

The peso has already devalued by about 40 percent from its levels in July 1997. The inflation rate in 1997 actually declined to 5.1 percent, but inflation is expected to increase to at most 8 percent in 1998. As in Thailand, weak domestic demand is expected to offset the inflation stimulus from the exchange rate devaluation.

The peso devaluation has raised the cost of imports. Retailing and manufacturing activities for the domestic market are having a particularly difficult adjustment and some bankruptcies in this sector are being seen. The high interest rate regime cum devaluation will sustain a barely noticeable increase of 3 percent in imports seen in 1997. Exports are expected to grow about 8 percent in 1998, based on the

TABLE 9.5   Rates of Growth of Key Sectors

Real Growth Rates	1991	1992	1993	1994	1995	1996	1997
GDP	-0.6	0.3	2.1	4.4	4.8	5.7	5.1
Agriculture	1.4	0.4	2.1	2.6	0.9	3.1	2.8
Industry	-2.7	-0.5	1.6	5.8	7.2	6.3	5.7
Manufacturing	-0.4	-1.7	0.7	5.0	6.8	5.6	4.0
Services	1.0	1.0	2.5	4.2	4.9	6.5	5.6
Personal	2.3	3.3	3.0	3.7	3.8	4.6	5.0
Government	-2.1	-0.9	6.2	6.1	5.4	5.2	3.6
Investments	-17.3	7.8	7.9	8.7	3.0	15.6	10.0
Exports	6.3	4.3	6.2	19.8	12.0	20.3	8.9
Imports	-1.1	8.7	11.5	14.5	16.0	21.1	8.7

projections of the Central Bank (*Philippine Star* 1998). This means that the trade deficit will be halved from $4.49 billion in 1997 to $2.2 billion in 1998.

Poverty rates had been declining steadily during the economic recovery in the 1990s. This trending downward will be halted with the crisis. Nevertheless, a sharp reversal of modest gains in the last few years is not expected because the increase in the unemployment rate should be modest.

In general, these immediate effects can be characterized as the occasion of deep disappointment in the Philippines, which had just began to reach Asian rates of growth. But there will be a relatively gentle descent in economic performance. The crisis will have more significant real effects if the current regime of high interest rates is maintained for more than one semester (i.e., half a year). This depends on the return of confidence in international markets and how the domestic authorities continue to respond to the crisis.

Philippine Responses to the Crisis

The Central Bank staged a vigorous defense of the peso after the Thai devaluation on 2 July 1997 (see Table 9.6). On 3 July it raised overnight interest rates from 15 to 24 percent. In defending the peso, the Central Bank devoted $2 billion

TABLE 9.6   Rates of Depreciation of Selected
              Asian Currencies

Local Currency	Exchange Rate to U.S. Dollar		Percent of Change in Dollar Value
	1 July 1997	24 January 1998	
Indonesian Rupiah	2,432.00	14,800.00	-83.6
Malaysian Ringgit	2.52	4.58	-44.9
Philippine Peso	26.37	43.50	-39.4
Singapore Dollar	1.43	1.76	-18.8
Thai Baht	24.53	54.00	-54.6
Korean Won	888.00	1,744.00	-49.1

out of its $11 billion international reserves, until it gave up on 11 July and let the peso float.[11] On 14 July, The IMF offered the Philippines $1.1 billion in financial support under the fast-track regulations drawn up after the 1995 Mexican crisis.

The Central Bank also attempted to directly dampen speculation against the peso. It imposed rules requiring prior clearance on the sale of non-deliverable forward contracts (of foreign exchange against pesos). This action was a weakening of the "guarantee" of an open capital account, which could have risked further capital outflows since these moves are often interpreted as attempts to prevent capital flight.[12] In hindsight, one might interpret the original opening of the capital account in 1992 as a good move. The resulting outward movement of residents' capital did not infuse too much short-term liquidity (in net terms) into the banking system that could be recklessly lent out in local currency, as happened in Thailand.

After the 1997 crisis erupted, under circumstances not of the country's own doing, the early opening of the capital account looked more questionable since the authorities were only left with two options: increase domestic interest rates drastically, which could mean sacrificing the soundness of the domestic banking system itself, or devalue. A third choice of trying once again to close the capital account is extremely dangerous, since standard economic models indicate that this will provoke further attacks on the exchange rate and reward the speculators (Montes 1998). One must understand, however, that in 1992 when it opened its capital account, the Philippines was engaged in a "beauty contest" with other emerging nations concerned with attracting the newly available investment funds from industrial economies.

The national government has ordered a 25 percent across-the-board reduction in spending. Fiscal 1997 results had been disappointing; the cash budget surplus was P1.6 billion in 1997 compared to P6.2 billion in 1996. Due to disappointing revenue performance, the surplus was significantly below the target of P11.4 billion for the year. Internal revenue fell short of the 1997 target by close to P20 billion. This was attributed to slower output growth, lower customs collections, and some confusion over the implementation by the Bureau of Internal Revenue (BIR) of a revised tax payment scheme. The new weakness in fiscal finances forced the government to accelerated the rolling over of its existing domestic debt and spurred higher domestic interest rates.

The severe fiscal contraction in response to the crisis sustains the prudent fiscal stance taken in the 1990s. In December 1997 the Congress finally passed the controversial comprehensive tax reform program. The delay in the passage had been due to the attempt of Congress to apply tax exemptions to higher tax brackets than had been proposed by the administration.

The tax program was a key provision of the Extended Fund Facility (EFF) reform program the administration had been undertaking with the International Monetary Fund (IMF). This program had been scheduled to end in June 1997, but the delay in the tax bill forced its extension to December 1997. The EFF program had been touted by the government as its "exit" program from the IMF, after an almost unbroken series of IMF programs since 1962. As the crisis deepened in the second half of 1997, however, the EFF program was further extended to end-March 1998. The government negotiatied a new IMF program, described by the government as a "precautionary arrangement," to begin immediately after the end of the current EFF program.

Restarting and retaining external private financing is always critical to a country whose savings rates have been stuck below 20 percent of GDP (Table 9.3), while its neighbors—except for Viet Nam (Montes 1996)—enjoyed savings rates near 30 percent of GDP. The regional crisis has had a significant impact on the economy precisely because of this dependence.

A public debate broke out in February 1998 over whether lending rates charged by the private banking system were grossly higher than their cost of funds, with the Central Bank governor and representatives of business chambers of commerce hurling this accusation. Local chambers of commerce throughout the country staged demonstrations against this banking practice. The president of the Manila chamber of commerce appeared in a popular morning television show in 14 March to complain about high deposit-to-loan margins. In the town of Midsayap in Mindanao, 150 businessmen and traders closed their accounts in several banks as part of the protest (AFP 1998). The protestors warned that mass withdrawals would occur everyday until 6 April. These protests—as the protests of exporters against the strong peso since the early 1990s—forced the Central Bank to acknowledge the demands of constituencies beyond the banks that it supervises and the government that it helps to finance.

The rather conservative stance of the private banking system helps to protect the soundness of the financial system, and the high margins provided by the high lending rates assists banks in writing off their non-performing assets. However, it is constricting investment. This is the resurfacing of a debate that broke out in the late 1980s, as explained above (Montes and Ravalo 1995). To reduce the cost of funds, the Central Bank scheduled the reduction of reserve requirements from 13 to 10 percent to take effect from 31 March 1998. The objectors to the conservative banking stance did not seem to be very confident that their protests would be heeded. Suggestions about permitting new foreign banks to enter the domestic market to increase domestic competition were also being raised by these objectors.

The Central Bank announced additional measures meant to improve the soundness of the banking system in early March 1998. Prudential rules had required banks to classify problem loans in descending order of quality in four grades: "classified," "especially mentioned," "substandard," and "doubtful and loss." Beginning 15 April 1998, banks had to make specific provisions for losses on "especially mentioned" and "substandard" loans, categories which used to be covered only under general loss provisions. The new provisions will be phased in. The reform was carried out under a $250 million World Bank financial sector reform program. The main objective of the program is to strengthen prudential monitoring in the financial system.

In the last two months of 1997, labor unions began to petition the Ramos government for legislated wage increases in response to the crisis. The impending national elections added timeliness to the request, which was in conflict with the strategy began in the Aquino administration of setting mandatory wage increases at the regional instead of at the national level. Regional wage setting creates competition between the regions and moderates wage increases. The Ramos administration resisted these demands until the adjournment of Congress in the run-up to the national elections.

As would be expected, the Asian crisis ignited policy debates over economic policy in the Philippines. The Central Bank, which had already come under heavy criticism from academics (notably from the University of the Philippines' School of Economics) and export groups for the undue strength of the peso, opened itself up to criticism for trying too hard to defend the peso at its onset. As the peso continued to fall beyond levels consistent with a competitive export sector, these criticisms became less sustainable.

The Ramos government, which had enthusiastically pursued and widened the reform programs begun in the last years of the Aquino government, also came under criticism from the same academics and research organizations associated with labor unions and the popular movement for premature liberalization of the capital account.[13] This issue, however, was too esoteric to become an important political issue among the masses. Furthermore, the rich and intellectuals—who could understand the arcane nature of capital account liberalization—supported the liberalization program because they could make money from it. The liberalization of the capital account can be very popular among asset owners. As had happened in the Philippines and elsewhere, capital account opening saw the influx of funds into the stock markets and the banking system (relent as property and car loans) which induced handsome capital gains for asset holders. In the case of the Philippines, the peso strengthened; this favored import-dependent industries, and residents were able to diversify their portfolio to include foreign assets. In the 1992 debates among *congnoscenti* on the issue, those who supported capital account liberalization made the argument that the Philippines should begin by accepting "hot money" flows to give foreign investors the opportunity to "learn more" about the Philippines. Eventually, the argument was that these flows would metamorphose into direct foreign investments.

The currency crisis affected the national election campaigns in specific ways. Its onset provided opposition candidates with an issue to tar the Ramos party. The issue also appeared to have reduced the power of a presidential endorsement, compared with the strong position enjoyed by President Corazon Aquino when she endorsed the candidacy of Fidel Ramos. The crisis provided a lot of grist to policy debates in connection with the national election campaign and the opportunity for nationalist posturing. However, the policy implications that emerged from these debates, except from the candidacy of Alfredo Lim (former mayor of Manila and the candidate endorsed by former President Corazon Aquino), have steered away from protectionist and regulatory strategies.

It appears that the economic reform process started in the last few years of the Aquino administration will continue. Like Presidents Aquino and Ramos, the new president will be inaugurated in 1 July to preside over an economy in crisis. It is a smaller crisis than ones previously, but one in which the country's destiny, unlike previous crises, is not completely in the hands of domestic actors. This pressure can be expected to prevent any significant backsliding in development strategy.

Conclusion

In 1993 a World Bank study pointedly excluded the Philippines from the list of Asian "miracle economies" (World Bank 1993). This list included Indonesia, now the economy with the deepest economic crisis in Asia. After protesting vehemently for a decade that it is an East Asian economy, not a Latin American one, the Philippines returned to the region's ardent embrace by being swept into the Asian currency crisis.

The difference is that, unlike its neighbors, the Philippines is well-acquainted with the drill (devaluation-inflation, tight credit-output contraction) of balance-of-payments crises. Moreover, the current crisis is generally expected to impose milder effects on the Philippines than its previous troubles.

Can the Philippines' previous experience provide lessons for the other countries in the region? In previous crises and the present one, Philippine authorities have thrown themselves fully into IMF responses to the crisis. In previous crises and the present one, this approach generated domestic controversy, not just due to the standard complaints that IMF programs have been contractionary and have forced all the adjustment on borrowers instead of forcing lenders to share in the burden, but also with regard to the technical appropriateness of the IMF programs themselves. For example, the 1985 program had been criticized for being so credit-constricting that it led to the disappearance of export credits (Montes 1987). In general, IMF programs have been popular inside government circles and unpopular among academics and the business sector. This pattern appears to be the case in both Thailand and Korea, but in Indonesia it appears that the government itself is balking against the IMF program.

It must be stated, however, that the IMF these days often appears as paralyzed as a doe caught in a car's headlights. Implicit assumptions about exchange rates in its single-country programs in Thailand, Korea, and Indonesia have been rendered obsolete within days after the start of the programs, as sympathetic devaluations in other currencies forced the further devaluation of the currency of the country under the program. The institutional assumptions regarding currency setting and capital movements have been overtaken by the speed and the size at which hedge funds respond to economic news (Montes 1998).

When Indonesia closed down sixteen banks immediately at the start of its IMF program in October 1997, the IMF and domestic authorities expected that this sudden policy would restore confidence in the remaining banks. Instead, a run on the remaining banks ensued, forcing Indonesian authorities to provide liquidity not calculated into the IMF program (Montes and Abdusalamov 1998).

IMF programs are meant to restore confidence so that external creditors are encouraged to roll over their short-term lending to the country; specially critical for the short-term are trade credits. However, for countries which have renounced control over selling their currencies in the future by opening their capital account transactions, exchange rates are heavily determined not by trade transactions but by asset movements of hedge funds, which can be very large in comparison to trade. Rapid changes in the exchange rate increase the uncertainty in the provision of short-term credits. They also weaken the banking system and the domestic corporate sector if they have incurred foreign liabilities after the opening of the capital account.

The inability of IMF programs to stabilize exchange rates (as had happened in Thailand and Indonesia) arises from the self-confirming loss of confidence in currency markets. Markets react quickly to fact and rumor and tend to over-react in both cases. In Asia, over-reaction would seem to have operated both during the boom and bust period. During the period of euphoria, capital poured into Asia—in spite of increasing instances of financial failure in Thailand and Indonesia and obvious institutional inadequacies such as the overly generous government bailouts and the lack of bankruptcy procedures.

In this kind of situation, one would expect that greater information flow, possible in more democratic settings such as the Philippines, would have an advantage: economic rumor and information are disclosed early, and citizens and the markets are able to discount equally early. The string of financial crashes in industrial economies suggests that greater information flow cannot prevent overreaction, but it can dampen it. It took a while for euphoria to set in the Philippines, and even when it did residents appeared to have considered investing abroad more remunerating or at least more prudent.

A more democratic setting also means that policies cannot be changed quickly, so the probability of policy suprises is smaller. This should offer a range of certainty to international investors. Checks-and-balances, and consequent partial paralysis, are part of Philippine democratic practice. As discussed earlier, the matter of strengthening the Philippine peso became a controversial political issue as early as 1992, just as high loan margins are now a political issue.

One might argue that these controversies prevented the relatively independent Central Bank from committing egregious policy errors. Since its founding in 1949, the Central Bank has enjoyed autonomy almost comparable to that of the Federal Reserve system of the United States, reporting to a Monetary Board chaired by the governor. Unlike the United States, however, the Secretary of Finance was an automatic member of the board. It was always the Central Bank governor, with a fixed term and the sworn duty to protect the value of the currency, who dominated Philippine monetary policymaking. Policy coordination between the Central Bank and the Ministry of Finance has been quite good, even after the martial law government.

The role of an independent Central Bank is critical when fiscal finances are weak, since the government customarily requires money creation to finance part of the deficit. Fiscal finances have been improving in the Philippines in the 1990s. In Thailand, the Central Bank enjoys enormous independence even though fiscal finances have normally been robust. Before the crisis, this independence played the role (as it also did in the Philippines) of permitting Thai authorities to pursue a strong peg to the dollar, irrespective of the consequences. When the strengthening of the dollar against the yen led to attacks against the peg beginning in late 1996, one of the consequences of independence was the use of Thai reserves to sustain the dollar peg of the baht. The Thai administration learned about the loss of reserves five days before the Thai devaluation, too late to address the problem (Bardacke 1998). There were only about $1 billion in reserves out of a total of $30 billion officially reported to the administration.

Philippine political and economic governance had been deemed too weak, or at least too un-Asian, to warrant its inclusion in the Asian miracle group, whose governments were identified as playing a key role in their development effort (World Bank 1993). Events in the 1990s reviewed in this paper, however, suggest that the less intrusive government role in the economy—erected as a result of economic reforms and political democratization interacting with the long-standing private sector preeminence in the economic sphere (Montes 1995)—dampened the potential for hothouse, Asian-style growth processes. This prevented the Philippines from growing too fast before the 1997 regional crisis.

Philippine investment sentiment was weak, and the capital account liberalization actually resulted in resident capital flowing out from the country. Governance was not good enough to permit faster growth, but it was good enough to prevent large policy errors from occurring. However, data beginning from 1996 suggest that the government and the private sector were beginning to succumb to the temptations that eventually undermined Thai and Indonesian growth. It also suggests that the peso had been appreciating more quickly in real terms than the other currencies in the region.

The failed attempt to amend the constitution to extend the Ramos presidency can also be viewed as a political counterpart to the hothouse alternative. That Filipinos, assisted by fate or at least by globalization's first major crisis, chose against the amendment in September 1997 provides another clue to future Philippine prospects. Unspectacular growth and unspectacular achievements in social and political institutions change might yet prove to be a more sustainable approach to economic development in the Philippines.

Notes

Early discussions about analytical points and assistance in obtaining up-to-date data from Josef Yap are heartily acknowledged.

1. Because of the heavy capital inflow, a stable rate is easy to sustain during an inflow period. In fact, during that juncture, because of the heavy capital inflow it is more difficult to prevent the exchange rate from appreciating too much (Montes 1998), so that achieving nominal exchange rate stability can actually be deemed a kind of achievement.

2. An example of a less orthodox interest liberalization was in Thailand, where lending rates were liberalized one year before deposit rates, reserving for the government the power to set deposit rates to protect small depositors (Nijithaworn 1995).

3. In 1991 the Philippine Central Bank was reorganized into the Bangko Sentral ng Pilipinas (BSP). The new bank was freed of the oustanding losses of the old Central Bank and the monetary board governing its operations slightly reorganized. In the narrative, the word "Central Bank" will often be used to refer to the BSP for convenience.

4. Recent work have raised questions about the presumed smaller volatility of direct foreign investment flows. See Claessens, Dooley, and Warner (1993); and Dooley, Fernandez-Arias, and Kletzer (1996).

5. See Gurria's chapter on Mexico in Ffrench-Davis and Griffith-Jones (1995).

6. Even though the official term of the new Ramos administration would end in 1998.

7. The Aquino government's natural suspicion of alternative large power projects from the Marcos regime after its decision not to complete the nuclear power plant were critical in this respect.

8. In a paper originally presented in 1993, Montes and Lim (1996) warned that attempting to grow too fast was a dangerous strategy and suggested aiming for rates of growth in the order of 4 or 5 percent per year, while carrying out economic reforms, including reforms more oriented to addressing equity and environmental issues.

9. See Montes (1992) for an analysis of this effort.

10. From the title of the piece by Montes and Lim (1996).

11. In contrast, Indonesia floated its currency more quickly. It appears that Indonesia used only $1 billion in reserves in its original defense of the rupiah (Montes and Abdu-salamov 1998).

12. See Montes (1998) for a discussion of the guarantee of an open capital account and its role in attracting foreign investment.

13. As an element of the flourishing of non-governmental organizations, there are now many professional research organizations serving the popular movements. These have provided analyses and criticisms not normally associated with the old Philippine "left" movement. For example, they have supported a weaker peso to assist exporters and tax reforms for redistributive and environmental purposes.

References

AFP. 1998. "Philippine traders close bank accounts in protest." *Straits Times*, 28 March: 6.

Bardacke, Ted. 1998. "Origins: The day the miracle came to an end." *Financial Times*, 12 January.

BSP (Bangko Sentral ng Pilipinas). 1998. *Staying on Course*. Manila: Bangko Central ng Pilipinas.

Cororaton, Cesar B. 1995. "Surge in Capital Inflows: Response of the Government, and Effects on the Economy: The Philippine Case." Philippine Institute for Development Studies (PIDS) Discussion Paper Series No. 95-24 (August).

Claessens, Stijn, Michael P. Dooley, and Andrew Warner. 1993. "Portfolio Capital Flows: Hot or Cool?" In *Portfolio Investment in Developing Countries*, ed. Stijn Claessens and Sudarshan Gooptu. Washington, DC: World Bank Discussion Paper No. 228.

Dooley, Michael, Eduardo Fernández-Arias, and Kenneth Kletzer. 1996. "Is the Debt Crisis History? Recent Private Capital Inflows to Developing Countries." *The World Bank Economic Review* 10(10): 27-50.

Ffrench-Davis, Ricardo, and Stephany Griffith-Jones, eds. 1995. *Coping with Capital Surges: The Return of Finance to Latin America*. Boulder, CO: Lynne Rienner.

Griffith-Jones, Stephany. 1997. "Causes and Lessons of the Mexican Peso Crisis." Working Paper No. 132. Helsinki: United Nations University/World Institute for Development Economics Research (UNU/WIDER) (May).

Hutchcroft, Paul D. 1993. "Selective Squander: The Politics of Preferential Credit Allocation in the Philippines." In *The Politics of Finance in Developing Countries*, ed.

Stephan Haggard, Chung H. Lee, and Sylvia Maxfield. Ithaca, NY: Cornell University Press.

Lamberte, Mario B. 1994. "Managing Surges in Capital Inflows: The Philippine Case." Philippine Institute for Development Studies (PIDS) Discussion Paper Series No. 94-20 (December).

Montes, Manuel F. 1989. "Financing Development: The 'Corporatist' versus the 'Democratic' Approach in the Philippines." In *The Political Economy of Fiscal Policy*, ed. Miguel Urrutia, Shinichi Ichimura, and Setsuko Yukawa. Tokyo: United Nations University: 84-148.

———. 1992. "The Politics of Liberalization: The Aquino Government's 1990 Tariff Reform Initiative." In *The Politics of Economic Reform in Southeast Asia*, ed. David G. Timberman. Makati, Philippines: Asian Institute of Management: 91-115.

———. 1995. "The Private Sector as the Engine of Philippine Growth: Can Heaven Wait?" *Journal of Far East Business* 1, 3 (Spring): 132-47.

———. 1996. "Country Responses to Massive Capital Flows." Working Paper No. 121. United Nations University/World Institute for Development Economics Research (September).

———. 1997a. "Viet Nam: Transition as a Socialist Project in East Asia." Working Paper No. 136. United Nations University/World Institute for Development Economics Research (June).

———. 1997b. "Public Responses to Private Capital Flows: Why, If, and How?" Unpublished manuscript. Helsinki: United Nations University/World Institute for Development Economics Research (June).

———. 1998. *The Currency Crisis in Southeast Asia: Updated Edition.* Singapore: Institute of Southeast Asian Studies.

Montes, Manuel F., and Muhamad Ali Abdusalamov. 1998. "Reaping the Market: Indonesia's Currency Crisis." Unpublished manuscript. Institute of Southeast Asian Studies (February).

Montes, Manuel F., and Joseph Y. Lim. 1996. "Macroeconomic Volatility, Investment Anemia, and Environmental Struggles in the Philippines." *World Development*, 24(2): 341-57.

Montes, Manuel F., and Johnny Noe E. Ravalo. 1995. "The Philippines." In *Financial Systems and Economic Policy in Developing Countries*, ed. Stephan Haggard and Chung H. Lee. Ithaca, NY: Cornell University Press: 140-81.

Nijathaworn, Bandid. 1995. "Central Banking Policies in Thailand in the 1990s." Paper presented at the "First International Conference on Forecasting the Singapore Economy and Annual Review of Central Banking Policies in the Asia-Pacific Basin," in Singapore, 10-11 August.

Philipine Star. 1998. "$1.1-B BOP Gap seen this yr." (10 March 1998): 17.

World Bank. 1993. *The East Asian Miracle.* Washington DC: World Bank.

Yap, Josef T. "Beyond 2000: Assessment of Economic Performance and an Agenda for Sustainable Growth." Unpublished manuscript. Philippine Institute for Development Studies (PIDS) (13 February).

10

Viet Nam: Ordeals of Transition

William Turley

Economic shocks stimulate economic policy reform, but it is history and institutions that do most to shape reform's long-term path. For Viet Nam, economic reform in the 1980s necessarily involved transition from a centrally planned economy to a market economy. Reform continued in the 1990s, albeit at a slower pace; however, the question was no longer whether Viet Nam would have a market economy, but what kind. Buoyant, open, export-oriented economies in neighboring countries provided models—until the Asian financial crisis of 1997 cast a shadow on their success. Although Viet Nam had some immunity from the difficulties afflicting its wealthier neighbors, the crisis and its backwash were bound to affect the debate that had, since the mid-1990s, deeply divided Vietnamese leaders over the pace and direction of further reform.

The question what kind of market economy Viet Nam will have is, of course, still being decided by the interplay of economic and political forces. In an effort to understand where those forces may be taking the country, we attempt here to answer three questions: (1) What policies must Viet Nam adopt to sustain growth at or near present rates? (2) What are the political variables and trends shaping the choice of policies? (3) What has been the impact of the current Asian financial crisis on Viet Nam's reform process? The first section of this chapter argues that while further growth is possible under present policies, significant changes are needed if Viet Nam is to catch up with its wealthier neighbors. The second section explores the interaction of politics and economics that will decide whether those changes are adopted. The third section discusses the current Asian financial crisis and Viet Nam's responses to it. The chapter concludes with a note on the political challenge of keeping reform on track.

270

Turley

The Way Ahead

The Viet Nam Communist Party (VCP) formally endorsed a program of "renovation," known as *doi moi* in Vietnamese, at its Sixth National Congress in 1986. No one attending that congress could have imagined what would transpire over the succeeding dozen years, although some must have realized that what was being discarded would not likely be resurrected. The congress ended central planning, freed prices, set limits on public sector spending, disbanded agricultural cooperatives, and loosened restraints on business activity. There may be no historical precedent quite as remarkable. Certainly there is no precedent in Viet Nam, where for the first time in two thousand years of recorded history, ordinary people had an opportunity to enjoy a permanent improvement in their lives. Among the results were a fall in inflation to single digits, an increase in the GDP growth rate to between 8 and 10 percent per year, and an increase in export volume of about 25 percent per year. The rate of investment doubled from 1990 to 1995 despite the loss of Soviet aid, thanks to dramatic increases in both domestic savings and foreign direct investment. All of this was achieved without leveraged prodding from the International Monetary Fund or significant support from international lenders (although, it is true, the IMF and the World Bank had supplied technical advice for years).

Pessimism about Viet Nam's reform process nonetheless has become pervasive among foreign observers. A Swedish study concluded in 1996 that "the potential benefits of past reforms are nearly exhausted" (Kokko and Zejan 1996: 53). In 1997 the Geneva-based World Economic Forum ranked Viet Nam forty-ninth out of fifty-three countries in "global competitiveness" and dead last in "openness." Even before the 1997 financial mess in Asia, Adam Fforde forecast growth to the end of the decade at almost five points below the 12 percent per annum forecast of the VCP's Eighth National Congress (Fforde 1997a: 178-79). A 1997 World Bank's report stated, "Viet Nam cannot expect to maintain its recent success or achieve its medium-term development objectives without deeper reforms. There are already indications that slow reform in key areas, notably the financial sector, the state enterprise sector and trade policy, are beginning to threaten macro-economic stability and jeopardize the achievement of medium-term objectives" (World Bank 1997: i). The IMF, the Asian Development Bank, and a succession of visitors, including Lee Kwan Yew, have echoed the World Bank in urging Hanoi to take up reform's unfinished tasks immediately.

Although past reforms hold potential for growth that pessimists fail to recognize, it is true that the pace of reform slowed in the mid-1990s, leaving much to be done. There is a ceiling on the growth that macro-stabilization and relaxation of controls alone can achieve. Viet Nam's resource base cannot long sustain constant growth in exports that are heavily weighted toward agricultural products and mineral resources. The sources of past growth (agriculture, oil, and commerce) cannot sustain growth in the long run; these resources are meager in proportion to the population, and in any case, commercial activities do not achieve productivity growth. Moreover, it will be difficult for Viet Nam to attract the $40 billion or more in foreign capital that it seeks by the year 2000 for infrastructure investment plans while it is $900 million in arrears to foreign commercial lenders. Foreign direct investment is declining as investors discover the difficulties of doing business in Viet Nam; and unreformed, ineffective state institutions have created and maintained inefficiencies in the market.

The only way ahead is industrialization, and that must conform to comparative advantage—that is, it must be labor intensive for the most part. And being labor intensive, it must be export-oriented because the market is abroad. Taiwan best exemplifies the elements of a successful export-oriented industrialization strategy appropriate for Viet Nam: (1) government provision of public goods and macro-stability; (2) high and rising saving and investment; (3) free trade, at least for exporters (that is, access to imported inputs and capital goods and a reasonable exchange rate); and (4) encouragement of private small- and medium-sized companies, the dominant form of industrial organization in the manufacturing sector. In Viet Nam the external constraints on this strategy are not significantly different from those that other countries in the region have faced, and there is no credible alternative. Certain steps therefore need to be taken. These areas of needed reform include:

- *Financial Sector.* The private sector needs access (presently hogged by state-owned enterprises) to medium- to-long-term bank financing for fixed investment, and efficiency needs improvement to increase the overall volume of savings available for investment.
- *Property Rights.* Private corporations need visible indicators that the government is not going to do them in once they succeed. To compete with state enterprises in attracting foreign investment, they also need laws allowing the use of land and real estate as collateral and of land-use rights as equity in joint ventures.
- *Tax Reform.* The multiplicity in kinds of taxes and rates, variations across categories of businesses and commodities, and administrative discretion must be reduced to discourage evasion of payment, duplicity in record keeping, and bribery.
- *Trade Policy Reform.* Current regulations that severely limit the number of licenses issued to private trading companies, impede direct trade, and protect inefficient state-owned trading corporations should be loosened. Tariff and nontariff barriers that protect inefficient industry in areas where Viet Nam lacks a comparative advantage should be lowered.
- *SOE Reform and Privatization.* The politically incestuous relationship between state enterprises and the agencies that "own" them, along with the

protection, privilege, and inefficiency this produces, must end. To become more efficient, state-owned enterprises (SOEs) need managerial autonomy, financial discipline, and exposure to competition. Privatization is also desirable but contingent on the parallel development of appropriate resources and institutions.

• *Institutional Issues.* The reforms recommended here will require improved professional administrative and technical capabilities, greater administrative responsibility and accountability, elimination of overlapping jurisdictions, procedures for impartial dispute adjudication, information services, and regulation of real estate, financial, and capital markets. They also require the accommodation of growth in civil society, particularly to facilitate participation by business, labor, and professional associations in economic policy making.

For years, Viet Nam's technocrats have understood the need for these reforms, but in the mid-1990s many of the country's still Marxist-Leninist leaders saw little point in strengthening market mechanisms while the economy was performing well. Moreover, leaders with a traditionalist bent perceived market economies as corroding ideological values. The powerful beneficiaries of earlier reforms were content with their gains, and policy making bogged down in acrimonious debate. Even relatively moderate leaders came to feel that change was outpacing the capacity of the party and state to guide it. As Do Muoi said on retiring as party chief in December 1997, "If you are extremely full, you cannot eat more." In the absence of visionary leadership or a shock like those that led to the initiation of *doi moi* in the first place, standing still with a cumbersome, bureaucratic economy like many in the Third World was a distinct possibility.

The Politics and Economics of Reform

To explain the slowdown in Viet Nam's recent reforms, this section examines the dynamics of the reform, its results, and the hurdles on the path to further liberalization.

The Road to Doi Moi

Because of the regime's continuity, reform in Viet Nam has been a process of discovering the hard way that the alternative to a market economy does not work.[1] Until 1976, the sole experience of Vietnamese leaders with development was to construct a rudimentary neo-Stalinist command economy in the Democratic Republic of Viet Nam (DRV), or North Viet Nam. This economy was heavily aid-dependent, partly because of the war and partly because, with a predominantly agricultural population and a chronic food deficit, it was unsuited for central planning. The government lacked the necessary staff and material resources, party discipline was lax, and localism thrived despite constant exhortation to place national interests first. The 1960 constitution, which accorded provincial and municipal state agencies and central government ministries equivalent status, created jurisdictional conflicts without institutionalized means to resolve them (Fforde 1997a: 149). Moreover, resources for control and administration were meager and unevenly distributed. In 1976 the party had 1,533,500 members (3.13 percent of the total population), but the membership in the South probably was no more than 200,000 (*Los Angeles Times,* October 18, 1978; Le Duc Tho 1976). Of 82,900 civil servants, only 16,100 (19.4 percent) were in the South (*NGTK* 1977: 61). The government could bolster its resources in the South by dispatching cadres from the North, which it did, but only by depleting resources needed for reconstruction in the North.

Nonetheless, central leaders were eager to fulfill long-deferred ideological goals and to extend the DRV model over the entire country. The VCP's Fourth National Congress in December 1976 therefore ratified a decision to proceed with full-scale socialization, and on this basis to take the entire country "from small production to large-scale socialist production . . . within about twenty years" (VCP 1977: 59). The vehicle of this goal was the Second Five-Year Plan (1976–1980). This plan began to fail immediately, only partly because of adverse international and climatic conditions. In the South, the state nationalized industry and suppressed private trade before it was able to provide alternative management and distribution. In both regions, the attempt to intermediate the flow of low-price inputs to industry while the state still lacked strong rationing capacity precipitated, as Fforde and de Vylder have shown, a spontaneous process of reform "from below," as state-owned enterprises went "outside the plan" to find needed inputs through direct relations with local suppliers. Sometimes protected by local authorities and ministries, such "fence breaking" activities became "rampant" (Fforde and de Vylder 1996: 129-30). The parallel and illegal "free" market grew along with these activities, diverting resources from the "organized" market, exacerbating shortages, and fueling inflation. From 1976 to 1980, real national income barely increased at all, but prices in the "free" market increased more than 60 percent per year (Do Hoai Nam 1989: 110-11). The weaker agricultural cooperatives, unable to obtain adequate supplies of gasoline and fertilizers from the state, began to dissolve in the North as well as in the South (Quang Truong 1987: 261-62). Staples output in the North, already down from an annual average of 303 kg per capita in 1960–1965 to 253 kg per capita in 1970–1975 (*NGTK* 1981: 48), continued to fall despite state investment and the introduction of miracle strains of rice (Chu Van Lam: 153).

Occurring at a time of acute isolation from all support except that of the Soviet Union and the Council for Mutual Economic Assistance, the economic crisis presented Viet Nam's leaders with a stark choice: they could rescue the Five-Year

Plan by strengthening enforcement, which was sure to make matters worse, or they could save the economy and restore public confidence by sanctioning some of the "fence breaking" that already had occurred. At its sixth plenum in August 1979, the Central Committee decided to do the latter, admitting that haste in the attempt to bring all production under centralized state management had led to "unnecessary confusion." Subsequent decrees relaxed some controls on private production and trade and temporarily suspended the campaigns to socialize the South. A number of adjustments in wages, prices, and currency followed, capped in January 1981 by authorization of output contracts *(khoan san pham)* in agriculture and a "three-plan system" for SOEs that allowed them to produce and sell goods not covered by quotas on a free-market basis.

In the minds of most top leaders these measures were a tactical retreat, not a strategic turn toward a market economy. They nonetheless afforded critics of hasty reunification and socialist transformation, and individuals who had been accused of holding "utopian" and "pseudosocialist" views, an opportunity to claim vindication (Turley 1980: 56).[2] Mid-level officials, paralyzed by orders to "implement unimplementable policies," welcomed the relief of partial liberalization (Beresford and Fforde 1996: 6). And producers now engaging legally in sideline activities were sure to resist any attempt to roll back the changes.

The measures triggered a fairly rapid economic recovery, but they also spurred inflation, speculation, smuggling, corruption, and a binge of sideline activity, which led to renewed controls. The concerns of leaders at the center tended to differ from those on the periphery, however. The reason lay partly in characteristics of the administrative system, inherited from the DRV, in which effective authority lay with territorial authorities. Government agencies at the subnational levels could own industrial and agricultural enterprises. At each level, the network of government offices that owned and managed enterprises constituted a "line ministry." Although the "functional" agencies of central government ministries had formal supervisory authority over all SOEs, the requirement to pass their orders through the line ministries gave the latter the greater power and authority. Line ministries had the capacity to defend enterprises against pressures from functional agencies (Vasavakul 1996: 44–45), and the policy shifts of 1979–1981 encouraged them to do this in ways that further consolidated the local state business interest. Some of the initiative for mobilizing and allocating resources shifted from central planners to the middle levels of government. Economic benefits trickled down and outward from these levels, providing mid- and lower-level party and state officials and even the military with a stake in expanding local autonomy in economic affairs.

Attempts by central planners since the late 1970s to "decentralize management" to the district level also exacerbated center-periphery frictions. The ostensible aim was to place resources so that the planners could best supervise the consolidation of agricultural cooperatives into "agro-industrial complexes." But the change directly threatened provincial, sectoral, and cooperative interests, which mounted a "concerted resistance" (Werner 1988: 154-55, 159). The potential for erosion of authority at the provincial level, particularly after orders came down to the provinces in 1984 to transfer their agricultural support services to the districts, gave provincial bureaucrats reason to search for allies among those who, for quite different reasons, were critical of highly centralized authority and planning.

Groups on the periphery therefore joined with technocrats at the center to create a base of support for reform, or at least for reforms that would increase the autonomy of the provincial governments. Reformers were not yet well established in the top echelons of the party, however. Nguyen Van Linh, who would later emerge as a leader of the reform coalition, recovered his post as party chief in Ho Chi Minh City but lost his seat in the Political Bureau. In March 1982 the Fifth VCP Congress retained a higher than usual number of members in the Central Committee; thus, the new committee represented continuity and, like its predecessors, was dominated by central party and state officials. The proportion of members from the party and state periphery, which stood to gain the most from further liberalization, actually declined.[3]

The Third Five-Year Plan (1981-1985) approved by the congress was an awkward compromise between an overall recentralizing direction and concessions to pressures from "below." The most significant concession was agreement that, for "a definitive period of time," Viet Nam would have a "multi-component economy" with regional differences (VCP 1982: 75). The plan also gave favorable attention to the "family economy" of sideline production, on which the country now depended for most of its food other than rice.[4] And it gave top priority to agriculture, conceding for the first time that an economy as poor as Viet Nam's could not skip an initial stage of agricultural development. However, it also reaffirmed the goals to "complete socialist transformation in the Southern provinces [and to] further perfect socialist relations of production in the North" (VCP 1982: 5). While temporarily accepting nonsocialist sectors and increasing managerial autonomy for producers, the Third Plan was also anti-*free* market (Fforde and de Vylder 1996: 132-35; Spoor 1988: 122-23; Vo Nhan Tri 1990: 123-80).

Like the Second Five-Year Plan, the Third Plan quickly exhausted its potential. State industry recovered, but mainly where it was allowed to respond to market demand by using domestic inputs. Food output increased from 273 kg to 304 kg per capita between 1981 and 1985 (*NGTK* 1985: 35), barely achieving self-sufficiency, but the increase was a one-time response to output contracting and the expansion of household plots beyond the 5 percent limit. Without continual productivity growth, population increase soon would nullify the gain. Inflation began spiraling out of control as the state raised wages for SOE workers and civil servants, boosted prices for rice needed to feed the urban population, continued paying out subsidies, and increased the money supply to cover its growing budget deficit (Do Hoai Nam 1989: 111).

The objective was to end two-track pricing without ending administrative resource allocation, and this had important political implications (Fforde 1998). The attempted recentralization of controls clashed with interests that now had a stake in market and off-plan activities. Efforts to halt the creeping commercialization of state business not only slowed output growth but irritated producers and their local government owners. The tide was running in reform's favor by June 1985, when the eighth plenum restored Nguyen Van Linh to the Political Bureau and announced some moderate reforms, including the intention to end two-track pricing. Conservatives, however, prevented implementation of the plenum resolution and engineered a currency conversion that confiscated wealth and tripled prices for some staples (Porter 1990: 77; Fforde and de Vylder 1996: 14). Exasperation with conservative obstructionism and incompetence almost certainly helped Nguyen Van Linh to become general secretary at the Sixth National Congress in December, with the support of secondary party and state officials. Representation by these officials in the new Central Committee rose from 30 percent to 40 percent (Thayer 1988: 187). Significantly, the addition of provincial VCP secretaries and deputy secretaries accounted for the bulk of this increase.

Nevertheless, the program of *doi moi* approved by the Sixth Congress was hardly radical or bold. Many delegates remained wedded to ideological orthodoxy, and the adopted reforms fell short of the gradualist measures China was then implementing. Although Sixth Congress documents sharply critiqued the "bureaucratic centralized mechanism based on state subsidies" and promised to bring the "multi-sector economic structure" into "full play," the "most *important thing*" (italics in original) was "to strengthen and develop the socialist economy, first of all, to enable the state sector to really play the leading role and control the others" (VCP 1987: 66). Policy innovations enhanced SOE autonomy, eliminated the state monopoly in foreign trade, and allowed private small-scale commercial activity. But the principle of a "socialist market economy" ruled out significant reduction of government control over SOEs, dismantling of the planning apparatus, and abolition of the dual price system. Failure to end dual pricing was particularly telling because producers had to go on selling to the state at artificially low prices and finance their losses through subsidies, which were financed by borrowing from the central bank, leaving the basic cause of macro-instability untouched.

Why the party moved toward reform at all in 1986 may seem the main question. But a more puzzling question is why *doi moi* did not break more decisively with the past, considering the history of chronic imbalances and the leadership changes that accompanied the policy shift. The answer lies in the boundaries of reform leaders' understanding and perceptions and in the political constraints of the time. In the first place, the "new" leaders were not political outsiders, free of all the commitments and liabilities of incumbency. Nguyen Van Linh already had served one stint on the Political Bureau, and Vo Van Kiet had joined it in 1982. No new or old member of the Political Bureau in 1986 could claim noninvolvement in previous policy making, even if the party ethos had allowed such a claim. Both the reformers and their opponents favored the smallest possible change in institutional framework that could promote growth; they differed mainly with regard to what that would consist of. Second, broad political support for policy radicalism was by no means assured. Support for reform was diverse and uneven, and the existing model still afforded many party members, officials, and bureaucrats their most credible source of economic security. It would take a greater and more credible threat to their security to induce them to accept the risks associated with a new model.

The Big Bang

Whatever its limitations, the Sixth Congress did allow change at the margins, including a reduction of the differences between free market and official prices, abolition of rationing for many commodities, and land use rights of at least fifteen years for farmers. But moves to relinquish administered pricing, unify exchange rates, substitute positive for negative real interest rates, and harden the budget constraint on state enterprises were conspicuously absent. This was reform by the path of least resistance—rewarding groups that had supported, or could be expected to support, a partial marketization, and postponing measures that might inflict real pain. The result was continuing macro-instability and an unsustainable burden on the state budget. Adjustment of some prices to market forces, along with growing private sector competition, cut into SOE incomes, as did the termination of the central government's foreign trade monopoly. Provincial authorities and enterprises that set up foreign trade organizations made large profits, but undervalued imports undercut domestic producers, adding to the pressure for subsidies (IMF 1995a: 55). In the absence of new forms of taxation, payment of subsidies implied a burgeoning deficit (which reached 40 percent of expenditures in 1988) and continuing triple-digit inflation. As if all that were not bad enough, a poor harvest in 1987 resulted in pockets of famine that lasted into the spring of 1988.

The VCP Central Committee held its sixth plenum in March 1989 to assess *doi moi's* first two years. Reporting on the meeting, the party newspaper, *Nhan Dan* (April 20), observed:

Conspicuous difficulties stem from the rate of inflation, . . . the large state budgetary over spending, the chronic scarcity of cash, and price fluctuations. . . . Many honest laboring people, particularly cadres, workers, administrative personnel, members of the armed forces, retirees, and social welfare recipients, have gained nothing. The living conditions of many people are extremely difficult. In the meantime, people who do business illegally make a great deal of money overnight. Consequently, social injustice becomes more and more acute with each passing day. . . . If we cannot promptly check the rate of inflation and significantly increase the state economic sector's efficiency, the situation may develop in a complex fashion.

But the plenum did not foresee the unraveling of communist regimes in Eastern Europe or the demonstrations in Beijing's Tiananmen Square that lay just weeks ahead. "Comprehensive cooperation" with the Soviet Union and with the Council for Mutual Economic Assistance was still the "guideline for expanding foreign economic relations" (VCP 1989). The collapse of Viet Nam's allies and the termination of the council's assistance stunned the leadership and fueled fears that reform could lead to turmoil and collapse. At this point, a decision to halt or repeal reform, at whatever cost to the population, was a real option. It is not uncommon, after all, for elites to choose survival in office over economic efficiency—the choice made at a similar juncture by the leaders of North Korea and Cuba.

Why did the Vietnamese respond differently? The answer has to lie in the characteristics of their leaders and of the milieu at the time. In 1989 Hanoi no longer faced a domestic rival capable of absorbing it if reform went wrong, as did Pyongyang; and Viet Nam's nearby large neighbor, unlike Cuba's, had no wish to overthrow it. Moreover, Viet Nam's civil society was extremely weak. Its leaders thus had some room for risk taking that existed in few other communist states. The reformers were now the incumbents, and the policies they felt obliged to defend were those of *doi moi*. If *doi moi* so far had produced unimpressive results, they argued, this was because it had not gone far enough. To choose autarky would be to admit error.

The pace and scope of *doi moi* quickly exceeded anything imagined by its proponents in 1986, matching and in some ways surpassing the reforms already under way in China. The stabilization program—"pure IMF orthodoxy, albeit without the IMF behind it" (Riedel and Comer 1996: 10)—was "shock therapy" in the accepted sense of seeking immediate solutions across several policy areas. In 1989 alone, the two-tier price system was abolished, interest rates were raised to real positive levels, the dong was devalued to near the market rate, gold trading was legalized, foreign exchange and trade rules were relaxed, and tax rates were equalized across economic sectors. Inflation came to a virtual halt in the latter half of 1989.

Transitional Boom

The outcome for Viet Nam was very different from that in Eastern Europe, Russia, and Latin America, where "big bang" referred to the big collapse in output that followed major reforms. Far from causing a transitional recession, the reforms unleashed exceptional growth. The real GDP growth rate rose from 5.1 percent in 1990 to 8.6 percent in 1992 and 8.8 percent in 1994, while inflation, after a spike in 1991, stabilized around 10 percent per year in 1993. Viet Nam had recorded some years of solid growth in the 1980s, but never as high or as sustained as in the first half of the 1990s; and growth in the 1980s invariably had been accompanied by accelerating inflation. The speed with which Viet Nam after 1990 lowered the inflation rate and raised the real growth rate is perhaps unprecedented.

Stabilization in a country like Viet Nam boils down to fiscal austerity, because the monetary expansion that fuels inflation invariably originates in public sector deficits. Given the weak tax base, the only way to reduce the public sector deficits was to curb public sector expenditures, which Viet Nam did dramatically between 1989 and 1991 by eliminating subsidies to SOEs, cutting the state investment program, restraining wage increases for state employees, and demobilizing a half million soldiers. However, the typical village household saw only benefit in the sharp decrease of inflation and the end to price controls, which offered new incentives to grow. Liberalization of agricultural prices and decollectivization yielded an overwhelmingly positive net result for most of the 70 percent of Vietnamese who were farmers, as Viet Nam went from being a net rice importer (400,000 tons in 1987) to a leading rice exporter (1.4 million tons in 1989, rising to 3.7 million tons in 1997). The vigorous response of the household sector far outweighed the recession in the public sector, and the rapidly growing private sector absorbed about one third of the SOE sector's 2.4 million employees (World Bank 1995b: 22-23). Reduced spending on social services and education raised alarms, but overall social costs were low; and the government remained committed to the containment of inflationary pressures by following a prudent fiscal policy.

Viet Nam's reforms also succeeded in attracting the investment on which growth depends. Gross domestic investment as a share of GDP doubled from 1990 through 1995, from about 12 percent to 27 percent. The dramatic increase in the rate of investment was accompanied by an equally dramatic rise in the rate of domestic savings, from 7 percent to about 17 percent, and by a massive inflow of foreign direct investment (World Bank 1996: 4). Moreover, impressive as the numbers are, there is reason to suspect that they fall short of the actual saving and investment activity during these years; a large proportion of saving and investment in the private sector, the most dynamic component of the economy, went unreported and unrecorded. The impact of private sector saving and investment on growth appears all the greater when one considers that the figures for foreign direct investment were the reported amounts based on official approvals, a significant proportion of which were never implemented.

The counterpart of the net inflow of foreign direct investment and other foreign savings is the current account deficit. A current account deficit of 10 percent to 12 percent of GDP is often the harbinger of a balance-of-payments crisis, although in Viet Nam's case such a crisis seemed less likely because the deficit had been financed primarily by foreign direct investment rather than by debt-creating foreign capital inflows. Nevertheless, given that Viet Nam by 1996 was about $900 million in arrears to international commercial lenders and needed more than $40 billion more in foreign capital before the year 2000 to undertake its infrastructure investment plans, the time had come for steps to improve its creditworthiness (Grant 1996). If the government responded to the growing trade deficit (from near zero in 1990 to more than $2 billion in 1995) by restricting imports, this would only make external financing more difficult.

Whatever the challenges ahead, the process of transition to a market economy in Viet Nam at least avoided the big collapse that occurred in Eastern Europe. It is routinely suggested that this was because Viet Nam had little inefficient industry to dismantle. But the main difference between Viet Nam and the socialist economies of Europe was its large rural labor force, which, like China's, was ready and willing, at a moment's notice, to go to work in export-oriented industries at wages only slightly above subsistence level. It is the abundance of human resources that has allowed East Asian countries to build dynamic, export-oriented industries side by side with inefficient, capital-intensive, often state-owned industries, and this was decisive.

Interests and Power

Economic success was bound to alter the constellation of interest and power that had generated reform in the first place. Some of the effects in four important sectors were as follows:

Agricultural Sector. Agricultural cooperatives vanished in areas where they had never been firmly established, such as the Mekong Delta. But in the Red River Delta and the central coastal areas, local leaders managed to hold a few cooperatives together by offering new services (Tran Thi Van Anh and Nguyen Manh Huan 1995: 202-3). The attachment of these cadres to the jobs and status that cooperative management afforded them accounts in part for their opposition to private land ownership and for the more recent advocacy by some provincial authorities of "new style" cooperatives.

Meanwhile, urban growth, peasant debt, and the relaxation of controls on population movement generated a market, technically illegal, in land use rights. A volatile mix of administrative irregularities, demographic pressure, unemployment, rising taxes, and corruption produced thousands of local frictions, called "hot spots," during the early 1990s.[5] The term "hot spot" was used to describe the situation in the North's Thai Binh Province, fifty miles southeast of Hanoi, where in May 1997 a peaceful protest of farmers in the provincial capital precipitated violent confrontations with local officials across six districts. Five other provinces also experienced turbulence. *Nhan Dan* investigated these events and reported in its September 8 issue that district and commune governments were the targets of popular wrath because of their corruption, bidding irregularities, and excessive demands for public contributions. In November, demonstrations by Catholics in the South's Dong Nai Province to demand the return of land previously owned by the Church led to clashes with police involving thousands of residents. The turbulence revealed rising popular discontent with the efforts of local officialdom to preserve its power and privilege. However, it played into the hands of party traditionalists demanding priority for stability over growth, and it gave occasion for the security and defense establishments to advocate strengthening of local militia units and the enlistment of veterans to maintain order.

Industrial Sector. Foreign trade liberalization brought competitive imports, rising unemployment, and downward pressure on wages in certain protected and inefficient industrial sectors (*Asia 1991 Yearbook*: 239; Kim Ninh 1990: 389). Not surprisingly, the affected enterprises—which tended to be SOEs involved in the manufacture of bicycles, household goods, textiles, electric fans, and clothing—demanded protection. Large state firms in sugar, construction materials, machinery, fertilizers, and steel were particularly successful in pressing the government to reimpose quotas and raise tariffs. SOEs in all of these areas made specific demands for protection during 1997, to which the government capitulated (Haughton 1997: 38). Interests seeking protection enjoyed success partly because many policy makers still believed in the infant industries argument, the importance of economies of scale and scope, the virtues of self-sufficiency, and the need to shield domestic enterprises from a hostile external environment (Kokko 1997: 28). The results were high levels of smuggling,[6] an overvalued dong, favorable tax and tariff rates to attract foreign investment in infant industries, and a rise of foreign trade taxes from 10.4 percent of budget revenues in 1992 to nearly 30 percent by 1995 (IMF 1995b: 22; Nguyen Tuan Dung 1996: 82; *Asia 1996 Yearbook*: 223). Viet Nam's trade regime thus became less, rather than more, liberal in response to the domestic effects of *doi moi's* "open door."

Finance and Banking Sectors. The finance and banking sectors continue to be virtually indistinguishable. Although there are a large number of small credit funds, a couple of finance companies, and since 1995 a treasury bill market, most finance operates through the banking system. The soundness of the banking sector is a matter of grave concern because of the rise in overdue loans (at 15 percent of credit in June 1997) and the weakening of banks' capital base, especially that of private joint-stock banks. Shortcomings in bank supervision make it difficult to assess the soundness of individual banks or to make adequate provisions against bad loans. The unwillingness of the authorities to undertake a thorough reform of the financial sector, at least so far, is a natural result of their continuing desire for a "market economy with a socialist orientation," in which the state occupies the "commanding heights." Although private banks are allowed to operate, reforms heretofore have avoided threatening the dominant position of the state-owned banks.

State Enterprise Sector. Serious reform of state enterprise began in 1989, when the government hardened the budget constraint and allowed the total number of SOEs to shrink by almost half, through mergers and liquidations, to about 6,000 by the end of 1995. The overwhelming majority of liquidations involved very small enterprises that were auctioned off to state or private bidders. It was the big SOEs under central management that had the best survival rate, despite performance levels that almost certainly were poorer than the available data suggest. A study in 1995 estimated that more than 25 percent of SOEs were operating at a loss (Le Hong Tien 1995). The number was estimated at 30 percent to 50 percent in 1997, a year in which three big SOEs—Nam Dinh Textiles, Hung Vuong Frozen Product Company, and Lam Son Lacquer—nearly sank in red ink and scandal (Reuters, January 19, 1998).

In mid-1994, ostensibly to centralize and streamline management of the many SOEs that were quite small, the government grouped a number of enterprises into eighteen "general corporations" and fifty smaller "special corporations." The Textile and Garment Corporation, for example, was created from fifty-five enterprises employing nearly 100,000 workers (IMF 1996: 35). The long-term goals were to reap economies of scale and to strengthen the government's capacity to guide development, in the manner of Korea's *chaebol*. Although the final design of these structures remains to be decided, the potential for duplicating the problems of the Korean model is clear.

SOEs derive substantial rents from operating in the most protected sectors of the economy. They also retain privileges in the form of access to land and to foreign trade licenses (World Bank 1995a: 98). In rural areas they often have local monopolies, maintained with help from the local units of government that own and manage them. The incestuous relationship between enterprises and line ministries is an especially serious problem. As regulators, government bodies should favor ease of entry and promote competition; but as owners and partners in joint ventures with foreign investors, they have an interest in restrictive arrangements (Dollar 1996: 181).

Because many SOE managers and directors are party members and many party committees have stakes in SOEs, state enterprises have political clout that private firms cannot match. SOEs also derive influence from the desire of VCP leaders to perpetuate the party's dominance of the political system. Without a vigorous state sector dominated by the party, some fear, power would follow wealth to the private sector, intensifying pressure on the party to share power (Bui Minh Thang 1995). Moreover, workers and managers in loss-making enterprises have resisted "equitization" (privatization) for fear this will lead to job losses. Attempts to implement specific demands to equitize have bogged down for lack of guidance from the central government and because of the impossibility—given the lack of clarity as to assets and property rights—of determining the value of firms to be equitized (Huong Lien 1997). Thus, equitization is not only a highly controversial process but one that many of its targets can easily impede. A pilot equitization project was launched in 1992; by mid-1996, only six enterprises had been equitized.

Political Quagmire

Doi moi itself thus generated impediments to reform. Although progress in structural reform continued (e.g., in the form of the State Enterprise Law, simplification of foreign trade procedures, and centralization of public investments and expenditures), caution overtook boldness in January 1994 at the VCP's Mid-Term National Conference, which identified "four dangers" to be avoided. These were (1) lagging behind other Asian countries in economic development, (2) deviating from the socialist path, (3) corruption and bureaucratism, and (4) "peaceful evolution." In truth, "the four dangers" was a coded reference to the pet projects of different and fractious segments of the party. The main cause of the tension thus expressed was the differential effects of reform across the party and the country. Decentralization made SOEs and the line ministries the prime beneficiaries of reform. Some party committees, state agencies, and military commands developed commercial interests in the new economic arrangements as well. Party members responsible for economic decisions slipped into the best jobs in emerging centers of wealth and power, while those responsible for political, ideological, and mobilization decisions lost status and found few opportunities for material advancement. Tension between these two currents of thought and preference found expression during the 1990s in the debate about what constituted a "socialist direction." Leaders in the government sector tended to express modernist views; the members of the party political work sector defended traditionalist ones.[7] The growing tension between these groups caused rancorous debate in the run-up to the Eighth National Congress.

More or less open skirmishing to control the congress surfaced in January 1995. In the course of formulating a resolution on ideological work, the eighth plenum deadlocked over a proposal to delete a reference to "proletarian dictatorship," and meetings later in the year turned on issues such as whether to extend rights of private ownership beyond those under the current "transition to socialism."[8] Obviously hoping to influence this debate, Prime Minister Vo Van Kiet in August 1995 sent a memo to his Political Bureau colleagues that soon found its way into more than one émigré journal.[9] The letter was extraordinary for the insight it provided into Kiet's thinking, its contrast with the views of party traditionalists, and its forthright identification of the contested ground. Kiet argued, for example, that no socialist or post-socialist country could serve as a model for Viet Nam; that it was "totally wrong" to view a guiding role for the state in the economy as a criterion of socialism; that state enterprises needed thorough restructuring despite "much resistance"; that *doi moi* should level the playing field between state and private actors; that Viet Nam should not hesitate to borrow from the institutions and practices of capitalist countries; and that the VCP should be content for the present to promote development and defer the goal of "building socialism." Kiet's statements had obvious appeal for results-oriented state cadres, closet liberals, and private businessmen. They directly attacked the cherished views of the traditionalists who were concentrated in the party-work sector. The inevitable counterattack took the form of stepped-up assaults in the press by ideologues and military figures, condemning "social evils," "peaceful evolution," and other supposed ill effects of haste in reform and loose control of markets.

The chairs of party organs with economic oversight functions weighed in with a defense of the state and cooperative sectors (Vasavakul 1997: 106). In April they issued a "political report" proposing to raise the SOE-and-cooperative share of the GDP to 60 percent by the year 2020 (Schwarz 1996b: 15-16). This, however, was the high tide for advocates of SOE dominance of the economy. Soon thereafter Political Bureau member Nguyen Ha Phan was accused (possibly by Kiet supporters) of revealing information to the enemy while imprisoned during the war in the South, and he was expelled from the bureau. Anger also boiled up against Political Bureau member Dao Duy Tung, chair of the Political Report Drafting Committee, for hijacking the drafting of the report on behalf of ideologues. The draft had to be reopened to revision.

General Secretary Do Muoi sided with the traditionalists, urging that the state sector "continuously grow to maintain its leading role in production, technology, and markets" (*Hanoi Moi*, May 8, 1996). At the Ho Chi Minh City party congress he applauded the rapid growth of the nation's economy but expressed fear that foreign competition could turn it into a "consumer market for foreign products and into a source of raw materials for foreign countries." Growth in the nonstate sector still was very much "uncontrolled"; evasion of taxes and business registration was rife; and corruption, product counterfeiting, and smuggling continued unabated. All of this, said Muoi, made the city susceptible to "conspiracies of 'peaceful evolution,' political destabilization, economic sabotage, and cultural and social pollution aimed at overthrowing the revolutionary regime." The party organization within the military also aligned with the traditionalists.[10] Delegates to the army's party congress reportedly agreed that strengthening the state and cooperative sectors was essential to staying on the socialist path, and that "disorientation" resulting from private sector growth would lead to political instability (Voice of Viet Nam Radio, May 7, 1996).

Heading into the Eighth National Congress, the VCP was deeply divided. Party members who opposed further liberalization had grown more assertive and perhaps more numerous. In a vote that included new members inducted at the Mid-Term National Conference in 1994, the congress elected a Central Committee that had the largest number of new members in two decades. A substantial portion of the new members were from the central party and state sectors, which increased those sectors' share of the total membership to 45 percent. This figure represented the highest degree of "centralism" in any Central Committee elected since the war's end. (The figure for the committee elected by the Sixth Congress, which launched *doi moi* in 1986, represented the lowest degree, at 32 percent.)[11] The rise in centralist representation implied a decrease in representation by the secondary party and state officials who had figured prominently in the reform coalition of the late 1980s. Furthermore, among the secondary-level officials, representation by heads of SOEs appeared to increase. The impression of a net loss for sectors that previously had provided the strongest support for change was further confirmed by the composition of the new nineteen-member Political Bureau. By most analysts' reckoning, the reform group within the bureau consisted of six or seven members, while the more cautious group had four or five members supported by a six-member military-and-security bloc, leaving the proponents of reform in a minority position. The reform group included all bureau members who held concurrent positions in the state structure, plus at least one municipal party secretary. The more cautious group represented the party-work and mass organization sectors.[12]

The resolutions passed by the congress require no detailed analysis. It suffices to say that the political report was close in tone and content to speeches made by Muoi prior to the congress. However, both the political and the socioeconomic reports contained concessions to reformers. Omitted, for example, was any target for an SOE share in the GDP and included was acknowledgment of the need for significant revamping of SOE management. The conflict during the initial drafting of the report and the awkwardness of the compromises revealed a weakening of collegiality in the leadership. The final documents were significant only as maps of the terrain on which the contest would continue.

After the congress, the July 1997 elections produced a National Assembly that was younger and better educated than any of its predecessors. The assembly proceeded to confirm the selection as prime minister of Pham Van Khai, a vigorous reformer with strong links to Vo Van Kiet. It also approved Khai's nominations for a reform-oriented cabinet and chose Tran Duc Luong as president (defeating Defense Minister General Doan Khue).[13] All of these selections gave the leadership of the state structure a distinctly reformist cast. At about the same time, however, the VCP apparently reached agreement on a successor to Do Muoi, although it did not formalize the decision until December. The new general secretary was Le Kha Phieu, who had spent his entire career since 1950 as a political officer in the armed forces. His public statements, which included the assertion in 1996 that capitalism was "obsolete" and would "soon be replaced," had been typical of the traditionalist wing of the party, known for its preoccupation with "hostile forces" and its ignorance of economics. On taking office in December, Phieu reaffirmed his commitment to *doi moi*, probably to appease reformers. But he and the party, its unity in tatters, had yet to face the full import of the regional crisis lapping on Viet Nam's shores.

The Asian Financial Crisis and Viet Nam

The financial crisis that erupted in a number of Asian countries in 1997 has raised serious concerns in Viet Nam.[14] The most immediate concern is that the crisis in neighboring countries will spread to Viet Nam. Even if Viet Nam can avoid a similar crisis, it is feared that negative spillover will harm the nation's economic prospects in the near- to medium- term. Finally, it is feared that the much-vaunted "Asian model" of economic development, on which Viet Nam has pinned its hopes for long-term growth, is less reliable than was believed, and that Viet Nam must rethink its long-term development strategy. All of these concerns are legitimate. Before we consider them individually, it will be useful to examine briefly the nature of the financial crisis in the region.

The Nature of the Asian Financial Crisis

The current regional crisis began, according to most reports, when the Bank of Thailand announced on July 2, 1997, that it was abandoning the peg of the baht to the U.S. dollar, sparking a sell-off of the currency. The weakness of the baht encouraged speculative attacks on other Asian currencies, some of which held their value while others collapsed. Six months after the onset of the crisis, the currencies of Thailand, Malaysia, the Philippines, and South Korea each had fallen about 50 percent in value. The Indonesian rupiah suffered the most, losing about 75 percent of its value. The currencies of Singapore and Taiwan each were devalued about 20 percent, mainly as a competitive response to the wholesale devaluations in the region. The Hong Kong dollar and the Chinese RMB remained unchanged in relation to the U.S. dollar. The Vietnamese dong has been devalued less than 10 percent during the past six months.

The massive devaluations in the "crisis-stricken five"—Thailand, Malaysia, Indonesia, the Philippines, and South Korea—were the product of a classic financial panic. In mid-1997 foreign investors and creditors suddenly realized that the assumptions they had made in the early 1990s were no longer valid. Back then it had seemed so easy: stock prices and property values were soaring, interest rates were high, and risks were assumed to be low because the currencies of these countries were pegged to the U.S. dollar. In the rush to cash in, European and American fund managers pumped enormous sums of short-term credit into the newly discovered "emerging markets" (Figure 10.1). Short-term foreign credit to Thailand amounted to 7 to 10 percent of the GDP every year from 1994 to 1996. By the end of 1996, short-term loans to Thailand by foreign banks stood at about $70 billion. In Malaysia the figure was $22 billion, in Indonesia $55 billion, and in Korea a staggering $100 billion (Chanda 1998: 46).

What went wrong? And could it have been anticipated? Of course, both borrowers and lenders should have remembered lesson one of international finance:

FIGURE 10.1 Capital Inflows to the Crisis-Stricken Five
(US dollars billion)

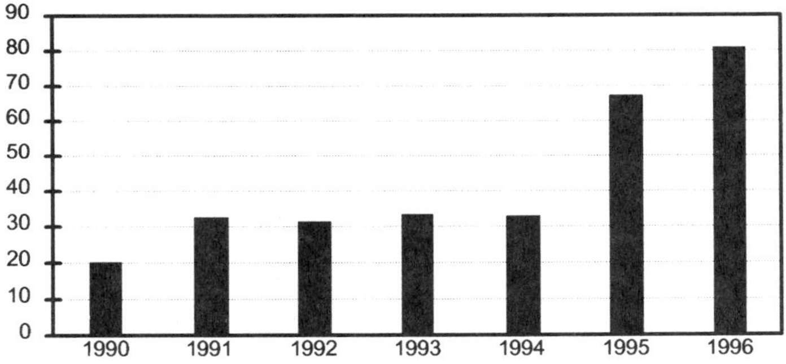

Sources: IMF, International Financial Statistics, selected issues; World Bank, Viet Nam database.

that a relatively high interest rate is associated with an expectation of currency depreciation. Even more basic, they should have remembered that every party comes to an end—and that the most raucous ones end most abruptly. It was no secret that real estate markets were overvalued, that many banks were over-extended, that foreign currency debt was accumulating rapidly. But nobody wanted to be the first to leave the party. It took the collapse of the Bangkok Bank of Commerce in 1996, the default on a Euro-bond by a major Thai real estate company in February 1997, and finally, revelations of trouble in Thailand's largest finance company in March to make investors run for cover (Chanda 1998: 48). China and Viet Nam so far have avoided the crisis mainly by avoiding international financial markets and relying on foreign direct investment for foreign capital.

The crisis was not, however, simply the result of panic by greedy investors. It was also caused by fundamental weaknesses in the economic and political systems of the stricken countries. Corruption, crony capitalism, and weak financial systems have been identified as the key culprits. Opening up to international financial flows exposed the political and economic weaknesses of the stricken countries—it did not create them. In exposing these weaknesses, the international financial markets rendered an invaluable service. The crisis may turn out to be a blessing in disguise, provided that Asian countries are willing and able to learn from their mistakes.

The ability of the crisis-stricken countries to make the necessary changes hinges mainly on the strength of their political systems. This undoubtedly is why Indonesia, which has perhaps the weakest political system of all, has fared the worst. Malaysia's economy may well have been the healthiest of the stricken countries, but the reluctance of Prime Minister Mahathir Mohamad to acknowledge that anything was fundamentally wrong, while blaming the problem on "immoral" currency traders, certainly made matters worse. The business community's cautiously optimistic reassessment of Korea's prospects is due in large part to the surprising resilience that Korea's political system demonstrated during the recent presidential election. Undoubtedly, the massive assistance offered by multilateral financial institutions and the United States government also helped, but this assistance was made possible by Korea's show of political will to deal with its fundamental problems.

Will the Crisis Spread to Viet Nam?

The fear that the crisis will spread to Viet Nam arises not just because of geographic proximity but because many weaknesses of the economic and political systems of the crisis-stricken countries are shared by Viet Nam. One in particular is the weakness of the banking system, which was at the root of the crisis in each of the affected countries. In Thailand, banks and finance companies affiliated with banks engaged in short-term borrowing in international financial markets to fund a speculative bubble in real estate. In Korea, banks were directed by bureaucrats to lend money for projects in sectors favored by government policy, and many of the projects proved unprofitable. In Indonesia, political connections dictated a large number of bank loans funded from abroad, which not surprisingly ended as a mountain of bad debt. In each of these countries the root problem was improper banking practices made possible by inadequate regulation and lax supervision. Although Viet Nam's banks did not hold bad loans collateralized by property—the Achilles' heel of banks in Thailand and Malaysia—they exhibited other shortcomings in common with banks elsewhere in the region.

Bank supervision is still at a rudimentary stage of development in Viet Nam, and many recently enacted regulations have not yet been tested. In the past, bank regulation and supervision were less important than they are now because the Vietnamese banking industry was entirely state-owned and under direct government control. The credibility of the banks rested on the credibility of the government. The banking sector is still dominated by the state-owned banks, but private banks are gaining ground and forcing their state-owned counterparts to become more competitive. Furthermore, with the opening of the economy, domestic banks, both state-owned and private, have been required to establish credibility not only with domestic depositors but also with their foreign counterparts, on whom they rely to finance trade. The loosening of government control over banking and the opening of the economy have produced an urgent need for transparency in the financial system. However, as one observer noted recently, "transparency has never been a strong point of Viet Nam, which regards even its level of foreign reserves as a state secret" (Golin 1998: 38).

This lesson was vividly underscored in early 1997, when Viet Nam experienced a so-called mini-banking crisis as a result of several defaults by state-owned and private joint-stock banks on deferred letters of credit owed to foreign banks. The difficulty of assessing the liquidity and solvency of domestic banks, and even of ascertaining the government's policy toward defaults on foreign letters of credit, rapidly undermined international trust in Vietnamese banking institutions. Only after the government was forced by events to disclose that the defaults occurred because of mishandling of several financial scandals, not because of bank illiquidity or government policy, was the matter laid to rest.

In summary, Viet Nam's banking system has the same weaknesses as the crisis-stricken countries, and perhaps even more. Under these circumstances it would be a great mistake for Viet Nam to open itself to the free flow of international capital. Fortunately, Viet Nam has maintained strict control on foreign exchange transactions and has restricted private capital inflows mainly to foreign direct investment. Indeed, since 1991 foreign direct investment flows have more than matched Viet Nam's current account deficit in every year except 1996 (Figure 10.2). However, while Viet Nam has avoided the peril of a hot money attack on its currency, it has also forgone the advantages of integration into international financial markets, including access to investment financing, which the country sorely needs. It is imperative, therefore, to prepare the domestic banking system to become integrated into international financial markets. What needs to be done to achieve this integration—and the consequences of not achieving it—can readily be learned from the experience of neighboring countries.

Will Spillover Effects Harm Viet Nam's Economy?

The spillover effect that has raised the most concern in Viet Nam is the increase in competitive pressure brought about by the large devaluations of currencies in the crisis-stricken countries. The degree to which Viet Nam suffers a loss of competitiveness from these devaluations depends on the extent to which it competes with these countries in world markets. A popular view is that the loss has been great and that the poor performance of exports at the end of 1997 is attributable to the regional crisis (Tran Mai Huong 1998: 2). However, an examination of the trade structures and the world market shares of the stricken countries suggests that the popular view may not be correct. The world market shares of these countries are small in most of the commodity categories that are important to Viet Nam; therefore, their devaluations are unlikely to affect significantly the U.S. dollar prices of Viet Nam's main exports (namely, petroleum, rice, coffee, and light manufactured goods). Where the competitive pressure is likely to be most acute is in the domestic market, where local goods compete with imports (legal and smuggled) from the crisis-stricken countries in the region. In this area there is, however, a compensation: the losses suffered by domestic firms that compete with

FIGURE 10.2 Current Account Deficits and Foreign Direct
Investment Inflows (US dollars millions)

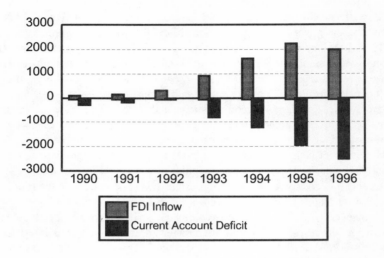

Sources: IMF, International Financial Statistics, selected issues; World Bank, Viet Nam database.

these imports are offset by the terms-of-trade gain that accrues to domestic consumers.

What this suggests is that the Asian financial crisis does not, in itself, provide a very strong case for a devaluation of the dong, contrary to popular opinion. A much stronger argument for devaluation rests on the real appreciation of the dong that has been under way for a long time. The relative dollar price of Vietnamese goods has risen 60 percent since 1992 (Figure 10.3). This, far more than the devaluations of regional currencies, is the main source of Viet Nam's declining international competitiveness.

Vietnamese authorities so far have resisted a devaluation, fearing that it could ignite inflation. Their fears may well be justified, especially if they are not willing to accompany devaluation of the currency with appropriate macroeconomic and structural policy changes, including reductions of planned public expenditures and steps to encourage export-oriented industrial development. Without such measures it is likely that a devaluation would result mainly in a higher domestic price level. The status quo is, however, equally unappealing. If no action is taken, the pressure on foreign exchange supplies will only increase, forcing the authorities to continue to restrict and compress imports, with deleterious effects on short- and long-term growth prospects. Furthermore, as expectations of a devaluation intensify, the black

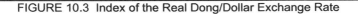

FIGURE 10.3 Index of the Real Dong/Dollar Exchange Rate

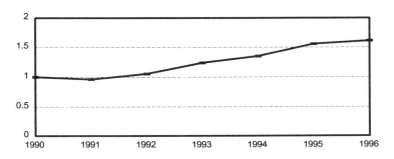

Note: A rise in the index indicates real appreciation. *Sources:* IMF, International Financial Statistics, selected issues; World Bank, Viet Nam database.

market rate will rise and more internal substitution of dollars for dong will take place, putting upward pressure on interest rates.

The impact of the Asian financial crisis on foreign direct investment in Viet Nam is perhaps more serious. There is great concern that foreign direct investment is drying up, in part because of the regional crisis and in part because of the growing hostility of foreign investors to the inhospitable business environment they face in Viet Nam. New foreign investment in 1997 totaled $4.5 billion, about half the record $8.6 billion licensed the preceding year. In response to these pressures, Prime Minister Khai called a meeting with foreign investors in February 1998 to reassure them that the government was taking steps to address their complaints.

The real impact of the crisis on foreign direct investment is hard to gauge, however. A slowdown might have occurred even in the absence of a regional crisis. Moreover, the available statistics on approved foreign direct investment have limited usefulness, as they vastly overstate the amount of investment that actually is implemented. Even if one takes the reports of decline at face value, the implications are far from obvious. Viet Nam cannot and should not rely on foreign sources to finance investment and to balance payments to the same large extent that it has in the past. A slowdown of foreign direct investment does not necessarily imply a deterioration of economic prospects.

Must Viet Nam Rethink Its Long-Term Development Strategy?

The concern that the crisis may require Viet Nam to rethink its long-term development strategy is based on two assumptions: that Viet Nam has such a strategy, and that its strategy resembles one pursued in the crisis-stricken countries.

These assumptions may be premature, as questions about industrial and trade policy and the roles of the public and private sectors in Viet Nam's economy are still hotly debated both inside and outside the government. Whether or not Viet Nam has achieved practical consensus on development strategy, there exists a strong consensus in the literature of economic development as to what Viet Nam's strategy *should* be, based on the experience of countries in similar circumstances. In both the crisis-stricken countries and those that so far have escaped crisis, an export-oriented industrialization strategy has been the route to rapid growth. This strategy is not called into question by the crisis. However, the tactics of the countries pursuing this strategy have varied in some important respects, and it is the tactical variations and their outcomes that offer some important lessons for Viet Nam.

The fundamental issues are crystallized most vividly in the contest between the "Korean model" and the "Taiwan model" of export-oriented industrialization. The Korea model, which features a high degree of economic concentration in the family-run *chaebol* system and a heavy-handed industrial policy of picking and promoting "winners," was a natural favorite of many in the Vietnamese government. Certainly it offers more of a socialist orientation than the Taiwan model, which features intricate networks of small and medium-sized private companies, and thus a low level of economic concentration and much less government guidance and support for industrial development. With the Korean model, so it seemed, Vietnam could have it both ways.

The contradiction inherent in the Korean model—a capitalistic system run by the visible hand of government rather than the invisible hand of the market—was revealed before the current crisis, most clearly in the late 1970s when government-led investment in heavy industry brought Korea to the brink of a debt crisis. But rapid GDP growth and booming exports made it easy to forget this lesson until six months ago, when history replayed itself with a vengeance. A similar pattern of massive investment in heavy industry, financed by short-term foreign borrowing with little regard for the bottom line, brought Korea past the brink this time. The nation's short-term debt reached a staggering $100 billion, and eight of its fifty largest *chaebol* faced bankruptcy (Chanda 1998: 48). Meanwhile, Taiwan came through these turbulent months mostly unscathed. It now finds itself in a good position to capture market opportunities from which its Korean competitors are being forced to withdraw. Thus, the contest between the two models should be seen as settled; but it would be naïve to expect agreement on that point.

Vietnamese leaders would do well to note that international investors, too, draw lessons from crises. The lessons investors see in the current crisis are apparent in the way they have discriminated among the stricken five. Why did people think that Korea would turn around within a year, but that Thailand might need two years and Indonesia perhaps as many years as Suharto remained in power? The answer is that the Korean system inspired faith in its ability to hold politicians accountable.

Investors had almost no faith in the power of the Indonesian system to check Suharto, his family, and his cronies, or to make institutions more credible and transparent. Investors, particularly banks, assume that a closed political process allows authorities to get away with more bad government, but they will settle for an honest, competent administration. If Vietnamese authorities believe that international investors will forever tolerate Viet Nam's deficiencies in these areas, they are mistaken.

The Political Economy of Late *Doi Moi*

Whether Viet Nam's political leaders and institutions have the qualities needed to adopt good policies and implement them is very much open to question. At its fourth plenum in December 1997, the Central Committee passed a resolution approving direct exports by private companies, trade in agricultural land-use rights, stronger emphasis on labor-intensive industries, and other progressive measures. The resolution did not address the implications of the region's economic difficulties for Viet Nam, however (Keenan 1998: 24). And the measures it instituted fell short of those that Viet Nam's own technocrats and international lenders had urged even before the region headed into crisis. The gradualism reflected in the resolution was the result of compromise, made necessary by the continuing rift over the pace and scope of liberalization, the continuing influence of Do Muoi in the role of official "advisor" to the party, and the power of satisfied interests.

Under these circumstances, reform policies in Viet Nam are bound to be incremental at best, with occasional backsliding. This has been the pattern— obscured by favorable economic outcomes—ever since Viet Nam's reform process began in the late 1970s. Only when deep crises seemed to require it did Viet Nam's leaders diverge boldly from the socialist path, into the dangerous and uncharted waters of a market economy. Moreover, there is no assurance that a particular level of pain for the economy as a whole will produce change. What matters is the impact of economic events on the interests and perceptions of those who wield power. The depth of crisis necessary to trigger change varies widely from country to country and time to time (Bates and Krueger 1993: 452). The usual triggers are balance-of-payments difficulties, accelerating inflation, and revenue losses; only the first of these has worsened recently in Viet Nam.

The economic difficulties Viet Nam seems likely to face in the short term do not immediately threaten the vital interests of any significant actor. And no emerging group with a stake in different arrangements (private small business owners, for example) is powerful enough to exert effective pressure for change, even at the margins. Powerful interests such as the SOEs are more committed to preserving their current privileges than to seizing the opportunities that a more efficient structure would offer. Without a sharp turn for the worse in the economy, no sudden switch from muddle to boldness should be expected. However, it is obvious that Viet Nam cannot sustain the growth rates of the recent past, much less approach the party's 9 percent target rate, without significant expansion of its reforms. Over the middle to long term, moreover, the country faces daunting challenges: population growth, diminishing marginal utility in agriculture, unemployment and alienation of youth, and rising demand for the development of human capital—all of which it must meet with very limited national resources at a time of sharpening competition for foreign inflows. The gap is bound to grow between the economic performance level of the present model and the level required if Viet Nam is to "catch up" with its wealthier neighbors. Inevitably, the growing gap will raise further questions about the adequacy of Viet Nam's political leadership and institutions.

Such questions increasingly come from members of the political elite itself.[15] But the present leadership seems determined to avoid meaningful political change, attempting instead to defuse pressure by showing sensitivity to popular grievances and emphasizing good governance. This approach was evident during the rural turmoil of 1997, to which the authorities responded peremptorily by replacing local party and state cadres accused of corruption, suspending onerous development schemes, and launching pilot projects in "democracy." Such measures are no substitute for effective restraints on officialdom. It was the lack of such restraints that allowed abuses to become widespread in the first place: Viet Nam, like China, increasingly is gripped by economic parasitism. Party members and relatives, state agencies and ministries, people's committees at the district and provincial levels, and the army own, control, or manage a very large slice of the economy, including most of the firms that operate in protected sectors.[16] In the face of growing resentment of the privileges and politically defended inefficiencies of the system, a rhetorical commitment to good governance is little more than a political holding pattern.

Viet Nam's political tensions are symptomatic of the tendency of economic reforms to outstrip the political systems that produce them. The new, decentralized Vietnamese economy requires strengthening of certain kinds of central control, particularly in fiscal, monetary, and revenue matters. It also requires improvements in transparency and accountability. These steps are more difficult politically than are reforms that concentrate on getting government out of the way. From 1986 to 1991, local governments strongly supported reforms that increased their autonomy; but they became ambivalent when their power was curbed by further reforms that enhanced the central government's macroeconomic management role (Rana 1995: 1166). Because they controlled many of the country's privileged business interests, local governments had reason to resist pressures to conduct their affairs with greater openness.

It was because of tensions like these between the central and local governments that proposals to reorganize local governments and their relationship to the center became a major point of contention during the drafting of the 1992 constitution. In the resulting compromise, the prime minister was authorized to dismiss local leaders but could appoint them only on the recommendation of the local people's councils (Thayer 1993: 54). The central government then launched a public administrative reform to clarify the functions and lines of authority within the state. It also relaxed slightly the screening of candidates for elections, producing a crop of younger, better-educated popular representatives. Thus, Viet Nam has moved—appropriately for its development needs—in the direction of greater centralization and collaborative means of social control, a course mapped out by the successful developmental states of Asia. The question is whether it will continue to move, and move fast enough, in this direction.

Notes

I wish to acknowledge the comments, materials, and other assistance received while preparing this study from Adam Fforde, Nguyen Mong Giao, David Marr, Lew Stern, Jonathan Stromseth, and Thaveeporn Vasavakul.

1. This section draws, in part, from J. Riedel and W. Turley, forthcoming, *The Politics and Economics of Transition to an Open Market Economy in Viet Nam* (Paris: Organization for Economic Cooperation and Development).

2. Party leaders in Ho Chi Minh City widely believed that the priority given to capital goods industry of the type that was concentrated in the North was essentially a North-first growth strategy. They also tended to believe that, because the city's economy was so heavily dependent on private commerce, early full-scale socialization would snuff out recovery (Tran Bach Dang 1995). In 1977 the city's party chief, Nguyen Van Linh, opposed the decision to proceed with nationalization of all the South's trade and industry, even though he was chair of the committee authorized to organize that campaign. Charged with "rightism," he was removed from the post in February 1978.

3. On change in the sectoral composition of party leaders, see Thayer 1988: 184, 187.

4. "In 1983, the family economy reportedly supplied 50-60 percent of the peasants' total income, more than 90 percent of the pork, chicken, vegetables, and fruits consumed by the peasants, and 30-50 percent of total foodstuffs" (Vo Nhan Tri 1988: 84).

5. For an excellent description of this turbulence, see Kerkvliet 1995: 73-80. Considering that Viet Nam in 1994 had 465 rural districts (*huyen*), and 8,774 communes (*xa*), with most communes divided into two to four hamlets, the phenomenon was quite prevalent.

6. Estimates of goods smuggled in during 1995 ranged from $500 million to $1 billion. As many as 500,000 tons of rice were smuggled out to China with the connivance of officials in the navy and the customs department (*Asia 1996 Yearbook*: 220). In 1994 it was estimated that the amount of rice smuggled to China about equaled official exports to that market (Nguyen Thi Khiem 1996: 38).

7. On sectors within the party, see Thayer 1997; for a refinement of Thayer's approach, see Vasavakul 1997.

8. Interview, Hanoi, November 1995.

9. For example, *Dien Dan*, Paris, January 1, 1996; *Viet Luan,* Sydney, January 5, 1996; and *Xay Dung,* San Jose, December 1, 1995. Thanks to Nguyen Ngoc Giao, David Marr, and Lew Stern for locating copies.

10. It is inaccurate to depict the military as conservative, as foreign news sources have tended to do, because there is no unified military interest or viewpoint on reform. It must be kept in mind that while virtually all officers are members of the party, those whose primary responsibility is political work have a separate career path and training from those whose primary responsibility is operations. It is mostly officers in the General Political Directorate who have made public statements identified as conservative. Many officers and units have benefited from *doi moi* by going into business on the side, sometimes illegally.

11. For a comparison of VCP Central Committees on which this paragraph is based, see Thayer 1997; also see Vasavakul 1997: 94-96.

12. The reformers, sometimes labeled "the government bloc" or "the technocrats," were Vo Van Kiet, Nong Duc Manh, Nguyen Manh Cam, Pham Van Khai, Tran Duc Luong, Truong Tan Sang, and possibly Le Xuan Tung. The more cautious "party bloc" consisted of Do Muoi, Nguyen Duc Binh, Nguyen Van An, Nguyen Thi Xuan My, and—representing the mass organization sector—Pham The Duyet. Le Duc Anh, Le Kha Phieu, Doan Khue, and Pham Van Tra represented defense; Nguyen Tan Dung and Le Minh Huong, the security forces.

13. The one reappointment the assembly did not approve was that of Cao Si Kiem as director of the State Bank, whom the assembly held responsible for the rising incidence of scandal and mismanagement in the finance and banking sectors. This gesture displayed some capacity for independent action and for collective rationality in economic matters.

14. Appreciation is expressed to James Riedel for his contribution to this section on Viet Nam and the Asian contagion.

15. The most significant recent examples, both from December 1997, are an open letter from retired General Tran Do to the party, the National Assembly, and the central government; and a speech by Phan Dinh Dieu to the Expanded Conference of the Presidium of the Vietnam Fatherland Front Central Committee. Both men called for a substantial reduction of the party's power and more competition in elections, among other things.

16. Businesses owned by the armed forces had revenues of $83 million in 1997, an increase of 30 percent from the preceding year. Average wages in that sector were nearly $70 a month, compared with the national average of about $40, according to the Viet Nam News Agency (reported by Reuters, January 22, 1998).

References

Asia Yearbook of *Far Eastern Economic Review*. 1991, 1996. Hong Kong: Review Publishing.

Bates, Robert H., and Anne O. Krueger. 1993. "Generalizations from the Country Studies." In *Political and Economic Interaction in Economic Policy Reform: Evidence from Eight Countries,* ed. R. H. Bates and A. O. Krueger. Cambridge, MA: Blackwell.

Beresford, Melanie, and Adam Fforde. 1996. "A Methodology for Analyzing the Process of Economic Reform in Vietnam: the Case of Domestic Trade." School of Economic & Financial Studies, Working Paper Series No. 2 (March). Sydney: Macquairie University.

Bui Minh Thang. 1995. *Tap Chi Cong San* (Hanoi), No. 15 (November): 14-18. Translated in Foreign Broadcast Information Service, Daily Report: East Asia (FBIS-EAS), April 2, 1996.

Chanda, Nayan. 1998. "Rebuilding Asia," *Far Eastern Economic Review* (February 12): 46-50.

Chu Van Lam. 1993. "Doi Moi in Vietnamese Agriculture." In *Reinventing Vietnamese Socialism: Doi Moi in Comparative Perspective*, ed. William S. Turley and Mark Selden. Boulder, CO: Westview: 151-63.

Do Hoai Nam. 1989. "The Real Situation and Sources of Inflation in Our Country." In *Van De Lam Phat o Viet Nam va cac Giai Phap* (The Inflation Problem in Vietnam and Solutions), ed. anonymous. Hanoi: Institute of World Economy.

Dollar, David. 1996. "Economic Reform, Openness, and Vietnam's Entry into ASEAN." *ASEAN Economic Bulletin*, 13, 2 (November): 169-84.

Fforde, Adam. 1997a. "The Vietnamese Economy in 1996: Events and Trends—the Limits of *Doi Moi*?" In *Doi Moi: Ten Years after the 1986 Party Congress*, ed. Adam Fforde. Political and Social Change Monograph No. 24. Canberra: Australian National University.

———, ed. 1997b. *Doi Moi: Ten Years after the 1986 Party Congress*. Political and Social Change Monograph No. 24. Canberra: Australian National University.

———. 1998. Correspondence with Turley, March 21.

Fforde, Adam, and Stefan de Vylder. 1996. *From Plan to Market: The Economic Transition in Vietnam*. Boulder, CO: Westview Press.

Golin, Jonathan. 1998. "Should You Bank on It? Assessing Viet Nam's Bank Credit Risk." *Vietnam Business Journal* VI, 1 (February): 37-39.

Grant, Jeremy. 1996. "Vietnam's Economy in a Political Trap." *The Financial Times* (October 4).

Haughton, Jonathan. 1997. "Trade Tension." *Vietnam Business Journal* V, 5 (October): 38-40.

Huong Lien. 1997. Article in *Nhan Dan* (*The People Daily*, Hanoi). (November 21).

IMF. 1995a. Viet Nam: Background Papers. Staff Country Record No. 95/92 (September). Washington, DC: International Monetary Fund.

———. 1995b. Viet Nam: Background Papers, Staff Country Record No. 95/93 (September). Washington, DC: International Monetary Fund.

———. 1996. Viet Nam: Background Papers, Staff Country Record No. 96/145 (December). Washington, DC: International Monetary Fund.

Keenan, Faith. 1998. "Half Measures." *Far Eastern Economic Review* (February 12): 24.

Kerkvliet, Benedict J. Tria. 1995. "Rural Society and State Relations." In *Vietnam's Rural Transformation*, ed. B. J. T. Kervliet and D. J. Porter. Boulder, CO: Westview: 65-96.

Kerkvliet, Benedict J. Tria, and Douglas J. Porter, eds. 1995. *Vietnam's Rural Transformation*. Boulder, CO: Westview.

Kim Ninh. 1990. "Vietnam: Renovation in Transition." In *Southeast Asian Affairs 1990*, ed. Ng Chee Yuen and Chandran Jeshurun. Singapore: Institute of Southeast Asian Studies: 383-95.

Kokko Ari. 1997. "Managing the Transition to Free Trade: Vietnamese Trade Policy for the 21st Century." Stockholm: School of Economics (May).

Kokko, Ari, and Mario Zejan. 1996. *Vietnam 1996: Approaching the Next Stage of Reforms*. Unpublished manuscript.

Le Duc Tho. 1976. Speech at the Fourth Party Congress as broadcast by Radio Hanoi. Translated in Foreign Broadcast Information Service, Daily Report: Asia & Pacific (FBIS-APA), December 23, 1976.

Le Hong Tien. 1995. *Tap Chi Cong San* 8 (July): 27-31. Trans. FBIS-EAS, October 3, 1995.

Le Xuan Tung. 1996. "About Four Dangers and Prevention Measures." *Tap Chi Cong San* 501 (August). Trans. FBIS-EAS, August 15, 1996.

Leung, Suiwah, ed. 1996. *Vietnam Assessment: Creating a Sound Investment Climate.* Singapore: Institute of Southeast Asian Studies.

Leung, Suiwah, and Vo Tri Thanh. 1996. "Vietnam in the 1980s: Price Reforms and Stabilization." Unpublished manuscript. Canberra: National Centre for Development Studies.

Marr, David G., and Christine Pelzer White, eds. 1988. *Postwar Vietnam: Dilemmas in Socialist Development.* Ithaca, NY: Cornell University Southeast Asia Program.

NGTK (Nien Giam Thong Ke [Statistical Yearbook]). 1997, 1981, 1985. Hanoi: Statistical Publishing House.

Nguyen Thi Khiem. 1996. "Policy reform and the microeconomic environment in the agricultural sector." In *Vietnam Assessment: Creating a Sound Investment Climate,* ed. S. Leung: 21-41.

Nguyen Tuan Dung. 1996. "Foreign direct investment in Vietnam." In *Vietnam Assessment: Creating a Sound Investment Climate,* ed. S. Leung: 69-89.

Nhan Dan [*The People Daily,* Hanoi] (April 20, 1989). Unattributed article, "Seeking to Understand the Resolution of the Sixth Plenum of the Party Central Committee—With Firm Confidence Let Us Strongly Push Forth the Renovation Process." Trans. FBIS-EAS, May 17, 1989.

Phan Dinh Dieu. 1997. "On the Need to Continue the Reform in the Current Period." Speech delivered at the Expanded Conference of the Presiding Committee, Vietnam Fatherland Front Central Committee, Hanoi, December: 12-13.

Quang Truong. 1987. Agricultural Collectivization and Rural Development in Vietnam: A North/South Study. Ph.D. diss. Amsterdam: Free University of Amsterdam.

Rana, Pradumna B. 1995. "Reform Strategies in Transitional Economies: Lessons From Asia." *World Development* 23, 7 (July): 1157-1169.

Riedel, James, and Bruce Comer. 1996. "Transition to a Market Economy in Viet Nam." In *Economies in Transition: Comparing Asia and Eastern Europe.* ed. W. T. Woo, J. Sachs, and S. Parker. Cambridge, MA: MIT Press.

Riedel, James, and William S. Turley. Forthcoming. *The Politics and Economics of Transition to an Open Market Economy: Viet Nam.* Paris: Organization for Economic Cooperation and Development.

Schwarz, Adam. 1996. "Economic Opening has Unleashed Corruption Scourge." *Far Eastern Economic Review* (July 11): 18.

Spoor, Max. 1988. "State Finance in the Socialist Republic of Vietnam." In *Postwar Vietnam: Dilemmas in Socialist Development,* ed. D. G. Marr and C. P. White: 111-32.

Thayer, Carlyle. 1988. "The Regularization of Politics: Continuity and Change in the Party's Central Committee, 1951-1986." In *Postwar Vietnam: Dilemmas in Socialist Development,* ed. D. G. Marr and C. P. White: 177-94.

———. 1993. "Recent Political Development: Constitutional Change and the 1992 Elections." In *Vietnam and the Rule of Law,* ed. C. A. Thayer and D. G. Marr. Political and Social Change Monograph No. 19. Canberra: Australian National University: 50-80.

———. 1997. "The Regularization of Politics Revisited: Continuity and Change in the Party's Central Committee, 1976-1996." Paper presented at the Annual Meeting of the Association for Asian Studies, Chicago, March 13-16.

Tran Bach Dang. 1995. Interview by William Turley. Ho Chi Minh City, November 13.

Tran Do. 1997. "The State of the Nation and the Role of the Communist Party." Unpublished letter sent to "the Party, National Assembly, Government and friends." Hanoi, January.

Tran Mai Huong. 1998. "Viet Nam Alert to Impact of Financial Crisis." *Viet Nam News* 11 (February 2).

Tran Thi Van Anh, and Nguyen Manh Huan. 1995. "Changing Rural Institutions and Social Relations." In *Vietnam's Rural Transformation*, ed. B. J. T. Kerkvliet and D. J. Porter: 201-14.

Turley, William. 1980. "Hanoi's Domestic Dilemmas." *Problems of Communism* XXIX , 4 (July-August): 42-61.

Vasavakul, Thaveeporn. 1996. "Politics of the Reform of State Institutions in the Post-Socialist Era." In *Vietnam Assessment: Creating a Sound Investment Climate*, ed. S. Leung: 42-68.

———. 1997. "Sectoral Politics and Strategies for State and Party Building from the VII to the VIII Congress of the Vietnamese Communist Party (1991-1996)." In *Doi Moi: Ten Years after the 1986 Party Congress*, ed. A. Fforde: 81-136.

VCP. 1977. *Fourth National Congress Documents*. Hanoi: Foreign Languages Publishing House.

———. 1982. *Fifth National Congress: Political Report*. Hanoi: Foreign Languages Publishing House.

———. 1987. *Sixth National Congress of the Communist Party of Vietnam*. Hanoi: Foreign Languages Publishing House.

———. 1989. "Overall Assessment of the Situation." Resolution of the Sixth Plenum, broadcast by Radio Hanoi, April 26-28. Trans. FBIS-EAS, April 28, 1989.

———. 1991. *Communist Party of Vietnam Seventh National Congress: Documents*. Hanoi: Foreign Languages Publishing House.

Vo Nhan Tri. 1988. "Party Politics and Economic Performance: The Second and Third Five-Year Plans Examined." In *Postwar Vietnam: Dilemmas in Socialist Development*, ed. D. G. Marr and C. P. White: 77-90.

———. 1990. *Vietnam's Economic Policy Since 1975*. Singapore: Institute of Southeast Asian Studies.

Werner, Jayne. 1988. "The Problem of the District in Vietnam's Development Policy." In *Postwar Vietnam: Dilemmas in Socialist Development*, ed. D. G. Marr and C. P. White: 147-62.

World Bank. 1995a. *Viet Nam: Economic Report on Industrialization and Industrial Policy*. Washington, DC (October).

———. 1995b. *Viet Nam: Poverty Assessment and Strategy*. Washington, DC (January).

———. 1996. *Vietnam: Fiscal Decentralization and the Delivery of Rural Services*. Washington, DC (October).

———. 1997. *Vietnam: Report on Deepening Reform for Growth*. Washington, DC (September).

Author Index

Subject Index